Cold War Frequencies

ALSO BY RICHARD H. CUMMINGS

*Radio Free Europe's "Crusade for Freedom":
Rallying Americans Behind Cold War Broadcasting,
1950–1960* (McFarland, 2010)

*Cold War Radio: The Dangerous History
of American Broadcasting in Europe,
1950–1989* (McFarland, 2009)

# Cold War Frequencies
*CIA Clandestine Radio Broadcasting to the Soviet Union and Eastern Europe*

RICHARD H. CUMMINGS

McFarland & Company, Inc., Publishers
*Jefferson, North Carolina*

Portions of Chapter 1 originally appeared as an article in
*The Intelligencer: Journal of U.S. Intelligence Studies*, December 1999,
Association of Former Intelligence Officers, Falls Church, Virginia.
Portions of Chapter 2 originally appeared as an article in
*The Intelligencer*, Summer/Fall 2007, and as an article in
*The Intelligencer*, Winter 2017–8. Portions of Chapter 7 originally
appeared as an article in *The Intelligencer*, Fall 2018.

LIBRARY OF CONGRESS CATALOGUING-IN-PUBLICATION DATA

Names: Cummings, Richard H., 1944– author.
Title: Cold war frequencies : CIA clandestine radio broadcasting
   to the Soviet Union and Eastern Europe / Richard H. Cummings.
Description: Jefferson, North Carolina : McFarland & Company, Inc.,
   Publishers, 2021. | Includes bibliographical references and index.
Identifiers: LCCN 2021006094 | ISBN 9781476678641
   (paperback : acid free paper) ∞
   ISBN 9781476640686 (ebook)
Subjects: LCSH: United States. Central Intelligence Agency—History—
   20th century. | Radio in propaganda—United States—History—
   20th century. | Propaganda, American—Soviet Union—History. |
   Propaganda, American—Europe, Eastern—History—20th century. | BISAC: HIS-
   TORY / World | PERFORMING ARTS / Radio / History & Criticism
Classification: LCC JK468.I6 C86 2021 | DDC 327.127304709/045—dc23
LC record available at https://lccn.loc.gov/2021006094

BRITISH LIBRARY CATALOGUING DATA ARE AVAILABLE

ISBN (print) 978-1-4766-7864-1
ISBN (ebook) 978-1-4766-4068-6

© 2021 Richard H. Cummings. All rights reserved

*No part of this book may be reproduced or transmitted in any form
or by any means, electronic or mechanical, including photocopying
or recording, or by any information storage and retrieval system,
without permission in writing from the publisher.*

Front cover image © 2021 iravgustin/Shutterstock

Printed in the United States of America

*McFarland & Company, Inc., Publishers
   Box 611, Jefferson, North Carolina 28640
   www.mcfarlandpub.com*

To those brave men who were killed in battle, sentenced to death, or imprisoned while fighting for freedom in their homelands behind the Iron Curtain and to their families and friends who suffered the loss of their loved ones.

# Acknowledgments

I wish to thank the following for their translation and analysis of relevant non–English documents: Liviu Tofan for Romanian; Vanya Petkova and Jordan Baev for Bulgarian; Prokep Tomek for Czech; Bohdan Nahajlo for Ukrainian; Ivan Tolstoi for Russian; Beata Blehova and Peter Jašek for Slovak.

For his advice and support, I wish to thank Dr. A. Ross Johnson, who died on February 2, 2021. He did extensive research into CIA archives, from which he provided declassified documents to the Wilson Center digital archive for online research. He also is the author of the book *Radio Free Europe and Radio Liberty: The CIA Years and Beyond*, based upon his research.

And for her advice and support, I wish to thank Katalin Kadar Lynn, editor and publisher of *The Inauguration of Organized Political Warfare: Cold War Organizations Sponsored by the National Committee for Free Europe/Free Europe Committee*.

And last but not least, I wish to thank the management and staff of my publisher McFarland for their support, not only for this book, but also for my first two books.

# Table of Contents

| | |
|---|---|
| *Acknowledgments* | vi |
| *Preface* | 1 |
| *Abbreviations and Acronyms* | 4 |
| 1. Genesis of American Clandestine Cold War Broadcasting | 7 |
| 2. Radio Free Europe: The American People's Counter Voice to Communism | 21 |
| 3. From Radio Liberation to Radio Liberty to RFE/RL | 47 |
| 4. Clandestine Broadcasts from Greece to Bulgaria and Romania | 67 |
| 5. A Seaborne CIA Fiasco and the Voice of Free Albania (VOFA) | 89 |
| 6. Black Radio to the Baltic States from Radio Nacional de España (RNE) | 108 |
| 7. Black Broadcasts to Ukraine from Greece and RNE | 137 |
| 8. Focus on Russia: Our Russia, Radio Free Russia and TsOPE | 151 |
| 9. Clandestine Radio to Byelorussia and to Slovakia | 176 |
| *Conclusion* | 195 |
| *Appendix A: Selected CIA Cryptonyms* | 197 |
| *Appendix B: National Security Council Directive 5412/2* | 205 |
| *Appendix C: Radio Nacional Propaganda Broadcasts* | 209 |
| *Appendix D: Frank Wisner Memorandum, November 22, 1950* | 211 |
| *Appendix E: Extracts from 1953 Jackson Report on Radio Free Europe—National Committee for Free Europe* | 215 |
| *Appendix F: Extracts from 1953 Jackson Report on Radio Liberty* | 218 |

## Table of Contents

*Appendix G: Termination of Voice of Free Albania Broadcasts—Termination of HTGRUBBY Broadcasts*     221

*Appendix H: Personal History of Ferdinand Durčansky*     224

*Chapter Notes*     227

*Bibliography*     253

*Index*     257

# Preface

> Radio affects most people intimately, person-to-person, offering a world of unspoken communication between writer-speaker, and the listener. That is the immediate aspect of radio. A private experience.
> —Marshall Mcluhan, *Understanding Media: The Extensions of Man*

As far back as I can remember, radio has played an important role in my life. My earliest recollection is that of a boy in greater Boston sitting on the floor listening to the large family Zenith console radio during the so-called Golden Age of Radio. There were adventure and detective stories to be heard, comedy shows to laugh at, news, documentaries, and music. In the mid 1950s, I heard rock 'n' roll music for the first time over the radio on the Arnie "Woo-Woo" Ginsburg show called "The Night Train." I first learned a little about Radio Free Europe in advertisements from the Crusade for Freedom that were broadcast over the radio and from those advertisements printed in newspapers, magazines, and posted in the subway cars of Boston.

In the 1960s, on a transistor shortwave model, I listened to Radio Luxembourg for pop music and to the Voice of America for Willis Conover's internationally famed jazz programs. I first heard that President John F. Kennedy had been killed over loudspeakers broadcasting the radio news in the college canteen. A few years later, I was a "voice intercept processing specialist" for the U.S. Air Force in West Berlin and learned of the deaths of Martin Luther King, Jr., and Bobby Kennedy via Armed Forces Radio broadcasts. I still recall listening to the last English-language broadcast of Radio Prague in August 1968 during the Soviet invasion of Czechoslovakia. In Turkey in August 1969, I heard Neil Armstrong say his famous words, "That's one small step for [a] man, one giant leap for mankind," live over the radio at 4 a.m.—almost no one heard the indefinite article "a" but Armstrong always insisted he said it.

## Preface

In the 1970s, as a graduate student at the CIA-supported Institute for the Study of the USSR in Munich, I listened to Radio Liberty and would walk by Radio Free Europe at the edge of English Garden, not knowing that I would one day become the director of security at Radio Free Europe/Radio Liberty in Munich in 1980, and then a security and safety consultant for RFE/RL for three years after it moved to Prague in 1995.

This book is a result of my research into my two earlier books: *Cold War Radio: The Dangerous History of American Broadcasting in Europe, 1950–1989*, and *Radio Free Europe's Crusade for Freedom: Rallying Americans Behind Cold War Broadcasting, 1950–1960*. Through my research for the two books and my blog https://coldwarradios.blogspot.com, I discovered that there was no book that detailed the subject of CIA's clandestine radio broadcasts to Eastern Europe and the USSR. The subject has been only briefly covered in academic journals and other books; for example, the ground-breaking 1986 book *Clandestine Radio Broadcasting: A Study of Revolutionary and Counterrevolutionary Electronic Communication* by Lawrence C. Soley and John C. Nichols contains very little on the subject.

The Open Society Archives in Budapest, Hungary (http://www.osaarchivum.org), houses many of the records of Radio Free Europe and Radio Liberty, including corporate records and digitized recordings of each station's programs available for online research as well as on-site research. The Hoover Institution Archives (HIA) (https://www.hoover.org/library-archives) at Stanford University in California, which includes corporate, broadcasting, and personal archives, proved to be an invaluable resource for my on-site research, not only for this book, but also for my first two books. I wish to thank Anatol Shmelev of HIA for his guidance and support in obtaining grants to allow me to do on-site research.

This book was made possible with the public release of more than 12 million pages of declassified documents available for my online research through the CIA's Freedom of Information Act Electronic Reading Room (https://www.cia.gov/library/readingroom/home). In addition, I had previously conducted research of the historical documents of the CIA Records Search Tool (CREST) system at the National Archives (NARA) in College Park, Maryland.

The first chapter gives an overview of the origins of clandestine radio broadcasts to Eastern Europe and the USSR. That is followed by historical overviews of the "gray" broadcasting of Radio Free Europe (Chapter 2) and Radio Liberty (Chapter 3). Clandestine or "black" radio broadcasts are covered in the chapters that follow: Radio Nacional de España in Madrid, Spain, broadcast to Estonia, Latvia, and Lithuania (Chapter 6), and to Ukraine (Chapter 7). From a secret transmitting site near Athens, Greece, CIA-sponsored broadcasts were made to Bulgaria and Romania (Chapter

4), Albania (Chapter 5), Ukraine (Chapter 7), and to the USSR, in Russian and other languages (Chapter 8). Clandestine broadcasts to Byelorussia and Slovakia are included, although the CIA did not directly sponsor them (Chapter 9). The seven appendices include a list of relevant CIA cryptonyms and extracts from declassified CIA documents.

What the book does not cover are details of the associated foreign intelligence (FI) operations, which included infiltration and exfiltration of CIA and other intelligence service agents into and out of the respective broadcast countries. This is a complex subject that goes beyond this book. I do bring up some examples, however, of the tragic story of those who sacrificed their lives "in the cause of freedom." It is hoped that this book will inspire others to dig deeper into the intelligence service archives, especially those that are now or perhaps will someday be available in the former Soviet bloc. There is much more research to do from the monitoring records of those countries to which the broadcasts were made. The various intelligence services made monitoring reports of radio broadcasts, some of which are mentioned in the book. But for the most part, the respective archives have not been published or are available only for on-site research.

# Abbreviations and Acronyms

**AD/ORE**—Assistant Director for Reports and Estimates (CIA)
**ADPC**—Assistant Director for Policy Coordination (OPC and CIA)
**AmComLib**—American Committee for Liberation from Bolshevism
**AVH**—Allam Vedelmi Hatosag (Hungarian State Security and Intelligence Agency)
**AVO**—Allam Vedelmi Osztal (Hungarian State Security Department)
**BND**—Bundesnachrichtendienst (German Federal Intelligence Service)
**CIA**—Central Intelligence Agency
**CIC**—Counter Intelligence Corps (U.S. Army)
**CIE**—Centrul de Informa'ii Externe (Romanian Foreign Intelligence Center)
**CSSR**—Czechoslovak Socialist Republic
**DCI**—Director Central Intelligence
**DDR**—Deutsche Demokratische Republik (German Democratic Republic—East Germany)
**DIE**—Directia de Informatii Externe (Romanian Foreign Intelligence Service)
**DS**—Drazven Sigurnost (Bulgarian Intelligence Service)
**FBI**—Federal Bureau of Investigation
**FEC**—Free Europe Committee
**FEP**—Free Europe Press
**FI**—Foreign Intelligence (CIA)

**IOD**—International Operations Division (CIA)

**KGB**—Kommitet Gosudarstvenoi Bezopastnosti (USSR Committee for State Security)

**LfV**—Landesamt für Verfassungsschutz (Land Office for the Protection of the Constitution—Land [State] Security Office)

**MfS**—Ministerium für Staatssicherheit (East German Ministry of State Security)

**OCI**—Office of Current Intelligence (CIA)

**OPC**—Office of Policy Coordination (CIA Division)

**ORG**—Gehlen Organization (German Intelligence Agency)

**OSO**—Office of Special Operations (CIA)

**OSS**—Office of Strategic Services (U.S. intelligence agency in World War II)

**NSC**—National Security Council

**PP**—Political and psychological, sometime paramilitary and psychological (CIA)

**PW**—Psychological Warfare

**RFE**—Radio Free Europe

**RFE/RL**—Radio Free Europe/Radio Liberty, Inc.

**RL**—Radio Liberation, Radio Liberty

**Securitate**—Departamentul Securității Statului (Romanian secret police)

**SNB**—Sbor narodni bezpecnost (Czechoslovak national security brigade)

**Stasi**—Staatssicherheit (East German secret police)

**StB**—Statni Bezpecnost (Czechoslovak state security service)

# 1

# Genesis of American Clandestine Cold War Broadcasting

> *Radio broadcasts directed behind the Iron Curtain are of three types: white, gray, and black. The first type consists of broadcasts made in the name of the American Government, such as the Voice of America programs, or by an overtly supported station such as RIAS (Radio in the American Sector of Berlin).*
>
> *The second type includes broadcasts by stations which are overtly supported by unofficial American organizations, but to which the Government gives covert financial support. Such stations are Radio Liberation, supported by the American Committee for Liberation from Bolshevism, Inc., which now broadcasts to Soviet occupation troops in Germany and Austria and the Soviet Union; Radio Free Europe (RFE), supported by the National Committee for a Free Europe, which broadcasts to the Soviet satellites; and until recently Radio Free Asia (RFA), supported by the Committee for Free Asia, which has now ceased broadcasts to Communist China.*
>
> *The last, or black, category includes CIA supported clandestine stations which purport to speak for groups inside the satellite countries.*[1]

The US State Department first broached the idea of American radio broadcasting in Russian to the Soviet Union from Germany in August 1946, other than from the official Voice of America. General Lucius D. Clay, then US military governor of Germany, rejected the idea: "I cannot agree that the establishment of a broadcasting station in Germany to broadcast to the Soviet Union in the Russian language is in the spirit of the quadripartite government" (Four-Power government of Germany).² Instead, Clay focused on sustaining the American supported German language radio station Radio in the American Sector (RIAS), for all Berlin and East Germany, which had started broadcasting in February 1946. RIAS' successful staff experiences, techniques, and programming became the model for the "surrogate home services" Radio Free Europe and Radio Liberty. The overt ("white") US government broadcasting service Voice of America began broadcasting in the Russian language in February 1947.

CIA's Special Procedures Branch for covert psychological operations was established on January 1, 1947, within the CIA's Office of Special Operations (OSO), the CIA department responsible for foreign intelligence collection. On February 24, 1947, Director of Central Intelligence Roscoe Hillenkoeter chose World War II OSS veteran Thomas C. Cassady to head this unit, which was renamed Special Procedures Group (SPG) on March 22, 1947. SPG was replaced by the Office of Special Projects on June 18, 1947.³

On December 17, 1947, the newly created United States National Security Council reported:

> The USSR is conducting an intensive propaganda campaign directed primarily against the US and is employing coordinated psychological, political and economic measures designed to undermine non–Communist elements in all countries. The ultimate objective of this campaign is not merely to undermine the prestige of the US and the effectiveness of its national policy but to weaken and divide world opinion to a point where effective opposition to Soviet designs is no longer attainable by political, economic or military means. In conducting this campaign, the USSR is utilizing all measures available to it through satellite regimes, Communist parties, and organizations susceptible to Communist influence.⁴

The National Security Council then issued NSC 4-A, which directed the Director of the Central Intelligence Agency to "initiate and conduct covert psychological operations designed to counteract Soviet and Soviet-inspired activities, which constitute a threat to world peace and security or are designed to discredit and defeat the United States in its endeavors to promote world peace and security."⁵ One aim of this psychological-war campaign would be to create surrogate radio stations that would broadcast to countries under the Soviet control yet not be officially connected with the United States government. These stations could broadcast programs and take positions for which the United States officially could deny responsibility—the doctrine of plausible deniability.

In 1948, career diplomat George Kennan was the director of the Department of State's Policy Planning Staff and the prime mover in creating Radio Free Europe and Radio Liberty. On May 4, 1948, Kennan presented a US State Department position paper to the National Security

## 1. Genesis of American Clandestine Cold War Broadcasting

Council titled "The Inauguration of Organized Political Warfare," which read in part:

> Political warfare is the logical application of Clausewitz's doctrine in time of peace. In broadest definition, political warfare is the employment of all the means at a nation's command, short of war, to achieve its national objectives. Such operations are both overt and covert. They range from such overt actions as political alliances, economic measures (as ERP), and "white" propaganda to such covert operations as clandestine support of "friendly" foreign elements, "black" psychological warfare and even encouragement of underground resistance in hostile states.[6]

Kennan proposed a program of support for "liberation committees, underground activities behind the Iron Curtain, and support of indigenous anti–Communist elements in threatened countries of the Free World."[7] The purpose of these "liberation committees" was

> to encourage the formation of a public American organization which will sponsor selected political refugee committees so that they may
> 
> (a) act as foci of national hope and revive a sense of purpose among political refugees from the Soviet World;
> (b) provide an inspiration for continuing popular resistance within the countries of the Soviet World; and
> (c) serve as a potential nucleus for all-out liberation movements in the event of war.[8]

Kennan further described "Liberation Committees" as overt operation, which; "[S]hould receive covert guidance and possibly assistance from the Government." Moreover, he proposed that

> trusted private American citizens be encouraged to establish a public committee, which would give support and guidance to U.S. interests to national movements.... [T]he American Committee should be so selected and organized as to cooperate closely with the government. The functions of the American Committee should be limited to enabling selected refuges leaders to keep alive as public figures with access to printing presses and microphones. It should not engage in underground activities.[9]

In February 1948, George Kennan's planning staff approved a study titled "Utilization of Refugees from the Soviet World (PPS 22/1)." The paper called on the U.S. "to encourage defections and better utilize refugees from the Soviet bloc in its intelligence, public information, and 'politico-psychological operations'—a euphemism for covert operations."[10] The author of PPS 22/1, John Paton Davies, met on March 1, 1948, with Thomas G. Cassady to discuss the paper's implementation. Davies and Cassady agreed that "the most effective method of penetrating the iron curtain would be via clandestine radio situated in an artificially created sterile area of our occupied zone."[11]

The CIA began to make physical preparations for the radio transmitter, codenamed "Project UMPIRE," which was a "psychological warfare project that provided the production and dissemination of covert propaganda against the Soviet Union and its satellites using radio broadcasts and printed material."[12]

On April 26, 1948, Davies gave tentative State Department approval to "Project ULTIMATE"—the plan for using weather balloons to drop propaganda leaflets behind the Iron Curtain. On the following day, however, Davies told Cassady that State Department cancelled approval for both projects. Apparently, George Kennan was concerned about certain operational details surrounding the two projects: what nationalities would be operating the radio transmitter, what they would be saying, and what sort of propaganda leaflets were going to be spread by the weather balloons.[13]

On June 18, 1948, the US National Security Council (NSC) Directive NSC 10/2 canceled NSC 4-A and directed that the task of confronting the Soviet Union clandestinely be given to the Office of Special Projects within CIA (the name would be changed to the Office of Policy Coordination [OPC] on September 1, 1948).[14] The NSC directive gave OPC a loose charter to undertake the full range of covert activities incident to the conduct of secret political, psychological, and economic warfare together with preventive direct action (paramilitary activities)—all within the policy direction of the Departments of State and Defense. NSC 10/2 defined "covert operations" as

> all activities ... which are conducted or sponsored by this Government against hostile foreign states or groups or in support of friendly foreign states or groups but which are so planned and executed that any U.S. Government responsibility for them is not evident to unauthorized persons and that if uncovered the U.S. Government can plausibly disclaim any responsibility for them. Specifically, such operations shall include any covert activities related to: propaganda; economic warfare; preventive direct action, including sabotage, anti-sabotage, demolition and evacuation measures; subversion against hostile states, including assistance to underground resistance movements, guerrillas and refuges liberation groups, and support of indigenous anti-communist elements in threatened countries of the free world. Such operations shall not include armed conflict be recognized military forces, espionage, counter-espionage, and cover and deception for military purposes.[15]

The position of head of OPC, Assistant Director of CIA for Policy Coordination (ADPC), was nominated by the Secretary of State (General George C. Marshall at the time) on the basis that he was to be acceptable to the Director of Central Intelligence (DCI) and appointed by the National Security Council (NSC). Frank G. Wisner was appointed the first ADPC in the summer of 1948. Wisner, who was a World War II Office of Strategic Services (OSS) veteran and lawyer. In September 1944, he had been sent to Bucharest, Romania, where he controlled an OSS operation that evacuated allied airmen downed behind enemy lines. Wisner remained in Bucharest until March 1945, witnessing the arrival of Soviet troops and the tragic

## 1. Genesis of American Clandestine Cold War Broadcasting 11

aftermath of the occupation.[16] After World War II, Wisner returned to private practice and joined the Council on Foreign Relations with Allen Dulles, former OSS Switzerland chief, as the Council's president.

In July 1948, Secretary of State George Marshall sent a telegram to US ambassadors in Eastern Europe and the USSR telling them of the plans to allow political refugees from Iron Curtain countries in the United States in official VOUSA (Voice of USA, later Voice of America) broadcasts to those countries. He asked for their opinions.[17] The Ambassadors were against the idea. The US Ambassador in the Soviet Union explained: "Under present circumstances, use of any Soviet refugees on VOUSA would not only be ineffectual but would undoubtedly excite resentment and ridicule against our broadcasts."[18]

## Project UMPIRE

In August 1948, CIA, State Department, Defense Department, and OPC officials met on the subject of broadcasting to Eastern Europe. They agreed to "the establishment of a democratic, philanthropic organization in New York under such name as the American Committee for Free Europe, which in turn would organize a committee of responsible foreign language groups in the western Zone of Germany and provide them with facilities of communication with their homelands." Specifically, "the New York committee was to make available to refugees in Germany: funds, radio equipment, and certain printing facilities to disseminate information, including news of developments within each country, discussions of the internal problems of each country, and material designed to undermine support for the existing regimes."[19]

Carmel Offie, OPC Special Assistant to Deputy Plans (SADO), sent a memorandum dated September 17, 1948, to ADPC Wisner, concerning Project UMPIRE:

> I wish to refer to the memorandum of the discussion at the Department of State on the establishment of an American Committee for Free Europe in New York in connection with the Umpire Project, and Mr. Kennan's comments thereon.... [I] should like to suggest that before the New York Committee or the Committee Groups in Germany request General Clay for permission to do any broadcasting, or to engage in any activities provided by the Umpire Project, General Draper should be acquainted with the entire proposal and, if possible, his full support be obtained in order that he may advice General Clay of the keen interest felt in Washington in this Project, stress to the latter its importance, and urge him to approve promptly the forth coming requests of the individual groups of the New York Committee, as the case may be, for permission to operate.... [I]n order to avoid confusion and misunderstanding with regard to the proposed establishment of the American Committee for Free Europe, I would suggest

that it not be referred to as UMPIRE Project and that some other appropriate name be applied thereto.[20]

Wisner wrote a memorandum to Director of Central Intelligence Hillenkoetter dated October 29, 1948, in which he outlined the OPC structure and explained why OPC had been assigned Project UMPIRE:

> During your absence, OPC has been holding a series of meetings of an Advisory Council which consists of high-level, security-cleared representatives of Army, Navy, Air Force, JCS and State. These representatives were nominated by the respective Secretaries to assist in formulating and coordinating policies for OPC in accordance with the charter outlined in reference (a). Although this preliminary planning has not yet been completed, the overall program is beginning to take shape along the following general lines of clandestine activity:
>
> Functional Group I—Psychological Warfare
>     Program A—Press (periodical and non-periodical)
>     Program B—Radio
>     Program C—Miscellaneous (direct mail, poison pen, rumors, etc.)
>
> Functional Group II—Political Warfare
>     Program A—Support of Resistance (Underground)
>     Program B—Support of DP's and Refugees
>     Program C—Support of anti–Communists in Free Countries
>     Program D—Encouragement of Defection
>
> Functional Group III—Economic Warfare
>     Program A—Commodity operations (clandestine preclusive buying, market manipulation and black-market operation)
>     Program B—Fiscal operations (currency speculation, counterfeiting, etc.)
>
> Functional Group IV—Preventive Direct Action
>     Program A—Support of Guerrillas
>     Program B—Sabotage, Counter sabotage and Demolition
>     Program C—Evacuation
>     Program D—Stay-behind
>
> Functional Group V—Miscellaneous
>     Program A—Front Organization
>     Program B—War Plans
>     Program C—Administration
>     Program D—Miscellaneous
>
> Until the overall plans and policies were formulated, it was obviously impossible to present an accurate or realistic outline for budgetary allocations as set forth in reference (b). However, the senior staff officers of OPC are currently working on such specific plans, which I shall be in a position to review with you in the very near future.
>
> In the meantime, we have had no alternative but to accept certain sub-projects, which have been literally thrust upon us, such as the old Umpire Project which was inherited from SPG, and Dr. Hilger, Czech Refugee Group. You may be sure that we have done everything possible to hold such emergency assignments to a minimum. In those instances where we had no alternative, we have limited our commitments and have set up earmarked funds to control expenditures.[21]

## 1. Genesis of American Clandestine Cold War Broadcasting 13

By November of 1948 there were only about 15 people in OPC, which was divided into an operation and plans and projects divisions, with foreign branches under each. The operations division was divided into broad geographical areas under the over-all direction of the Chief of Operations (COP). But, OPC was so small that only the branches handling Germany/Austria and the Balkans were actually operating.[22]

The organization and some of the known personalities of OPC in 1949 consisted of:

| Assistant Director for Policy Coordination | (ADPC) | Frank Wisner |
| Deputy ADPC | (DADPC) | Merrett Ruddock |
| Special Assistant to ADPC | (SADO) | Carmel Offie |
| Executive Assistant to ADPC | (EAD) | Charles C Hulick[23] |

In November 1948, OPC was divided into an Operations Division and a Plans and Projects Division, with Foreign Branches (FB) under each (FB-I, FB-II, etc.). The Operations Division was divided into broad geographical areas under overall direction of the Chief of Operations (COP). The Foreign Branches Division was divided into:

FB-I was responsible for Yugoslavia, Rumania, Trieste, Bulgaria, Albania, Greece, Hungary, and Malta
FB-II was responsible for Finland, Poland, and Czechoslovakia
FB-III was responsible for Germany and Austria.[24]

In May 1950 the following changes were made:

FB-I became EE-1,
Hungary transferred to EE-2 (Czechoslovakia also but date unknown)
Germany and Austria became EE-3
USSR, EE-4[25]

According to a declassified CIA history of OPC:

> To the United States and to OPC, the conduct of political and psychological warfare in peacetime was a new art. Some of the techniques were known but doctrine and experience were lacking. OPC was to learn by doing.... The secret war provided an immediate area of confrontation and, as a consequence, there was much governmental pressure to "get on with it." Operations grew apace, some successful and some not.[26]

By then the Soviet domination of East Europe was complete, there was the Berlin airlift, the Marshall Plan, and the Iron Curtain. Eastern, Central, and Western Europe were physically divided by barbed wire, armed patrols, land mines and guard towers. The Communist Party monopoly and censorship of the domestic media effectively cut off and prevented the free flow of information to the peoples of East Europe and the USSR. U.S. Government officials, Congress, and the American corporate world decided to act in a secret relationship to bring news and information to the "peoples of the captive nations."

## *May 1952 Princeton Meeting and Future of Political Warfare: A Few Martyrs*

An extraordinary weekend meeting took place May 10–11, 1952, at Princeton University, New Jersey. Radio Free Europe president C.D. Jackson moderated a high-level meeting of persons from the CIA, State Department, Radio Free Asia, Radio Free Europe and the National Committee for Free Europe (NCFE), and others. Jackson, NCFE, and RFE had apparently called for such a meeting out of frustration with the Truman administration for failing to give RFE a guidance policy for its broadcasts. C.D. Jackson begin the meeting with:

> You Washington men are in Princeton; we New Yorkers are in Princeton; the occasionally mysterious CIA people are here; the also occasionally mysterious State Department people are here; Admiral Miller, who is President of NCFE, and Bob Lang, head of Radio Free Europe, are just back from Europe. But everyone is off home field. And the reason for that was that I desperately hope that although all of us are here representing some kind of organization, at the same time I hope that the atmosphere will be such that people can say things to each other, and about someone else, and even their own organizations, with complete frankness and without any defense mechanisms being set up or hurt feelings quivering on the table. This is, I hope, a group of individual professionals of good will, interested and concerned with this problem.[27]

Each participant had been given a packet of four discussion documents to be reviewed before the meeting:

1. Memorandum from Lewis Galantiere
2. 1952 William (Bill) Griffith: Memorandum on Czechoslovakia
3. Copy of magazine *Economist* editorial, April 26, 1952, "Containment Plus"
4. Copy of April 16, 1952, newspaper column by Joseph and Stewart Alsop.[28]

C.D. Jackson explained the problem to be discussed:

> I don't know how many times in the last 18 months, but certainly close to ten times, our guys have gone to Washington and in their very friendly and helpful talks with, say, the Central European Desk in the State Department, have said, "Look, tell us what you want us to do." And those guys quite honestly said, "We can't tell you what to

## 1. Genesis of American Clandestine Cold War Broadcasting

do. Go ahead and do you want you want to do. We will tell you if you are getting into trouble."

This is a U.S.A. long-term "think session," and if it is long-term, and a political warfare will can be developed, the how-to and the coordinating, and all the other implementery things can follow reasonably smoothly. So I pitch it to you: do all of you really want to do it? And if you do, it can be done.

We created one or more salient—into the hearts and minds of our friends behind the Iron Curtain, into the fears and mistrust of Communist officials behind the Curtain, and possibly created a frown on Uncle Joe's brow. Well, then these salients have been created, and we look around for who was to close up on the flanks—the U.S. or the West—there was no one there.

It comes to this—that arising not merely of the operation of RFE, but out of our posture with respect to German, Eastern Europe, and Russia itself, it is felt that a gap exists in the understanding of the nature of the American objectives and that this gap contributes to apathy and weakens the dynamism of any effort to see that part of the world move without war toward a shape, which is in the American interest.[29]

Adolphe Berle, director of NCFE's Mid-European Study Center, reiterated RFE's frustration and need for specific, concrete policy guidance:

> Something must happen—either we tell them to go home, or start composing music, or drop out of the picture, or we suggest a goal for the U.S. or West. Without that, I don't see how the boys in Munich can make noises and increasingly make trouble there without getting themselves hated for their pains.... We can no longer take ad hoc action. All this has to go somewhere, and we must have a hypothesis. It must be flexible, but we must be able at least to have some picture of the eventual result we expect to do. That is not a "statement of objectives." Enough ideas have been stated, be we ought to have a blue-print, flexible, of what we expect to do.[30]

Allen Dulles, CIA Deputy Director, Plans, commented, "As I said before, you have got to have a few martyrs. Some people have to get killed. I don't want a bloody battle but I would like to see things started. I think we have got to take a few risks. We have got to move on with caution and foresight." C.D. Jackson concluded, "I hope that you will agree that in pulling it off, political warfare, or whatever you want to call it—which deals with the minds of men everywhere (the only thing we can get at in many places)—may be the way in which we can pull the neatest trick of this century."[31]

On June 30, 1953, the Presidential Committee on International Information Activities, under the chairmanship of William Harding Jackson, former Deputy Director for Central Intelligence, submitted a report to President Eisenhower. The Presidential Committee, which first met on January 30, 1953, "interviewed over 250 witnesses, including many representatives of government departments and agencies. It also consulted with members of Congress, studied much highly classified material furnished by various agencies, and received a large volume of correspondence both from government officials and from members of the public and private organizations."[32] Surveys and evaluations of both Radio Free Europe and Radio Liberty were included. Specifically on Radio Free Europe, the report read:

> In the original plan the various national councils were to be responsible for broadcasts over RFE facilities to their respective countries. Since the complexities and rivalries of émigré politics made the organization of national councils difficult, it was decided to set up RFE on a non-political basis. Émigré staffs were hired for competence rather than political affiliation and programs to various countries are now identified as the Voice of Free Czechoslovakia, Poland, and so on. Although this reason for the national councils no longer exists, they do have potential value in exile relations. If the émigré leaders are prepared to create national councils of their own volition, NCFE should assist them to engage in such propaganda activities as they may be qualified to conduct. Primary attention, however, should be given to the broadcasting phase of NCFE activities. The Committee recommends that the rest of these activities be reviewed by CIA to determine whether they should be continued or modified.
>
> Certain specific problems arise in connection with NCFE activities, particularly RFE. There is first the question of cover. It has been suggested that, because the present cover has worn thin, RFE's official connections be freely admitted. Such a course, however, would vitiate the principal reason for the existence of RFE as a separate organization. So long as its government connections are not officially admitted it can broadcast programs and take positions for which the United States would not desire to accept responsibility. The Committee believes that the present cover is adequate for this purpose.[33]

The recommendations for radio in Chapter 4, Operations against the Soviet System, included:

- All broadcast material to the Soviet system for which the United States government does not wish to accept responsibility should be handled by Radio Free Europe (RFE), Radio Liberation or other covert channels.
- The American Committee for Liberation from Bolshevism, Inc., should concentrate on the improvement of Radio Liberation and reduce expenditures on the émigré coordinating center.
- CIA's clandestine radio operations should be continued.[34]

## *CIA and Clandestine Radio Stations*

### Radio Nacional de España

In 1949, officers of the Office of Policy Coordination (OPC) began discussing the use of Radio Nacional de España (RNE) as a tool in the psychological warfare campaign against the USSR. EDUCATOR was the OPC psychological warfare project set up in Germany for the production and dissemination of covert propaganda against the Soviet Union and its

## 1. Genesis of American Clandestine Cold War Broadcasting 17

satellites using radio broadcasts and printed material. An "official dispatch" OPC message dated May 30, 1949, on the subject Radio Nacional Propaganda Broadcasts contained the outline of how to use RNE:

> [W]e have studied the matter not only in regard to the immediate problem of applying background material but also relative to the larger, long range possibility of utilizing Radio Nacional as a channel for operational broadcasts, to which EDUCATOR creative personnel in Germany might contribute both program material as well as programs themselves, including possibly special recordings.
>
> Information here indicates that Madrid is heard reasonably well in satellite areas. If the Spanish Government, through proper covert arrangements, is willing to place the facilities and broadcast time of the station as the disposal of (redacted), this would clearly open up the possibility of using Madrid as an operational outlet for broadcasts, whether sponsored by or accordingly produced by the U.S. Government.
>
> Assuming the broadcasts can be heard satisfactorily in the target areas and time and facilities could be made available to (redacted), it would seem there are four problems to be met:
>
> a. Cover for the operation.
> b. Policy control.
> c. Type of broadcasts in relation to audience reaction.
> d. A competent production organization.
>
> In regard to (a) above, through negotiations with the proper Spanish Government levels, I should think a suitable operational cover could be arranged—as, for example, the Spanish Government, in its desire to oppose religious persecutions in satellite countries, has accorded broadcasting time to refugee Catholic groups in Spain in order to permit them to talk to their fellow countrymen.
>
> In regard to (b) above, periodic policy guidance from the home office, together with a close monitoring watch over the broadcasts, should provide adequate policy control, especially if the cover and security of the operation are well maintained and the U.S. Government is not linked in any way with the broadcasts.[35]

At the German OPC site near Frankfurt, there were Hungarian and Czechoslovak language personnel who could "prepare and transmit to Madrid, programs either in rough or finished form, for actual broadcasts. These might include occasional recordings of a special nature." The OPC author of the memorandum optimistically wrote, "I believe that by 1 July (1949) we could begin furnishing with rough or finished scripts for periodic broadcasts in Hungarian, and possibly in a more limited way, in Czech."[36]

There is no record that CIA used RNE to broadcast to Czechoslovakia, or Hungary.

### Greece-Based Clandestine Radio Broadcasts

OPC clandestine broadcasts from Greece were initially via two or three mobile units close to the Bulgarian border. In spring 1950, the Greek government gave the CIA approval for the construction of a permanent communications installation near Athens for the purpose of psychological warfare broadcasting—the installation for transmitting and monitoring gained the cryptonym WEMCA, with a broadcasting operation of up to nine language units known as PYREX. Eventually, PYREX broadcasts were made to Bulgaria, Romania, Albania, Ukraine, and to the USSR, in Russian and other languages.

## Effectiveness of Clandestine Radio Broadcasts

One method CIA used to measure the effectiveness of the clandestine radio broadcasts was to examine how the East Bloc regimes reacted to them. For example, at the 21st Congress of the Communist Party of the Soviet Union, in January 1959, Politburo member and Minister of Culture Yekaterina Furtseva spoke about strengthening Marxist-Lenin ideology and Communist consciousness of the peoples of the USSR: "At the service of the organizers of the Cold War are all sorts of private committees, funds, and unions, and numerous radio stations with provocative names like Bajkal, Kavkaz (Caucasus), Nova Ukraina, Nasha Rossiya, Osvobodoshdenie (Radio Liberation), Svobodnaya Evropa (Radio Free Europe) and so forth."[37] Radio stations Bajkal, Kavkaz, Nova Ukraina and Nasha Rossiya were CIA clandestine radio stations in Athens, Greece. The author of this information added, "The fact that Furtseva found it necessary to mention the 'diversionary' work of our black radios, thus publicizing them before the great masses of listeners and readers of her speech is proof of the significance the ruling clique of the USSR-CPSU attaches to the role of these radios in the overall Psychological War effort of the Free World against Communism."[38]

In Washington on September 15, 1959, there was a meeting between Yuri Zhukov, Chairman of the State Committee for Cultural Relations with Foreign Countries, and George Allen, Director United States Information Agency (USIA). Zhukov began the meeting by telling Allen that Voice of America's broadcasts were no longer being jammed. He then added: "This was an experiment—whether the Voice of America would cease pursuing the cold war and be the real voice of America."[39]

Zhukov then spoke about Radio Baikal, Radio Free Russia, and Radio Caucasus: "The Soviet Government hoped the American Government would put a stop to these transmissions and, if so, the Soviets were ready to stop jamming altogether. Mr. Zhukov said: 'We are ready to establish altogether normal relations in radio' … jamming and broadcasting efforts designed to break through jamming were a waste of money on both sides."[40]

They then spoke briefly about Radio Free Europe and Radio Liberty. Zhukov said, "All these were established for the purpose of overthrowing

Soviet power." Zhukov then again spoke about Radio Baikal and Radio Caucasus:

> Radio Baikal emanated from Okinawa and Radio Caucasus from a ship near Rhodes. In the ensuing discussion, Mr. Zhukov read some excerpts from Radio Caucasus broadcasts which indicated that it was an NTS station, purportedly giving directions to an underground in the Soviet Union. Mr. Zhukov said that Radio Free Russia emanated from Frankfurt and went on to say that he could publish all of the material at hand but did not wish to continue the cold war by doing so. Mr. Allen noted that these stations were not under his control and said he was not certain that the United States had anything to do with these stations. He questioned whether any of them emanated from a ship near Rhodes, as the only ship of that kind was a USIA ship which transmitted only VOA broadcasts.[41]

During a meeting between KGB and East German Stasi intelligence officers on November 13, 1969, KGB First Deputy S.K. Zvigun mentioned CIA sponsored clandestine radio stations:

> A particularly important role in the struggle against the Soviet Union is played by radio propaganda. In addition to legal radio stations like the BBC, RFE, and "Voice of America," there are also illegal stations directly run by intelligence services like "Radio Baikal," "Radio Caucasus," "Free Russia," and "Free Ukraine."
> Some of them are mobile stations broadcasting from ships or trucks. They broadcast daily for many hours the vilest slander in Russian and the different languages of the Soviet peoples. They exploit certain negative phenomena from Soviet life based on the central and local press. Also they receive information from émigré circles. It is difficult to rebuke this slanderous propaganda. Usually the broadcasts are shrewdly embedded in music. Wavering people, youths in particular, are getting softened up by this, and individual people are led in the wrong direction.
> In Krasnodar, a 21-year-old citizen was arrested after he produced and disseminated anti–Soviet leaflets. During interrogations he said his political opinions were formed when he was 14 and he began to listen to Western radio stations. When he listened to those stations he dreamt about the Western lifestyle and freedoms. He committed his criminal actions influenced by this type of bourgeois propaganda.[42]

Radio Caucasus (Kavkaz) was CIA's black radio to the Georgian SSR, under Project AEPARADE. There is little information available about this CIA Soviet Russian Division project. There was some sort of "informal contact" between AEPARADE and the émigré group Georgian National Democrats in New York. One member, cryptonym AEHUNTER 7, of this émigré group was assessed in 1952 for possible foreign intelligence operations under CIA's REDSOX project—operations involving the illegal return of defectors and émigrés to USSR as agents.[43]

Program tapes were pouched from CIA domestic operations base (DOB) to Athens for broadcasting. For example, during September 1957, AEPARADE broadcasts from Athens were aired to Tbilisi, Georgia, from 18:00 to 18:30 and 02:15 to 03:15 GMT, for a total of 39 hours.[44] The number of tape runs was 76. For December 1959, there was a total of 38½ hours.[45]

For February 1958, there was a total of 35 transmitting hours with a total of 40 tape runs.[46] Also in February 1958, the two frequencies for the programs aired at 18:00 were changed to one and two used at 02:15 were changed but remained two frequencies.[47]

There is not much information available about the operations of the clandestine radio station Radio Baikal: a mention of the radio station in a study of "counterfeit broadcasters" and in the 1959 KGB report on jamming: "In the suburbs of Khabarovsk, programs of the radio station 'Baikal' were listened to regularly on one to two frequencies. These programs were also listened to in the suburbs of Petropavlovsk, Kamchatka, Chita, Tashkent, Tbilisi, and in such cities as Artem, Suchane, Nakhodka."[48]

# 2

# Radio Free Europe

*The American People's Counter Voice to Communism*[1]

> *RFE is a group of complete radio stations, with all the elements of any normal western radios—news, lecture, music, education, sports, comedy and political commentaries. These stations must be capable of entertaining and thereby holding their audience on their own, entirely from their propaganda impact. Furthermore, such a placing of propaganda in its proper setting—one element of a complete whole—acts as a deliberate and profitable contrast to the unending strident yells which characterize Communist radio.*
>
> *Since each RFE station is a "home service" it must be different for each country. It cannot be one radio station, each "Voice" (e.g., The Voice of Free Czechoslovakia) must be adapted to the listening habits of the country and set up in accordance with the country's national characteristics.*[2]

## Greenwood Project

UMPIRE as a Special Procedures Group (SPG) project was CIA's first psychological warfare project that provided for the production and dissemination of covert propaganda against the Soviet Union and East European countries behind the Iron Curtain using radio broadcasts and printed material. The project designation was later changed on December 1, 1948, to EDUCATOR and then QKDEMON. The Special Procedures Group became the Office of Policy Coordination (OPC) in August 1948, which then took over the SPG projects, including UMPIRE. The Greenwood Project was a sub-project of UMPIRE.

The first OPC radio broadcasting site was located at Lampertheim, Germany—midway between Heidelberg and Darmstadt. Elements of the U.S. Army Security Agency (ASA) constructed the site under the cover of a "Communications Ionosphere Research Unit." The military unit cover designation was "7989 Special Technical Unit, Weinheim Sub-post, Heidelberg, Germany."[3]

By November 1948, construction at the transmitting site in Lampertheim was completed on two class E rhombic transmitting antenna bearing 70 and 112 degrees. "The antennas were complete with transmission lines and dissipation lines. Also completed was the erection of masts for class 'E' rhombic transmitting antennas bearing 130 degrees and two folded di-poles bearing 70 and 120 degrees. No additional work was done to these antennas due lack of material for the rhombic and lack of frequency information for folded di-poles."[4]

The offices for the broadcasting site headquarters were set up at No. 4 Bobostrasse, Weinheim, by converting the living space into offices. A files room included three-combination cabinet-type safes for classified documents. The Quartermaster, Heidelberg Military Post, provided the office furniture, which included desks, chairs, tables, etc.[5]

ASA built and then loaned to OPC 15 radio towers, 63 and 90 feet tall, to the project. They were loaned to OPC with the understanding that they would be returned to ASA or replaced when new ones from the U.S. arrived. Reportedly, "tower directional pattern permits broadcasting to all major satellite areas." Electricity was provided by a 50 KW generator and two transformers connected to 20,000-voltage line 4 kilometers away.[6]

By December 1948, the main building of the transmitting site consisted of:

- transmitting studio. which took up one entire end of the building
- sleeping rooms 12 sq. m.,
- one large shower room,
- dining room and
- kitchen

The blueprints of the main building were titled "Lampertheim Project. There were five guard personnel protecting the installation, including the buildings, towers and antennas. Project UMPIRE was discontinued on December 1, 1948 and succeeded by projects EDICT and EDUCATOR."[7]

On December 20, 1948, OPC Washington sent a message to OPC Karlsruhe: "Recommend return to towers to ASA as soon as possible with thanks and appropriate explanation. Retain other Greenwood property for future use."[8]

On February 23, 1949, OPC Karlsruhe advised Policy Coordination

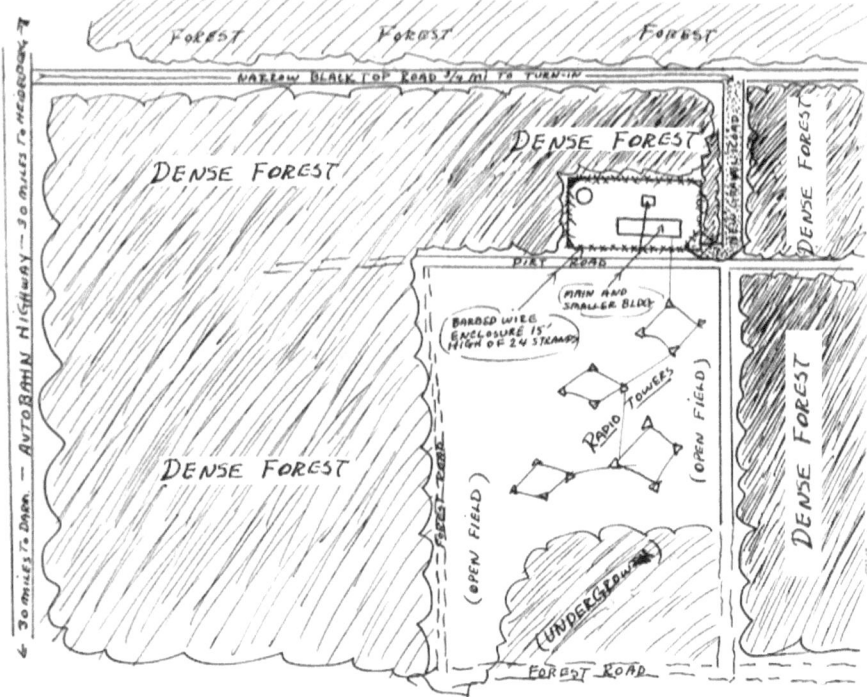

Pen and ink drawing from 1948 showing the layout of the Office of Policy Coordination transmitting site near Lampertheim, Germany. It eventually become the site first for Radio Free Europe and later Radio Liberty.

that Lt. Colonel Walker, ASA, said, "He was willing to forget whole dismantling project if we agree to replace masts and wire borrowed from his unit as soon as practicable."[9] On March 14, 1949, OPC headquarters informed Karlsruhe OPC and Heidelberg OPC branches: "Unless dismantling not already under way, leave entire installation in place. We will supply ASA with replacements for all equipment. If dismantling in progress, use your best judgment as to whether it can be halted diplomatically."[10] Dismantling had not begun.

The Karlsruhe OPC office sent a message on March 17, 1949, to OPC headquarters: "Lt. Colonel Walker agreeable to allow site to remain intact as his outfit was not looking forward to dismantling. Would appreciate some indication of shipping date of replacement as he is planning new construction for coming summer and replacement items scheduled for this new site."[11] On March 31, 1949, Karlsruhe OPC sent this message to Washington: "Wire borrowed from ASA did not comprise complete rhombic antenna kits. ASA willing to accept three antenna kits minus transmission line, dissipation line, and pole line kits and consider matter closed. No other items required."[12]

In an internal memorandum to ADPC Frank Wisner dated February 4, 1949, an OPC officer wrote about the negative developments of the project:

> The ill-coordinated and frequently ill-advised series of moves resulted in the premature establishment of OPC's activities in Germany and a consequent series of operational misfires.
>
> It is true that the unfortunate series of circumstances surrounding the Greenwood Project caused a certain amount of hard feeling in the theater, but this was primarily at the level of the functional commands which did a lot of work on this project without being fog, aware of the reasons for having started it in the first place or for later abandoning it. Inasmuch as General Walsh supported the concept of the old UMPIRE operation, and was, to a large extent for the rush orders, which went out for Greenwood.[13]

U.S. Air Force General Robert LeGrow Walsh was director of intelligence of the European Command, Office of Military Government at Berlin, Germany.

## *Mobile Transmitting Equipment*

On June 9, 1949, OPC headquarters sent a message to Heidelberg OPC on the subject of mobile radio operation EDUCATOR Project, which was an answer to a message from Heidelberg OPC, April 29, 1949 (copy not available):

1. The essential reason for delay in answering your dispatch of 29 April enclosing the plan for mobile radio operation is due to the fact that we have given a considerable amount of study and discussion to the proposal. It is a well thought out paper.
2. There are a number of considerations that enter the picture and a number of questions we should like to put to you with reference to it, but we think this is not the time for it since the entire policy of black radio is still under review here. We know that the technique is being used by the opposition forces, but the advisability of our engaging in the work is still faced with some doubt.
3. The plea, which you propose, will be brought out again for consideration when a determination of policy is made here. In the meantime, thanks for submitting it. You will be advised at once when policy is laid down.[14]

A December 29, 1949, CIA memorandum makes mention of mobile broadcasting equipment in storage:

1. The Chief of Communications has requested that he be advised as to the foreseeable requirements, which would necessitate the use of the mobile broadcasting equipment procured and built under the Project UMPIRE,
2. The equipment has been on 10-day call since it was built and the maintenance under such condition is such that two men are required full time and considerable warehouse spece is allocated for it.
3. The cost of maintenance and the use of the space is justified if there will be urgent need for the equipment at some future time, but (redacted) informs me that UMPIRE is dead and if the equipment is needed by him in the future it will be known at least one month in advance.
4. Therefore, if there is no immediate existing need for the equipment, it is suggested that the Chief of Communications be notified and that he be allowed to have the equipment mothballed and stored for future use.[15]

It is probable that the mobile broadcasting equipment referred to in this exchange was the mobile unit "Barbara" used to broadcast Radio Free Europe's first program on July 4, 1950, to Czechoslovakia. "Barbara" was not one vehicle, but a set of seven vehicles: studio van, the transmitter van, generators, a fuel supply truck, jeep and trailer, camping and housekeeping equipment, and a flatbed truck for the antenna towers. The first programs consisted of news, information and political analysis.

Ten days later, on July 14, 1950, "Barbara" sent its first broadcast to Romania. In August 1950, shortwave broadcasts began to Hungary, Poland, and Bulgaria. It is doubtful that anyone heard the first programs due to the low power of the mobile transmitter. Thus the idea was borne for a powerful medium wave transmitter south of Munich for Czechoslovakia, a new transmitting site at Bibis, Germany, and a huge transmitting site in Gloria, Portugal, outside Lisbon.

*Time* magazine reported on July 17, 1950, under the rubric "Urgent Whisper":

> This week Czech and Rumanian radio listeners could hear music, plays and satires forbidden by their Communist masters—as well as the voices of men long exiled. These forbidden broadcasts came from a Radio Free Europe transmitter deep in Western Germany.
> RFE's lone 7 1/2-kilowatt transmitter is only a whisper compared to the worldwide-station network of Voice of America. But RFE, a branch of the National Committee for a Free Europe founded last year by a group of private U.S. citizens, expects to make up in pungency for its lack of volume. Explains Banker Frank Altschul, chairman of RFE: "Unhampered by diplomatic restrictions, we can slant our programs in a more definitely anti–Soviet way than the Voice."

Welcomed by the State Department as a freewheeling, free-speaking ally in the propaganda war, RFE plans to boost its power with five transmitters now on order. It intends, eventually, to speak strongly to every Communist satellite from the Baltic to the Black Sea.

The *New York Times* reported "New 'Voice' Talks to Europe Like Member of the Family." Some grass-roots newspapers in the United States printed this editorial about Radio Free Europe and its secret-location transmitter:

> Many wise statesmen have been appealing insistently to the free world to exert greater effort to the grimy "struggle for men's mind." They have pounded repeatedly on the idea that it isn't enough to combat Russian Communism with economic and military measures: that freedom must be shown to be the great cause it really a way of life eminently superior to the slavery imposed by Moscow.
>
> The first imaginative stride in this direction has now been taken. From a secret radio transmitter in Europe, a new series of programs is being beamed to the countries behind the Iron Curtain.... Radio Free Europe, as the new transmitter is called, is the product of the National Committee for Free Europe, which was organized about a year ago by outstanding American citizens.
>
> We must make plain to decent people everywhere that the language of Communism is the language of falsehood, that Russia's words can never be believed because words to the Soviet Union are simply weapons in the psychological theater of war.

Initially, the first Radio Free Europe broadcasts were prepared in RFE's New York studios and air transported to Germany, but this was time consuming and soon the entire broadcast operation would be moved to Munich, Germany. The administrative and editorial offices were located at Sieberstrasse 4, in Munich, where there were two studios, two newsrooms, a tape library, a recorded music library, a control room installed in the kitchen, offices for the staff, and the workers found space in the passage ways of the building.

On Labor Day, September 4, 1950, General Dwight D. Eisenhower, then President of Columbia University, passionately called for an American Crusade for Freedom in a nation-wide radio broadcast from Denver, Colorado, covered by the four major radio networks (ABC, CBS, NBS, and Mutual):

> I speak tonight [...] about the Crusade for Freedom. This Crusade is a campaign sponsored by private American citizens to fight the big lie with the big truth. It is a program that has been hailed by President Truman and others as an essential step in getting the case for freedom heard by the world's multitudes. [...] We need powerful radio stations abroad, operated without government restrictions, to tell in vivid and convincing form about the decency and essential fairness of democracy. These stations must tell of our aspirations for peace, our hatred of war, our support of the United Nations, and our constant readiness to cooperate with all who have these same desires. [...] One such private station, Radio Free Europe, is now in operation in Western Germany. It daily brings a message of hope and encouragement to a small part of the masses of Europe.[16]

## 2. Radio Free Europe

## *NCFE and CIA at Odds*

The Committee for a Free Europe, the parent organization of Radio Free Europe, was set up in New York on May 17, 1949, when the articles of incorporation were signed. Directors and officers included future CIA director Alan Dulles and future president Dwight D. Eisenhower. The corporate name was changed to the National Committee for a Free Europe (NCFE) on June 1, 1949.

At the end of September 1950, Dewitt Poole, President of the NCFE, had a telephone conversation with Allen Dulles in which he expressed concerns about the NCFE and CIA'S Frank Wisner. Dulles told Poole that it was time to "re-examine" the position of the NCFE, in particular "policy guidance" from the Office of Policy Coordination.[17] As a follow up, on September 28, 1950, Poole wrote to Dulles giving details of his displeasure with the existing relationship. He quoted from a "fundamental memorandum" from October 1949, in which Allen Dulles, Frank Altschul, and DeWitt Poole had agreed, in part, to the following (FW is Frank Wisner):

> All activities directly or indirectly affecting (governmental or State Department policy) official policy guidance will be given or confirmed through (FW's office) and (FW's office) shall be the sole channel for the purpose.
>
> On the programming side of the radio we have received scattered "directives" from FW's staff, but the directives, or some of them, don't' make too much sense, and here the situation cannot be said to be satisfactory at all. Nor has the coordination between us and the Voice been worked out as it should be and I think can be.
>
> Relations with the exiles and the national councils constitute obviously a most important area in which close working contact with Washington is essential. Experience so far has been anything but satisfactory.
>
> The whole NCFE operation has outgrown by far original conception and arrangement. As this marks the success of the original idea, everybody ought to be happy about it and join gladly in the readjustments consequently needed. I am glad you are opening the way for the needed top-level discussions.[18]

On October 23, 1950, W.H. Jackson, Deputy Director of the CIA, DeWitt Poole and Joseph Grew met at Joseph Grew's house in Washington for two hours in a "very constructive session" to discuss CIA, NCFE and Radio Free Europe. The next day, DeWitt Poole reported to the NCFE Directors the results of the meeting and told them that the NCFE was "entering a new chapter. How consultation and coordination can be more closely organized than they have been in the past." Poole wrote a letter to W. Hl. Jackson on October 25, 1950, telling him about the meeting with the NCFE Directors:

> My brief and highly selective report to the Directors yesterday was received with marked gratification. I concluded by saying that I thought we were entering a new

chapter. Someone corrected me to say that he thought we were opening a new volume.... I believe the Directors I spoke with yesterday fully accepted the fact that "orders are orders" with each being at liberty, of course, to withdraw according to judgment and conscience; and all seemed to agree with an observation on my part that in practice the important thing was the preparation of decisions—specifically, how can consultation and coordination be more closely organized than they have been in the past? I hope to be able to prepare some specific suggestions under this head within the next few days and perhaps send them along to you.[19]

Frank Wisner and the CIA's Deputy Director of Central Intelligence, W.H. Jackson, met with Radio Free Europe directors at the Union Club in New York on November 2, 1950. RFE's directors were asked to "reexamine its radio activities and prepare a statement of the aims and objectives of Radio Free Europe for study by the Deputy Director of Central Intelligence." Frank Wisner wrote a summary report to W.H. Jackson on November 22, 1950, which in part read:

> To accomplish the purpose of bringing hope to our friends and confusion to our enemies, Radio Free Europe has been developing programs aimed at: [C]reating doubts and fears among the quislings of the satellites by character assassination and talk of ultimate retribution; and at the same time drawing a distinction between Communist puppets and those who follow the party line in order to survive, thereby encouraging high-level defections among the latter.
>
> As a result of five month's experience, emphasis has shifted from the use of distinguished political and intellectual exiles, whose personal prejudices and protracted absence from their native lands render them of questionable current value, to timely news items and commentary slanted to accomplish Radio Free Europe's purposes.[20]

Dewitt Poole resigned as President of the NCFE on January 18, 1951. C.D. Jackson of *Fortune* magazine replaced him. On January 25, 1951, the Undersecretary of State for Public Affairs Edward Barrett wrote a memorandum to the Deputy Secretary of State on the subject of Radio Free Europe, part of which read:

> It is inevitable that some people must know the full background of the Committee, this number should be kept to the absolute minimum as one of its principal advantages will be lost if the general public, particularly in Europe, has grounds for belief that RFE has any official or semi-official connection with the United States government.... Every precaution should be taken by Department officers to keep overt contacts with RFE officers at a minimum and such cooperation as is necessary and desirable should be carried on in the most discreet manner as possible.
>
> I believe that Mr. Jackson, as an experienced propaganda warfare expert, will give the Committee and RFE the leadership and drive which has been needed.[21]

At the Undersecretary's Meeting on February 2, 1951, Barrett reported on NCFE and said, "During the past few months it has not been too effective. However, General Smith has persuaded Mr. C.D. Jackson, Editor of

Fortune, to head the Committee, and it is now hoped that some progress will be made."[22]

The new Radio Free Europe medium-wave transmitter site was dedicated on May 1, 1951, at 10 a.m., in Munich's Bayerische Hof Hotel. Ferdinand Peroutka, a Czech journalist, who had been imprisoned in the Nazi prison camps Dachau and Buchenwald, fled Czechoslovakia in 1948 to the United States. Peroutka, who helped found the Council of Free Czechoslovakia, read the following message to those in attendance:

> The Communist government in our country is the biggest attempt, which has ever been undertaken to turn things upside down to deprive words of their meaning. Jailers sing songs of freedom and officials of the secret police lecture on humanity. The loss of freedom is officially called independence in our country, aggression is called peace action, plunder of the country "benefits," forced exports to Russia "building up of Czechoslovakia," enslavement of women in heavy industry is called their liberation.
>
> We know how much effort the Communists stake on reforming your souls..., But we also know that in the evening when you return home from the daily drudgery ... between your four walls you say to yourself: "They are telling lies."[23]

Radio Free Europe began broadcasting to Czechoslovakia, as the Voice of Free Czechoslovakia, on medium wave (AM band) frequencies on that day from the newly constructed transmitter station, nicknamed "Carola" at Holzkirchen—less than 20 miles south of Munich, Germany. The new transmitter station had four antenna towers, which reached 400 feet, and, at that time with 135,000 watts of power, was almost three times more powerful than any commercial radio transmitter in the United States. The broadcast schedule was then increased to 12 hours a day to Czechoslovakia. After Holzkirchen, transmitter stations were constructed in Biblis, Germany, and in the town of Gloria, Portugal.

The first broadcast from Munich actually began at 5 a.m. on May 1, 1951, and was just music until the first program, read by Czech exile Pavel Tigrid, aired at 11 a.m. from a studio in the RFE building. He said, in part,

> Dear Listeners:
>
> Today, a terrible enemy rises against all communist informers, agents provocateurs and stool pigeons, all inhuman guards in prisons and work-camps, all judges and members of communist jurisdiction, all propagandists of communist ideology: Radio Free Europe, who will reveal their names, one by one; all of them will be blacklisted by the democratic world and will be dumped on the rubbish heap of contempt by the Czech and Slovak people.[24]

Pavel Tigrid would become the Czech Republic's first Minister of Culture, after the 1989 Velvet Revolution.

## Project Troy

Project "Troy" began in October 1950 as a government-academic partnership in the early days of the Cold War. As in most partnerships, there was disagreement as to how the partners perceived their roles:

The Government View was that

> under this project, the Massachusetts Institute of Technology assembled 30 of the nation's top scientists and other experts to explore all means—conventional and unconventional—for penetrating the Iron Curtain. The report endorses the large-scale expansion of radio facilities, already initiated, and calls for even further expansion along lines, which should facilitate further piercing the curtain by means, which will not interfere with other telecommunications channels (military).[25]

The Academic View was in contrast:

> In 1950, as war raged in Korea and the U.S.S.R. tested its atomic bomb, the Soviets were jamming Voice of America (VOA) radio propaganda broadcasts. Undersecretary of State James Webb asked MIT President James Killian to assemble a team to solve the jamming problem.
> 
> Killian and Humanities and Social Studies Dean John Burchard assembled a diverse group (including professors from Harvard and other universities) to address not only the technical issues but also matters of political warfare: what the VOA should broadcast, to whom, and to what effect, once the jamming was circumvented.... [P]roject Troy resulted in the establishment of a research center at MIT funded by the CIA.... [P]roject Troy had not only led to a solution of the jamming problem, but also to the creation of an inter-disciplinary center where scholarly expertise would be applied to foreign policy issues.[26]

A committee report titled "Project Troy, Perforating the Iron Curtain," dated February 1, 1951, was submitted to the US Secretary of State. Chapter 1, Part II of that report, Communication into Shielded Areas, dealt with

> means of communication for piercing the Iron Curtain, mentioning, besides radio and balloons, and other existing ways, the use of direct mail to send professional journals and industrial and commercial publications and questions "Impulsive emotional blockades of this kind of communication, such as the recent ban on shipments of The Iron Age." It also mentions sending of objects, typical of American life, drugs, flashlights, fountain pens, small radio receivers, etc.[27]

Chapter III of the Troy Report dealt with the "urgent" use of balloons to send information over the Iron Curtain:

> An area of a million square miles could be saturated with a billion propaganda sheets in a single balloon operation costing a few million dollars.... If the area of dispersal in such an operation were restricted to 30,000 square miles, which may be practicable, there would be a leaflet laid down, on the average, for each area of 30 by 30 feet. The dispersion of balloons in flight and the dispersion of leaflets in falling from altitude both lend themselves to saturation operations.
> 
> The operational testing and production program should be undertaken now. It may

cost about one million dollars.... In order to coordinate balloon use with other political warfare operations, organizational planning for the final operations should start now.... A stockpile sufficient for an actual operation should be created now, and the questions of size and type of stock should be reviewed periodically as the program develops.[28]

## *"Winds of Freedom"*

In August 1951, NCFE created the Free Europe Press, which was used not only for the printing of various publications in the US and Europe, but also for the printing of leaflets and launching of balloons to carry them to the countries in Czechoslovakia, Poland and Hungary. Permanent launching sites were constructed set up in Fronau, Freying, and Hohenhard, West Germany.

The first balloons were launched on August 13, 1951, in an open field along the Czechoslovak border. This test operation, known as the "Winds of Freedom," was on an experimental stand-alone basis, i.e., the launching of the balloons was not fully part of a coordinated programming effort with Radio Free Europe broadcasts. The Free Europe Press printed up millions of propaganda leaflets to be launched. The leaflets contained such slogans as "A new hope is stirring," and "Friends of Freedom in other lands have found a new way to reach you." The schedule and frequencies of Radio Free Europe's broadcasts to Czechoslovakia were on the reverse side of the leaflets. Over 11,000,000 leaflets were dropped behind the Iron Curtain during the two weeks of the "Winds for Freedom" operation at a cost of $233,041.89.

From August 1951 to November 1956, the skies of Central Europe were filled with more than 500,000 balloons carrying over 300,000,000 leaflets, posters, books, and other printed matter that were sent from West Germany over the Iron Curtain to Poland, Czechoslovakia, and Hungary.

## *Operation STONE (Akce Kámen): The Tragic Theater of Communism*[29]

On August 31, 1951, Radio Free Europe's Czechoslovak broadcast service, the "Voice of Free Czechoslovakia," aired a radio drama in the hard-hitting series titled *All This We Know*. This program series identified secret police officers and agents as well as agent-provocateurs, blackmailers, informers and "quislings" in countries behind the Iron Curtain. This particular program identified a "Dr. Evzen" and went into details of a

Czechoslovak intelligence service (StB—Státní bezpečnost) scheme known as Operation STONE (Akce Kámen). It used agent provocateurs not only to arrest, try, imprison or execute potential escapees from Czechoslovakia, but also to steal anything or "wealth" from the victims. STONE referred to the border markers used to identify the German-Czech border.

The criminal scheme involved a false German-Czechoslovak border, according to an official U.S. State Department protest note on June 15, 1948, to Czechoslovakia:

> For approximately four weeks, representatives of the Czechoslovak State Security Police (S.N.B.), dressed in full uniform with insignia of officers of the United States Army, have been conducting an office in a house on Czechoslovak territory in the western outskirts of the village of Vseruby. In the conduct of their business, these representatives are seated behind a desk on which there is conspicuously displayed a bottle of American whiskey, packages of American cigarettes and a small American flag. On the wall behind their desk is a large American flag and pictures of Presidents Truman and Roosevelt.
>
> These S.N.B. representatives, dressed in uniforms of the United States Army, are assisted by other S.N.B. representatives who are dressed in uniforms of the German border police. According to factual evidence in the possession of the Government of the United States, the purpose of this office, as well as of the fraudulent misuse of the uniform of the Army of the United States and of the German border police, as well as the display of the American flag and pictures of the former and present presidents of the United States, is to supplement other measures taken by the Czechoslovak Government to prevent illegal departures from Czechoslovakia.[30]

The Czechoslovak government not only denied the allegations but also "hinted that the Americans were being somewhat paranoid." Moreover, "most minute investigation in Vseruby has failed to find the smallest trace or suspicion of a misuse of American insignia or portraits of US statesmen. We maintain that the protest is based on a report of an unreliable informer."

Researchers into Communist Czechoslovakia crimes have convincingly proved that the Americans were not paranoid and scores of Czechoslovak citizens were victimized. Information about the scheme and the false border station that were detailed in the 1948 protest note were revealed to the United States through Stanislav Liška, an American agent for the U.S. Army Counterintelligence Corp (CIC). Liška was later arrested in December 1948, but he was released for lack of evidence. In August 1949, Liška, his wife and three children escaped to West Germany and after a time in a displaced persons camp in Ludwigsburg, they resettled in Canada.[31]

One variation of how the scheme worked in general: previously identified wealthy persons were approached by agent provocateurs and told they were about to be arrested by the secret police. To avoid this, they should leave Czechoslovakia immediately and take only cash and jewelry. They were driven at night to a "border" with border markings. Believing they were at the German border, the victims would then cross on foot, when they would be met by StB agents acting as smugglers, or bribed German border police. From there, the victims would be brought to the house described in the 1948 U.S. protest note. They believed they were then in the care of the American military.

Another StB officer speaking fluent English and Czech named Amon Tomašoff (Code name "Tony") greeted them, offered them a glass of whisky, cigarettes, and chocolates to any children. He then proceeded to ask them who they were and why they wanted to leave Czechoslovakia. The victims answered questions about their past, their associates and contacts, and any anti–Communist activities. This was reduced in writing in the form of an official protocol and signed by the victims.

After a certain period of time, the victims were told that their asylum request would be further processed at a nearby refugee camp. They left the border point in the darkness of night with the protocol in hand and headed to what they thought was a refugee camp, sometimes alone or accompanied by a "guide" who somehow managed to get lost. Their personal items and valuables were left behind.

But this time, instead of meeting West German border police, the victims were met by Czech border guards who arrested them. The victims returned to Prague to face trial, imprisonment or death. The evidence used was the protocol they had signed in the "American" house. Their personal property including house, apartments, and villas were then confiscated. Some of the victims were sent to work in the uranium mines and certain death.

Some victims' request for political asylum were denied and they were handed over to the Czech border guards. The news that the United States had turned down some asylum requests leaked out of prisons and labor camps and thus potential escapees thought twice about attempting to leave Czechoslovakia.

Similar operations were acted out in Cheb, Marienbad, Domaylice, and other Czechoslovak locations near the German border.

It would appear that the operation finally stopped after the 1951 RFE program. "Dr. Evzen" in Radio Free Europe's program was StB counter-intelligence officer Evzen Abrahamovič, code-named "Dr. Breza" and "Evzen." He was born on July 7, 1921, and was one of the main players in the STONE criminal activities. According to Boston University history professor Dr. Igor Lukes:

> Abrahamovič ultimately continued on to a long and happy life as a director of a large department store. He was still alive as of October 2010, at the age of 89, living in the Czech Republic. Until some two or three years ago, undisturbed by any of the geopolitical upheavals that beset his country after the Velvet Revolution of 1989, he could be seen lunching regularly at the same place as the notorious traitor Karel Köcher.[32]

On December 24, 1951, the US State Department sent the following information to all American diplomatic and consular missions:

> It is emphasized that Radio Free Europe is a private, non-governmental agency supported from contributions solicited in the United States by "The Crusade for Freedom." It concentrates its radio broadcasts on the captive countries behind the Iron Curtain.
>
> Radio Free Europe cannot be construed under any circumstances to be speaking for the United States Government. Any suggestion by other nations that the United States Government assumes responsibility and endeavor to control the output of Radio Free Europe has been rejected as contrary to democratic procedure and the principle of freedom of information.[33]

On January 17, 1952, there was another top-level meeting with CIA, the State Department, and C.D. Jackson of the NCFE and Abbot Washburn, executive vice chairman of the Crusade for Freedom.[34] Mr. Barrett reminded the group that NCFE had started as an organization to look after and make use of the various Eastern European refugee groups. He recalled that giving these groups a radio voice was something of a later development.[35]

RFE Police Advisor William E. Griffith in Munich 1952–1958 wrote in February 1952: "RFE is therefore a group of complete radio stations, with all the elements of any normal western radio—news, lecture, music, education, sports, comedy and political commentaries."[36] Griffith has been credited with developing the concept of radio "surrogate (home service) broadcasting," when he postulated four essential elements to surrogate broadcasting:

1. A saturation "home service"—Radio Prague and Radio Bucharest, for example, as they would be if the countries were free and democratic;
2. A nimble Front-Line operation able to monitor Communist media quickly, interview refuges, and imbue a sense of morale and élan among the broadcasters;
3. Avoidance of exile politics allowing professional broadcasters to set forth both conservative and liberal democratic processes; and
4. Empowerment of exile broadcasters by American management as equal partners "who know more about how to talk to their own people than do the Americans themselves."[37]

Griffith also contrasted the New York and Munich RFE operations: "RFE's New York operations have clearly and finally demonstrated that exile politics and successful psychological warfare do not mix. Political patronage, party 'representation,' and incomprehensible but destructive intrigues are the only result. On the other hand, RFE Munich as shown that exile radio men and journalists, selected primarily for their professional competence, can come close to excluding the crippling aspects of exile politics form their radio work."[38]

## The Eagle

At 04:50 a.m., December 2, 1953, Radio Free Europe put a 50 kw, mobile, medium-wave transmitter, code name "Eagle," on the air with the playing of Beethoven's Egmont Overture.[39] This transmitter was in addition to the medium wave transmitter operating in Holzkirchen, near Munich, which was so heavily jammed that RFE decided to add the second transmitter. The mobile transmitter complex, located in Cham near the Czechoslovak border, consisted of seven trailers: a cooling van, studio van, frequency receiver, power supply van, diesel tanker, shop van, and an RCA 50 kw transmitter, and was identified as MB-50.[40]

The frequency chosen for its broadcasts was 854 kHz, which happened to be the primary frequency of Radio Bucharest. That frequency also had been used with low power by the Armed Forces Network (AFN) in Berlin for the American military stationed there. High-level negotiations were required to get the station to agree to dropping the frequency so that RFE could use it. AFN moved to another frequency, and almost immediately began complaining that coverage was not as good as it had been previously on 854 kHz.[41]

It is doubtful that RFE's programs were heard as interference from Radio Bucharest was severe and two Czechoslovak jammers began interfering with the frequency within minutes after it went on the air. Romanian protests to the United States and to Germany eventually forced RFE to close down the transmitter.[42]

The "Eagle" was quietly shipped to the Germany port of Bremenhaven, where it remained in storage for several years, until CIA thought it would be useful to move the transmitter into the Caribbean and begin a black radio operation beamed toward Cuba as "Radio Americas." The medium wave transmitter, still inside its van, was shipped to Swan Island, where it broadcast to Cuba for the next eight years. The transmitter was then moved to Vietnam, where it conducted clandestine operations until 1974. While in Vietnam, the transmitter operated from an airplane, and was often referred to as "The Blue Eagle."

## Shortwave Radio Broadcasting to Hungary

The first Radio Free Europe program to Hungary as the Voice of Free Hungary (VOFH) took place on August 4, 1951, Monsignor Bela

Varga, former President of the Hungarian National Parliament, advised listeners:

> To attempt no futile uprisings at this time. Pending the day of liberation, which will permit them to use their strength effectively, ... the free world knows and feels that their own battle is their battle. It is no longer indifferent or neutral. It is wholeheartedly allied to us in this great crusade, which is being waged for world freedom.[43]

One example of the Voice of Free Hungary's "Black Book" provocative series identifying Communist agents and informants is a 1951 VOFH broadcast that singled out factory official Vilmos Vizi as a sexual predator:

> The mills of God grind slowly, but thoroughly. Each day new voices are added to our Black Book. No traitor, no helper of the Russians should believe that his acts will remain unknown. Disgusting, treacherous eyes are persecuting the pretty girls working at the textile factor of Ujszeged. They are sly, these eyes, and the unfortunate young girls do not know which of them will be the next victim of the Almighty Activist of the factory organization. For by now you will have discovered, Comrade Vilmos Vizi, that I am talking to about you. Aren't you ashamed, Vilmos Vizi, of using the advantage originating in your party position not only to exploit physically the working women and to torture their minds, but to lay claim to their bodies in order to satisfy your filthy urges. How many young women have you denounced, Vilmos Yizi, as reactionaries and enemies of popular democracy and of the party merely because they had sufficient courage to refuse your immoral and dishonorable suggestions? ... You are worse than a beast, Vilmos Vizi.... The mills of God grind slowly but thoroughly. We know everything. We are watchful.... Someday everything will have to be paid for. Tomorrow it may be too late, but you can still find in yourself the human being, the Hungarian. The free Hungarians are looking at you with open eyes and will not forget.[44]

The script was based, in part, on Information Report, No. 9812, October 24, 1951, from on an interview in the summer 1951 from a source listed as "fairly reliable" and the information as "possible, unconfirmed":

> Vilmos VIZI is a trade-union activist in the factory. He has come from Romania to Szeged. He leads an immoral life. He keeps on chasing the girls in the factory with improper advances. If they resist, he denounces them to the communist party as being reactionary or lewd. His wife, who is also an active communist, has an office job in the factory. She conducts a rather loose way of life. She is passing from one male to the other among her colleagues in the office. The Vizi couple lives in the "Hatházak" settlement in New Szeged.[45]

Famed espionage/intelligence writer Ladislas Farago was employed in New York City as a consultant to the RFE Hungarian Desk from October 1, 1950, to January 31, 1952. He used the name John L. Carver, as RFE did not want his connection known to the outside world. He worked out of two hotel rooms not at the Radio Free Europe office. Thus the name Desk X was used in reference to him. He was paid $700 a month for his consultancy.

"Colonel Bell" was an important fictional character created by Ladislas

Farago. One representative script used for broadcasting by other RFE language services was one dated 6 September 1951: "Colonel Bell's Military Analysis 42: 'The Plan in Secret Warfare'" (excerpt as written in the radio script):

> This is Radio Free Europe, the Voice of Free _____. Today Colonel Bell continues his review of secret warfare with a Discussion of The Plan and its significance in preparation for an effective resistance movement. ... Colonel Bell's report will be read by a staff member of the _____ Desk of Radio Free Europe.[46]

## Bela von Liszka: A CIA Double Agent Game

Bela von Liszka was born on October 31, 1895, in Kecskemet, Hungary. After serving in the Austro-Hungarian Army in World War I, he graduated from the University of Budapest with a PhD in law. He was the mayor of Kecskemet, Hungary, from 1938 to 1944. He fled Hungary in May 1945, first to Austria and then to Munich, West Germany. In 1951, he started working as an actor-announcer for RFE in Munich. For unknown reasons, RFE terminated him in November 1951, only to re-hire him in April 1952.[47]

On December 6, 1955, von Liszka was in his apartment in Munich, when his doorbell rang at 7:30 p.m. He opened the door and found a man standing there, who spoke in German. He said his name was Miklos Rosner and he had a letter for von Liszka, purportedly written by his son, Georgy, a physician in Budapest. Von Liszka then invited the man in. For a few minutes, they both spoke German. Then Miklos switched to Hungarian, after he was convinced of von Liszka's identity.[48]

Unknown to von Liszka, CIA previously identified Rosner as Karoly Rose, a presumed officer of the Hungarian Intelligence Service ÁVH.[49] Karoly Rose in September 1955 questioned Miklos Szabo, exiled leader of the Independent Smallholder's Party about his possible return to Hungary—Szabo had openly told others that he desired to return to Hungary (he eventually returned in 1957). On December 7, 1955, Rose made a similar pitch to RFE Hungarian Service employee Laszlo Bery, who rejected it.[50]

Rose said he had delivered the letter as a favor for a Hungarian Foreign Ministry civil servant. Von Liszka read part of the letter and said it was not really from his son or was obviously written under pressure and he had no further interest in reading it. Rose did not deny the possibilities.

Rose than pitched von Liszka by offering to pay all his expenses to return to Hungary, including for the shipment of his furniture and personal belongings. He also said he had "direct authority" from the Foreign Ministry to promise von Liszka that he would be given "complete amnesty." Rose added that he could not resume his position as mayor, but would be given employment as chief librarian, or assistant chief librarian, chief bookkeeper, or assistant chief bookkeeper in the State Library. Arrangements for von Liszka's return to Hungary would be made through the Hungarian Consulate in Vienna, Austria, or Berne, Switzerland.

As Rose left the apartment, he told von Liszka that someone else would contact him in January or February 1956, and that Liszka "better not rebuff."[51] Von Liszka then called an RFE co-worker, who reported the incident to his CIA contact. He in turn then telephoned the RFE security officer, who went to von Liszka's apartment. The security officer interviewed von Liszka later that night and again the next day. The security officer told von Liszka not to discuss the Rose meeting with anyone else.

CIA would wait to see if Rose would try again or if another agent would come in his place. If so, von Liszka was to say that he was afraid to return to Hungary but did not want to put his family in danger, so he would agree to try to perform small favors. The Munich Operations Base (MOB) also ran traces on von Liszka and wanted to evaluate his fitness to be a double agent.

In January 1956, CIA met von Liszka. He agreed to cooperate regarding any contacts from Rose, or anyone else from Hungary, and work as a double agent.

One of the results of the CIA trace showed that a West German double agent (UJDROLLERY #305, "Pfeifer") told his AVH handler that he had met von Liszka in August 1955 in Munich, and von Liszka told him that "all employees of RFE had to sign an agreement that they would not allow themselves to be employed by an intelligence service. If they were approached by any intelligence agent, they were to report this to the RFE Security Officer. If they did not to his they were subject not only to dismissal but also investigation." Based on this conversation, CIA assumed that the AVH was aware that if von Liszka did agree to "perform missions," he was probably a double agent.[52]

"Pfeiler" in 1954 was also tasked by the AVH at one meeting to provide information about "Operation Focus," the balloon/leaflet program of NCFE's Free Europe Press combined with RFE's Hungarian Service broadcasts. "Focus" began October 1, 1954, and ended in March 1955, by which time over one million balloons carrying 16,000,000 leaflets were launched.

Because of the von Liszka-Rose meeting, CIA instituted a mail intercept of letters coming to and from von Liszka. This resulted in the intercept of 18 Hungarian language letters, which were duly read and translated. In early February 1956, von Liszka received a letter purportedly written jointly by his wife and son. Under CIA control, von Liszka sent them a letter dated February 25, 1956, which read in part:

The first thing in your dear letters I would like to answer regards the problem of returning home. Every person thinks about it, that in the soonest possible time he should be able to see those that are dear to him, if fate was such that it has separated them from each other. The individual who lives in a foreign land also desires that he once more under the old conditions be together again in his homeland and with those to whom blood and relatives tie him. These desires are the only things that give momentum to his life.

Neither do I wish to renounce this wish to see you again happily, however there are some other things and other problems tied in with this question. These problems have to be resolved with concrete assurances since only their resolution could assure one re going home. Only the most important ones will I point out: That the returnee will find without any consequences personal liberty and security, and that he will be able to live together with those who belong to him and remain with them if all so desire. Then (that there exists) the freedom to choose employment, that the individual receives work which is in line with his ability and with his physical strength and that the returns are sufficient to support his family. And finally that there would be security in old age or sickness, and in case of unemployment.

From my viewpoint, these are inseparable pre-conditions which are very important, because these things still don't exist, therefore it does not give me that security and assurance, which would be necessary for me to consider a return home. And exactly because of that I still don't see that the time to return home has arrived.[53]

Von Liszka received another letter dated March 5, 1956, which told him that he was incorrect in believing that conditions for returning to Hungary were not already present and he should reconsider his decision not to return. The writer said that when von Liszka's wife is lonely, she listens to Radio Free Europe to hear his voice. She looked forward to a "sweet reunion." The letter went on, "She says she is only interested in your health and that he should come to the Pfarrhaus, where he will be received as if he were returning home. He can rest in the yard under the apple trees and regain his health."[54]

Von Liszka received another letter dated March 21, 1956, postmarked in Vienna, with the request that he travel to Switzerland:

> Received your letter from George, which showed when I should meet you. Since your last letter to George, there has been a change in my itinerary; I will be in Switzerland Only in early April in Bern.
> If it is convenient, please meet me on 5 April at 1400 on Casino Platz on the stairs in front of the Casino Restaurant. If the 5th is inconvenient, then the same time and place on the 6th.
> I trust that you will be able to respond to George's questions, and that I will be able to tell you of the things which he and I have discussed.
> Kovacs Miklos[55]

The AVH tried again for a meeting in Switzerland with a follow-up letter:

> In my letter I let you know where and when to meet me. Apparently, you didn't get that letter, and thus did not keep the appointment. Since the talks at Bern have been

extended, there is still a possibility for you to talk to me. If convenient, meet me at the Casino Restaurant, on 12 April at 1400, on the stairs. If it is more convenient for you, then on the day before I will be at the same place at the same time. I shall take time to meet you. I would like to discuss my friend George's problem with you, and do what I can to keep my promise to George.[56]

Since there was no meeting in Berne, the AVH tried another tactic. In April 1956, von Liszka received a letter from his wife advising him that she had just taken a job with the Red Cross and would be traveling to East Berlin at the end of May. She hoped that he would go to Berlin to meet her. Von Liszka believed that this was a way to have his wife personally appeal to him to return to Hungary. The CIA was against this meeting, as it was believed that they could not control the meeting, even if it were held in West Berlin. With CIA concurrence, von Liszka wrote a letter stating it was impossible for him to travel to Berlin and she should travel to Munich after arriving in Berlin.[57]

Von Liszka received another letter dated May 17, 1955, which again cryptically asked him to travel to Berlin for a meeting:

> When my friend arrived and told me he could not talk to you, the news disturbed me greatly. He told me how his itinerary changed, and how many times and ways he tried to reach you. Even though Miklos and I are good friends, I still doubt his words. A few days after Miklos's arrival I received your letter, for which I thank you. This letter convinced me that my friend Miklos is a decent and trustworthy fellow.
>
> Miklos also said that present plans are for travel to the place he has already mentioned, between 20 and 26 May. I ask you urgently to talk with Miklos. I would like you to inform him of the family's status. I think you will be able to help us. My friend has promised to take time for this. Please let me know when you will be able to meet him at the place he mentioned in his last letter to you.[58]

Another letter dated June 5, 1955, contained no references to a meeting in Berlin. Von Liszka assumed that the AVH dropped its interest in him. But he received two more letters from his wife respectively dated June 23, 1955, and July 4, 1955. The gist of the letters was that because von Liszka was working for Radio Free Europe, she had lost her job and although von Liszka was working against his homeland, he should return to Hungary. The CIA concurred with another letter from von Liszka, in which he said there was no question of his returning to Hungary.[59]

In May 1956, von Liszka learned that his December 1955 meeting with Rose was known in the émigré Hungarian community in Munich.

CIA's Munich Operations Base chief wrote this comment about von Liszka in August 1956:

> In brief, we do not believe him capable of maintaining in the course of personal meetings with the AVH the fiction that he is not an AIS [American intelligence service] double agent. Our course in the past few months has thus been to disentangle

ourselves from Subject although maintaining the appearance of being at all times willing to advise him on what steps to take vis a vis the continued efforts to redefect him. We intend to continue to see Subject as he professes the need, since this is not costing any great effort on our part. Our one present single objective is to monitor further developments on the chance that we may find **an** opportunity to induce the AVH to make a further personal meeting with Subject and we may thus be able to identify another AVH asset. We intend to report further on Subject's *case* only in the event of significant new developments.[60]

On March 27, 1957, CIA's Deputy Director of Security (Investigations and Support) reported:

Reference is made to your memorandum wherein you request a Proprietary Approval for Subject's use as an actor-announcer under Project TPTONIC.[61] Subject's activities are to be closely controlled and supervised, He is not to have access to any classified information, he is not to be used operationally or be witting of Agency/Project relationship and his status may not be changed without the prior concurrence of this office.[62]

One of the "results of local processing" of von Liszka in April 1957 included this comment: "There are numerous references to subject in local files. Although subject was approached by Karoly ROSE, he is apparently loyal to RFE."[63]

On June 30, 1961, RFE went through a reduction in force in Munich and terminated von Liszka's employment. Bela von Liszka died in Munich on March 30, 1978.

## Radio Free Europe and the 1956 Hungarian Revolution

There are 13 days (October 24 to November 4, 1956) of still unclear and controversial events in and outside Hungary. One of the everlasting controversies is the role of Radio Free Europe (RFE) broadcasts as the Voice of Free Hungary in fermenting the Revolution.

According to a post-mortem RFE internal study of 308 Hungarian language programs, "There were relatively few real policy violations. All of them occurred in the first period (before November 4)." There were four violations of RFE's broadcast policies and, 20 programs involved "misapplications or distortions of policy or serious failure to employ constructive techniques of policy application." Examples of the four programs that were "policy violations" included

Borsanyi's "Armed Forces Special" #A1 of 27 October violations the letter and spirit of policy in effect at the time. The program gives detailed instructions as to how partisan and Hungarian armed forces should fight. It advises local authorities to secure stores of arms for the use of Freedom Fighters and tell the population to hide Freedom

Fighters who become separated from their units. It advises the population to provide food and supplies for Freedom Fighters. The writer tells Hungarians to sabotage ("disconnect") railroad and telephone lines. It fairly clearly implies that foreign aid will be forthcoming if the resistance forces succeed in establishing a "central military command." ... [T]he program concludes with some rather complex formulations that could be interpreted by listeners as implying help from the outside.[64]

Colonel Bell again surfaced in broadcasts during the critical days in October and later were identified as another clear violation of Radio Free Europe's Broadcasting Policy that should not have been broadcast.

"Armed Forces Special" #B1 of 28 October gives detailed instructions to Hungarian soldiers on the conduct of partisan warfare. The author states at the beginning of the program that Hungarians must continue to fight vigorously because this will have a great effect on the handling of the Hungarian question by the Security Council of the UN. Without saying so directly, he implies that the UN will give active support to Hungarians if they keep on fighting. The program is over-optimistic in tone.

The opening announcement states: "Colonel Bell will tell Hungarian soldiers how ingenious and smart leadership can counterbalance numerical and arms superiority.

Colonel Bell has told Hungarian soldiers how to obstruct large forces by small ones and by simple means." In the light of subsequent events the program grossly underestimates the ability of the Soviets to move new troops into Hungary. Borsanyi implies that the most the Soviets can bring in is about four divisions and that it might take as long as two or three weeks for the Soviets to secure the Danube line if Hungarians fight effectively against them.

This program of Borsanyi's constitutes a serious policy violation, for the author in no way makes any effort to demonstrate that he is basing his advice on opinions or even information coming from within the country. Here at its worst is the émigré on the outside, without responsibility or authority, giving detailed advice to the people fighting at home.[65]

The post–Revolution Hungarian government issued a "White Book" on the events of the Revolution and clearly blamed Radio Free Europe as one of the main players not only in inciting the revolution but also in allowing to continue longer than necessary, a charge and myth that continues to have believers even today:

The subversive broadcasts of Radio Free Europe-backed by dollars, directed from America, and functioning on the territory of West Germany, played an essential role in the ideological preparation and practical direction of the counter-revolution, in provoking the armed struggle, in the non-observance of the cease fire, and in arousing the mass hysteria, which led to the lynching of innocent men and women loyal to their people and their country.[66]

On November 4, 1956, Free Europe Committee issued a 113-page report titled: *The Revolt in Hungary: A Documentary Chronology of Events based exclusively on internal broadcasts by central and provincial radios, October 23, 1956–November 4, 1956.* The preface began:

This document records the story of the Hungarian people's revolt as broadcast day-to-day, hour-by-hour. The record begins with the Radio Budapest account of student demonstrations on October 23, 1956, continues through the Soviet military intervention on November 4, 1956, and includes significant excerpts from broadcasts through November 9, 1956. The source materials for these transcriptions are the broadcasts of all central and provincial radio stations of Hungary, and edited to give a running account of the most important political, economic and military events of the revolt. Passages have been selected only on the basis of their significance in the sequence of developments; they have been given as completely and in as great length as possible, with a particular eye for materials, which have not been published elsewhere.[67]

The Free Europe Committee issued a press release on November 16, 1956, under the name of Joseph C. Grew, Chairman, Board of Directors that defended the broadcasts of RFE:

Since the uprising in Hungary the Soviet Press has falsely accused Radio Free Europe of inciting the rebellion. Fears that this may have been the case have also been expressed in some free world newspapers and radio comment.

A Radio Free Europe directive, issued as long ago as December 12, 1951, stated categorically:

"Speakers are warned not to yield to a natural impulse to bring hope to their compatriots by promising armed intervention by the West. To raise the hopes of our audience in this fashion would be to do them a cruel disservice: it would also constitute radical misrepresentation of the present policies of the western powers. Such talks by not be broadcast on RFE."

Over the years since that time, Radio Free Europe has not deviated from this essential policy and practice.[68]

Both the United Nations and West German governments investigated these and other allegations against Radio Free Europe and concluded differently. The West German government finding, as announced at a January 25, 1957, press conference of Chancellor Konrad Adenauer:

This investigation has shown that the assertions which appeared in the press, that Radio Free Europe promised the Hungarians assistance by the West-armed assistance by the West-are not consistent with the facts. However, remarks were also made which were liable to cause misinterpretations. But a discussion, an exchange of views, took place which also resulted in personnel changes and I believe that the matter can be considered settled for the time being.[69]

The United Nations report concluded: "It would appear that certain broadcasts by Radio Free Europe helped to create an impression that support might be forth coming for the Hungarians. The Committee feels that in such circumstances the greatest restraint and circumspection are called for in international broadcasting."[70]

The CIA officer directly responsible for RFE, Cord Meyer, probably best summarizes the role of RFE in the Hungarian Revolution, when he wrote:

> From my own exposure to these events and from the findings of the working group within the Agency that reviewed the taped RFE broadcasts, I am satisfied that RFE did not plan, direct, or attempt to provoke the Hungarian rebellion.... The spontaneous combustion of a popular revolution does not fit easily into the conspiratorial theory of history, but in this case it is the best explanation of what occurred.[71]

Former Director of Radio Free Europe George Urban has written:

> There can be no escaping the truth that in the psychological climate of what must be considered wartime conditions everything the free world said in its broadcasts was liable to incite or, at least raise the hopes on a very large scale. ... A "positional" kind of incitement was inevitable. Surrogate broadcasting from Munich ... a form of encouragement simply because they and the sentiments they reflected, existed.... Incredibly, the risk of being misinterpreted in a revolutionary environment had not been foreseen.[72]

## *RFE and the Soviet-Led Invasion of Czechoslovakia 1968*

The USSR-led military operation using cryptonym "Danube" began at 23:00 August 20, 1968, when hundreds of thousands of soldiers using thousands of tanks, trucks, and other vehicles, plus airplanes, invaded Czechoslovakia putting an end to the short-lived freedoms known as Prague Spring. Almost immediately, the battle for men's minds using radio began.

Radio Free Europe went on an emergency broadcast basis in the early morning hours of August 21, 1968, that lasted to September 5, 1968. The emergency contingency planning sessions that took place in July foresaw twenty-four-hour continuous news, commentary, and American management tight control of program content. They had used the events surrounding the 1956 Hungarian Revolution as a lessons-learned exercise.

The actual date and time of the Soviet-led invasion caught Radio Free Europe off-guard as many of its top managers were on vacation and had to be recalled. Even the President of the Free Europe Committee, William Durkee, was in Spain and had to fly back to New York, where he was based. A policy task force was set up in the RFE Central News Room, with a 24-hour management presence for control and guidance.

All information fed to Broadcast Departments was screened for content, any of which was objectionable and/or alarmist information was either eliminated on identified as "Background Information Only" (BIO). All program scripts devoted to Czechoslovakia were previewed for approval, or not, by the American policy staff. "Background Information Only" material, i.e., not for broadcasting, included:

- All names of traitors and collaborators
- Alarmist reports of upcoming KGB arrests or Czechoslovak intellectuals. All mentions of names of those arrested or about to be arrested.
- All Czechoslovak clandestine radio reports (and subsequent Western media pick-up of these reports) of the rejections of the Czechoslovak-Soviet Moscow agreement
- All references to calls for a neutralist policy of Czechoslovakia.
- Alarmist reports of possible Soviet invasion of Romania or Yugoslavia.
- Alarmist reports of current danger of World nuclear war.
- Reports on, or anything, which might be interpreted as encouraging resistance by Czechoslovaks, unless this clearly qualified as passive resistance.
- Any material which, by an stretch of the imagination, could have been interpreted or understood by RFE's listeners as a hint that the U.S. or the West would intervene militarily to alter the situation in Czechoslovakia or to prevent Soviet action against Romania.
- All but moderate, factual and limited reports on the presence and fate of Czechoslovak refugees in the West. While reporting official western government statements, we were are careful as we could be in order to avoid giving the impression of encouraging defections.[73]

Normal broadcasting was altered by all Broadcast Departments: popular music was eliminated and services consisted primarily of serious music, news, and information, plus whatever commentaries were believed essential. The commentaries were reviewed in English translation prior to their being broadcast. Arrangements were made to keep all the language services on the air 24 hours a day. This meant a reduction in normal transmitter strength to Poland and Hungary, allowing for full coverage to Bulgaria and Romania. No news items on Czechoslovak subjects were issued prior to clearance by top management. The intention was to keep tight control, even if from time to time clearance procedures might have caused slight delays in news programming.[74]

In the afternoon of August 21, 1969, RFE sent two teams of journalists to the border points Germany-Czechoslovakia and Austria-Czechoslovakia. The teams were under "rigid instructions" not to enter Czechoslovakia under any circumstances whatsoever—teams of RFE personnel had entered Hungary in 1956 and some were even detained by Soviet troops. The teams also were under instruction "to find out what is going on, behave as normal journalists and in no way push themselves off as representatives of

RFE." After their arrivals, the teams announced that there was no evidence of mass flights of refugees across the borders.[75]

On August 23, 1968, a mobile monitoring and recording team was sent to the German-Czech border to monitor the low-powered local radio stations that sprang up after the invasion. This team augmented the large RFE monitoring station outside Munich at Schleissheim. The purpose of the team, told to be inconspicuous, was "to get best possible coverage of remaining Czechoslovak radio stations and any new clandestine broadcasting, which develops."[76] Although RFE also had monitoring stations in West Berlin, Vienna, and Thessaloniki to monitor RFE transmitter strength and quality, they also could have been used to monitor Czechoslovak radio broadcasts, but there is no record that they were used that way.

RFE saw it role in the crisis as a watchful observer, commentator, and cross-reporter. Soon after the invasion, Soviet and other East European communist media began to develop a pattern of attack similar to that mounted around the 1956 Hungarian events. A major effort in this connection was the attempt to link RFE directly with the clandestine or free Czechoslovak radios still operating. It was claimed that RFE directed the activities of these stations, counter-revolutionaries, etc.

On August 23, 1968, RFE withdrew the news team from Austrian-Czech border, as refuges flow simply did not occur. The German border team under Bill Marsh remained a few days afterwards, in case the flow of refugees increased. It did not and eventually this team also returned to Munich.

Although the Bavarian government set up a fund to financially help Czechoslovaks who were unable to return to their county, RFE set up its own fund to help those, who did want to contact Bavarian government officials and found themselves in need: "A relatively small cash account to be used in extraordinary circumstances to help those who cannot, or perhaps should not, be referred to some other source for aid."[77]

As Radio Prague's freedom further increased, RFE's audience went down. This was clearly demonstrated by the downward trend in listenership size between 1967 and August 1968. Inasmuch as it is RFE's aim to contribute to the development of free communications media in its broadcasting area, RFE had come close to fulfilling its mission. Therefore, the drop in RFE's Czech and Slovak audience was fully to be expected and constituted success rather than failure. The careful planning and execution of RFE'S crisis response activities paid off.

# 3

# From Radio Liberation to Radio Liberty to RFE/RL

> "The help that every man of good will, every day can give Radio Liberation is to water the arching tree of liberty, of which Radio Liberation is a branch."
> —*Sparks into the USSR* (1956 Radio Liberation Information Booklet)

## Creation of Radio Liberation/Liberty

On August 21, 1951, Frank Wisner sent to Allen Dulles DDP a history of developments that led eventually to the creation of Radio Liberation / Radio Liberty, especially the cover of the CIA involvement:

> In the summer of 1950, the Department of State through Mr. George Kennan, who was then Counsellor of the Department, requested CIA/OPC to undertake the development of a political center among the emigres from the Soviet Union.
>
> Certain general principals were also decided upon in relation to the establishment of the cover committee in New York ... [T]he committee should be strictly a "front" and that at the outset this should be made very clear to them so that there would be no misunderstanding at a later date.... [T]he committee would not publicly solicit funds.... [A]t the present time, a Foundation is being established in the Midwest to act as one of the ostensible funds for the committee.
>
> The largest and most difficult problem is that of establishing the radio facilities and programming necessary for large-scale broadcasts to the Soviet Union.[1]

The American Committee for Freedom for the Peoples of the USSR was founded in the United States on January 18, 1951, in Delaware. Newspaper columnist Eugene Lyons was the first president. Unlike the National Committee for a Free Europe, the American Committee for the Freedom

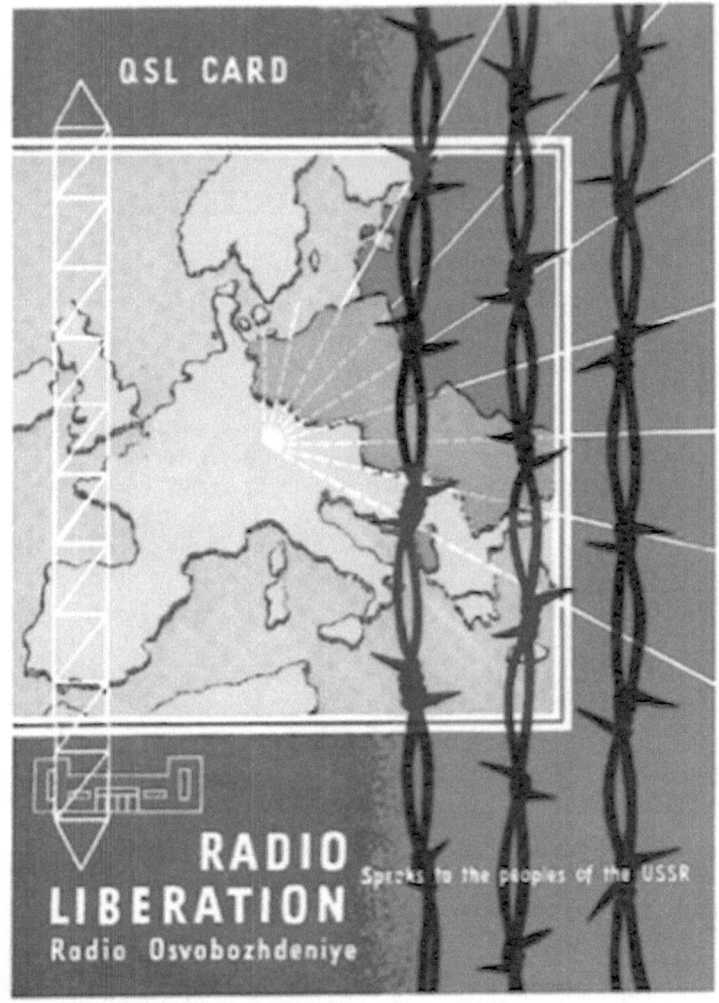

**A Radio Liberation QSL card. This was sent to listeners to record broadcast audibility, times and frequencies in the 1950s.**

of the Peoples of the USSR decided not to raise public funds in the United States, which would have "aided in providing plausible cover for its true sponsorship."[2]

The Committee would undergo names changes to American Committee for the Liberation of the Peoples of the USSR, and American Committee for Liberation from Bolshevism in March 1953, and, finally, in 1964, Radio Liberty Committee. The American Committee's position was that the most effective psychological war against the Soviet regime would be

## 3. From Radio Liberation to Radio Liberty to RFE/RL 49

conducted by former Soviet exiles united in speaking out against Communism. However, there were difficulties in the way of accomplishing this aim: one was the extreme hostility between Great Russian groups and non–Russian nationalities of the USSR. The other difficulty was the basic political differences between Marxist and non–Marxist exiles, regardless of their nationality.

After long and arduous negotiations among the émigré groups at meetings held throughout Germany, agreement was finally reached in October

A 1956 Radio Liberation 48-page booklet cover for "Sparks into the USSR."

1952, for the formation of a Coordinating Center, composed of four Great Russian and five nationality groups. This was not a unified émigré agreement: certain Great Russian émigrés (NTS for example) and representatives of important minority groups in the USSR, including Ukrainians and Byelorussians, did not join the Coordinating Center.

A CIA ten-page paper dated January 22, 1953, contained, in part, these editorial policy guidelines:

1. The American Committee for the Liberation of the Peoples of Russia, Inc., will sponsor radio broadcasts beamed to Soviet occupation personnel and to the peoples in the USSR proper, enabling the representatives of these peoples in the non-communist world to speak to their counterparts under Soviet control in terms denied official radio activities....
2. Radio Liberation, sponsored by the *American Committee,* is an organ of the peoples of the USSR.... [I]ts voice will be solely that of the total Russian and Nationalities emigration, so that it may achieve credibility and accomplish maximum results.
3. The aim of the anti–Soviet Russian and nationalities emigration, whose members are staffing Radio Liberation, and who, under American supervision, are responsible for the programming, are simpler and more specific:
    a. To overthrow the Soviet regime
    b. To establish a new regime (or regimes) which will reflect their political and ethnic concepts.[3]

"Radio Liberation" (Radiostantsiya Osvobozhdeniye) first broadcast from transmitters in Lampertheim, Germany, on March 1, 1953, with a 20-minute program that was rebroadcast for the next 12 hours. It opened with Soviet émigré Sergey Dubrovsky giving the station's broadcast times and frequencies. This was followed by a political and moral proclamation read by Boris Vinogradov that began: "Listen! Listen! Today, a new radio station, Liberation, begins its broadcasts" (Слушайте! Слушайте! Сегодня начинает свои передачи новая Радиостанция Освобождение!). The program continued with, "The radio would advocate 'complete freedom of conscience and the right to religious preaching,' as well as 'the elimination of exploitation of man by a party or the state.'" World news followed and was read by Ekaterina Goby and Sergei Dubrovsky. The program ended with a historical program read by Sergi Dubrovsky that focused on the anniversary of the 1921 Kronstadt Rebellion when disillusioned revolutionary sailors, soldiers and workers rose against Bolshevik power.

Sergei Dubrovsky unexpectedly died at age 57 on October 25, 1955, after being hospitalized for what could be termed "acute liver failure." He was buried in Munich. Some Russian Service broadcasters were so affected with his death that RL headquarters in New York sent a telex message to Munich telling the managers to do what they could about controlling the rumors among the émigrés that Sergei Dubrovsky had been murdered.[4]

The prime suspect was Boris Vinogradov, who had been a successful Shakespearian stage actor in the USSR in the 1930s. In the Second World War, the acting ensemble of which he was a part got caught behind the German lines. They performed for German army officers and Russian prisoners of war. As the German army retreated, the ensemble went with them to Berlin. Vinogradov then remained in Germany as the others eventually moved to occupied France. After the Second World War, Vinogradov remained in Germany, eventually joined Radio Liberation as an actor/announcer, and married a woman who had escaped from the Soviet controlled area of Germans to Bavaria in the American sector. Vinogradov reportedly was never happy in the West and acting opportunities for a Russian actor were limited. He apparently contacted Soviet authorities in Paris and arranged to return to the USSR. Vinogradov then returned to USSR in July 1956 by driving his Volkswagen Beetle car.[5]

There was some propaganda in the Soviet media after his return. He was given a state apartment and renewed his acting career in Leningrad until the mid 1960s. Vinogradov eventually moved to Kazakhstan in 1967 and continued with his Soviet film career. It is not known when and where he died.

The two 10 KW transmitters purchased from Radio Free Europe were so low-powered that only the Soviet armed forces in Germany and Austria were targeted. There was no record that the first broadcast was actually heard in the target area. Yet, within ten minutes, the Soviet Union started jamming the broadcasts, and the jamming of Radio Liberty's broadcasts would continue uninterrupted until 1988. It has been estimated that the Soviet Union and other communist countries spent $4 for each $1 RL expended on broadcasting.

Dana Durand, chief of CIA's DDP/SR Division responsible for Radio Liberation, in a memorandum dated May 18, 1953, to the Deputy Director (Plans), Frank Wisner, wrote, "The fundamental issue is whether to continue the effort to bring about the unification of the Soviet emigration on a broad base.... With a considerable measure of reluctance, we have come to the conclusion that this effort, however desirable, is probably not feasible, and that continuation of it may well serve only to intensify and advertise existing differences.... [T]he Agency is confronted by a mounting body of evidence that the security situation in (redacted) is very grave, and that Soviet penetration of the Coordinating Center is effective and damaging."[6]

On June 30, 1953, a Presidential Commission issued a Top Secret report to President Eisenhower on International Information activities ("Project Clean Up"). The Commission's recommendations included:

> In a situation short of war, the project can probably make its greatest contribution by de-emphasizing its political activities and devoting its major effort to the improvement of broadcasts from Radio Liberation. This station should use Soviet émigrés in an effort to weaken the Soviet regime and should concentrate on the Soviet military, government officials, and other groups in the population, which harbor major grievances against the regime. The American Committee for Liberation from Bolshevism, Inc., should concentrate on the improvement of Radio Liberation and reduce expenditures on the émigré coordinating center.[7]

Historian and journalist William Henry Chamberlin, and one of the first members of the Board of Trustees of AmComLib, visited Radio Liberation in Munich in July 1953 and wrote:

> A visit to the editorial section of the station (the transmission is from another part of Germany) reveals an atmosphere of pioneering enthusiasm among the 250 persons, of whom 25 are Americans, who are taking part in the operation. To anyone who has lived in Russia and sensed the iron weight of a single propaganda viewpoint, hammered in with every resource of the printed and spoken word, there is something thrilling in this spectacle of the "Radio Liberation"—David going forth to battle with the Soviet mass indoctrination Goliath.[8]

By the summer 1953, the Coordinating Center was dissolved and any idea that the émigré groups would run their own radio station faded into history. Ukrainian, Belarusian, Kazakh, Kyrgyz, Tajik, Turkmen, Uzbek, Tatar-Bashkir, Armenian, Azeri, Georgian, Chechen, and Ingush language broadcasts were added to RL's programming.

William H. Chamberlin wrote in 1954:

> But another cause which this Committee has tried to advance has not fared so well. This is the combination in a single organization, with a joint platform, of representatives of all Soviet refugee groups, Russian and non-Russian, with the exception of pro-Communists, Fascists and Monarchists, who are regarded by the Committee as a liability, rather than an asset, in a united front.
>
> This effort ran into many snags from the beginning and the Coordinating Centre which was finally set up in Munich soon split into two warring and irreconcilable groups. For the time being the attempt to create a united political representation for the political emigration from the Soviet Union has been shelved and attention is being concentrated on practical enterprises, such as the radio station, broadcasting in Russian and in some of the languages of the Caucasus and Central Asia.[9]

In September 1954, Alex Karas of RF's Belorussian Service was found dead in Munich's Isar River. In December 1954, Abo Fatalibey was murdered in his apartment. Both cases were never solved but were presumed to be the work of Soviet agents.[10]

## Russian Broadcasts from Taiwan

On Sunday, August 13, 1950, the Chinese Nationalist shortwave broadcasting station, the Voice of Free China, began transmitting on 7159 kilocycles, 09:00–09:15 GMT. The content of the broadcast was short items of international news presented in a straightforward manner, without comment. The announcer reportedly spoke fluent Russian, but with a Chinese accent. The broadcast was promptly and effectively jammed by a transmitter, which was of the same types of jammer used against the Voice of American and the BBC broadcasts.[11]

Radio Liberty on Taiwan (Formosa) was on the air for almost 20 years. An agreement was signed on December 4, 1954, between RLC and the Broadcasting Corporation of China which allowed RLC to use certain transmitting facilities owned by the corporation. The agreement provided that the corporation furnish the land and personnel for operation and maintenance of the facility and that RLC provide and maintain the antenna system and related equipment and parts. Under the agreement the corporation assigned transmitting time blocks to RLC for its use for eight hours each day. RLC was required to pay the corporation $16.50 an hour for each transmitter provided. The initial broadcasts went on the air on shortwave on May 1, 1955, from a transmitter at Panchao, located just beyond the western edge of the capital city, Taipei. This was an interim location, while a new base was constructed at Pali, on the coast 20 km north of Taipei.

The programming from Radio Liberty Taiwan was beamed to the eastern areas of Russia and Siberia. A 1959 Soviet KGB report of jamming included this mention of RL's Taiwan broadcasts: "In Petropavlovsk-Kamchatka, Khabarovsk, Chita and such cities as Artem, Suchan and Nakhodka (Primorsky region), programs from a branch office of this radio station, located on the island of Taiwan, were broadcast freely on frequencies 15345 and 17755 KHz."[12]

News programs were produced locally. While some feature programs broadcast from Taiwan were flown from Munich or New York, this was a time-consuming process, so a local program department was established in Taiwan, supplemented by a correspondent in Hong Kong. Eventually there was a staff of 16 persons working for RL. To monitor the effectiveness of its broadcasts originating from the site in Taiwan, Radio Liberty had a monitoring facility in Sapporo on the island of Hokkaido, the northernmost island of Japan. Radio Liberty's Taiwan stopped broadcasting on December 31, 1973, due to cutbacks in RL's budget.[13]

Two Russian émigré groups, NTS and TsOPE (Chapter 8) also broadcast from the same site.

One of the first known American newspaper accounts of Radio

Liberation appeared in the *Christian Science Monitor* on February 2, 1955. The article, written by George W. Neill, began by quoting from a RL program:

> Attention!
> This is Radio Liberation.
> Listen to the free voice of your brother fighters from abroad.
> Listen to our true information, which the Kremlin tyrants and their lackeys conceal from you.
> Pass along what you hear on Radio Liberation to your relatives, friends and acquaintances.
> This is Radio Liberation.

The radio station's name was changed to Radio Liberty in 1959. Former Presidents Herbert Hoover, Harry Truman, and Dwight Eisenhower were "honorary chairmen" of Radio Liberty at that time. The AmComLib press release gave the ideological justification for the existence of Radio Liberty:

> Radio Liberty's broadcasts analyze events and developments in the Soviet Union and the acts and policies of the Soviet government from the point of view of the best interests of the peoples of the Soviet Union. Radio Liberty's writers and speakers seek to give expression to the innermost feelings, thoughts and repressed aspirations of their fellow countrymen.[14]

On March 23, 1959, Radio Liberty transmitted its first broadcast from the beautiful beach Playa de Pals, on the Mediterranean coast, north of Barcelona, Spain.[15]

## The Book Program

The man chosen to try and unite the diverse émigré groups in Germany was Isaac Patch, who had been a career diplomat in Moscow in World War II and later in Prague, from where he was expelled on 24 hours' notice in October 1949 for having been involved in anti-Communist underground activities in Czechoslovakia. Patch joined RLC in Munich as "director of émigré relations" or "political coordinator," in a failed attempt to unite the émigré groups. In his memoirs, he wrote,

> My job as émigré relations advisor had run its course. Although I had been unsuccessful in bringing the Russians and non-Russians together in a committee to serve as its sponsor, I did help in recruiting people for the various Radio Liberty desks.[16]

Patch then took over the Special Projects Division that published a newspaper and quarterly journal for the Russian émigré community. In 1956, Patch transferred to RLC headquarters in New York to begin the Book Project, the purpose which was, "To communicate Western ideas to Soviet citizens by providing them with books—on politics, economics, philosophy, art, and some technology—all denied them by the Soviet dictatorship."[17]

Howland Sargeant was then president of RLC. He heartily endorsed Patch's program and presented it to the CIA for financial support. The CIA responded with an initial grant of $10,000 to give cover to the book program.[18]

The Bedford Publishing Company was initially created as a "private venture" to publish Western books that had not been previously translated into Russian. The Bedford Publishing Company remained physically separate from Radio Liberty operations. Patch, although no longer officially associated with Radio Liberty, attended its regular staff meetings in New York. The Bedford Publishing Company had offices in London, Paris, Munich and Rome. Book translations were made in France and England and publishing was done in Italy. Soviet visitors to cities such as London, Paris, New York, and Rome were given books, as were Western travelers to the Soviet Union. In the 14 year-long book program associated with Radio Liberty, over one million books were delivered to the USSR this way. In his memoirs, Patch broke down this number:

35 percent were given to Soviet travelers to the West:
- Engineers,
- Teachers,
- Artists,
- Students and
- Journalists.

40 percent were given to Western travelers to USSR:
- Doctors,
- Lawyers,
- Teachers and
- Engineers

10 percent were mailed to people authorized to receive book packages from the West.

15 percent found their way by special routes to the USSR.[19]

Although CIA funding for the Bedford Publishing Company, as a unit of the Radio Liberty Committee, ceased in 1970, support continued for it until the program was consolidated with the International Advisory Council (IAC) into the International Literary Center (ILC) in July 1975.

Patch has written, "There was no evidence that the Soviet government made any concerted attempt to disrupt our efforts." He added,

> The Book Program was a rewarding endeavor for me and everyone else who was involved. Americans in the Department of State approved of the project, and Walt Raymond, who was my liaison with CIA, told me years later that the Book Program

was highly regarded by his agency. It was great fun dealing with books and ideas and working with other book lovers who enjoyed searching for titles and translators. Those of us working on the Program were thrilled to think that those hundreds of thousands of books perhaps helped to broaden Soviet minds and horizons toward democracy and western economic ideas.[20]

Isaac Patch died May 31, 2014, at age 101.

## *American Friends of Russian Freedom (AFRF)*

In the early Cold War years, a myriad group of organizations, associations, and foundations in the US and Europe were formed to aid and assist those persons known as exiles, émigrés, refugees, escapees, and defectors from the USSR: the International Rescue Committee, the Tolstoy Foundation, and the American Friends of Russian Freedom (AFRF [CIA cryptonyms CAMANTILLA and AECAMANTILLA]), to name but a few. Some were short-lived, some were covertly financed by CIA, and some were supported overtly by private and public sources, e.g., the United States Escapee Program (USEP) under the US State Department direction.

In January 1950, the National Security Council (NSC) issued Intelligence Directive No. 13 titled "Exploitation of Soviet and Satellite Defectors Outside the United States." This directive specifically defined defectors as

> individuals who escape from the control of the USSR or countries in the Soviet orbit, or who, being outside such jurisdiction or control, are unwilling to return to it, and who are of special interest to the U.S. Government
> - Because they are able to add valuable new or confirmatory information to existing U.S. knowledge of the Soviet world,
> - Because their defection can be exploited in the psychological field.[21]

NSC authorized and directed that "the Central Intelligence Agency shall be responsible for the covert exploitation of defectors, and shall … coordinate all matters concerned with the handling and disposition of declared defectors from the Soviet Union and the satellite states in order to assure the effective exploitation of all defectors for operational, intelligence, or psychological purposes by the U.S. Government."[22]

NSC Directive No. 13 included these extracts:

> 7. Subject to over-all direction of the Chief of Mission, CIA representatives in the field shall have operating responsibility outside U.S. occupied areas for:
>    a. Providing secure facilities and preliminary assessment of a defector's bona fides and his intelligence or other potential value to the U.S. Government.

  b. Assuring that the other IAC (International Advisory Committee) agencies have adequate opportunity to exploit a defector for intelligence or operational purposes, including immediate access to the defector in the field.
  c. Arranging secure movement of defectors as required.
8. In U.S. occupied areas CIA shall establish, together with the Department of State and that military department having executive authority in the area, adequate procedures designed to carry out the obligations listed in paragraphs 7 a-c.[23]

In 1948, CIA's Mission to Germany set up a small operation with the cryptonym HARVARD to "provide safe house and operational aid facilities for all CIA activities in Germany" near Frankfurt.[24] Project HARVARD was expanded in 1952, when CIA set up "Defector Reception Centers" (DRC) near Frankfurt and Kaiserslautern.

Also, in 1948, an association of American intellectuals and literary personalities was formed New York under the name Friends of Russian Freedom (FRF) as an organization, "entirely independent of the United States government and policy." But beyond some organizational meetings and public statements, the group otherwise was not actively engaged.[25]

Another group consisting of prominent Americans was formed in New York on February 18, 1951, under the name Friends of Fighters for Russian Freedom (FFRF) with Mrs. Henry Hadley as Chairwoman of the Organizing Committee and Mrs. Ivan Tolstoy as Secretary and Treasurer. The *New York Times* reported on the forming of the FFRF with this headline, "To Aid 'Russian Freedom'; New Anti-Red Unit to Stress Amity for the People."[26] A *Washington Post* newspaper editorial of April 5, 1951, "Friendship for Russians," listed two objectives of FFRF: "To mobilize American support for anti–Communist elements inside Russia and to provide material aid for refugees from that land and for Red Army deserters."

Local newspapers in the US also covered the formation of FFRF by quoting from the press announcement: "There can be no lasting peace and no source of freedom for any people until the Russian people have regained their freedom and returned as free and equal partners to the community of nations. It revealed that it already had begun to send financial aid and guidance to runaway Soviet citizens now in central Europe."[27]

The name of the group was changed to or the group was superseded by the American Friends of Russian Freedom (AFRF) in late 1951. The president was retired Foreign Service Officer Felix Cole, who was the American Consul in Archangel, Russia, during the Russian Revolution. Other members included Mrs. Ivan Tolstoy, Eugene Lyons, Albert (Bert) Jolis, and William (Bill) Casey. Lyons was editor of *Reader's Digest* magazine and the first president of the American Committee for the Liberation from Bolshevism responsible for radio. Casey was a former member of the International Rescue Committee (IRC) and a future CIA Director in President Ronald Reagan's administration.

According a biography of Bill Casey, he recruited Frank R. Barnett as director the New York AFRF office in 1951. Barnett had been a Russian interpreter for the U.S. Army in World War II. He later described AFRF: "The idea was to get Red Army personnel in Berlin and Vienna to desert, to get them papers, find them jobs, resettle them in the West and make propaganda hay out of their defections."[28]

Barnett later wrote about the opening of a new AFRF "Friendship House" in Munich in November 1951 as

> the first reception center in West Germany exclusively for the use of escapees from the Soviet Union. Activities in a new and larger hostel include: language classes in German, English, and Portuguese; chess, ping pong, motion pictures, and a library of Russian, English, and German books; legal counseling and, of course, hot meals, not only for residents but transients enroute to some technical training center or to the AFRF center at Kaiserlautern for job placement with U.S. Army installations in that area.[29]

Mckinney Russell was the first director for the AFRF center in Kaiserslautern 1953–1955. He later described his experiences in an oral interview:

> I met in Munich, an organization with an odd name, American Friends of Russian Freedom, AFRF. The Tolstoy Foundation existed to help Russian refugees, ex-Soviet refugees but it had a religious coloration which AFRF did not. And the president of AFRF, a woman named Sheba Goodman, tracked me down, found out where I was assigned and invited me to meet with her in December of '52 or so. She said we are opening up a resettlement center, AFRF, with money from the PEP. What's the PEP? The Presidential Escapee Program was started to make it easier for all of the escapees from communist tyranny in Western Europe: mainly give them a place to live, a place to get a chance in life and help them prepare to emigrate eventually to the U.S. or Australia or Canada or some other place.
>
> [A]t that time there was a major NATO build-up and consequently there were lots of jobs for drivers, plumbers, electricians and security guards, and so on. As Center Director I was in charge of finding jobs for the escapees and running the Center, a rather challenging job because I was still younger than most of the people I was responsible for.... They would arrive speaking barely any German, and it was my job, through the German Labor Office, to persuade the Germans to give them a reference to the American office that was hiring for the U.S. Forces build-up. It turned out to be a very tough job. There were some rowdies and drunks among the Russians who were very hard to manage.[30]

McKinney Russell left AFRF after two years and first took a job as a manager at Radio Liberation in Munich to 1962 and then became a State Department career foreign service officer.

## 3. From Radio Liberation to Radio Liberty to RFE/RL     59

AFRF was primarily supported as a voluntary agency (VOLAG) under the U.S. Escapee Program (USEP) directed by the U.S. Department of State that was formed in March 1952. USEP was established to "provide escapees from Communist countries in Europe and other areas of the world with reception, supplementary care and maintenance, resettlement, and local integration support."[31] USEP had two stated objectives: "(1) to supplement the basic shelter and sustenance provided by refugees by voluntary relief agencies and the countries first giving them asylum and (2) to assist in permanent resettlement of escapees in free countries."[32]

The Psychological Strategy Board (PSB) estimated that there were 12,000 persons who "fled the Soviet Orbit" from 1950 to 1951, with another 6,000 due to "cross the Curtain" in 1952, mostly in Germany and Austria, for a total of 18,000 to be processed for resettlement. But of that number, it was estimated that only 50 would "have sufficient intelligence value" to qualify as defectors as defined by NSCD-13.[33]

AFRF did not publicly campaign for funding as did the Crusade for Freedom, in support of Radio Free Europe, but was not averse to publicity for donations. For example, in her March 24, 1953, nationally syndicated column, Inez Robb not only praised AFRF but also included an appeal for donations. For this newspaper column, she interviewed Mrs. Sheba Goodman, European Director, AFRF in Frankfurt, who said, "The number of Russian escapees may be small but we feel they are the very crux of the stubborn determination of men to be free, and that their defection is the ultimate condemnation of Communism."[34] She added,

> For years, escaped Russian citizens lived in real misery in camps in the American, British and French zones of Germany. For some reason, they were regarded with hostility and suspicion. Bitterness and frustration grew among these people who, we feel, are the key to our whole psychological warfare program.... We have a $25,000 grant from the governments escapee program fund. And with another $150,000 in the next twelve months from private contributors, we think we can almost work miracles.[35]

The column ended with this donation appeal: "If you would like to help that miracle—from ten cents to $10,000—the address of the American Friends of Russian Freedom, Inc. is 279 Park Avenue, New York City."[36]

The AFRF "Friendship House" in Kaiserslautern, with 34 deserters in 1955, was described by Norman Lindhurst, American correspondent for the North American Newspaper Alliance (NANA) as a "Freedom House":

> An effort to provide a homelike atmosphere for the defectors until they can get settled in the West.... Freedom House has 22 rooms, including a kitchen and recreation room. Defectors pay 19 marks ($4.50) a month for their rooms. They can get breakfast and dinner for two marks a day. More important to the defectors than having a roof over their heads, however is the psychological sense of security provided by the Kaiserslautern center.[37]

Lindhurst quoted the defectors as saying, "The Allies cast defectors aside and take no more interest in them after Allied intelligence interrogators have squeezed them dry of information."[38]

In a 1955 Memorandum from the Acting Chief of the International Organization Division to CIA's Deputy Director (Plans), AFRF was described as

> active in Europe in assisting, feeding, rehabilitation, and resettling new refugees from the USSR, including the two barracks in Munich.... The AFRF receives funds for its European activities from ... USEP, and has frequently requested additional support from the Agency (CIA), the American Committee for Liberation from Bolshevism, and from private foundations.
>
> In May 1952, Mr. Dulles (Director CIA) requested that the American Committee continue the subsidization it had been granting since June of 1951 to AFRF ... the subsidy continued until February 1953.
>
> It is our view that no further funds should be granted the AFRF by the Agency directly or through the American Committee. The AFRF is a regular recipient of USEP funds and can and should be overtly supported. It is our understanding that such welfare activities, although beneficial to our covert programs, are not to be covertly supported.[39]

In her March 18, 1953, syndicated columnist Inez Robb wrote: "Part of each day's program is a talk by a Russian refugee who has escaped to the West. He contrasts what the Kremlin told him of the West with what he actually found on this side of the Iron Curtain. The committee is now making tape recordings of refugees who are happily resettled in the United Stated, Western Europe, South America and Australia."[40] She quoted RL manager Theodore Steele, who said,

> Our object is to fight Bolshevism. We want the listener to defect from Russian Bolshevism or Communism. We hope his defections, if he hears the truth, will be mental and emotional. We hope he is capable of sabotage. And we want this man or woman, who is risking so much, to know that other sympathize with him in his terrible plight and are with him in spirit.[41]

Six years after it opened, the Friendship House reached a low when in November 1957 Munich police raided it looking for criminals. The raid was reported in the Munich newspapers *Muenchener Merkur* and *Sueddeutsche Zeitung*. The raid was apparently conducted in response to a series of break-ins and burglaries in the previous two months in Munich. Reportedly two Russian gangs were living in the apartment building. One was led by Semion Maximov, aka, Monach—"The Monk." The other gang was led by Genadiy Alexyev, aka Ruka, Odnorukiy—"The Hand," "The One-Armed."[42] The inhabitants were identified as low-level criminals and/or suspect KGB agents. Some of those who lived there had returned to the USSR and one was convicted in Germany for being a KGB agent.[43]

One example of CIA-AFRF cooperation is detailed in a September 7, 1960, internal CIA memorandum:

> The expenditure of some (redacted) per year in project AEMANTILLA enable our DRC resettlement officers in Frankfurt through contact with the chief of the AFRF Frankfurt office to resettle on the German economy or prepare for immigration to the U.S. anyone of interest to the Clandestine Services, but primarily defectors and ex-agents in a secure manner and with a minimum of delay. Particularly difficult or sensitive cases which we could otherwise handle only at a great expense and the labor of several case officers have been turned over to AFRF with excellent results.[44]

From January 1, 1959, through April 1960, AFRF processed 52 resettlement cases, with 35 of the cases "integrated" into the German economy and 24 cases (36 people in total) were given assistance to the United States.[45] The breakdown by nationality of the 35 cases was:

21 Russian,
2 Hungarian,
1 East German,
5 Polish,
3 Korean,
2 Chinese, and
1 Bulgarian.

For these 35 persons, AFRF and CIA resettlement officers arranged for:

- Language lessons,
- Job placement,
- Housing,
- Purchases of clothing,
- Medical and dental services, police registration, and
- Subsistence until the first paycheck was received.

Of the 24 persons sent to the United States, the nationality breakdown was:

11 Polish,
2 Russian,
1 Lithuanian,
4 Czech,
1 Hungarian,
1 Romanian, and
2 Bulgarian.

AFRF representative in New York met many of these persons, helped them clear through Immigration and Naturalization Service (INS) procedures at the airport, secured hotel accommodations, and arranged for transportation to their final destinations.[46]

## *AFRF and Redefections*

Not all cases handled by AFRF and the DRC resulted in settlement in the West. For example, in 1960, AFRF handled 12 Soviet defectors. Some of them returned (redefected) to the USSR. CIA's Chief SR/3 wrote a memorandum to the International Organizations (IO) division downplaying this:

> [T]he entire organization's staff (including the secretary) went out of its way to effectively resettle these people. Excessive amounts of time, effort, and money were expanded by AFRF and the resettlement case officers to help these individuals become Western-orientated and happily resettled. DRC Resettlement is of the opinion that without AFRF's assistance those who have remained in the West would most likely have redefected.[47]

A well-publicized example of how news of defection was domestically "exploited in the psychological field" under NSC No. 13 by raising public opinion, can be illustrated with this example: In August 1964, two Soviet jazz musicians, Boris Midney and Igor Berukshtis, defected in Tokyo, Japan by asking for asylum at the U.S. Embassy. They were then sent to Frankfurt for processing as defectors destined to the United States. AFRF sponsored them. When they arrived in New York in October 1964, there was a press conference at Kennedy airport. It was announced that AFRF found them a manager in New York and they then appeared on television shows and performed in jazz clubs in New York, and, with two other musicians, formed a jazz group known as the Russian Jazz Quartet.[48]

In November 1964, the *New York Times* reported on their musical tour as part of the Russian Jazz Quartet and wrote: "The two Russians, both graduates of the Moscow Conservatory, were introduced to jazz by Willis Conover's broadcasts over the Voice of America. They are being sponsored here by the American Friends of Russian Freedom, an organization that usually deals with defecting scientists."[49]

There was nationwide newspaper coverage of their defection, e.g., the *Billboard* magazine issue of November 7, 1964, used the headline, "2 Red Jazzmen are U.S. Sit-ins." The music magazine *Down Beat* featured an article about them in December 3, 1964, edition: "A Day in the New Lives of Two Russian Defector Jazz Musicians."

After Midney and Berukshtis formed the music group the Russian Jazz Quartet, their album *Happiness* was released. Midney went on to a successful music career in the U.S: as a producer, arranger, composer, and conductor, whose trademark was a "blend of strings, horn and percussion created a sound as deep and lush as any heard during the disco era."[50] Igor Berukshtis was later heard on Radio Liberty's Russian Service broadcasts commentating on jazz.

### 3. From Radio Liberation to Radio Liberty to RFE/RL 63

It is not known when AFRF stopped functioning with CIA support but for renewal plan for fiscal year 1964, but project renewal exchange messages between CIA East European Division at CIA to Chief of Station Germany contained this information:

> One reason for including CAMANTLLLA with the others is that the prime activity for which we are paying under this Project takes place right in Frankfurt.... Headquarters' functions have been and are limited to three routine support activities:
> - Our subsidy is routinely channeled to the New York Office through Finance on a quarterly basis;
> - CAMANTLLLA accountings are routinely forwarded through KUVEST to Finance; and
> - The Desk maintains occasional contact with the New York Office for administrative and support purposes. In our view, these facts characterize CAMANTILLA as being primarily a field type Project.[51]

CIA's Chief of Foreign Intelligence recommended renewal of the HARVARD Project, when he wrote,

> Should the State Department withdraw funds for support of the United States Escapee Program (USEP), HARVARD would be faced with an increased burden in the resettlement of CIA cases. We use extensively one of the USEP voluntary agencies, the American Friends of Russian Freedom, for the resettlement of CIA cases. This organization receives a CIA subsidy therefor. should USEP support be withdrawn from the American Friends of Russian Freedom, CIA will NOT (emphasis added) attempt to maintain it unilaterally.[52]

CIA had another defector project at the Frankfurt DRC, CABEZONE, which was, since its inception, administratively and financially separately supported from HARVARD and CAMANTILLA. Actual debriefing and interrogation of defectors and potential defectors, including use of the lie detector, was the responsibility of CABEZONE officers. Afterwards, if approved by CABEZONE, they would be turned over to HARVARD for relocation and resettlement, with assistance from AFRF.

In fiscal year 1963, since there were fewer bona fide defectors processed by CABEZONE, the number of HARVARD case officers was reduced from four to two and project costs reduced.[53] For FY 1964, both HARVARD and CAMANTILLA projects were merged into Project CABEZONE. The budget was approved in July for 14 months, with next renewal request due August 1, 1965.[54]

With 1965 changes to the Immigration and Nationality Act of 1952, the US Escapee Program under State Department ended. And with that, funding for AFRF from both CIA and State Department ceased, thus bringing an end to AFRF operations.

## From RFE and RL to RFE/RL

A major turning point in the history of Radio Free Europe and Radio Liberty occurred in 1967 when *Ramparts* magazine publicly revealed the RFE-CIA relationship, which would subsequently lead to a congressional decision that the CIA would no longer finance RFE and RL.

> Within the United States there are many elements, including large ethnic groups with close ties to many of the countries to which the Radios broadcast, for whom cessation of broadcasting would seem a serious and incomprehensible decision, especially in light of the Soviet invasion of Czechoslovakia. The attitudes of the ethnic groups would probably add significantly to the likelihood of adverse publicity attendant on termination, and would lend themselves to domestic political exploitation. Strongly negative Congressional reactions were encountered when the Director of Central Intelligence discussed the possibility of termination with key members of Congress in late 1967. A number of Congressmen are likely to show particular concern for the fate of RFE and RL because of their traditional responsiveness to the interests of domestic European ethnic groups, and because of their considerable knowledge of and belief in the work of the Radios.[55]

Richard M. Nixon was elected President on November 5, 1968. The Johnson administration deferred any decision on the fate of the radios to the Nixon administration. President Nixon on February 22, 1969, approved the continuation of covert CIA funding for both radios. In December 1969, Nixon decided to terminate Radio Liberty. CIA appealed this decision to National Security Advisor Henry Kissinger, who in turn appealed to President Nixon. One of his arguments was "unilateral termination of Radio Liberty would be a major political concession to the USSR with no quid pro quo and might result in the early demise of Radio Free Europe." Kissinger recommended the continuation of CIA funding for Radio Liberty; Nixon agreed.[56]

On March 20, 1970, there was a meeting in the White House, with President Nixon, Richard Helms, the director of the CIA, and Henry Kissinger, the president's national security advisor. The future of Radio Free Europe was one of the topics discussed. After the meeting, Helms wrote: "With respect to black operations, the President enjoined me to hit the Soviets, and hit them hard, any place we can in the world. He said to 'just go ahead,' to keep Henry Kissinger informed, and to be as imaginative as we could. He was as emphatic on this as I have ever heard him on anything. He indicated that he had had a change of mind and thought that Radio Free Europe should be continued."[57]

In response to this meeting, CIA wrote a paper titled *Tensions in the Soviet Union and Eastern Europe: Challenge and Opportunity*. The paper, which Kissinger described as "excellent" in a note to President Nixon,

### 3. From Radio Liberation to Radio Liberty to RFE/RL

supported the continuation of Radio Free Europe and Radio Liberty. CIA's report included mention of jamming of both RFE and RL:

> A measure of the Soviet concern over Western broadcasts is the extent of the Soviet jamming effort. At this time, Czechoslovakia and Bulgaria also extensively jam RFE broadcasts. According to a VOA study, the Soviets use 2,000–2,500 jammers at an estimated annual cost of $150,000,000. As indicated above, however, the jamming is marginally effective inasmuch as the target audiences hear the radios on one or more frequencies. The cost of the Soviet jamming effort can be put into perspective by comparing it with the annual operating costs of RFE, Inc., and RLC, Inc., $21,723,000 and $12,770,000 respectively. The radios represent a 20-year investment of over $400,000,000.[58]

President Nixon appointed a commission in August 1972 to study international radio broadcasting to review alternative arrangements for funding RFE and RL.

In his letter to Dr. Milton Eisenhower confirming his appointment as Chairman, Nixon wrote:

> As you are undoubtedly aware, the operations of Radio Free Europe and Radio Liberty have been thoroughly debated by Congress during the past year. Throughout this period of intense review, the radios have continued to receive overwhelming support from the majorities of both houses of Congress, the news media, and many of our leading citizens from all walks of life.... [I] believe the Commission should undertake a critical examination of the operation and funding question and recommend methods for future maintenance and support of the radios, which will not impair their professional independence and, consequently their effectiveness.[59]

The presidential commission published a report in 1973, *The Right to Know*, which formed the basis of legislation to consolidate RFE and RL into a new hybrid organization: a private nonprofit corporation funded by Congress. The summary of the report read, in part, "Radio Free Europe and Radio Liberty are unique in the entire spectrum of international broadcasting.... [W]e therefore recommend that the stations be continued until the government of the countries to which the stations are broadcasting permit a free flow of information and ideas, both internally and between the East and West.... [T]he Commission there believes that the stations must continue to be financed mainly by United States appropriated funds."[60]

The Commission report listed 13 "restraints" to Radio Free Europe's tone in its broadcasts, some of which to be avoided were:

- Vituperation, vindictiveness, belligerency, stridency, pomposity, emotionalism, arrogance, pretentiousness and condescension.
- Programming the content of which is or could be legitimately construed as inflammatory or unrealistic.
- Blatant, propagandistic argumentation.
- Any comment or broadcast of any material, which would amount

to or could be reasonably construed as incitement to revolt or other violence.⁶¹

Included in the Commission's report, were Radio Liberty's role: "An independent radio devoted to the dissemination of objective, balanced information.... [T]o this end, Radio Liberty attempts to put at people's disposal specific, relevant information and ideas as a basis for formulating their own ideas and funding their own solutions. It serves Soviet citizen as a channel for airing and exchanging their own views, which are denied an opportunity for expression in public media under tight censorship controls." Radio Liberty's "six basic techniques" were listed:

1. Effective broadcasting consists of presenting the truth, hard facts and cold analysis.
2. A question mark is a good ending for a script.
3. RL avoids direct comparisons, which can be odious and counterproductive.
4. The more brutal the facts, the less emotional should be the presentation.
5. RL avoids polemics with the Soviet media.
6. RL does not engage in pejorative use of terms or phraseology acceptable to Soviet listeners nor use obsolete terminology.⁶²

CIA ended financial support to RFE and RL on June 30, 1971, and all supervision and other involvement on March 30, 1972. State Department took over funding of the radios until 1975, when the Board for International Broadcasting was created. Final physical and administrative consolidation of the two radio stations in Munich took place in 1975–76, as RFE/RL, which moved to Prague, Czech Republic in 1995 and continue to broadcast from there.

# 4

# Clandestine Broadcasts from Greece to Bulgaria and Romania

## Introduction

The Office of Policy Coordination's (OPC) clandestine broadcasts from Greece were initially via two mobile units close to the Bulgarian border in 1950. Arrangements were completed with the government of Greece in the spring of 1950, which permitted CIA to create a permanent communications installation in the Athens area for the purpose of black broadcasting. The cryptonym was PYREX. CIA-sponsored programs were eventually transmitted from PYREX in Albanian, Bulgarian, Romanian, Russian, Ukrainian, and in some of the languages of the Caucasus region of the USSR. In addition to clandestine radio broadcasts, the PYREX site would also be used in balloon/propaganda leaflet operations against Albania and Bulgaria.

## Bulgaria

### Radio Goryanin: The Voice of Bulgarian Resistance

In September 1945, the Red Army invaded Bulgaria and a reign of terror began under Sovietization of the country. Thousands of Bulgarians, who took up armed resistance to Communism, were known as the Goryani (Горяни—also transliterated as Goriani), or "Man of the Forests" or "Ones of the Forest."

In January 1950, CIA's Office of Policy Coordination (OPC) "Plan of Operation for Bulgaria" was approved by the Assistant Director Policy Coordination (Frank Wisner), Director of Central Intelligence, and by the U.S. Department of State in February 1950.

The OPC "Operational Plan" for Bulgaria using the cryptonym QKSTAIR was submitted through CIA channels on April 18, 1950, and authorized on April 24, 1950. The objective of QKSTAIR was, "To conduct psychological warfare operations against the Bulgarian regime, and to establish in the country resistance organizations capable of paramilitary activity of various types." One of the objectives of the plan was "Undertake at the earliest possible date a large scale (clandestine) propaganda and psychological warfare campaign against Bulgaria." One of the lines of action was, "This will necessitate the immediate establishment of covert broadcasting facilities as near as possible to Bulgaria and simultaneous preparation for the distribution of printed material with the target area."[1]

The operation was under control of OPC headquarters in Washington, which approved and authorized all significant operations. The OPC-subsidized Bulgarian National Committee in the United States acted as "cover" for the OPC activities.[2]

The radio plan included the use of three crews to operate mobile shortwave transmitters with trucks and power units and one crew of six men to operate a medium wave transmitter also with a power unit. Two mobile units were to broadcast two different propaganda lines. One station was to be set up to broadcast "nationalist-communist propaganda" and the other station would "broadcast propaganda aimed at increasing the discontent and resistance of the masses of people."[3]

The mobile units in July 1950 were constructed on CIA facilities near Bethesda, Maryland, at a cost of $15,000, including labor, for each unit. The range of the transmitters was estimated at 300 to 500 miles.[4] The project financial plan called for a total of 55 persons at a cost of $254,000 in fiscal year July 1, 1951, to June 30, 1952.[5]

The original mobile shortwave station Radio Goryanin was similar to the "Barbara" broadcasting unit of Radio Free Europe in Lampertheim, Germany: broadcast truck, trailer containing power source, and transportation jeep, a 500-watt transmitter, and other broadcasting equipment. The difference was that Radio Goryanin consisted of two units broadcasting simultaneously on two different frequencies. Although this technique was to outmaneuver the jammers, it created difficulties for the listeners, who had to keep turning the dial to try and find the broadcasts.

In July 1950, the issue of cover was discussed within OPC: "On the basis of the type of equipment used and the proposed use to be made of it, is the cover adequate to meet the requirements of our charter, namely: that the operation be carried out in such a way that it cannot be traced to the U.S. Government and if so traced can be plausibly disclaimed?"[6]

Radio Goryanin shortwave programs over the two mobile transmitters began April 1, 1951, with 30-minute broadcasts in the 6 MHz band. The exact frequency was changed every few minutes to avoid jamming transmissions. The programs opened with the militaristic, nationalist anthem "One Covenant" and ended similarly with the anthem "Shumi Maritsa."

The Bulgarian Directorate of State Security (DS) reacted to the broadcasts of Radio Goryanin by trying to locate the station. For example, on May 5, 1951, a DS report contained this passage: "There is still no accurate data on her whereabouts, and who has created and manages it. Intelligence suggest that it is located somewhere in the country, near the Greek border, or on a ship in the waters of the Mediterranean."[7]

It is possible that the DS had an agent in Radio Goryanin as CIA reported in June 1951:

> Evidence recently received indicating that the chief scriptwriter and announcer may be a Bulgarian agent was sufficiently strong that Athens has been directed to (a) remove him and (b) lay on an exhaustive interrogation. If it is determined that this man is an agent, a complete revision of the operation of Goryanin will probably be necessary. He was subsequently removed and handed over to Greek authorities for interrogation as a suspect Bulgarian intelligence agent.[8]

CIA's East European Division (EE-1) "Report of Operations for the Quarter Ended June 30, 1951," included this information:

> Two new 500-watt transmitters, similar to the two already operating but not mounted on tracks, have been procured and shipped to Greece to augment the effectiveness of Radio Goryanin. It is planned that these additional transmitters will be installed in July. Because of the obvious success of Radio Goryanin even with its present limited facilities and because of the need to circumvent the extensive jamming efforts of the Bulgarian Government, two new 500-watt transmitters, similar to the two now operating, have been procured and shipped to Greece. The technique of interrupted and irregular broadcasts is being used in order to lend greater credence to the claim that the radio is broadcasting on Bulgarian soil.
> 
> A basic Propaganda Guidance for Radio Goryanin was completed in June and will be sent to the field in the beginning of July. An extract of this Guideline is also being sent to C/SP for transmittal to Radio Free Europe.[9]

The July 1951 monthly QKSTAIR project status report contained this comment: "Further reports were received regarding the clear reception and widespread popularity of 'Radio Goryanin.' To prevent touching off any premature popular revolt PYREX was instructed to avoid stating that the broadcasts were originating 'in the forest,'" and imply instead only that they emanate from somewhere in Bulgaria.[10] In early July 1951, "Freedom Brotherhood" stickers were posted simultaneously throughout Bulgaria, presumably by agents, who had previously been infiltrated into Bulgaria. Radio Goryanin broadcast announcements of the sticker postings.[11]

For August 1951, the project status report included, "Black propaganda broadcasts over Radio Goryanin … continue on a routine basis."

The QKSTAIR project status report for September 1951 included this statement:

> Black propaganda broadcasts over Radio Goryanin and the QKSTAIR mailing campaign continued. In accordance with instructions issued in August, Radio Goryanin programs have begun avoiding explicit claims that broadcasts originate within Bulgaria. However, the programs are so worded that credulous listeners can readily believe that the situation is inside the country. Program content has been continually improved to bolster the impression that Radio Goryanin enjoys close contacts with developments inside Bulgaria.[12]

In Sofia in September 1951, six OPC agents, who had infiltrated into Bulgaria, were put on trial in Sofia. Three of the agents were sentenced to death and the other three to long prison terms. OPC believed that the men were caught as a result of "(a) information furnished the militia by a defector (b) faulty operational judgement on the part of some of the agents, and (c) militia ambushes." The OPC analysis was that the trial did not cause serious damage to the operations because the information that the agents presumably told Bulgarian authorities was already known through other agents, who had defected or were captured in previous missions.[13]

In October 1951, a schoolteacher escaped Bulgaria to Greece. During an interview with a Radio Free Europe correspondent stationed in Greece in November, the teacher said that he had listened to Radio Goryanin frequently and "heard it giving coded instructions to 'couriers.'" He added, "Radio Goryanin signs off all its broadcasts with a warning to the people not to trust anyone who claims to be a Goryanin partisan. The station also reads of the names of hated Communists and advises its hearers to send anonymous letters to those persons warning them that the day of reckoning is drawing near." The RFE interviewer considered his comments to be "reasonable and corresponded to the truth."[14]

OPC's October 1951 project status report included this comment:

> A report was received through an Italian diplomat that diplomatic circles in Sofia know that Radio Goryanin is located near Athens and is controlled by American intelligence. This suggests that Goryanin may be the target of a future Bulgarian propaganda blast. Therefore, precautions are being taken to avoid the pinpointing of the transmitters and/or disclosure of contacts of OPC personnel with the transmitter installation. Recently Goryanin has been stressing the theme "we may go off the air at any time without warning, but we shall always be back," to cover that eventually should it be necessary.[15]

In the EE-1 monthly project status report for November 1951, instead of "black" the term "gray" was used to describe the propaganda radio broadcasts. Specific targets of the broadcasts were the peasants and the army, with stress on the theme of Bulgarian nationalism. The project name was changed to BGCONVOY, which was considered to be in "its informative

## 4. Clandestine Broadcasts from Greece to Bulgaria and Romania

and organizational phase." Radio broadcasts were to continue through the winter but agent infiltration operations were suspended until Spring 1952.[16]

In 1952, the Bulgarian Intelligence Service DS identified the following as working for Radio Goryanin and branded the three men and one woman as "traitors to the motherland":

- Dimitar Stanchev Baharov, born in the Lyubenova neighborhood, N. Zagorsko, he fled to Greece in 1950;
- Zlatka Assenova Vlaycheva, a native of Sofia;
- Emanuel Georgiev Kozhuharov a native of the town Burgas and lived in Sofia, and
- Ivan Hristov Mitev, born in Balgarovo, Haskovo.[17]

It is probable that the DS learned the identities of the staff through the chief announcer and scriptwriter, who was removed from duty under suspicion of being an agent.

In January 1952, the BGCONVOY project status report concluded:

The Radio Goryanin staff has been handicapped by a dearth of information on recent local events within Bulgaria, other than that which can be obtained by monitoring the Bulgarian radio and reading the Bulgarian press. However, information has been obtained through refugee debriefings, which has enabled Radio Goryanin to publicize many of those policies and actions of the Bulgarian regime, which the Communist rulers has sought to conceal. A fairly rapid turnover of Goryanin's indigenous staff members in encouraged with replacement from among the refugees recently arrived from Bulgaria, to give the programs a local flavor, which is desirable in such a clandestine radio station.

The difficulties encountered in maintaining the radio voice of a resistance movement are considerable, when that voice is unable to carry on frequent contact with resistance nets inside the country. But Radio Goryanin has at least partly succeeded in achieving the objectives of its first phase of operation—to give hope and courage to the Bulgarian people, to keep them constantly angry and resentful at the injustice of the Communist regime, to inject some suspicion and fear into the minds of the opportunists and even to some real Communists, and to prepare the whole country psychologically for cooperation with the resistance forces in the event of either war or revolution.[18]

By February 1952, Radio Goryanin, with its daily program repeated five times during the day, had made a total of 273 broadcasts. Broadcasts continued on a daily basis. Sample scripts were reviewed by two covert consultants who made their analyses and recommendations for improvement of the scripts and additional subjects for inclusion into the broadcasts.[19]

By April 1952, Radio Goryanin had made a total of 335 broadcasts. In response to OPC headquarters suggestion, Goryanin stressed certain timely themes such as economic exploitation of Bulgaria in connection with the recent Moscow Economic Conference. CIA took steps to correct the damage, if any, done if an exhaustive interrogation of the former chief scriptwriter and announcer revealed that he was a Bulgarian agent. After about two weeks of surveillance by Greek authorities, the man was picked up and isolated for the interrogation on April 24, 1952.[20]

Throughout the summer 1952, Radio Goryanin 15-minute broadcasts continued on a daily basis that included morning, evening, and night broadcasts, and was subjected to heavy jamming with two or three jammers being heard simultaneously. By September 1952, the total number of broadcasts reached 486.[21] In September, there was a conference with representatives of NCFE and CIA SE and International Organizations divisions. The results included, "Closer and more frequent liaison between SE and NCFE desk officials handling the Bulgarian National Council affairs."[22]

By October 1952, at least 14 jamming transmitters were in operation against Radio Goryanin resulting in 20 repeat 15-minute programs per day.[23]

In November, programming was temporarily stopped due to the review and reorganization of the station. The decision made in December 1952 was to continue the broadcasts: "Radio Goryanin activities have been reviewed both from a security standpoint and effectiveness of programming by (redacted) and visitors from Washington. There is indication that the transmissions have a more telling effect that was previously realized. It was, therefore, decided to continue the operation along the lines currently being followed with special concentration on the peasant audience."[24]

In 1953, the mission statement of the CIA project for clandestine broadcasting to Bulgaria was:

- Use psychological warfare assets of the Project (radio and written propaganda material) to break the Communist stranglehold on Bulgaria,
- Bring about the downfall of Communist officials and their followers,
- Keep alive the hope of eventual liberation in the minds of the Bulgarian people,
- Encourage the people to resist apathetic acceptance of Communist slavery by passive resistance.[25]

The year 1953 was an important one for Radio Goryanin broadcasts as the mobile stations were changed out to a recently installed high-powered transmitter. Radio Goryanin was reorganized due to a serious security breaches, including one when radio staff members made an unauthorized visit to a housing complex where Bulgarians, who had been trained to infiltrate Bulgaria as agents, lived.[26]

In January there were a series of interviews of recent Bulgarian

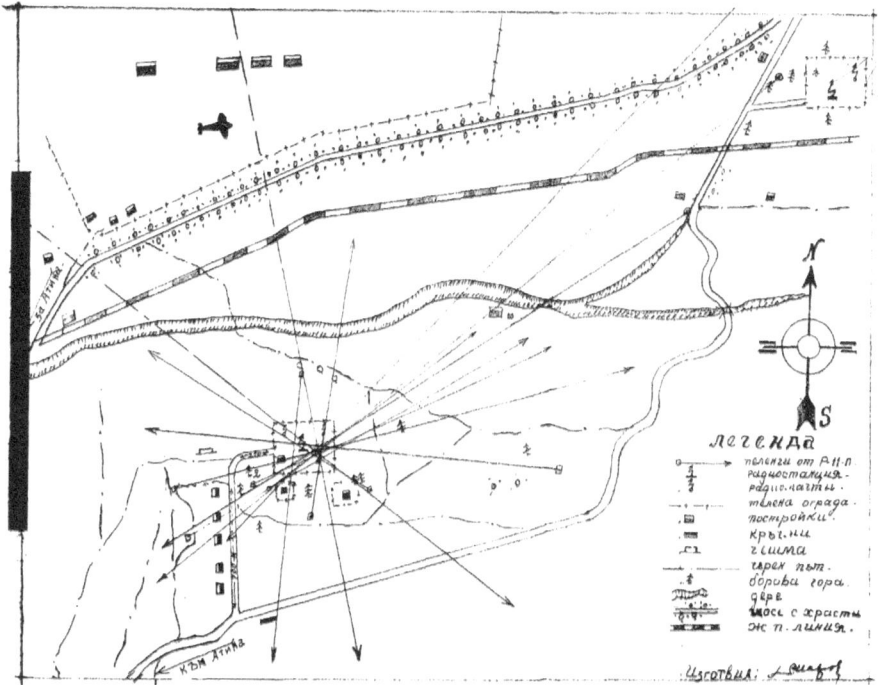

**A Bulgarian intelligence drawing of the CIA's clandestine radio complex outside Athens, Greece.**

refugees by a sociological expert on Balkan peasant life, who was sent to Athens as an advisor on psychological warfare activities. He indicated that Radio Goryanin continues to be effective and could be considerably strengthened within the existing framework of its operations. His suggestions for improvement of the programs included "modification of world affairs broadcasts to give a local twist, emphasis on Bulgarian historical heritage rather than 'political programs,' and concentration on the principal theme that Bulgarians are slaves under Soviet colonialism."[27]

In February 1953, Radio Goryanin made a daily average of 28 repeat broadcasts of the 15-minute programs.[28]

During the week following Stalin's death on March 6, 1953, Radio Goryanin gave major emphasis to the consequences of Stalin's death in the upsetting of the present Satellite hierarchies and to forecasts of the replacement of Chervenkov, the Stalin appointed Bulgarian Premier. The previous average of two jammers per broadcast was steadily increased to a maximum of eleven monitored on one broadcast of March 9, 1953. To increase the credibility of Goryanin's predictions, a story predicting the purge of Chervenkov, crediting Goryanin broadcasts monitored in Germany, was planted on the front page of the *Berlin Telegraf* of March 22, 1953. Both VOA and RFE were requested to exploit the article in their broadcasts to permit Goryanin to cite their broadcasts in furthering their anti–Chervenkov campaign.[29]

The broadcasts of Radio Goryanin continued in April 1953 to play the theme of impending purges in the Communist hierarchy and to stress the importance to Bulgaria of the Balkan Pact. Broadcasts were shortened and items repeated and summarized in subsequent broadcasts to obviate the effect of constant Soviet jamming of the programs. After several months of negotiations for resettlement of six locally hired Bulgarians working on psychological warfare programs in Athens, arrangements were made with the Greek Government for direct resettlement to either Argentina or Brazil.[30]

Radio Goryanin continued in May 1953 operating on an emergency basis due to the discovery of various serious security violations, which required the disposal of the entire staff of indigenous employees before a reorganization with new personnel could be undertaken. A decision was made that the Goryanin would be taken off the air sometime between July 1 and August 1. A new program was being formulated in CIA Headquarters, would be resumed in the fall under the supervision of a new station psychological warfare director and under the immediate direction of a staff employee—both of whom were scheduled to arrive in Athens in August.[31]

In June 1953, in addition to the standard broadcasts CIA headquarters suggested that broadcasts make use the recent disturbance in East Germany and Czechoslovakia—with emphasis on the spontaneity of the outbreaks, the defections of East German police and the brutality of the reprisals—but with warnings against premature action.[32]

Also, in June, there was a CIA meeting with a National Committee for Free Europe representatives that ended with the decision to "cease attempting to reorganize the present strife-ridden Bulgarian National Committee, and make an attempt instead to organize a group of young emigres, who would subscribe to U.S. interests. If such a group proves viable and attains prestige, it would be transformed into a new Council or Committee to be used as an operational 'front.'"[33]

Radio Goryanin transmitted broadcasts on nineteen days during July 1953 that included news from the West, from the Satellites, and from inside in Bulgaria, Broadcasts also were made to Russians in Bulgaria. The scripts were coordinated between CIA's Soviet Russia (SR) and SE/2 Divisions. Some programs were made for:

- peasants to resist collectivization and to sabotage production norms,

### 4. Clandestine Broadcasts from Greece to Bulgaria and Romania 75

- intellectuals to resist Communist control, and
- other distinct social groups.[34]

Radio Goryanin transmitted broadcasts on nineteen days during August 1953 with a sufficient number of programs that had been taped in order to continue broadcasts until the scheduled station termination in early August for complete reorganization.[35]

The Field Project Outline for the operation of the reorganized Radio Goryanin was received in September 1953. The new set-up was designed to guard against security violations by proper compartmentation of the operation, with locally hired Bulgarians completely isolated from the operation and each other. No operations report was received for September. However, a cable received on September 10 indicated that broadcasts of Radio Goryanin at that time were on the air averaging four short reports and special appeals per week.[36]

During October 1953, a new program format was inaugurated to broadcast "nationalist-communist propaganda." The new program eliminated the old recorded introductions and made references to the "Brotherhood for the Freedom of Bulgaria." The radio station now was called "Hristo Botev." A new schedule of broadcasts was set up with occasional programs broadcast on a high-powered transmitter.[37]

The monthly report on activities of Radio Goryanin for the month October 15 to November 14 stated that the radio was on the air 24 days during the period. The programs for ten of these days, however, were repeats of the preceding days' programs. The main themes stressed were: Communist mismanagement and corruption, encouragement of passive resistance, insecurity and fear of the present regime, and Sovietization of Bulgaria.[38]

On December 1, 1953, a new broadcast schedule (05:00, 12:30, 18:00 and 23:00 local time) was inaugurated with the use of high-power transmitters on three of the broadcasts, and with each broadcast being repeated two times. The main themes stressed during this period were: Communist mismanagement and bungling in Bulgaria and the Soviet Union, encouragement of passive resistance, the ridiculous falsity of Bulgarian elections and the "Sovietization of Bulgaria." During the broadcasts 19 different jammers were monitored.[39]

## Project METAPHOR

Project METAPHOR was approved on January 12, 1954, with the objective to "Create the illusion of a clandestine shortwave broadcasting station operating within Bulgaria."[40] Project MENTHOL was created for the leaflet and other written material sent into Bulgaria. Two indigenous agents were later approved for immigration to the United States under the CIA Act of 1949, which allowed CIA to bring up to 100 persons per year, without going through normal immigration procedures. The agents were trained in the US and returned to Greece for use on Project METAPHOR.[41]

In the period, January 15, 1954, to February 15, 1954, Radio Goryanin was on the air 29 days. Programs were repeated ten times per day. An average of five jammers was reported on all programs; nineteen separate jammers were monitored. Program themes included:

- Sovietization of Bulgaria.
- Exploitation of Bulgarian economy by the USSR.
- Prediction of a purge to be announced at the BCP Congress in March.
- Counterattack aimed at Communist denunciation of "hooliganism" among Bulgarian youth.
- Instructions for passive resistance, malingering directed to textile workers.
- Appeal to listeners to protest the New State Loan through anonymous letters.[42]

In the course of Fiscal Year 1955, basic elements of the psychological and political warfare program BGCONVOY were projected out separately into Project METAPHOR (clandestine radio) and MENTHOL (leaflet and other written material). Personnel of BOCONVOY were under official cover of Department of Army staff or unofficial cover as a commercial enterprise in Athens. All personnel covered by BOCONVOY were security cleared and were witted of their CIA relationship.[43]

Project BGCONVOY was terminated effective June 30, 1955, and all personnel, who were carried on it, were disposed or assigned to other programs. CIA personnel in Greece then consisted of one staff employee, two staff agents, and four contract agents. The salaries and allowances of the staff employee and staff agents were $41,400, and those of the four contract agents were $40,400.[44]

Clandestine radio to Bulgaria consisting of broadcasts of Radio Goryanin and Hristo Botev continued respectively as METAPHOR and METAPHOR I, which "embody basic elements of the PP Program and with any PM project which may be initiated directed toward Bulgaria."[45]

Both stations continued normal broadcasting until October 2, 1959, when a request under cost savings was made to phase out black broadcasts from Greece to "denied areas," which included Albania on October 31, 1959, and Romania on October 21, 1959, and downgrade the broadcasts to USSR and Bulgaria:

[T]his officer has done a fine job in building up a revisionist program and in maintaining an anti-Communist program. We recommend continuing the METAPHOR 1 program using DOCEKAB (meaning unknown), who—as a former Communist agit-prop writer—is almost unique for revisionist propaganda. We do not like to give up the anti-Communist program, which is not written by a field agent and which has provoked such angry reactions by the Communist regime ... we can phase out this program too sometime after 31 October—when budgetary pressures and other considerations so require.[46]

The answer from CIA Chief, EE, was to terminate the Romanian, Albanian, and Radio Goryanin broadcasts. METAPHOR 1 (Hristo Botev) broadcasts were to continue.

## Bulgarian Intelligence Service Activity

In May 1954 the Bulgarian Intelligence Service DS created a special directorate, "Radiooko" (radiokontrarazuznavane), with the task of clarifying and working on signals for available illegal hostile radio stations. In one report there was this comment: "The broadcasts of the radio station 'Goryanin' in their goals and purpose are divided into two types. The first addressed the couriers of the radio station and the second—the population. Of course, the ones addressed to the couriers have coded form."[47]

The report on "the subversion of the radio station 'Goryanin' against our country" from December 1956 read, in part: "A radio station 'Goryanin' was created by US intelligence in 1951 to assist its subversion of our country. For the purpose enemy propaganda is made through which they deny all the achievements of the people's power, blood and fire and brimstone are poured against the Party, the Government, our friendship with the Soviet Union, against individual party and government events, and large and small figures. In addition, this radio station is headed by American agents in our territory. This was established by the captured agents and the periodical broadcasts of five number encrypted messages."[48]

The scripts and tapes of both Radio Goryanin and Hristo Botev are presumably lost or not available publicly to research, but the following are representative sample programs attributed to Radio Goryanin or Hristo Botev taken from Bulgarian Intelligence Service Reports:

May 29, 1951: "Transmitting for forester C. Pass through the specified area without contacting the local members of the brotherhood. Give message to couriers AP-15 and TV-3. The innovation for obtaining secure information is approved. End of message for couriers AP-14 and GP-3. Get new material from 'Snowdrop'! If necessary, seek cover in those couriers."

June 13, 1951: "The whip: talk about courier Lyubo. I repeat: for courier Lyubo. Lyubo. After five days meet with Assen. Repeat Assen.... The water is very cold. The dog is not barking. Penka called Misho. End."

October 1, 1951: "The whip will deliver a message to one of the messengers of the Free Brotherhood. Warning! Speaking to the courier Stone, Stone. The sun rose. You have a new backpack. Watermill No 3. At 4, 8, 3, 4, 1. Cut branches up to 4, 2, 8, 6, 5. The pine trees. End."

July 5, 1954: "It is reported that BTA cannot keep track of radio programs from Goryanin due to SS jamming policy. It is recommended that Department IV of the SS provide secure premises outside the range of jamming devices, with proper equipment to monitor transmissions."

October 27, 1954: "In the course of our work it became known that radio 'Goryanin' transmits five-digit messages of the telephony in Bulgarian recommended for agents under the pseudonym 'Balkan' and 'Lyulin.' Broadcasts intended for agent 'Balkan' start with a blast of waltz by Strauss. After playing the waltz, the speaker says: 'Balkan, I start' or 'Hello, Balkan.' After these words, he says the number of the groups and begins to announce numbers in groups of five."

May 9, 1955: "Attention! Attention! Here is Radio Goryanin—the Voice of Bulgarian resistance. Radio Goryanin welcomes Bulgarian Resistance! The Brother of Bulgarians, Goryanin radio, calls all real Bulgarians! Let's be ready always, Brothers, to prepare for the day of freedom and to free the earth of Bolshevik slavery. Brother Bulgarians, the future is ours, freedom will shine! Death to barbaric Communism! Long live Bulgaria!"

August 12, 1955: "Listen to a cycle of practical tips. Be ready to avoid failures like those that happened so far due solely to the nonsense and the enthusiasm of our youth. When selecting adherents, there are two rules. The first is: Do not judge for your friends only on their anti-communist speeches. Judge their deeds, examine their character, study their lives, establish their vices. Full and comprehensive judgment is unnecessary. The second one is this: Never bring your closest friends to work illegally because the failure of one of you will mean a failure of the whole group."

August 17, 1955: "Five-digit coded message intended for 'Mousalla'"—Experts state: "the radiogram was disguised with a special code pad, which we do not have, so we cannot decipher."

January 3, 1956. "This is Radio Goryanin. Brother Bulgarians, 1955 brought us the accession of Bulgaria as a member of the UN. Should we be disappointed? Should we lose hope? No, Bulgarian brothers! Our accession to the UN does not mean recognition of the Communist regime. Communist dictatorship today is renounced more than ever. The fact that our country will be represented by a communist is of no importance, because the shadow of our people will hang over their shoulders and the people shall not stop to expose and accuse the communist oppressors of our homeland. The accession of Bulgaria to the UN, however, has brought us something else. It made us, the people—stronger, our voice—more powerful, our borders—more open to international scrutiny over the atrocities of the communist clique on our enslaved nation. Today, as a member of the UN we, the people, must raise our voices against communist oppression and deprivation of rights and receive support at the United Nations."

October 31, 1956: "The so-called Radio Hristov Botev has its first broadcast demanding dissolution of cooperative farms and reinstatement of private property, disbanding of state security structures and reorganization of the state system."

March 19, 1957: "Radio Station 'Goryanin' broadcasts daily at 6.30, 12.00, 17.30 and 22.30 hours. The station operates with two transmitters simultaneously. The first one transmits within the range from 6000 to 6400 kilohertz and the second one from 6600 to 6800 kilohertz. This radio station is used for malicious propaganda against the PR

Bulgaria (People's Republic of Bulgaria) aimed at undermining the measures of the people's rule. With regards to different campaigns and events carried out by the government, radio station 'Goryanin' tries to bring confusion, mistrust and desire for hostile activity among the population of our country. During the events in Poznan and Hungary radio station 'Goryanin' was making open appeals for performing enemy activities against the people's rule."

February 5, 1958: "In order to avoid the communist jamming we are forced to change the lengths of the waves to which we transmit, so if you stop hearing our voice, turn the knob slightly to the left or to the right from the spot where you have heard us and you will continue hearing radio 'Goryanin'—the voice of the enemies of communism."

June 8, 1959: "The technical facilities are 17.5 km north of Athens. The radio center covers an area of 10,000 square meters and is guarded by US military personnel under the code names 'Owl' and 'Raven.' It broadcasts in Albanian, Bulgarian, Romanian and Russian."[49]

"Hristo Botev" last known broadcast was on July 30, 1962; on August 9, 1962, "Radio Goryanin" terminated its broadcasts.[50]

## Romania

Radio Free Europe began short-wave "gray" broadcasting to Romania from the mobile transmitter station "Barbara" in Lampertheim, Germany, on July 14, 1950. It is doubtful that anyone in Romania heard the early broadcasts as the power of the mobile transmitter was too low to reach that far.

### Vocea Padurii (Voice of the Forest)

A clandestine or "black" radio station known as "Vocea Padurii" (Voice of the Forest) was broadcasting in 1951. It is not known if this was an early experimental CIA clandestine radio station or a domestic Romania propaganda station operated by partisans in the mountains and forests, who were fighting the Communist regime. In September 1951, one Radio Free Europe interviewer of refugees from Romania in Turkey wrote this about clandestine radio transmitters in Romania (Romania).

> More and more news from inside Romania shows that the mysterious radio broadcasting station called Vocea Padurii (Voice of the Forest) is very much listed to and is growing increasingly popular. The broadcasts are starting almost daily about 0200 hours (Romanian time) and many people in Bucharest especially wake up to hear it. They are made in the name of General DRAGALINA, who achieved great popularity in 1949 as head of the first spontaneous marquis in Romania. Since then contradictory news about his death reached the outside world, but refugees who listened very recently to the broadcasts claim to recognize his voice and his manner of speaking. The style of the broadcasts is extremely vindictive. Many traitors and collaborators are

named in these broadcasts and are promised very quick vengeance. The broadcasts seem to be well informed especially on local affairs. The wavelength is 6,700 kilocycles or 49,60 kilocycles on the 41-meter band.[51]

General Dragalina refers to Lt. General Corneliu Dragalina (1877–1949), who was a highly decorated Romanian army officer, who fought against the USSR in World War II and later opposed the Communist takeover of Romania. RFE's evaluator commented: "Source: reliability unknown; Information: unknown, wait for confirmation. It should be mentioned that western monitoring has not yet been able to locate this station and unless further confirmation could be obtained, accounts of this matter should be taken with a certain reserve."[52]

In May 1952, Radio Free Europe's field operations in Istanbul, Turkey, sent another information report:

> While still in Romania, a 57-year-old Armenian immigrant who arrived at Istanbul on 2 April 1952, listened many times to a clandestine radio station, conducting a campaign against the Communist regime. He said that he always heard the broadcast in Romania but at various hours of the day or night, since the stations had no fixed time for broadcasting. Most of the time, however, he was able to listen to it at night, usually after 2000 hrs. He tuned in to the station on shortwave, between the 16- and 25-meter bands, night next to the BBC on the dial.
>
> Only one man spoke over this station, starting every broadcast with the words: "Romania speaking." The station attacked the regime very severely and quoted facts and names. It seemed to give people courage especially because it was within Romania and because it never repeated what the Western radio stations said. Our informant said that he did not know where the clandestine radio was, but people generally believe it to be located in the vicinity of the town of Cluj, capital of Transylvania; at any rate, they believed it to be in Transylvania.[53]

RFE's evaluator commented: "No reliable confirmation available."[54]

## "România Viitoare—Vocea Rezistenței Naționale" (Future of Romania—Voice of National Resistance)

An undated (presumably early 1951) 39-page Office of Policy Coordination (OPC) proposal included these comments:

> To institute covert operations within Communist held Romania. Such actions will be carried out by free Romanians in the name of a Free Romanian Council headed by King Michael.
>
> After the volunteers have been properly processed, they should be introduced one by one into a room where the ceremony of swearing in shall be officiated. Each man will take an oath of allegiance to King Michael and free Romania in a proper and formal ceremony similar to the swearing in procedure in pre–Communist Romania. A Romanian priest and a high-ranking free Romanian officer should officiate under the Romanian colors. The oath of allegiance should be carefully worded and studied by members of Council before final approval by King Michael.

Undoubtedly some of the broadcasts of the Free Europe program and some of the Voice of America broadcasts are listened to by quite a few Romanians in the hope that they may grasp some information as to early liberation of their country. We believe and recommend that intensive propaganda by means of a "black" radio be instituted as soon as this plan is approved with a radio station in the vicinity of our proposed forwarding base in Greece. From Greece the free Romanians assigned to this radio work, will be in a position to listen daily to the Bucharest Communist radio broadcasts and pick up any points which will be useful in countering the false propaganda spread by the official Communist station. This powerful "Black" radio directed to Romania from Greece, whether on a long or medium wave, will no doubt be subjected to jamming in certain areas of the country but according to past experience they will be unable to extend this all over Romania. Consideration should also be given to the dropping of throw away radios to the local population. It is very gratifying that quite a good many free Romanians now in the United States have had opportunity to receive proper training and indoctrination as to the making up of programs directed to Romania under the auspices of the National Committee for a Free Europe. These people will no doubt above very helpful in setting up and running the black radio program with the assistance of U.S. technicians. Attempts should also be made to shadow broadcasts or inject adverse ghost talk into the Communist broadcasts emitted from Bucharest.

In addition to the black radio, consideration should be given to the dropping in of leaflets and posters in various parts of Romania. One of the primary objectives of the black radio should be to uncover the Communist "bullies" and threaten any further Communist crimes with measures of retaliation. Once bases in Romania have been established, it will be easier to carry out threats made by radio and, in fact, carry out acts of reprisals against Communist leaders and those threatened. Information shall be collected from all possible sources emanating from Romania and from those recently out of the country, in order to piece together the pattern and set up of as many Communist organizations and towns as possible. In this way we will have correct information as to the Communist leaders in various towns and follow-up their doings. Should a Communist official or Militia chief embark on a terror campaign against the local population in some areas, then both by radio and by leaflets we could uncover him, threaten him and actually abduct him and leave his body exposed in the "Red Square" of the village or town.[55]

John C. Campbell, Officer in Charge of Balkan Affairs, US State Department, met with ADPC Frank Wisner and other staff members of OPC in January 1951. One of the OPC proposals, based on this meeting, was "to establish a black radio station within Greece for the purpose of beaming propaganda material into Romania. This station will operate under the guise of an underground radio, broadcasting from Romania, and will employ such methods as 'ghosting' Radio Bucharest as well as scheduled newscasts and commentaries."[56] The meeting was then reported in CIA channels and the following considerations were listed in the OPC project plan dated April 23, 1951:

> The Romanian people are held in line by repressive Communist police and political controls, which have ensured a pace of Sovietization exceeded only in Bulgaria. Over the past five years Romania's traditional orientation toward the West has been

vigorously undermined, as Romania becomes progressively more isolated from the Western world and absorbed into the Soviet complex, the confidence of the people in eventual liberation must continue to dwindle and their will to resist be replaced by increasingly passive resignation.

It is not anticipated that the Romanian people can summon sufficient psychological and material strength to overthrow the host regime under existing circumstances. Nevertheless, their detestation of the regime and its sponsors represents a basic vulnerability of Soviet control, which, if properly exploited, would impede the utilization of Romanian resources as either a covert or overt base of Soviet operations in the Balkans.[57]

OPC's psychological warfare plan for Romania with the cryptonym QKBROIL was approved on August 7, 1951. The major objectives of QKBROIL were:

a. To fortify the hope of liberation among the Romanian people and to strengthen their will to resist Communism.
b. To establish a clandestine underground for the implementation of U.S. policy toward the Soviet orbit in cold war and hot war situations.
c. To undermine by a combination of covert operations including psychological warfare the political, economic and military structure of the Communist regime.
d. To develop a political center as a point of attribution for overt activities and as a covert operational support arm for projected operations.[58]

One line of action to meet the objectives was "the preparation and initiation of a coordinated psychological warfare programs against Romania including covert radio broadcasts, propaganda leaflets and mailing campaigns intended to discredit various public figures associated with the regime." And "the development and strengthening of a united Romanian refugee organization—within the framework of the National Committee for Free Europe to unify the Romanian resistance effort and cover various activities."[59] However, "efforts were made to establish a field headquarters and propaganda center for QKBROIL in Turkey but because of the attitude of the Turkish authorities this has so far been impossible. It now looks as though radio propaganda activities will have to be postponed until the question of a permanent base has been decided."[60]

In a proposal dated June 22, 1951, for fiscal year 1952, the purpose of QKBROIL was defined as:

To encourage the hope of liberation and will to resist of the Romanian people to establish a clandestine underground in Romania to hamper Soviet/Satellite military operations and to serve as a medium for wartime resistance; to undermine the political, economic and military structure of Communist Romania; to form a NCFE Political

Center for refugee Romanians to give cover and support for OPC activities.... In lieu of existing organizations, which appear unable to unite, it is possible that a new organization will be formed to assist OPC.[61]

In another proposal document, there was further discussion of the difficulties in uniting the Romanian émigré organizations: "The Romanian refugees have so far been unable to unite into a single, effective organization. The formation of such a group is considerably hindered by personal rivalries, factionalism, and the hesitancies of King Michael in assuming a more positive role in its creation. Initially, however, the present National Committee and/or its rival the Free Romanian Association could provide adequate cover for OPC activity."[62]

The June 1951 Monthly Status Report contained this information:

> The actual undertaking of covert operations against the Communist Regime in Romania, while considered as both important and desirable, has been subordinated to the mounting of certain other operations due to:
> a. The necessity for concentration of effort by this Branch on the more vulnerable perimeter Satellites, and
> b. The absence of a mechanism or vehicle representative of all Romanian political factions in exile which could act as an overt sponsor for operations. Generally, the program of psychological warfare against Romania will parallel that undertaken against Bulgaria. Existing facilities will be enlarged where this is possible to obtain black radio coverage of Romania. It is planned that the establishment of the proposed fifty kW radio station in Greece will provide coverage for Romania as well as other Balkan states. As an interim measure, two small 500-watt transmitters are on order for this Project.[63]

The OPC EE-I Report of Operations for the Quarter that ended June 30, 1951, contained this operations comment: "Clearances have been obtained for *two other* operations officers, a communications instructor, the chief of the broadcast staff, three spotter-recruiters, and one translator. Present plans call for dispatching the three broadcast staff personnel to Greece in the latter part of July to inaugurate PW activity."[64]

On August 2, 1951, the Consultant Board, which included U.S. State Department and Defense Department personnel, approved Project QKBROIL. CIA finally approved the project on August 28, 1951. The CIA project officer expected that the station would be manned by the end of February 1952 and operating by the end of March 1952. That expectation changed, with a new one: the first broadcast of 15 minutes was expected on June 1, 1952.[65] Included in the project approval request were these points:

> Preparation and initiation of a coordinated PW program against Romania.
> This will necessitate the immediate enlargement of covert broadcasting facilities established under BGFIEND (Albania) and QKSTAIR (Bulgaria), in order to extend these clandestine broadcasts to Romania. As soon as additional personnel for the transmitters now in Greece are available on the spot, the beaming of black

transmissions to Romania can be coordinated with those presently directed against Bulgaria.

Psychological Warfare

In general, PW activity during Phase 1 will aim at bolstering popular morale fostering the people's hopes in ultimate liberation, and undermining Communist leaders, policies and propaganda. This phase will comprise black broadcasts from Greece and adjacent areas., as well as spectacular airdrops of propaganda leaflets.[66]

For a briefing of CIA's Soviet/East European Division, dated January 1952, it was written,

> There has been no single refugee organization representing the Romanian people since November 1950.... [A]lthough the NCFE has supported the Association, QKBROIL has taken the position that neither the Romanian National Committee nor the Association of Free Romanians as presently constituted is acceptable for our use. Our continuous efforts to effect unification have been unavailing.... [I]n connection with the refugee problem, NCFE's open support of the Association has made it extremely difficult for us to convince the refugees that unification is the only way to obtain American backing. NCFE'S partisanship has widened the breath between the two groups and has done nothing to alleviate the personal differences that existed prior to the break and that have developed since then. This has also affected the attitude of the King toward us.[67]

By September 1951, CIA selected the broadcast team to run the clandestine radio station in Greece:

> Brutus Coste will depart, as soon as his immigration status is clarified, for a three-week trip in Europe, under NCFE European University cover, to spot personnel for the PW unit. He will return to the ZI before proceeding to Athens. He, his wife, and Pogoneanu, his assistant, should depart for Athens by December 15 in order to make preparations for the broadcasts. Broadcasts and leaflets will be initiated prior to agent drops, which probably will start in early 1952.[68]

Brutus Coste (1910–1985) was an important personality in the Cold War émigré politics. As a former diplomat in pre–World War II Romania, he prepared foreign policy comments for NBC broadcasting network and wrote numerous articles on propaganda, including the 1950 book, *The Political Premises of Successful Propaganda to East Europe*, published by the Mid-European Studies Center. In 1954, Coste became Director of the International League for the Rights of Man and representative at the UN. He then worked on "Democracy in Russia" and received $300 per month from the National Committee for Free Europe. From 1954 to 1965, he was Secretary General of the Assembly of Captive European Nations (ACEN). From 1967 to 1976, he was a professor of international relations and world history at Fairleigh Dickinson University, New Jersey. Brutus Coste died in New York on September 3, 1984.[69]

The OPC Aims of QKBROIL Operations 1952 were: "Accomplish the objective of the QKBROIL Project, the weakening of the Romanian link in

## 4. Clandestine Broadcasts from Greece to Bulgaria and Romania

the Communist chain of Satellites, falls into two categories; cold war operations and intensified cold war or hot war operations."[70] One of the cold war operations was, "Initiation of psychological warfare against the Communist regime and of a black propaganda program for the Romanian people." The Psychological Warfare Program was defined as

> a carefully designed covert propaganda and pw program has been developed and will be initiated approximately 45 days prior to first agent drops in Romania. It is necessary that the propaganda phase be initiated prior to agent drops in order to prepare the Romanian people psychologically to receive and assist our agents. The Romanians have developed fear and distrust of any sort of clandestine matter because the Communist regime has planted and fostered resistance groups in an effort to uncover opposition and potential resistance leaders. Black broadcasts and distribution of leaflets will have the dual aim of building up the will to resist on the part of the Romanian people and of raising doubts and fears in the minds of the Communists and their tools. The propaganda staff will be based temporarily in Athens.[71]

The year 1952 was a period of establishment and consolidation rather than action. Active operations were to be developed in 1953. For Fiscal Year 1953, which began on July 1, 1952, CIA planned to conduct a psychological warfare campaign, with the intention: "Raise the morale of the Romanian public through providing tangible evidence of the existence of a Romanian anti–Communist effort working from the outside on behalf of the Romanian people and to foster sentiments of national solidarity and participation in this effort by instituting a covert propaganda program consisting of radio broadcasts, leaflet drops and mailing campaigns."[72] It was also proposed to "continue work through NCFE on the establishment of some type of unified front representing the politically acceptable refugee groups."[73]

By December 10, 1953, there were still no clandestine radio broadcasts to Romania and the psychological warfare Project QKBROIL was broken down in smaller projects, including the clandestine radio project with the cryptonyms: SHELLAC and SHELLFIRE. The clandestine radio broadcasts were to have "the primary aim of disaffecting the Romanian Communists and it is planned to supplement these broadcasts with an 'intruder voice' program to be established in 1954. This project will utilize a technical installation already established in Greece."[74]

Approval of the project by DDP/O/OPO, dated December 18, 1953, was made contingent upon "individual clearances of each and every unconventional broadcast and approval in advance by DDP.... The Office of Communications however, has told us informally that, in addition to limitations on 'intruder' broadcasts, national policy prohibits two ether type of broadcasts, i.e., those which have the effect of jamming enemy broadcasts and those which employ 'deception' tactics."[75]

The July 1954 proposal to extend Project SHELLFIRE for fiscal year 1955 included these negative comments about NCFE:

> The Romanian emigration was often handled by NCFE in a haphazard, devious and frequently frustrating matter. The task could have been performed more effectively, perhaps, by an individual who had not only a thorough knowledge of the political and social history and development of the country and the personalities concerned, but who also was in the position to follow closely OPC-Romanian emigration operations, such as a qualified OPC staff officer, under NCFE cover.
>
> Much exhaustive effort was spent to develop a NCFE Political Center as a cover for overt activities and a covert operational support arm for projected OPC operations. This effort met with consistent failure. One of the difficulties encountered stemmed from the fact that the financial support the Romanian emigration received from U.S. sources rendered it attractive to exploitation by those refugees who were interested in furthering their own or their parties' political aims.[76]

CIA in 1954 chose Mugur Valahu (1920–2003), attorney and journalist, as chief of the new clandestine radio station. Valahu had escaped Romania in 1948. He first settled in Paris and eventually worked for Radio Paris, BBC, and Radio Free Europe. For Radio Paris, Valahu was responsible for broadcasting "coded messages" to non-existent persons in Romania that gave the impression that the West had links with a fictitious anti-Communist resistance. Romania protested these broadcasts and Valahu was forced to leave Radio Paris.[77]

In an interview given to Radio Romania's Center for Oral History on October 25, 2010, Valahu talked about his broadcast experiences in Athens: "There were, for example, prosecutors and other fervent communists whom we attacked personally, warning them—'be wary, things do change, we are here, and you, traitor to the country, will pay for your crimes.'"[78] He added,

> This was a clandestine radio broadcast, fifteen minutes maximum, in Athens, and had special transmitters for broadcast variable wavelength of 49 meters. These issues were generally made at night, were sporadic, unannounced, to surprise jamming stations in the country, which were extremely numerous.... [O]ur language was very violent, Romanian nationalist, so we substituted somehow for the people who could speak neither in public nor in writing. Welcome anti–Russian slogans and asking the independence of Bukovina and Bessarabia.
>
> All information we collected from journals in the country we received from the American Embassy. Furthermore, we listened to Radio Bucharest every day. From time to time, I met some Romanians who barely left the country and told us what the situation was in Romania. So, I was very well informed. We had the names of all Securitate Communists, the ones we could find out, right? We had names of Prosecutors, different names of diehard communists whom we personal attacked, pointing out: "Pay attention! Things are changing, we are here, you are traitors to the country, you have to pay for all your crimes...." "Are you not ashamed?" "You are murderers, traitors! "In Pitesti this happened..." "At Sighet died such..." "They were tortured..."
>
> I wanted to leave the impression that we were even in Romania. Our programs had little to do with broadcasts of Radio Free Europe and Voice of America, which were

broadcast, so to speak, stylish, moderate, pure information.... [I]n our programs, incitement was our very clear intent. Not only did I attack the government, accusing them as gypsies, foreigners, servants, ax tails, etc. but also as the end of broadcast, we said: "Death to the government's executioners! Down with Dej's Gypsies!" A very violent language which was, after all, the language that I think people would have had if it had not been gagged.

(Program of "Voice of Freedom–Organ of Refugees from Romania," Athens, March 1, 1957)

Brothers! Here is the clandestine post Romania Future-Voice of Despair! Let the red beasts of our land go! We want freedom and reassurance! Let go of Moscow's servants from the helm of the country! We want freedom and justice! We want a national government chosen by workers, peasants and civil servants! We want a responsible government! We want the end of the Russian occupation! To Break the Securitate! We want to punish Drăghici's beasts! Brothers! Here is the Voice of Romania's Future—the Voice of Despair! The Communists dig their grave! Keep your trust in freedom! Brothers! Let's step up the strike of laziness and bureaucracy! To boycott the orders of the government servants! Through continuous struggle for freedom and independence! Communists! Listen to the warning of the Romanian people! Break away from Moscow! Break the heavens of the Romanian people! Give us the proof that you are not the occupants of the invaders! Give the country a truly socialist government! Quickly earn the mercy of the people! Stop the terror, stop looting and exploitation![79]

Valahu also said, "Americans never made any comments with all our violent language. We had all the freedom to say what we wanted, which was extremely gratifying for us as Romanians."[80]

During the 1956 Hungarian Revolution, Valahu broadcast to Romania with this message: "We urged people to become aware of Romanian pride, of the fact that Hungarians were about to rebel and that Romanians could not sit idly by. We just had to do something, we had to hold strikes and street rallies.... We advised people to carry out individual acts, so as not to give way to reprisals against potential groups."[81]

## Jamming

In 1957, Soviet jamming of broadcasts from Athens was a major problem for CIA and after studying the problem, CIA decided that the jamming was skywave and was not effective in the target areas. CIA assumed that "the main purpose of this skywave jamming was to create confusion and force us into using drastic measures such as constant changing of frequencies during a broadcast, making it extremely difficult for a potential listener to find and/or follow our broadcasts. We had indeed obliged the Soviets by using these evasion tactics." CIA sent an "agent" in Bucharest to monitor the "Future of Romania" broadcasts. He had been given a schedule of fixed times and random times of the broadcasts and data of the skywave jammers heard in Athens. He spent three months in Romania. The "agent" discovered that the skywave jammers were not heard but ground jammers were in central Bucharest. The jamming was less effective in the outlying areas of the city and was weak of nonexistent in a large area of Romania where the broadcasts were heard. He recommended random times and not to use evasion tactics as that made "listening to a broadcast extremely difficult and must have discouraging effect on potential listeners."[82]

CIA chief at the Athens transmitting site recommended that a similar system be set up in the USSR and added this comment:

> The weakest point of our radio activities has been almost complete lack of information regarding the degree of audibility and intelligibility of our broadcasts in the target areas. This uncertainty regarding the degree of penetration of Soviet jamming by our broadcasts has been responsible to a large degree for lack of enthusiasm toward our radio propaganda activities among Headquarters personnel. Consequently, radio propaganda has been demoted to the level of "marginal activities," with only a half-hearted effort being made to keep it going.[83]

CIA decided to close down "Future of Romania" broadcasts on October 31, 1959.[84] Mugur Valahu left Greece for Paris and afterwards spent many years in Africa. He went on to become a successful author of books about Africa, including, *The Katanga Circus: A Detailed Account of Three UN Wars*. Migur Valahu died in southern France on February 24, 2003; he was 82 years old.

# 5

# A Seaborne CIA Fiasco and the Voice of Free Albania (VOFA)

> The best laid schemes of mice and men
> Go often askew,
> And leave us nothing but grief and pain,
> For promised joy!
> —(From the 1786 poem "To a Mouse" by Robert Burns, in modern English)

## Albania

> Although losses have been severe, amounting to a third of the men sent in, and although it has been decided to change our operational methods as a result of this experience, it should not be concluded that these earlier operations represent a waste of effort. Not only have we secured a mass of valuable information, but we have also obtained a great deal of the most valuable experience which could not have been obtained in any other way. This has given us a very much better understanding of the problems with which we are confronted.[1]

The original OPC Plan for Albania was based upon the following statement of overall United States policy: "Current U.S. policy with regard to Albania has as its objective the restoration of Albanian independence through the overthrow of the Moscow-controlled regime and its replacement by an enlightened government acceptable to the people of Albania. Such a government would enjoy the support of the United States as long as it remains friendly to the U.S. and its objectives and hostile to the Soviet Government and its objectives."[2]

Because of its isolation from the Soviet Bloc, its military and political weakness, and the hostility of its people to the Communist regime, Albania is the Communist state which would be easiest to defect from the Communist Bloc and is the one in which a rollback of the Iron Curtain could be undertaken at the lowest cost and with the best chance of success. In view of its geographic location and internal situation, Albania also presents an ideal proving and training ground for OPC type activities. It can serve as a sort of Aberdeen proving ground for CIA.[3]

When the Albanian project BGFIEND was first under consideration by CIA in 1949, it learned that the British had initiated project VALUABLE with substantially the same objectives. CIA's project was thereafter developed "as a result of discussion and close coordination with the Department of State, the Joint Chiefs of Staff, the Foreign Office, and the British Intelligence Service in the spring and early summer, with the maximum ultimate objective: the overthrow of the Soviet dominated Albanian Government."[4]

CIA/OPC operations against Albania were originally approved by the Assistant Director for Policy Coordination (ADPC) Frank Wisner and the Department of State (undated). The Outline for the Operational Plan for Albania was approved by Wisner on May 23, 1949. From May 20, 1949, to May 26, 1949, there were meetings in Washington between Wisner and his staff, the Department of State, British representatives, during which Albanian operations were discussed.[5] An OPC project began that aimed at "placing the Soviet position in Albania under great strain and which, if ultimately successful, might result in the overthrow of the Hoxha regime."[6]

The 1949 OPC Project BGFIEND foresaw a coup d'état to overthrow the Hoxha regime:

Preliminary to this objective were

- the formation of a political committee,
- the execution of a propaganda campaign, and
- the training and infiltration of agents into Albania.

Corollary objectives, independent of the ultimate goal of the plan, were

- to eliminate Albania as a training and holding base for Greek insurgents,
- to deprive the USSR of an outpost on the Mediterranean,
- to stimulate resistance activities within other satellite countries, and
- to provide OPC with a fund of experience in clandestine operations involving the coordinated explication of several techniques against a single target.[7]

On August 15, 1949, the first objective was completed with the formation of the Committee for Free Albania in Paris, France, with the participation of three Albanian political parties that had participated in resistance movements in World War II. The propaganda objective envisaged a

## 5. A Seaborne CIA Fiasco and the Voice of Free Albania (VOFA) 91

comprehensive campaign that included the use of a radio ship in the Adriatic and the dropping of propaganda leaflets.

## Seaborne Broadcasting Fiasco

In October 1949, the Office of Policy Coordination ((OPC) planned to use a "sea-borne broadcast transmitter" to transmit recorded programs to Albania with "live spot" announcements. The OPC plan included the use of a 1000-watt, medium wave transmitter to reach the largest possible audience in Albania by using a signal strong enough to overpower Radio Tirana's domestic frequency:

> It has been agreed that these broadcasts shall be based, for various technical, security and political reasons, on a ship to cruise in and around the Adriatic and Ionian Seas.... [T]his vessel with minor modifications can be converted into a floating broadcasting station capable of sending medium-wave broadcasts into all points in Albania. It will be operated in a 100-mile arc at the end of a 300-mile radius from the farthest point to be covered in the country. The broadcasting arc will be well below the heel of Italy, near Malta, and approximately 180 miles from the nearest Albanian port.[8]

The rationale for using a vessel carrying a medium wave transmitter was that there were, at that time, no OPC land-based transmitters in Italy or Greece. Medium wave broadcasts were chosen because of an estimate that of the approximately 50,000 radios in Albania, between 30,000 and 37,500 were medium-wave sets. It was also estimated that 10,000 to 12,000 short-wave radios receivers were in Albania, most of them owned by Communist officials.[9]

The idea was that a vessel would be purchased and outfitted for radio broadcasting. In November 1949 four prospective vessels were located, with one finally identified as being suitable enough for the operation. The cost of purchasing this vessel was put at $56,000 and OPC was to pay for it. The British were to "provide cover for the purchase, refit, and operation, plus arrange for the transfer of the title of vessel and cancel the ownership through a cover owner." The British were also to provide the crew and costs of refitting the boat for broadcasting and the operating costs were to be split "fifty-fifty."[10]

A joint British-American Memorandum dated December 6, 1949, was approved by the ADPC Frank Wisner and the U.S. Department of State with the objective of "proceed immediately with the setting-up of facilities for clandestine broadcasts in the name of the Committee for Free Albania."[11]

In April 1950, OPC, using the outline of the British plan for Albania code-name VALUABLE, decided to seek a vessel in the United States rather than in Great Britain as originally agreed upon with the British, to be put into operational use in August 1950. The OPC propaganda project was given the cryptonym BGSPEED, a subproject of the Albanian country plan BGFIEND, that was "for the purchase, equipping and operation of a vessel to be used for radio broadcasting beamed at Albania.... This is a direct OPC undertaking, whose program comprises the preparation, editorial processing, and transmitting of black propaganda to Albania."[12]

The plan including sailing the propaganda vessel to Marseilles, France, with the original crew, where it would that change the name, "flag" and ownership.[13] The requirements for this vessel included:

- Ability to support a propaganda staff of five men in addition to a full complement of the crew.
- Ability to carry sufficient water, fuel, and food to remain on station of the heel of Italy for at least twelve consecutive days with a full complement aboard, between return trips to Athens, Greece.
- Sufficient stock of engine parts and spares aboard to operate overseas independently for one year.
- Sufficient space aboard to permit installation of radio equipment and one compartment to be used as a recording and broadcasting studio.[14]

It was decided to use a "yacht-type vessel" because it was

- the more suitable for reasons of flexibility of operation,
- private cover potentialities as viewed against commercial cover,
- height of masts in relationship to size for accommodation of the radio broadcast antennae.[15]

By May 1950, two yacht brokers were asked to locate an appropriate vessel and three yachts were identified: one was in Acapulco, Mexico, one in Miami, Florida, and one in Gloucester, Massachusetts. OPC then used a cleared "cutout" for the purchase of the yacht. He had already owned two yachts and bought and sold yachts for years.[16] The "cutout" was to be financed by OPC, receive the title to the yacht and deliver it to the Smith Boat Yard in Baltimore, Maryland, for refitting and conversion to include "decking, placing of copper sheathing on the hull, ... broadcast studio, and other repairs necessary for extended operations." The "cutout" owner then was to transfer the vessel to Panamanian registration. A Panamanian-licensed ship master named Leslie Holmes, who was undergoing OPC security clearance processing, would then chose the crew. $150,000 was budgeted as the maximum cost for the purchase.[17]

After inspection of two of the vessels, the "motor sail/ketch" IRMAY in Gloucester, Massachusetts, was chosen as the one most, "Adaptable from the point of view of broadcast requirements, maneuverability,

## 5. A Seaborne CIA Fiasco and the Voice of Free Albania (VOFA) 93

accommodations for the crew and staff and can be outfitted in the least time and expense." The Irmay was purchased for $80,000 ($870,000 equivalent in 2020). The captain of the Irmay and crew were experienced and reportedly had been involved in several scientific expeditions in the Caribbean and South America.[18]

OPC Assistant Director for Policy Coordination Frank Wisner approved the project on June 14, 1950. However, he wrote this handwritten comment on the cover sheet "This project has been approved, with much trepidation.... I have seen this kind of thing tried twice during the last war with eventual abandonment of the project in each instance."[19]

The operational cover included the chartering of the vessel to a fictitious "Institute"—the Marine Biological Research Institute, Inc. (MBRI), which was incorporated in Maryland as a non-profit organization engaged in research of marine biology. The Charter included in the articles of incorporation was to

> promote generally the accumulation, analysis, and dissemination of scientific knowledge in the field of Marine Biology by undertaking, sponsoring, participating in studies, research projects, and field expeditions in any part of the world—making loans and gifts for such purposes—and to make such knowledge available through articles, lectures, books, letters, motion pictures, etc.[20]

MBRI was listed as incorporated foundation that was not authorized to issue capital stock so "funds for this foundation have consisted entirely of donations by a fictitious person purportedly of eccentric habits and keenly interested in this field of science."[21]

The "Institute" also made a letter of endorsement to the Chief OPC officer on board the vessel indicating that he was employed in "scientific explorations in the Mediterranean."

Final arrangements for the cover "Institute" were made. A lawyer in Baltimore was cleared to set up the articles of incorporation in the State of Maryland. His office was listed as the official address of the "Institute" for any correspondence. Four Directors of the "Institute" were listed, three of whom were pseudonyms. The printing of the letterheads, issue of bona fide stock to the Directors, chartering of the vessel (including the actual transfer of funds), and the establishment of a bank account in Baltimore for "Mediterranean Marine," through which funds to pay personnel aboard and to operate the vessel would be transferred regularly to a bank account. A part-time trusted bookkeeper was hired to maintain double-entry booking records of both the overt and covert expense accounts.[22]

In June 1950, a joint Bulgarian-Albanian propaganda center was set up in Athens, Greece. The Albanian broadcasts were to be prepared there, based on a joint propaganda policy-directive approved with the British. However, the British were not involved on an operational level. One of the stations in the Athens broadcast system would transmit to the propaganda vessel a daily teletype broadcast of the next day's program. Spot broadcasts would be transcribed on board the vessel.[23]

The Irmay left Baltimore for Miami on or about December 12, 1950, with OPC engineering personnel on board. On the way, there were "shakedown" tests conducted of the medium (sky-wave) transmissions. Rough seas off Cape Hatteras, sea sickness of the chief operator, and mechanical problems ensued, but in general the tests were considered positive: "Salt spray and heavy seas at no time handicapped the radiation efficiency of the installation." The conclusion of the testing was: "It can be seen that there are no technical radio factors, which might limit the effectiveness of the BGFIEND project as originally planned."[24] While in Miami, Captain Holmes made an unknown security violation and the Office of Naval Intelligence (ONI) became aware of the OPC connection to the Irmay. The Miami office of the Bureau of Customs wanted to inspect the vessel. The Assistant Deputy Commissioner of Customs was contacted with the request to stop the inspection.

ADPC Frank Wisner sent a message to Navy Rear Admiral Leslie C. Stevens giving some details of the BGSPEED operation.

> In view of the extreme sensitivity of the proposed mission of the covert vessel Irmay, the Eastern European Division, OPC, has handled this project from its inception in a manner believed consistent with the highest security precautions, and has purchased, overhauled the vessel, and installed all special equipment with a minimum revelation of government interests.... [T]he Irmay was purchased through private channels, which cannot be traced to the U.S. government.[25]

Admiral Stevens, coincidentally, would later become President of the American Committee for the Liberation of Bolshevism—the parent organization for Radio Liberty. Wisner promised Stevens and the Bureau of Customs that any future operations having any bearing on those agencies would be advised by OPC.[26]

OPC decided to let Captain Holmes continue to hold his position until the first port of call in Europe, when he would be replaced and returned to the United States—possible to face prosecution. In St. Thomas, Virgin Islands the name of the yacht was changed to "Juanita," and the registry changed from US to Panamanian. The OPC cryptonym for the yacht was KMHYMNAL.

The Juanita departed from Barbados on February 1, 1951, crossed the Atlantic Ocean for Europe and, after a few stopovers in various Mediterranean ports, arrived in Patras, Greece, on March 25, 1951, to perform the following mission under Project BGSPEED:

> At the time the JUANITA was purchased there was no certainty that permission would be granted by any country for her to operate within that country's coastal waters. It

## 5. A Seaborne CIA Fiasco and the Voice of Free Albania (VOFA)   95

was understood, therefore, that the broadcasts might have to be conducted from open sea, that the vessel obtained for this role would have to be sufficiently seaworthy for open sea operations, and the equipment capable of broadcasting from a considerable distance at sea. The JUANITA was equipped, accordingly, to broadcast medium wave into Albania, utilizing the skip wave technique.

This skip wave, unlike the ground wave, which exists both day and night, becomes effective as darkness falls and the ionosphere descends, and becomes ineffective as the sun rises and the ionosphere ascends. During the night hours the beam from the antenna strikes the ionosphere and bounces back to earth, permitting reception much farther from the transmitter than is normally possible by ground wave—which follows the ground sixty or seventy miles or so, depending on terrain, and grounds out.[27]

After JUANITA's arrival in Greece, serious problems were identified, some of which were:

1. From March 25 to June 9, no tests of the radio equipment were made, although it cost between $4,000 and $6,000 per month to maintain the crew and vessel.
2. A contract engineer was sent to Greece to review the JUANITA operation. He wrote: "The JUANITA was intended to broadcast medium wave—skip wave into its target from a distance of 175–300 miles, came to light during a meeting with Washington communications men two days before my departure to Athens.... On arrival in Athens I found that the men (both operations and communications) had apparently been unacquainted with this intention.... They expressed surprise, in fact, that Washington intended to depend on skip wave, for they believed skip wave had never been depended on before for medium wave broadcast."
3. The Albanian area is greater than the noise level off the U.S. east coast. Radio stations in the Balkans make a Babel of voices, move up and down the dial ... and operate with many times the power the JUANITA was given.
4. Communications equipment: The equipment was built for shore installation, however, which permits immovable foundation. The rolling, pitching, and constant vibration of the vessel caused abuse to the equipment, which it was not built to take.
5. JUANITA was designed for coastal yachting, not for constant Mediterranean service. The duty, to which she has been subjected, not so strenuous as actual operations, has already rendered her temporarily inoperative.
6. The chance, ever present in open sea operation, of a wave through the wheelhouse door or through the hatch over the transmitting room threatened to fry the communications men at their posts and disable the equipment permanently.

7. The distance between masts does not permit reasonable antenna length.
8. While the space allowed for sleeping quarters is more than ample, the space allowed for communications operation is so small that it denies the operators minimum movement. There is no ventilation in the transmitting room. The heat and smell when the equipment in operation is intense enough to cause sickness, a condition aggravated by semi-tropic weather and the violent movement of the ship.
9. Rigging and handrails become electrified during transmission endangering the life of all men topside.
10. The vessel's house-type wiring causes repeated fires. The vessel was delivered in the U.S. with its original wiring, which is of the house type, and is not suitable for marine use. This is evidenced by numerous minor fires which have occurred on board, and the extreme difficulty which the engineer has had in maintaining electric current throughout the vessel.
11. Generator power is insufficient both for communications operation and for ship's housekeeping.
12. Navigational charts of the Hydrographic Office and the British Admiralty are frequently based on surveys of the last century. There are numerous uncharted rocks and shoals. Lights are frequently found too weak to be seen the listed distances, if they are lighted at all. The risk of the loss of the vessel would be less important if the vessel were the best in design and condition. For any vessel in these waters the risk exists. For a black broadcasting ship seeking secluded coves on outlying islands the risk is accentuated.
13. At anchor in a sheltered island cove, one finds oneself but a few hundred yards from village dwellings. After fall of darkness the large white yacht, whose presence has brought excitement to the otherwise dreary existence of the islanders, lights up (when transmitting) like a Christmas tree. Spreader lights and running lights begin to glow, and brilliant flashes play about the rigging.
14. In May 1951, the JUANITA sailed to the Corfu, Greece, area to survey the coastline for a sheltered cove suitable as a permanent operating base for medium wave-ground wave broadcasts into Albania. The Corfu survey necessitated a 28-hour passage through a mined area, 14 hours through Greek and Albanian mine fields, and passage through a channel 500 meters from the Albanian coast. The rudder went out in the middle of the minefield, necessitating 20 minutes repair. The JUANITA went aground off Corfu—at a point where the chart showed 29 fathoms of water. Pertinent to grounding, as noted above, a vessel lending assistance to a vessel in trouble has the right

## 5. A Seaborne CIA Fiasco and the Voice of Free Albania (VOFA)    97

to tow her to any port of the salvager's choosing. In this case it might easily have been Albania, several miles away.

15. A radar set, weighing 4,288 pounds (not including cable, weighing an estimated 500 to 600 pounds), was purchased for the JUANITA at a cost of $15,000. The set was air freighted in thirteen crates to Greece at a cost of $1,500. Men sent from headquarters, whose mission included installation of the radar, found the set to be large enough for a Navy Light Cruiser. It was not suitable for the JUANITA.
16. In August 1951, the JUANITA was docked in the Piraeus harbor with,
    (1) One engine gone,
    (2) The other engine half-gone,
    (3) Dry rot under the galley,
    (4) Water tanks ready to collapse into the bilge, and
    (5) A winch, which, endangering the fingers of the man who uses it, will raise only the starboard anchor.[28]

There was an estimate of $20,000 to $30,000 and two months in Greek shipyards to make the necessary repairs.[29]

One ironic OPC conclusion of the Juanita's history read: "It was not necessary to buy a yacht, equip her, man her, sail her across the Atlantic, and maintain her in Greece for half a year to demonstrate that her transmitting equipment would not work."[30] The report had this recommendation: "Because of the failure of the transmitting equipment and the unsuitability of the vessel, there is no reason to reinstall the transmitter on the JUANITA. Since no other mission is contemplated by the field station for which she might be used, the JUANITA should be made available to other divisions of this organization. If other divisions find no use for her, she might best be sold in the field."[31]

In another OPC report, there was this comment:

> I wish to reiterate my belief that there need be no apologies by anyone for a decision now to liquidate this particular experiment. It has provided a number of people with valuable experiences and has taught a number of lessons that could not have been learned had not the basic proposition been tried out in actual practice. It has, however, taken up a great deal of time that might better now be directed to more pressing and fruitful activities.[32]

In March 1952, Acting Assistant Director for Policy Coordination wrote a memorandum to the Assistant Director, Office of Communications, in which he summarized the principal failures of Project BGSPEED, part of which read:

> A great many things have gone wrong in the implementation of this project, and it was finally terminated in October 1951. No actual broadcasting ever took place.
> Much of the onus for the failure can be attributed to shortcomings within OPC.

These include lack of seasoned judgment on the pert of various OPC officers concerned with the project, lack of continuous, adequate supervision unfortunate selection of a vessel: etc. On the other hand, the communications equipment provided proved totally inadequate for the contemplated operation.

This constitutes an expensive lesson for OPC.[33]

The JUANITA, which was purchased for $80,000 in 1951, was put up for bids and finally sold in May 1953 for $10,000 to Greek businessman Charilaos D. Petropoulos: "In summary, it appears that the field did everything possible to dispose of the yacht at the best price and that the sale to Petropoulos was in the best interests of the government."[34]

## *Voice of Free Albania (HTGRUBY)*

Although Project BGSPEED was considered a failure, that did not stop OPC from transmitting clandestine psychological warfare (PW) broadcasts into Albania as the Voice of Free Albania (often interchanged with Radio Free Albania) from the CIA radio transmitting site near Athens, Greece. One CIA declassified July 1954 document gives a good summary of how VOFA began at 10 p.m. local time on September 18, 1951:

> After repeated efforts to engage in clandestine PW against Albania covert radio broadcasts from the high seas, arrangements were completed with the government of Greece in the spring of 1950, which permitted CIA to create communications installation in the Athens area for the purpose of PW broadcasting to the satellites. On 18 September 1951, the Voice of Free Albania was activated and has broadcast on an almost daily schedule into Albania since that time in the 43- and 46-meter bands.
>
> The establishment of VOFA was based on the belief that as a corollary to the National Committee for Free Albania (NCFA), a supplementary PW effort was necessary, which would direct it efforts entirely to the creation of a feeling of hope in the minds of Albanian people inside the country. Consequently, with propaganda guidance from Headquarters, VOFA broadcasts into Albania news from the Free World, advice to the populace, encouragement for passive resistance and justification of the hope of ultimate liberation.[35]

Radio Free Albania is often used as the name of the clandestine station, but the official name was Voice of Free Albania. The first broadcasts were monitored by CIA's station in Italy. The CIA Information Report was distributed in November 1951 with the subject: *Albanian Clandestine Radio Station* and contained details of the initial broadcasts:

1. A new Albanian clandestine radio station, which has been vigorously denouncing the Albanian Communist regime, and is known as the "Voice of Free Albania," has been heard recently on short wave.
2. The station has advised its listeners that it will broadcast instructions for sabotaging the regime.

## 5. A Seaborne CIA Fiasco and the Voice of Free Albania (VOFA)

3. Although the location of the station is unknown, it is believed that it is in Albania itself, since it appears extremely well-informed on Albanian matters.[36]

A subsequent Information Report titled *Clandestine Station "Radio Free Albania"* gave more details:

- "Radio Free Albania," an anti–Communist transmitter directed to Albania was first heard on 10 September and intermittingly to 21 September at approximately 20:15–20:45 GMT on a frequency varying around 8200 kilocycles. Transmissions were obviously in the nature of tests in preparation for regular broadcasts and consisted of repeated anti–Communist slogans and announcements in the Albanian language to the effect that shortly it would broadcast the truth to the people of Albania.
- It purported to be on Albanian soil and stated its sponsor to be the "Free Albania Committee." The first bars of the old Albanian national anthem were used as a signature tune.
- On 21 September, the station began regular broadcasts at 20:00–20:30 GMT on a new channel of 6980 kilocycles, opening with the following announcement: "This is the Voice of Free Albania—for Albania, for Freedom, for the Red and Black Flag. Brothers and sisters, listen to the Voice of Free Albania; the Voice of Free Albania talks for all Albanians who love their country and want it strong and free…." This was followed by news items and commentary critical of the present Communist regime.
- On 22 September it called its listeners to spread the news of "Radio Free Albania," which came from the "free radios of the world and our trusted sources." However, it advised them to do so with caution because of spies and informants. It also warned all would be informants "to think twice" before doing any harm to their fellow citizens or betraying them.[37]

During the operational year 1952, VOFA, attempted to transmit its program three times daily over two different frequencies, but there were one or two days. out of every month when they could not broadcast. The main propaganda themes centered around the following topics:

- The failure of the Communist system and the subsequent misery of the Albanian people.
- The exploitation of Albanians by the Soviets.
- The atrocities being committed by the Albanian Communists.
- The growing strength of the anti–Communist feeling toward the West and its manifestations in the Mediterranean area.

- The growing effectiveness of the N.C.F.A. and its operations.
- Denunciation of and warnings to Albanian Communists and pro-liberation instructions to the Albanian people.
- The main objectives of the V.O.F.A. have been to give hope to the Albanian people that eventual liberation is certain and to convince the Albanian Communists that they are doomed unless they join the liberation movement spearheaded by the N.C.F.A.[38]

VOFA attempted to avoid general anti-Communist propaganda and concentrated on conditions and events inside Albania. Information from infiltrated teams in Albania and reports from monitoring stations confirmed that VOFA was audible within Albania, for at least a major portion of the year. It was heard by and made a favorable impression on at least a few Albanians. But there was no information that indicated VOFA was heard regularly by a large portion of the relatively small percentage of Albanians, who owned radios. VOFA changed the antenna design and used more powerful transmitters. To improve programming content VOFA directed messages to various social groups within Albania with the aim of causing specific anti-Communist action by that particular group.[39]

In late June 1952, a leaflet was dropped into Albania that called on Albanians to listen to R.F.A., which was presumed to refer to Radio Free Albania. A memorandum dated July 7, 1952, to OPC headquarters from the field was critical of the reference to R.F.A.: "[H]as inadvertently helped to increase the confusion between the Voice of Free Albania and Radio Free Europe."[40]

In September 1953, National Committee for Free Europe notified the National Committee for Free Albania that, owing to budget cuts, financial support of the NCFA would cease on October 1, 1953. Although financial support of the NCFA was continued through other channels, salaries were cut and other support reduced. At the same time, Radio Free Europe Albanian programs, which began on June 1, 1951, were discontinued.[41]

Also, in September 1953, CIA's monitoring station at Bari, Italy, reported continued jamming of VOFA. The monitoring station believed the jamming was due to the VOFA defection appeal to Albanian being repeated daily. The defection appeal was, in part, "Albanians—you are forcing the regime to the wall! Continue to demand what is due you. The despots are weakening and fearful of the next orders from Moscow. Enlightened and repentant Albanian Communists there is no security in a regime of traitors that uses scapegoats to explain its failures, but there is haven for you in the Free World."[42] There were indications that the jamming originated from Bulgaria; despite jamming, the regular broadcast schedule was maintained.[43]

## 5. A Seaborne CIA Fiasco and the Voice of Free Albania (VOFA)  101

"Radio Announcement Leaflet": 500,000 copies were dropped on July 28, 1952, and then again on October 10, 1952. The leaflet text began with "By means of a clandestine radio transmitter the NCFA fights to eradicate the Communist lies which fill and poison the Fatherland…The Voice of Free Albania."

Examples of program content can be seen the list of topics in 24 broadcasts from June 15, 1954, to July 14, 1954:

- the anniversary of the Berlin uprising,
- the Elections of the People's Assembly in Albania,
- Churchill's visit and discussions with President Eisenhower,
- the overthrow of the Communist regime in Guatemala.
- Other topics such as the rumored. rivalry between the Soviet and China, defections of Communists to the West, and appeals to the Albanian Communists, messages to our fighters for freedom, etc., also were part of our attempts to convince the Albanian Communists whom we believe form the major part of our listening audience that they had better change their loyalty while there was still time to do so.[44]

Jamming continued to be a major concern and the PYREX transmitting site decided to add two 2,500-watt transmitters to the two existing 500-watt transmitters for simultaneous transmissions over four frequencies.[45]

During operational year 1955, VOFA daily broadcasts were morning, noon, late afternoon and evening over two different frequencies. The number of new programs written per week varied from four in summer, when conditions were better for broadcasting to two in winter. VOFA did not concentrate on straight news items since VOA, BBC and other Albanian language broadcasts did so. Instead, VOFA tried to interpret world news in the light of its significance and meaning for the Albanian people. VOFA also concentrated on Albanian internal activities as monitored from Radio Tirana, Albanian publications, and refugee interviews conducted in Athens.

In order to avoid the disruptive effects of jamming and evasion tactics, the format of the VOFA broadcasts was changed from 2 or 3 four-minute talks and instructions to the people to ten or more very brief items and slogans. CIA believed that these shorter messages were more likely to be heard in their entirety.[46] Although there was a scarcity of reaction reports on the effect and popularity of VOFA within Albania, CIA felt that project OBTEST should continue, although perhaps at a reduced level, for the following reasons:

a. The direct attack on HTGRUBBY by Radio Tirana on 17 December 1955 and several refugee reports would seem to support the possibility that HTGRUBBY is both a thorn in the side of the regime and is still regularly heard by those anti–Communist Albanians, who have the means to do so.
b. The number of radios inside Albania will continue to grow whereas the leaflet raids, for reasons mentioned previously, may actually decrease.
c. Monitoring reports and other intelligence available indicates that in spite of enemy jamming HTGRUBBY is audible from at least the beginning of March until the end of October.
d. Since a minimum of one Psych ease officer and one indigenous agent (or one contract employee) would be needed for the leaflet program, the actual additional expense for continuing HTGRUBBY, with possibly fewer new programs per week, would be one additional indigenous agent at salary and expenses of not over $2,500 per year. The safe house would be required for the leaflet production by indigenous help and the recording and monitoring equipment with adequate spares is already on hand.
e. Even if QKIVORY (NCFE) should resume broadcasts to Albania, HTGBUBBY could continue with a presentation, interpretation and content which could not be done under QKIVORY sponsorship. Or, after a brief period off the air, broadcasts could

be resumed under notional or no specific attribution, or even on a blacker basis, possibly as some type of national Communist radio.[47]

Efforts continued to obtain more complete evaluations on VOFA through interviews of refugees as well as by monitoring from the Bari-Brindisi areas and selected points on the Greek-Albanian border, and reaction reports from the Italian and French Ministries in Albania.[48]

On January 28, 1954, CIA's International Operations Division presented a Free Europe Committee memorandum relative to the formation of a new Committee to be called the "Free Albanian Committee," with suggestions for the liquidation of the NCFA at such time as an agreement is reached to terminate the NCFA. It was agreed that prior to the implementation of these proposals, it would first be necessary to obtain the approval of the Department of State. On the advice of the SE representatives, IO agreed to convene a meeting for this purpose with appropriate Department of State officials.[49]

One propaganda leaflet dropped into Albania was one which contained information about the NCFA and Voice of Free Albania:

### Radio Announcement
Albanians!

By means of a clandestine radio transmitter the NCFA fights to eradicate the Communist lies which fill and poison the Fatherland. "The Voice of Free Albania" transmits each evening at 6:30 and 9 o'clock, as well as every afternoon between 1 and 2 o'clock. Through these transmissions, patriotic Albanians may hear:

The TRUTH on the filthy crimes of the Tirana Communist clique and of their Russian patrons which they serve.

The TRUTH on the strives and fight of your national Committee to bring honor and freedom to Albania.

The TRUTH of the immeasurable strength of our friends and Allies Nations in the free world.

Albanians!

Those of you who have radios may assist in the Fight for Freedom by listening to the "Voice of Free Albania" and by passing the news secretly to a trusted friend.

It must be emphasized that everything should be done clandestinely and with the greatest protection. You must be aware of every danger and especially the Sigurimi. (Secret police)

Take note again. "The Voice of Free Albania" transmits to the Albanian People from a secret place. These transmissions will be given on 49m and between 1 and 2 p.m., and 6:30 and 9 p.m. In the event the hours have to be changed, we will attempt to notify you beforehand.

The National Committee for Free Albania.

For Albania, For Freedom, For the Red and Black Flag![50]

On April 28, 1956, CIA informed the Executive Committee of the NCFA in Rome of its termination of financial support and relations with the Committee—ostensibly for budgetary reasons and because of the ineffectiveness for political warfare purposes of the existing arrangement. The CIA told the Executive Committee that the FY 1956 budget would be honored, but financial support would cease at the end of June 1956. The Committee also was informed that CIA action to terminate support to the Committee was not taken until it was first ascertained that the National Committee for Free Europe planned to resume limited activities in the Albanian field, including the organization of a small Albanian Committee and publication of an Albanian language newspaper. CIA recommended that the NCFA and Albanians in exile look to the NCFE in the future: "That private organization would continue its leading role in helping exiles in their struggle against Communism."[51]

VOFA broadcast a 16-minute program, four times daily over two different frequencies simultaneously. Each program was repeated one or more times for a total of 185 hours of broadcasting per month. On the average, three new programs were written each week.

The Hungarian Revolution of 1956 resulted in an increase of program hours to 220 per month. Program themes in 1956 became "less militant anti–Communist" as "the attacks on Communist personalities have given way to reasoned refutation of the failure of Albanian Communism with concrete examples of such failure throughout the world and especially in Albania." The main theme was "pressure-from-below campaign wherein we try to convince the Albanian people they should use non-violent legal and united methods to force concessions from the regime."[52]

Also, in 1956 CIA planned for the establishment of a black "National Communist" (NATCOM) radio program as "National Socialist Albania." It would be aimed at medium and lower level Communist Party and government officials. The programs were said to come from Socialists and Communists, who "disillusioned with the present regime and have fled their Albania." With the creation of "National Socialist Albania," VOFA's air time was reduced but was said to "continue to be anti–Communist in nature," but with a "pressure-from-below theme with emphasis on peaceful and evolutionary means of obtaining concessions."[53]

In 1957, VOFA averaged four-fifteen-minute programs per day over two frequencies for an average of 300 hours per month, including repeats. Between two and three new programs were broadcast weekly.

Nationalist Socialist Radio (NATCOM) averaged 55 hours per month in 1957, after its first program in May 1957. Programs averaged 15 minutes and were broadcast twice daily over two different frequencies. The broadcasts were designed to encourage Albanian Communists to seek more freedom by "tailoring" Communism to their national interests. Reportedly, "The quality and quantity of the programs was maintained with a good

## 5. A Seaborne CIA Fiasco and the Voice of Free Albania (VOFA)

measure of success, this effort was nevertheless at the expense of other fields of activity. Our plans for 1958 are therefore predominately affected by this fact: we have very reluctantly cut our Albanian/PSYCH activity to the bone with the hope of still achieving the best remits commensurate with our limited Case Officer time."[54]

It was decided to terminate VOFA broadcasts mainly due to the lack of a qualified psychological officer. Three staff members in Athens were let go on February 28, 1958, and returned to the United States. NATCOM became the sole psychological warfare radio effort. An ex-Communist intellectual, CIA cryptonym AIPLEBE, was retained and prepared about 30 scripts for NATCOM broadcasts. Each script, about fifteen minutes in length, was broadcast twice each day; each program was simultaneously broadcast on two wave lengths. The programs were designed "to encourage Albanian Communists to strive for more freedom from the USSR by tailoring Communism to their national situation."[55]

With the termination of VOFA February 28, 1958, CIA hoped to have NATCOM assume part of the function of an anti–Communist radio. This was to be accomplished, in part, by identifying NATCOM programs less and less with international "Communism" and by sharpening the attack on Albanian Communism in particular by encouraging the type of "self-criticism" used to some extent by Poland and Yugoslavia and to a lesser extent in Slovakia. CIA also planned to emphasize and precisely attack the numerous "built-in vulnerabilities" of 20th century Communism: "It does not appear that this projected transition will be difficult because AIPLEBE has already given indications in several scripts that although he maintains a consistent Nationalist Socialist approach he may be already slowly turning from Communism itself." The program must always be within the limits imposed by KUBARK (CIA) by existing PBRIME (U.S. government) policy.[56]

The field agreed to the termination of VOFA broadcasts and outlined the difficulties of maintaining a national socialist radio program: "It is obvious that the NATCOM program cannot be run properly for any long period of time unless proper guidance, direction, and support is given to AIPLEBE. To be effective, the program must be timely in its presentation; it must offer concrete and realistic proposals which can be acted upon by the listening audience thereby bringing about the desired changes."[57]

Cold Meyer, Chief of CIA's International Organization Division (IOD), responsible for NCFE and Radio Free Europe, sent a memorandum to the Chief SE Division on or about December 3, 1957, with the subject "Proposal that RFE Broadcast to Albania," which read

1. By memorandum of 12 November 1957, SE/CPP requested consideration of a resumption of broadcasting service by Radio Free Europe to Albania. The request

is based on the desirability of providing anti–Communist radio propaganda to take the place of the present broadcasts transmitted in Athens, and which are to be discontinued.

2. In discussions with representatives of SE, this Division has stated the position that, in the absence of compelling policy reasons, it would be inadvisable for RFE to undertake such broadcasts at this time. The principal bases of this position are:

   a. Budget limitations on RFE in this fiscal year and ceilings on ensuing fiscal years, coupled with increasing administrative costs the most important of which relate to anticipated wages adjustment, are expected materially to reduce RFE's present operational funds.

   b. The acquisition of competent Albanian exile desk employees and Albanian speaking American supervisors, while not insoluble, is a difficult problem.

   c. The proposal envisions that RFE would pick up the straight anti–Communist line of the present broadcasts, leaving to the present broadcasts the treatment of "national communism." This would place RFE in a difficult position vis-à-vis its exile employees who would question the difference in program lines to Albania as compared to the present five target countries.

   d. It is doubtful that RFE, from a policy point of view, should undertake broadcasts at this time to Albania. Obviously, the U.S. policy toward Yugoslavia would have important and possibly controlling bearing on the matter.

Consideration has been given to the suggestion that this proposal might be appropriate for action by the Radio Broadcasting Policy Committee. This Division believes that for the present budgetary and administrative problems must be looked upon as the controlling factors and recommends against referral of the matter to the Committee. It is pointed out, however, that in the relatively fluid East European situation, it is conceivable that there might arise a need for broadcasts to Albania which would justify a re-examination of present targeting by RFE, with a view to finding some means which would be within practical capabilities or which would necessitate the allocation of additional funds.[58]

In May 1958, the cryptonym for NATCOM was changed OBTEST/1. For FY 1959, the project outline described OBTEST/1 as "extremely limited in its activity (a very small target, limited transmitter facilities) … well-geared to make the best advantage of this one specific area of PW activity—black radio propaganda." The cost of the program was listed as $21,085.00. The plan originator admitted that there was "no specific information relating to the effectiveness of the program"[59]:

The budget for FY 1959 was approved in September 1958 but with this caveat:

Although mention is made of plans under way to attempt to determine if these broadcasts are reaching the targets, and what effect, if any, they are having on their listeners, it would seem that in its fifth year, we should at least know for certain if the transmissions are reaching their destination. Unless this can be determined, there would seem to be little point in continuing the project.[60]

A review of OBTEST/1 operation, written in April 1959, had this comment:

## 5. A Seaborne CIA Fiasco and the Voice of Free Albania (VOFA)

OBTEST/1 is a black revisionist radio program which was instituted in May 1957. It is directed to middle-level members of the Albanian Workers Party (Communist). At present OBTEST/1 is broadcasting between 220 and 250 hours monthly and is airing one new script every five days. We consider this level of script production to be optimum so long as we have only one script writer.[61]

An August 26, 1959, report gave the gave the purpose of OBTEST/1: "Assuming the guise of Albanian revisionists, we attempt to loosen the ties between Albania and the Soviet Union, foster disruptive tendencies in order to weaken the Regime, and encourage modification of the harsher and more unenlightened policies of the Regime." 15-minute broadcasts were produced every five days:

CIA decided to terminate its communications base outside Athens in September 1959 resulting in a phasing out of black broadcasts to "denied areas" including Albania. The field planned then to stop broadcasting to Albania on October 21, 1959, with this comment, "We believe this has been a good program but realize that Albania is a relatively minor target."[62]

OBTEST/1 broadcasts were terminated on November 20, 1959, but the project continued through June 30, 1960, to cover outstanding funding obligations due to the termination as well as re-location of agents carried under Project OBTEST.

# 6

# Black Radio to the Baltic States from Radio Nacional de España (RNE)

## Estonia

> *Estonia is a country of some 16,370 square miles with an estimated population of 1,200,000 as of 1950. It has a coastline of 276 miles fronting on the Baltic, but otherwise Is completely surrounded by Soviet-controlled territory [...] Since the time Estonia proclaimed its independence from Russia after World War I, it was twice occupied by the Soviets. The first occupation occurred in 1940, as a sequel to the Molotov-Ribbentrop agreement, and the second toke place in 1944, following defeat of the German armies. The country has since been incorporated into the Soviet Union— an action not recognized by the United States [....] Their hope of eventual liberation is presumably kept alive by news of growing resistance to Communism in the West and by anti-Communist activities of Estonian emigre organizations on this side of the Iron Curtain.*[1]

CIA wanted to have Radio Free Europe broadcast to the Baltic States (Estonia, Latvia, and Lithuania) in 1951. It first was approved by the U.S. State Department in May 1951 and again in August 1951. RFE started to plan for the broadcasts, including the selection of personnel for the broadcasts, but then the US Department of State vetoed the idea in November 1951: "There is nothing that needs to be said to the Baltics that cannot be said quite adequately by Voice of America."[2] Also, "compared to the Czechoslovakian broadcasts, which were estimated as costing $0.762 per radio set per year, broadcasts in Estonian, Latvian, and Lithuanian would cost on average $18.22 per radio set per year." Radio Free Europe broadcasts to the Baltic Republics were not considered to be cost effective.[3]

## OPC Project LCHOMELY

The original Office of Policy Coordination (OPC) project LCHOMELY was submitted for approval on January 4, 1950, and aimed at utilizing Estonian émigré groups, leaders and organizations for the purpose of contacting underground resistance forces in the Estonian SSR and to infiltrate agents into the area. The project's objective was to provide funds for the support, development and exploitation of the Estonian Resistance Movement. The rationale behind LCHOMELY was:

1. During the first two post-war years there were frequent reports relating to extensive partisan activity in Estonia. "However, except for isolated bands with no centralized control, it is doubtful if there is any significant resistance today although there is unquestionably much latent resistance and there are probably several hundred Estonians living in the woods where they escaped in preference to deportation." This lack of a resistance element that we can definitely place is not due to any deficiency in the anti–Soviet mood of the people; it is rather because of: (1) A failure on the part of the West to come to the aid of the Estonian resistance as they expected in the first post-war period, and (2) the thorough repressive measures by the Soviets.
2. Failing a good lead on a group inside Estonia, a proper approach is the development of a relationship with an Estonian émigré element that is capable of developing operational contact with the homeland […] General exile endorsement of any émigré element with which we would want to deal would also be important to the success of that group in making contact with the homeland. In both of these respects, the Estonian National Council (ENR) and its President August Rei seemed to offer the most significant potential.[4]

For three days in November 1950, an OPC officer stationed in Germany conducted a series of meetings with ENR President August Rei (CIA pseudonym Curtis F. Freely) to determine what potentialities there were for establishing and maintaining contact with any underground organization, which might exist in Estonia (CIA cryptonym FJKHAKI). Rei expressed "great interest" to put Estonian-language broadcasts on the air, either via Voice of America or Radio Free Europe. The Estonian Information Center Helene Purre of the Estonian Information Center wrote to NCFE expressing interest in making some connection with NCFE, which would permit Estonian broadcasts to be put out over RFE. Helene Purre also was a Stockholm representative of the Free Europe Press service, English translator for *The Baltic Review* and the editor / translator of the *Newsletter from Behind the Iron Curtain*.[5]

When questioned as to whether the Estonian National Council and the two other Baltic (QKCOAST) émigré political groups would be interested in membership in NCFE, Rei stated that they would be so interested. Rei expressed a strong preference for individual membership but indicated that if this were not possible for whatever reason, he was open to the idea of joining NCFE as a group member.⁶

## *AEBASIN*

The October 16, 1952, OPC Project outline for LCHOMELY included this statement: "This project is constructed to include all CIA operations into the Estonian SSR and. all activities connected with this objective, including both, the FI (Foreign Intelligence) and PP/W missions and responsibilities of the SR (Soviet Russia) Division. It embraces the development of Estonian émigré groups outside of the USSR for support operations, covert political activities and psychological warfare directed against the Estonian SSR."⁷

LCHOMELY objectives included:

- To assist in the organization, development, and execution of covert political and psychological warfare operations against the Soviet regime in the Estonian SSR for the purpose of placing a maximum strain on the Soviet structure and of widening the existing wedge between the Estonian people and the Soviet regime.
- To achieve a world-wide united Estonian émigré front.
- Through controlled entrée to this organization to assist it in the carrying out of political and psychological warfare activities against the Soviet regime.⁸

The project was approved by DCI on 31 January 1953.

Project LCHOMELY was replaced by Project AEBASIN. The objectives of Project AEBASIN/PP for Fiscal Year 1955 were expanded to include:

- To preserve and strengthen the pro-Western orientation of the majority of the people of the Estonian SSR and to bolster their hope of ultimate liberation.
- To develop potential PP assets within the Estonian SSR and continue developing existing assets among Estonian émigrés.
- To help weaken the prestige and effectiveness of the Soviet Communist complex, with special emphasis on Soviet organizations, activities, and individuals in Estonia.

## 6. Black Radio to the Baltic States 111

Operations directed toward the target area included:

> Radio Estonian émigré groups as such have no radio facilities of their own for broadcasts to Estonia. (Note: The VOA broadcasts, of course, are not included in this statement. They consist of three 10-minute spots daily from Munich and Algiers and are used occasionally by AEBASIN personnel on specific and limited topics acceptable to VOA.) Radio Free Europe, likewise, has no Estonian facilities at the present time.
>
> An attempt was made in August 1953 by the Principal Agent of AEBASIN to secure independent radio facilities from the Pan-American Broadcasting Company, but the arrangement fell through because of complications between that company and the Department of State. Similarly, on Headquarters instructions, Estonian émigrés in the U.S. have been negotiating with radio stations in Madrid and Hamburg. Radio-Hamburg is handicapped by Allied restrictions, while Madrid is prepared to make daily radio time available as of October 1954, when additional transmitter facilities will be ready.
>
> Establishment of radio broadcasting facilities will be coordinated with the Radio Advisory Panel.
>
> *Non-CIA Funds.*
>
> The Estonian National Committee and the Legion of Liberation are expected to provide approximately $6,000—from their own resources, by means of public contributions. A fund-raising drive for the support of the radio effort ... is expected to get underway throughout the Estonian emigration. The bulk of the funds is expected to come from emigres in the U.S. and Canada. These contributions will not affect the Agency's control of the operation. [P]ayments to foreign radio stations for radio time will be made by check by Covert Associate (redacted), in his capacity of president of the Legion of Liberation.
>
> A contact in Madrid, AEBASIN/2, has been promised a sum of money (unspecified) if he should be successful in procuring air time on Radio-Madrid.
>
> At least 60 broadcasts have been made by (redacted) and (redacted) over VOA and beamed to the Estonian SSR.[9]

The September 29, 1954, CIA internal memorandum to Cord Meyer, Chief IO, Division included these comments.

> The question of RFE undertaking broadcasts to the Baltic area was reviewed several months ago, and the arguments against such an undertaking seam pertinent to the present proposal. At that time the joint decision of the Agency and the Department was restated, i.e., that it is preferable to have broadcasting to that area handled by VOA.
>
> In view of current German sensitivities with regard to Baltic emigre activities I further question the desirability of attempting at this time to obtain facilities on Radio Hamburg.[10]

Broadcasts to Estonia began on October 16, 1955, from Radio Nacional de España. In January 1956 there was an internal CIA SR/PP staff evaluation of the broadcasts, which included:

> The undersigned has read in translation a large number of AEBASIN scripts dating from the inauguration of the broadcasts to 16 October. In general, they are more than adequate for the audience. It is believed that if they get through the jamming networks, the programs would fulfill an important function in maintaining the morale of whatever individuals and groups in Estonia are favorably disposed towards the West and which harbor anti-Communist resentments. All in all, their tone and character is surprisingly moderate and calm, considering the atmosphere of Radio NACIONAL.
>
> (The daily feature items discuss the anti-Communist activities of émigrés of all nationalities in the West, and occasionally religious messages with political implications—e.g., the illegitimacy of tyranny—are included.)
>
> Other scripts refute Soviet propaganda regarding the peaceful motivation of Soviet policies and point up matters like the exploitation of individuals in the concentration camps, factories, and on the collective farms. The scripts are singularly entirely free from anti-Russianism, as distinguished from anti-Soviet sentiments, and the theme of eventual liberation is mentioned, but is sensibly not over stressed. There is, however, a great deal of indiscriminate criticism of Soviet accomplishments, which would hardly please members of the Soviet intelligentsia. Since, however, the broadcasts are in Estonian, and, since it would be foolish not to play on Estonian nationalism, there is no basic objection to the project's line [....] The current AEBASIN line, however, acceptable and useful, need not rule out future black programs employing forms of deviation of the left or right.[11]

The June 1956 request for Renewal of AEBASIN for FY 1957 included the following accomplishments and effectiveness estimates:

> a. Daily 15-minute Estonian language broadcasts over three frequencies were beamed to the Estonian SSR via facilities Radio Nacional, Madrid.
> b. It has not been possible to date to establish what proportion of these programs succeeds in penetrating through Soviet jamming facilities to the listening audience. However, the programs are consonant with the objectives of the project.[12]

Another 1957 document for AEBASIN renewal included this description:

> This project provides for the exploitation of existing Estonian emigre organizations and their personnel. Present assets include the Estonian National Committee and the Legion of Estonian Liberation. Funds are to be provided for the support of a PW workshop in the U.S. and an Estonian short-wave radio program directed to the Estonian SSR under cover of these emigre organizations.
>
> The Division has agreed with the PP Staff that a project redocumentation will be carried out by 15 October, reflecting changes in the objectives of the project and a narrowing down of tasks.[13]

This comment appeared in the SR Division October 1958 Request for PP Project Renewal: "The AEBASIN operations have been conducted through the Estonian section at Radio Nacional, Madrid. Contact with Radio Regional is maintained through the Voice of Estonian Freedom, a cover organization located in New York City."[14] There were some problems in Madrid:

## 6. Black Radio to the Baltic States

AEBASIS/2, one of the two Estonian broadcasters at Radio Nacional, was dropped from Agency contact because of a disagreement over salary. He was still active at Radio Nacional and reportedly interfered with the activities of the other Estonian broadcaster, who was a CIA contract agent. Agency control over the broadcasts has thus deteriorated. Two solutions to this problem are under study:
1. The former agent may be required to resign from Radio Nacional because of financial difficulties arising from the fact that his salary from Radio Nacional is only $20 per month.
2. Negotiations may be renewed to bring this former agent back under Agency control.[15]

Broadcasts to Estonia were 15 minutes per day in the evening and beginning in May 1958, programs were rebroadcast for another 15 minutes in the morning, for a total of 30 minutes per day. However, "it has not been possible to obtain an adequate picture of technical reception or audience reaction for the past years."[16] CIA then decided to comprehensively review the Estonian broadcasts:

Headquarters is preparing a guidance directive for use by assets at Radio Nacional. Assets will be required to comply strictly with this directive. Special courses in broadcast technique and preparation will be conducted in West Germany or elsewhere for the broadcasters. Finally any incompetent personnel will be replaced. It is expected that the above measures will make the Estonian language broadcasts a worthwhile operation.

The cover organization for contact With Radio Nacional, the Voice of Estonian Freedom, has no popular membership. It claims to receive its funds from an "anonymous" donor. These points . are not considered to be significant weaknesses and sound sufficiently plausible. In addition, this arrangement permits much greater control than would be possible if this organization bad a popular base with selected leadership. Operational difficulties have been encountered because of lack of case officer contact with the assets at Radio Nacional. This weakness will be remedied by giving special training to these assets

Propaganda guidance is sent from Headquarters via the Voice of Estonian Freedom to Radio Nacional through the open mall. This is a limiting factor rather than a security problem. Certain material obviously cannot be sent in this fashion; however, the flow of guidance from the Voice of Estonia Freedom to Radio Nacional is a perfectly normal action in consonance with their relationship.

[H]eadquarters will review and critique the scripts on a continuing basis in order that broadcast content and technique may be constantly improved.[17]

AEBASIN was consolidated into Project AEFREEMAN and was defined in the November 1958 project action sheet for FY 1959 as

a psychological warfare type operation, AEBASIN supports the activities of Estonian emigres and emigre groups directed against the Estonian SSR. These activities include radio broadcasts, mailing operations, liaison with emigre organizations, PP briefings for legal travelers, and exploitation of other media which have PP potentialities.

Continue to exploit the foreign broadcasts facilities of Radio Nacional and to improve, without impairing their Spanish flavor, the effectiveness of their broadcasts to the Sino-Soviet bloc.

It has been almost impossible to evaluate the effectiveness of the radio operations of this project. Consequently, the Division has initiated a program to attempt to determine the effectiveness of its radio operations. It is expected that prior to FY' 1960 renewal time the Division will have sufficient data so that the value of these operations will be known.[18]

The 1960 Request of PP Project Renewal AEBASIN, Soviet Russia Division, Estonian Desk, was approved in March 1960. The project objectives included:

(a) To preserve the national identify of the Estonian people thereby helping them to resist assimilation into the Soviet society.
(b) To maintain among the Estonian people an attitude of irreconcilability toward International Communism and the Soviet regime dominating Estonia today.
(c) To maintain and enhance the pro–Western and pro–American orientation of the Estonian people.
(d) To encourage revisionist tendencies among the Estonian Communists.
(e) To foster evolutionary changes by encouraging the Estonian people to seek continuous concessions from the Soviet regime in Estonia.
(f) To contribute by all possible means to the growth of intellectual ferment among the Estonian people.[19]

The operational mechanisms of the project were:

(a) Estonian section of Radio Madrid (Radio Nacional de España).
(b) The Voice of Estonian Freedom (a cover organization in New York, which sponsors the Estonian broadcasts from Radio Madrid) continues to supply adequate cover.... Control has been strengthened by establishing more rigid requirements with respect to broadcast content.[20]

The analysis of the program effectiveness showed: "Radio broadcasts were continued from Radio Madrid with a 15-minute original broadcast and a 15-minute repeat per day ... technically on a per with VOA broadcasts. Last year a total of 95 reports on Radio Madrid were obtained from Balts and from Spanish repatriates, who had listened to these broadcasts in the Soviet Union."[21]

For FY 1961 project renewal, programs continued on a 15-minute original basis and 15-minute repeat broadcast. The general guidance directive and special guidance on current issues were sent to Radio Madrid during the past year. As a result, "considerable improvement in the radio broadcasts has been noted and their content is now considered to be satisfactory. The Voice of Estonian Freedom continues to supply adequate cover for the Estonian broadcasts. Control has been strengthened by establishing more rigid requirements with respect to broadcast content."[22]

In 1960, CIA headquarters sent a general guidance directive to the

## 6. Black Radio to the Baltic States 115

Estonian Section of Radio Madrid, along with special guidance as needed. There was some discussion at CIA about seeking to establish Estonian language broadcasts over Radio Rome (RR) but there is no record that Radio Rome did so.[23]

The project objectives for FY 1962 included "improve the quality of Radio Madrid's Estonian language broadcasts in relation to ODYOKE propaganda objectives will continue, specifically through a greater degree of cooperation by Radio Madrid Estonian section personnel with their Lithuanian and Latvian counterparts and through a new series of specific propaganda directives."[24]

This self-praising comment was included in the FY 1963 project FREEMAN renewal request:

> Baltic covert action operations can also claim effectiveness since of late there has been a great increase in the viciousness of the Soviet attacks against the propaganda activities and the Baltic leadership which sponsors these activities. The Baltic people refuse to become apathetic, to surrender to Russification, to give up their religious beliefs, or to admit they are part of the Soviet empire.[25]

On the questionable effectiveness of the AEFREEMAN programs, particularly radio broadcasts, CIA's Office of Communications, which was asked to monitor AEFREEMAN broadcasts, stated the following on March 26, 1963:

> Based on the results of the peripheral monitor conducted by our Communications Officer at Warsaw, Helsinki and Stockholm, he concluded that if the signal is heard at all is the target area, it is beard sporadically and with difficulty. This conclusion, admittedly, *is* based on a cursory monitor conducted from the fringes of the target area by persons not versed in the language of the broadcasts. However, the monitors are professional communicators using professional equipment with antennas and operating conditions far superior to the "average" home listener. We, therefore, believe the conclusion, above, is valid.
>
> It is not believed that the principal activity under AEFREEMAN, radio broadcasting, has been highly effective.... [T]he quality of the scripts used has been on the order to fair to good. What the actual effect has been within the Baltic states cannot be adequately measured. Although the principle of broadcasting to the Baltic States in the Baltic languages is subscribed to, it is not felt that the program which we have been subsidizing for this purpose has been performing satisfactorily.[26]

Effectiveness of the radio broadcasts remained a major issue:

> The effectiveness of the activities undertaken by this project must of necessity remain largely clouded in speculation, for it is most difficult to measure or assess the impact or reaction of such operations. Within realistic hounds, however, it is believed that the project is effective and that the Soviets would much prefer its activity to cease. Soviet jamming of the five Baltic Program funded under this project has increased and *is* more intense than ever before, in itself an indication of the effectiveness of the transmitted propaganda.[27]

The fiscal year 1963 project renewal contained this remark about the lack of information about the audience and the effectiveness of the broadcasts:

> A serious effort should be made to collect information on audience reaction to radio broadcasts to the Baltic countries particularly to those carried by Radio Madrid. The assistance of Radio Liberty's and RFE's audience analysis facilities may be of value in this connection. The continuation of the Radio Madrid programs beyond FY 63 should be reconsidered in the light of results achieved, as well as with reference to the political situation in Spain.[28]

The reconsideration resulted in the decision to terminate the program effective the end of October 1963. One of the reasons for termination was that the Voice of America was already broadcasting in the Baltic languages and negotiations were underway on the question of Baltic broadcasts from Radio Liberty or Radio Free Europe. Another reason was "it is not believed that the principal activity under AEFREEMAN, radio broadcasting, has been highly effective although estimates on this question are primarily conjecture." Moreover,

> the quality of the scripts used has been on the order of fair to good, we believe. What the actual effect has been within the Baltic States cannot be adequately measured. Although the principle of broadcasting to the Baltic States in Baltic languages is subscribed to, it is not felt that the program, which we have been subsidizing for this purpose been performing satisfactorily.[29]

AEFREEMAN was terminated on October 31, 1963, effective December 31, 1963. Staff and families in Madrid were returned to the United States or Germany.[30]

Shortly before the merger with Radio Free Europe, Radio Liberty inaugurated weekly broadcasts in the three Baltic languages: Lithuanian, Latvian, and Estonian. By September 1975, all three services were broadcasting daily form RFE/RL in Munich, Germany and then from Prague, Czech Republic, after RFE/RL moved there in 1995. RFE/RL stopped broadcasting to Estonia on January 31, 2004; the Voice of America stopped broadcasting to Estonia on February 27, 2004.[31]

## Latvia

> Latvia is a country of about 25,700 square miles with an estimated population of 2,100,000. It has a coastline of shout 310 miles fronting on the Baltic and is otherwise surrounded by Soviet-controlled territory. The Latvian people belong to the ethnic group of Malta and are not a member of either the Germania or Slavic races. They have their own language, which belongs to the Baltic branch of Indo-European language. The Latvian tribes settled down along the shores of the Baltic Sea in pre-historic

times. For many centuries they were governed by various foreign nations, i.e. Germans, Swedes, Poles, and Russians. Throughout all these centuries, the Latvian people preserved their national identity and their language. In 1918, Latvia became an independent republic, which it remained until 1940 when it was occupied by the Soviet Union. In July 1941, the Soviets were driven out by the German army, but after the defeat of the latter in 1944, Latvia was once more occupied by the Soviets end has since been incorporated into the Soviet Union, an action not recognized by the United States Government.

Mass deportations of Lutvians took place in 1941 and also in 1948 end 1949. A small percentage of Latvians were able to escape to the West during the war years and only very few after the war. According to the testimonies of escapees and news received from behind the Iron Curtain, there is strong and bitter resentment among the remaining Latvian against the Soviet political and economic oppression. Their principal aim is to survive in the hope that liberation might same day come.[32]

## Institute for Latvian Culture

CIA's Soviet Russia Division Administrative Plan dated November 30, 1953, for Project AEMARSH contained these objectives:

The purpose of this project is to utilize all possible existing legal means to penetrate the Latvian SSR in the gathering of intelligence on the Soviet regime. Specifically, the objectives of the project are:

- To spot, develop and train long-range covert personnel with specialized qualifications who will be or are strategically placed within the periphery. of the Soviet Union and its satellites, and who would be engaged in exploiting an legal channels which lead into or out of the Latvia SSR;
- To spot and develop all existing cultural, academic and recreational ties with the Latvian SSR for intelligence exploitation;
- To spot and develop all commercial ties, with the Latvian SSR for intelligence exploitation; and.
- To spot and develop all postal and other legal communication facilities with the Latvian SSR for utilization in the covert transmission of intelligence as well so the interception of all overtly transmitted intelligence.[33]

As a cover for its covert activities, CIA created the Institute for Latvian Culture (ILC—CIA cryptonym AEMINX) as a "non-profit culture organization engaged in the preservation and development of Latvian national culture, Collection and classification of information on Latvian national life and the safeguarding and preserving the physical, spiritual and moral condition of Latvians, who are separated from their homeland."[34] The Institute for Latvian Culture was also known as the Latvian Cultural Institute (LCI).

Radio Vatican began weekly 15-minute broadcasts to Latvia on October 2, 1948. Radio Nacional de España began broadcasting to Latvia on

February 1, 1955, as the "Voice of Free Latvians" (Brīvā Latviešu Balss) with 20-minute programs, three times a week. On March 1, 1955, the time was reduced to ten minutes, six days a week.[35]

## *AEFLAG*

On April 7, 1955, CIA's Chief SR/2 submitted a memorandum in which he wrote: "Project AEFLAG is being formulated and will be submitted for approval upon its completion. This project as presently envisaged will provide for all phases of conducting agency-controlled broadcasts from Madrid."[36]

As part of the Operational Plan, travel to Madrid was contemplated "in order to enter into negotiations with Roberts Kampus, the Latvian Charge d'Affaires to Spain" (CIA cryptonym AEFLAG/3), who was then was responsible for Latvian language programs over RNE. CIA wanted to get Kampus to agree to give up his role in the broadcasts to a person controlled by CIA.[37]

CIA's operational plan dated July 18, 1955, for Project AEFLAG had this purpose: "Activation of a Latvian language short-wave program directed at the Latvia SSR under cover of a Latvian émigré organization." The daily scripts and tape recordings were prepared at CIA headquarters by "covert associates" and pouched to Madrid. The name "Daugava" was contemplated for the name of the radio programand because "it was the largest river in Latvia and has a patriotic connotation for all Latvians."[38] The objectives of the RNE radio programs were listed as:

1. To preserve the national identity of the Latvian people.
2. To promote an attitude of irreconcilability among the Latvian people toward Communism.
3. To foster pro–Western orientation of the Latvian people.[39]

The basic themes of the broadcasts included:

- Condemn and discredit the Soviet regime, leaders, personalities and policies inimical to the Latvian people and the free world.
- Discredit Soviet foreign and domestic propaganda inimical to US interests.
- Inform listeners that the peoples of the western world are aware of, and hold deep sympathies for the suffering of the Latvian people as the result of cruelties and atrocities, oppression and exploitation visited upon them by the Soviet regime.

## 6. Black Radio to the Baltic States

- Nourish the listeners' hope for ultimate liberation from the Soviet yoke without rousing undue expectations of early action.[40]

The Latvian Cultural Institute then "negotiated" with Kampus to take over the broadcasting. He agreed to initial support for the broadcasts, but since there were no staff members in Madrid, the initial support for the broadcasts, e.g., raw material, script writing, preparation of special tapes and features, was to be furnished by unpaid members of LCI.[41]

Operational control of the radio programs was ensured by the fact CIA financially supported the scriptwriters in Madrid: "All financial transactions and expenditures in connection with these broadcasts will be under Agency supervision. The content of individual programs and the policy line will be examined and evaluated periodically."[42] The format of the initial ten-minute daily broadcasts was:

- Introduction (1 minute)—introduction of the program, Musical signal: several bars from the Latvian Anthem "Dievs, Sveti Latvlju" and the frequency and time of day.
- News and Comments (3 minutes)—Factual coverage of principal news events within the Soviet orbit and in the free world, which are ignored by the Soviet press and radio. These news items are to be supplemented by comments to make them better understandable to listeners behind the Iron Curtain
- Guiding Thoughts of the Day (4–5 minutes)—Commentary based on ideological or instructive themes.
- Entertainment (music, anecdotes, etc.) (1–2 minutes).[43]

CIA headquarters support including funding for procurement of the following media and publications for use as source and content material for the broadcasts:

1. Texts of Latvian SSR radio broadcasts monitored by the Latvian Information Center in Sweden
2. Latvian Language newspapers and magazines published in Canada, US, Sweden and Germany.
3. "Sovetskaya Latviya" and "Cina," published in Soviet Latvia.
4. Soviet publications on Latvian matters.
5. Special broadcast material from Latvian émigrés.
6. Latvian instrumental and choral music, now prohibited in the Latvian SSR, performed by émigré artists.[44]

The mechanism that will be utilized to provide cover for the transmission of the required financial support and guidance will be the ILC organization. This is a cultural organization established under Fl Project AEMARSH in order to provide cover for covert activities as required. The funds required for maintaining ILC as an organization will be borne by Project AEMARSH.[45]

CIA's Chief, Information Coordination Division in a memorandum dated March 27, 1957, expressed doubt about the effectiveness of the RNE broadcasts to Latvia: "We have found that little evidence exists dated after 1954 to substantiate claims of either the program or technical effectiveness of Radio Nacional. We are now studying by what means both the program and technical effectiveness of Radio Nacional might be improved. However, we believe that the lack of effectiveness data at present should not influence the continuance of Latvian broadcasts as proposed in AEFLAG."[46]

For Fiscal Year 1957, $10,000 was authorized for Project AEFLAG and for FY 1958, there was a proposal for an increase to $19,000. The purpose of AEFLAG was to maintain the 15-minute daily programs over two short-wave frequencies with the following objectives:

- To preserve the national identity of the Latvia people in the Latvian SSR.
- To promote an attitude of irreconcilability among the Latvian people toward Communism.
- To foster the pro–Western orientation of people in the target area and to harass the Soviet regime in the area.[47]

It was acknowledged in the renewal plan that "inasmuch as the radio programs—in order to lend them tone of authenticity as expression of genuine free Latvians in exile—may occasional indulge in mild criticism of U.S. actions, an adverse reaction can be expected in the U.S. press in the event our sponsorship of these programs ever becomes public."[48]

CIA's Principal Agent of the operation in Madrid was AEZERO/1, who was a covert associate for foreign intelligence activities under Project AEMARSH as well as for psychological warfare activities: "Collecting materials and providing scripts and guidance for the Latvian radio broadcasts from Radio Nacional.... [T]ransmitting checks in payment of feature article to Latvian writers in the United States, as well as monthly remuneration checks to the subagents in Madrid, and maintaining the accounts of the Institute for Latvian Culture (ILC), a cover organization, in whose name such payments are being made." For his services he had an annual salary of $6,000.[49]

The announcer and script writer was a CIA contract agent (AEFLAG/1), who had been employed at Radio Riga in Latvia. For the renewal plan for FY1958 contained this positive comment on his contributions to the broadcasts over RNE: "The placement of a contract agent in the Latvian section of Radio Nacional Madrid has resulted in an improvement of the 15-minute daily broadcasts to Latvia and in better response to guidance on themes and substance."[50] AEFLAG/1 was described as: "[A] professional radio announcer and script writer. The broadcasts are composed of news on world events and on the activities of Latvian emigre organizations, followed by a commentary elaborating on news presented. The major obstacle to effectiveness of the broadcasts has been the continuous jamming of our broadcasts by the Soviets." To overcome the jamming, CIA planned to ask RNE for a second short wave frequency in FY 1958.[51]

The AEFLAG renewal plan for FY 1959 defined it as a "psychological warfare type operation" with "propaganda through Radio Nacional Madrid, legal traveler contact operations, and mailing operations based in West Germany utilizing Latvian émigrés and émigré groups—aimed at the people of Latvia SSR." CIA's analysis of effectiveness of the broadcasts included "radio broadcasts were continued from Radio Madrid with a 15-minute original broadcast and a 15-minute repeat per day. In December 1959 an appeal to listeners was broadcast requesting those individuals in the Latvian SSR, who listened to the broadcasts, to inform the station by writing letter to one of two addresses in the West. Ten replies were received in response to this request. All of the replies commented favorably on the broadcasts."[52]

CIA decided to replace AEFLAG/1 In FY 1960 with someone who had been recruited in Europe and would be paid one-third less than AEFLAG/1. With cost savings, broadcast quality was expected to improve based on guidance provided by the ILC. At the same time, negotiations were underway with the Italian government for Latvian broadcasts over Radio Rome in FY 1960. The estimated costs for the Radio Rome broadcasts was $7,200.[53] The response from the Italian government was positive, but they could not begin until FY 1961 as facilities were not available.[54]

CIA decided to terminate project AEFLAG in fiscal year 1964, when CIA's Covert Action Staff decided at that time against introducing Baltic broadcasts on Radio Free Europe or Radio Liberty, based on cost and policy factors. Plus the fact that VOA was broadcasting to the Baltics.[55] Another factor was that management and administrative policies at RNE made content quality irregular and weak at time.[56] Latvian Broadcasts over Radio Nacional de España ceased on October 31, 1963, as did broadcasts to Estonia and Lithuania.

Radio liberty began broadcasting to Latvia on July 5, 1975, before consolidation with Radio Free Europe as RFE/RL and continued from Munich until January 31, 2004.

## Freds Ziedonids Launags: A Cold War Tragic Hero

CIA's Soviet Russia Division used Latvian born Freds Ziedonids Launags as a contract agent from "1951 through 1959." He had been a member of the Latvian underground targeting Soviet interests and operated under military cover according OPC and CIA Pseudonyms and cryptonyms for Freds Ziedonids Launags included:

CHURGIN, Raymond S.
LAUNAGS, Alfredo
VANAGS, Alfreds (penname in 1950)
GANGIS, Alfreds
JANSON, Arnold (alias)
GOLTEDOE, Louis G.
TAURENS, P. (penname in 1952)
CAMBARO/1
LAGZDINS, Alfreds (during the mission in Spain1955/56)
HAHN, Cleveland O.
AEHAWKEYE / 1 (cryptonym)

Immediately after World War II, anti–Soviet partisans known as the "Brothers of the Forest" were active in Estonia but by the end of the 1940s, their activity was limited due to the success of the government forces. Launags was one of the Brothers and reportedly killed a Soviet officer in the summer 1945. He and 17 others managed to escape to Sweden on a small fishing boat on October 31, 1945.[57]

OPC recruited Launags in Sweden in 1951 and transported him to Germany to participate in training of OPC REDSOX agents, who were dispatched in Latvia in 1952. REDSOX operations included "illegal actions directed at Soviet targets that included but was not limited to intelligence gathering, recruitment of sources, and using agents for spot targets for sabotage"[58] However, all other agents used in these operations were exposed and the Soviets "either killed or captured" all of them.

Launags was utilized two years for "general support purposes" and in 1955 he indicated on an official medical history that he had been nervous since the end of World War II and "attempted suicide in 1951". After examination by official medical staff, he was "found to have had a brief psychotic episode in 1951 and always had a schizoid type of relationship with people with many obsessive-compulsive defenses." His coworkers referred to Launags as a "character" and he was assigned temporary duties in 1955.[59]

CIA officials subsequently sent him in Spain on a six-month assignment to perform propaganda broadcasts to Latvia via Radio Madrid:

> Louis C. GOLTEDGE, who is a covert associate under contract with Project AEMARSH, is being sent to Madrid, Spain, for 3–4 months on a temporary assignment involving a PP activity. A PP project covering this activity is being formulated and will be submitted for approval upon completion. However, since it is

anticipated that there will be some delay involved before a fully qualified PP expert can be recruited for the new project, GOLTEDGE has been assigned to Madrid temporarily to provide the required assistance, so that the necessary work may be started immediately.[60]

During his assignment in Madrid, Launags "had many paranoid projections and felt that he was under constant surveillance and that even his colleagues hated him."[61] Moreover, "he got involved in an argument and broke off relations with the local Latvian diplomat, felt that Spanish officials were suspicious of him ... because of his acid criticism of the Spanish way of life and the Franco regime."[62] After three months, he returned to the United States.

Launags wrote an undated report titled "Review of my activities in 1956/57" that included the following passage:

> Briefing of K.VIDENIEKS for his work in Madrid as well as interviewing him during his stay here (February–May, 1957) on many persons of interest in Latvia as well as abroad discussions about the broadcasts from Madrid. However, I have got no instructions whether I should participate at these broadcasts (by writing features, for instance) or not; in Oct./Nov., 1956, I prepared only four features though in the previous six month (April to September) I had prepared 27 features for the broadcasts from Madrid. Since nobody has told me whether I am supposed to participate in this project or not, I have stayed out of it almost completely mainly because 1 don't want to disturb my colleague, Mr. SINGER, who is in charge of this project. I am not sure whether my attitude is right or wrong.[63]

CIA returned Launags to the United States because "his behavior became erratic, he began to imagine he was being followed and then, less than one year after his arrival, he had to be returned to the U.S. because he had come to the attention of the local authorities and began to cause a series of embarrassing problems."[64] Although Launags was seen as a possible danger to CIA operations and himself, the Agency continued to use him for years. For example, the CIA reassigned Launags in 1958 to Germany, where he performed foreign intelligence operations in the Baltic under the direction of CIA's Frankfurt Station, including recruiting and debriefing. One documents states, "The same pattern of paranoid projection, loss of contact with reality, and a constant delusional framework of reference occurred in his recent PCS to Germany."[65]

After nine months Launags was forced to return from his German assignment in 1959, after he displayed evidence of mental instability: "An acute paranoid schizophrenic reaction with depressive features."[66] Agency mental health experts diagnosed him as "a paranoid schizophrenic" and placed him in a hospital.

A related document using Launags' pseudonym Raymond S. Churgin stated, " This same pattern of paranoid projection, loss of contact with reality, and a constant delusional framework of reference occurred in his recent PCS to Germany. The Subject apparently again experienced an acute paranoid schizophrenic reaction from which he recovered during the time that he was under examination by the Psychiatric Staff."[67] Moreover, "he feels inferior and markedly inadequate because of his incomplete education and because of his futile efforts to effect the freedom of his homeland. He feels guilty for having deserted 'the real battleground' which is in the area of his own homeland."[68]

CIA dismissed Launags effective December 31, 1959, once they had repeated confirmation of his psychological instability:

> Subject is considered unsuitable for further operational usage and will very likely never be cleared for any overseas activity in the future. He presents a management problem in regard to further assignment or termination of employment. It is unlikely that he will give up the dream of freeing his homeland by clandestine means despite the fact that he may no longer be employed as a contract agent of CIA. As such, he presents a security problem.[69]

A month following his dismissal Agency employees met with Launags to relieve him of a 7.65mm German made Walther automatic pistol that he had retained and to gather information about his current activities. CIA used the false pretense of wanting to give Launags an assignment to meet with him and CIA had multiple employees from the Medical Staff and Office of Security present for this gathering.[70]

After repeated employment losses he began to consider repatriating back to Latvia, but CIA sought to prevent this by persuading him to seek mental help domestically. This action was most likely due to the possible exposure of past clandestine plots and the negative publicity should they be revealed. A draft memorandum dated January 18, 1959, prepared for the CIA's Deputy Director for Plans, with the subject: Freds Z. LAUNAGS' Possible Repatriation to Latvia contained this comment:

> Should subject decide to return to Latvia, the damage of revelations to the Soviets would be extensive: not only is he knowledgeable in great detail of Latvian REDSOX activities during 1951–1954, but he is also well-informed of our involvement with black radio broadcasts beamed to Latvia over the Spanish Government owned Radio Madrid. Our role in those broadcasts is not known the Spanish Government and Soviet revelations to that effect could prove to be very embarrassing.[71]

The draft memorandum was re-worked and on January 29, 1965, David E. Murphy, Chief, SR Division sent a memorandum to ADDP, in which this summary paragraph was included:

> From 1954 through 1956 Subject was used for general support purposes by the Baltic Branch of SR Division. In 1956 he spent several months in Spain in connection with CIA-sponsored propaganda broadcasts in Latvian over Radio Madrid. In 1958 he was

sent to Frankfurt for Baltic operations run by the German Station but was returned in 1959 when he showed evidence of mental instability. Agency psychiatrists subsequently diagnosed him as a paranoid schizophrenic and he was hospitalized for a short period. A plan was then devised for termination and job placement and Subject *was* finally terminated in late 1959.

The Latvian REDSOX operations in which Subject was involved in 1952–54 were fully exposed to the Soviets when all of the agents were either killed or captured, and the Soviets later made propaganda use of some of the facts. Thus, Subject would be able to provide primarily confirmatory information on these operations if he were to repatriate to Latvia. He knew a number of SR case officers but as far as we can determine, only one of them in true name. The fact that he assisted in anti–Soviet Latvian broadcasts from Radio Madrid as a CIA agent could be somewhat embarrassing if the Soviets were to publicize this facet of his activities. While the extent of potential damage involved in Subject's repatriation is not excessive, we believe it appropriate nevertheless to take reasonable measures to prevent or at least delay his repatriation.[72]

For years afterwards, Launags traveled around the United States in search of permanent employment but was unsuccessful in his attempts. In 1967, one internal CIA memorandum included this comment:

At first we attempted to monitor and control Subject's activities indirectly through his former friend who is still employed by the Agency on contract. We also furnished Subject modest amounts of money which ostensibly were hand-outs given him by his friend.

Despite the efforts of CIA and many of his friends to assist him financially and to help him find suitable employment, he has not been able to hold a job for more than a few weeks and has turned most of his former friends against him by his irrational behavior.[73]

In 1965, Launags wrote a threatening letter to President Johnson if he did not take actions to liberate Latvia. CIA contacted the US Secret Service: "[W]e notified the Secret Service and other appropriate agencies at the end of 1965 that we considered Subject a possible threat to the President. The Secret Service interviewed Subject shortly thereafter and found him to be rational at that time. Since than we have kept the Service and the other appropriate agencies advised of any outstanding incidents concerning Subject."[74]

Launags visited the Soviet Mission at the United Nations in New York at least here times seeking a visa to visit Latvia as a journalist to report on conditions in Latvia for émigré publications in the West. These visits resulted in a Riga Radio broadcast on June 26, 1967, about Launags. This was followed up in an article in the official newspaper of Latvia "Cina" on July 1, 1967, "Why a Visa was not issued to him." This article was republished in in newspapers in the Latvia SSR and in the West. CIA determined the original article was accurate in Launags's biography. He was accused of being a Nazi war criminal and CIA agent who was involved in the sending of other CIA agents into Latvia.[75]

CIA was not concerned about these articles because "if he discussed his CIA activities with the Soviets, or if he should disclose them in the future, he could provide no current operational information. The only historical item he could provide which still retains some degree of sensitivity is that CIA was behind the black broadcasts to Latvia which were made by the Spanish Government Radio from 1957–1961."[76]

Another relevant episode in his troubled life took place in December 1968, when Launags was arrested in Olympia, Washington, on the charges of vagrancy/trespassing.

He called the CIA Portland Resident Agent (PRA) (name unknown) collect and told him about the arrest and that he was in the Thurston County jail. The FBI was notified and sent an agent to arrange Launags release from jail and give him travel expenses. The FBI agent gave the police $13.05 ($3.05 for a bus ticket to Portland and $10.00 for living expenses) to give to Launags upon his release from jail; he was released on December 18, 1968. Although the County Deputy Prosecutor wanted to press trespassing charges against Launags, the Sheriff requested that he not do so and the charge was dropped.[77] Launags then worked in Oregon in various low-skilled jobs, the last known ones were in tree reforestation projects in 1969.

During subsequent years, Launags apparently received some of the necessary medical and/or psychological treatment or gained stability in his life, because he was later positively referred to as a writer, poet, and member of the Latvian resistance in Latvian émigré and other publications. In 1986, Launags was the editor of the weekly newspaper *Brīvā Latvija (Free Latvia)* published in Münster, Germany. Copies of the newspaper could be ordered at this address:

BRĪVĀ LATVIJA pasūtināma
Postfach 15 02 61
Salzmannstr.152
D-4400 Münster
WEST GERMANY[78]

Freds Launags eventually returned to the United States but it is not known when and what he did afterwards. He died in Los Angeles on November 22, 1991.

## *Lithuania*

> *The Regime of the USSR has controlled the former Republic of Lithuania with an iron hand since occupying and annexing the nation in June-July 1940. This control was*

broken only by the German occupation of the area during 1941–1944. The United States has not and, on the basis of the evidence of public and classified policy declarations, does not intend to recognize the legality of the Soviet absorption of Lithuania as a constituent "republic" of the USSR. While the Soviets have killed and deported a significant portion of the Lithuanian population, and many fled to the West in 1944–1945, the great majority of those remaining in Lithuania today are nevertheless thoroughly anti–Soviet. The policy of the United States is to seek the eventual liberation' of Lithuania by peaceful means.[79]

## Project AEGEAN

AEGEAN was the cryptonym for the joint OPC-OSO project that began in November 1948 with support for the Lithuanian resistance group Vyriausiasis Lietuvos išlaisvinimo komitetas (VLIK)—The Supreme Committee for Liberation of Lithuania. OPC supported VLIK for both political and psychological warfare (PP) operations; OSO was primarily responsible for foreign intelligence (FI) support:

1. Procure information from Lithuania and the Baltic generally.
2. Procure information from other parts of the USSR.
3. Use the Lithuanian facilities as channel for two-way movement of personnel in OSO service, and, as necessary, for the movement of equipment, documentary data and instructions.
4. Use the Lithuanian facilities for such intelligence activities of OSO interest as may become necessary, to which the Lithuanian facilities, in the West or in the homeland, will lend themselves.[80]

The clandestine group (Bendras Demokratinio Pasipriesinimo Szjudis)—Board of the Democratic Resistance Movement (BDPS) led the underground movement in Lithuania.[81] OPC Project AEGEAN was approved on June 21, 1949, with two objectives in the project plan that was under control of the Munich Operational Base (MOB) in West Germany:

1. Procurement of intelligence from the Baltic States and contiguous areas.
2. Development of support base in the Lithuanian SSR as a transit point for agents to be dispatched into RSFR, Belorussian SSR and Ukrainian SSR.[82]

Targets of the plan included:

1. Development of OSO-controlled w/t (Morse code) communications from the Lithuanian SSR to American Zone in Germany and Sweden.
2. Development of sea, land and/or air courier routes—between

American Zone in Germany and the Lithuanian SSR for the two-way movement of personnel, materiel and information.
3. Development of safe areas, houses and routes in the Lithuanian SSR for the transit of personnel, materiel and information to and from RSFSR, Belorussian SSR and Ukrainian SSR.[83]

Project AEGEAN was to start on July 1, 1949. Lithuanian General Paulius Plechavicius then residing in the British zone of West Germany was to be the contact person and moved to Munich. Plechavicius had been chief of the operating (military) section of VLIK, who had experiences in Lithuanian during World War II in anti–Soviet activities. VLIK Operational Section personnel in Sweden were to be integrated into the project as were VLIK operational personnel selected by the French intelligence service for the parachuting covert operations into Lithuania.[84]

On July 29, 1949, Frank Wisner approved OPC's PP Project BGLAPIN for Lithuania.

The first year of the AEGEAN project, was devoted primarily to the recruitment, training and briefing of agent personnel. On October 4, 1950, one team was dropped by parachute into the area of Branischusen, Kaliningrad Oblast. Their mission was "to establish w/t as well as secret writing communications with the American Zone of Germany, and to reorganize the underground organization in Lithuania into a support organization for American-controlled procurement activities."[85] The first agents were Juozas Albinas Luksa (pseudonym Skrajunas), Benediktas Trumpis, and Klemensas Sirvys. They had originally been selected by French Intelligence for a mission in 1949, but then the French decided to abandon the mission. After being dropped into Lithuania, Luksa made initial contact with CIA, but the last contact was in January or February 1951 and by 1953, CIA believed he was dead.[86]

On April 18–19, 1951, for the second infiltration, Julijonas Butenas and Jonas Kukauskas-Kukis ("Jack") were dropped into the Kaunas area of Lithuania. Their mission was:

a. Establishment of contact with the underground resistance forces in Lithuania.
b. Reorganization of the underground resistance forces along more effective lines.
c. Establishment of reliable w/t and s/w communication between Lithuania and. the American Zone of Germany.
d. Procurement of positive and operational intelligence.[87]

Kukauskas reported that he and Butenas were separated and Butenas and the commander of the underground unit were killed in a farmhouse

## 6. Black Radio to the Baltic States 129

in the village of Altoniskiai, by Soviet security forces on or about August 1, 1951. The farmer was supposedly drunk and gossiped with his neighbors, one of whom reportedly informed the security forces. Kukauskas sent his first message on June 15, 1951, and continued sporadically until November 29, 1951. He went silent and renewed contact in April 1952. CIA believed it was likely that Kukauskas was under control of the security forces. In 1956, CIA learned that Butenas was alive and in a forced labor camp after being caught security forces, put on trial and sentenced to 25 years imprisonment.[88]

With the merging of OPC and OSO in 1952, the OPC functions under the project were given CIA's Soviet Russia (SR) Division. The project cryptonym was then changed to CAPSTAN.

Early in March 1953, CIA was informed by one of its agents in Lithuania that strong local security measures in December 1952 resulted in the destruction of a large segment of the Lithuanian resistance movement. The CIA agent himself claimed he was wounded in a skirmish with security troops and forced to go into hiding with friends. The primary effort for 1954 AECHAMP FI was to infiltrate another agent into Lithuania and have both of them exfiltrate through Finland. CIA learned, however, that the agent in Lithuania was being controlled by the intelligence service and the plan was abandoned.[89]

Voice of America broadcast to Lithuania for the first time on February 16, 1951. CIA decided to coopt the VLIK broadcasts. One of the early mentions of "black radio broadcasts" to Lithuania was in the renewal of the CAPSTAN Basic Plan October 1951 to June 30, 1953: "Psychological warfare activities will be centered on the support of indigenous organizations through which black radio broadcasts, distribution of leaflets and the support of newspaper and pamphlets can be carried out."[90] The cryptonym of the project was changed to Project AECHAMP effective May 15, 1953.[91] CIA's Summary Report as of July 1, 1953, on AECHAMP PP (political and psychological) contained the following:

> SR has been in continuous contact with the AECHAMP Organization since August 1949. Our collaboration with this national Lithuanian group was initiated primarily in the interest of FI (Foreign Intelligence) operations. Up to approximately nine months ago the PP value of the group remained largely dormant. The group prepared and signed two leaflets, which were dropped into LSSR in 1950 and 1951. It also published a few books of value in the English, French, German and Lithuanian languages, And prepared occasional materials for broadcasting into Iron Curtain territory over VOA, RFE and other available European facilities, but otherwise confined its work to political activity in connection with friendly governments and the Lithuanian community in the western world. Only since the turn of the year have AECHAMP PP activities assumed more serious proportions. Now they appear to be of great potential merit.[92]

AECHAMP'S activities were listed in this report as:

> [B]roadcasting to Iron Curtain areas in the Lithuanian language on seven-day weekly schedules over the following short-wave facilities:
> Radio Rome and Radio Vatican—20 and 15 minutes daily respectively and 15 minutes daily over Radio Madrid. This time is available to the AECHAMPS free of charge. To Radio Vatican they pay an occasional subsidy of $100 to $200 of the own will.
> Both on demand and at their own initiative they are supping texts, tapes, and speakers to
> - VOA (Radio Center Munich and New York)
> - RFE Munich (Polish Section)
> - RIAS (Radio in the American Sector, Berlin)
> - Radio Stuttgart (Südwest Rundfunk)
> - NWDR Hamburg
> - Deutsche Well Köln
> - AFN (Armed Forces Radio for the American military)[93]

AECHAMP monitored and recorded the daily output of Lithuanian radio stations from a monitoring station at Scherbeuts, near Lübeck, Germany. AECHAMP in Reutlingen, West Germany had a staff of five salaried officials, who composed the Executive Committee and 12 editorial, technical and clerical employees. There was one AECHAMP member at Radio Rome, Radio Vatican, and Radio Madrid. It was believed that Madrid might possibly require three employees and Rome and Vatican two additional employees each. In summary:

> Because of a lack of time and facilities AECHAMP radio activities have not been monitored for content during delivery or checked prior to delivery on the air except in isolated cases of major addresses or news stories. However, the general and specific lines used are apparent at all times, in the overt ARCHAMP news bulletins and other publications. The AECHAMP attack line has been consistently stronger than that of the VOA or the overt U.S. governmental line without contradicting it in spirit or intent.
> From any point of view AECHAMP radio activities must be regarded as still being in the stage of infancy and experiment. One of the early needs is to obtain some data for an estimate of the probable audibility of Rome, Vatican and Madrid shortwave facilities in end around the main AECHAMP target areas. This is a completely unknown matter. As of the summer of 1951 scattered sources from the LSSR reported hearing rumors that Radio Vatican could be heard there in a non–Lithuanian language, but nothing further has been learned to substantiate this.[94]

The CIA cryptonym for the political and psychological operation involving Lithuania was added as AEPOLE. The February 19, 1954, document "Extension of AECHAMP (PP portion)" signed by Richard Helms in behalf of Frank G. Wisner, Deputy Director (Plans), included these objectives:

> (a) To provide financial support for AEPOLE /1—a leading émigré organization in Germany—in order to maintain that organization as an effective instrument of political and psychological warfare against the USSR.

## 6. Black Radio to the Baltic States 131

(b) To deceive and confuse the Soviet Regime in Lithuania
(c) To maintain the morale and devotion to the West of the Lithuanian people.
(d) To preserve and support the spirit of resistance in the Lithuanian SSR.

Toward accomplishing the foregoing, this Agency is providing guidance, financial assistance and other forms of support to the leading Lithuanian émigré organization in Europe.

Rendering support and guidance for AEPOLE / 1 regular daily broadcasts to the homeland via Radio Vatican and Radio Madrid; assisting in the expansion of other AEPOLE/1 broadcasting and PP activities.[95]

The advisability of moving VLIK Headquarters to the US was discussed with officials of the U.S. Department of State. The CIA position was that the geographic location of VLIK was immaterial so long as it performed the functions that were required of it. The "situation" in 1954 listed in the extension request was

> the regime of the USSR has controlled the former Republic of Lithuania with an iron hand since occupying and annexing the nation in June-July 1940. This control was broken only by the German occupation of the area during 1941-1944. The United States has not and, on the basis of the evidence of public and classified policy declarations, does not intend to recognize the legality of the Soviet absorption of Lithuania as a constituent "republic" of the USSR. While the Soviets have killed and deported a significant portion of the Lithuanian population, and many fled to the West in 1944-1945, the great majority of those remaining in Lithuania today are nevertheless thoroughly anti-Soviet.
>
> The policy of the United States is to seek the eventual liberation' of Lithuania by peaceful means. The objectives set forth above constitute covert implementation of this policy.
>
> Duration
> (1) CIA association with and support of VLIK is viewed as a continuing activity and an integral part of cold war operations, so long VLIK continues to be a suitable instrument for the implementation of US cold war policy.
> (2). The maintenance of our support personnel in assisting the PP effort is viewed as a continuing activity. In the event of open hostilities, the covert personnel will be used to support hot war operations.[96]

The Chairman of VLIK and the members of VLIK's Executive Committee were aware of US Government support: funds were given individually to the Chairman of VLIK, who then transferred the money to the Lithuanian National Fund in Germany, which then handled all VLIK expenses. The members of the VLIK assembly in Germany only were aware that contributions to their fund come from a major Lithuanian organization in the U.S. and from other private and public Lithuanian sources.[97]

Daily broadcasts to Lithuania over Radio Nacional de España began January 1, 1955:

During the past year the activities under this project with respect to radio broadcasts have expanded considerably. Under the aegis of AEPOLE/1 there are now maintained regular daily ten to twenty-minute broadcasts to the target area via Radios Rome, Vatican and Madrid.... [T]hese broadcast activities are especially the new broadcasts require expansion of the AEPOLE/1 Radio Section headquarters as well as the establishment of a Radio Section office in Madrid.[98]

By 1955, VLIK maintained the following radio broadcast schedules to Lithuania:

- Radio Vatican, Sunday, Tuesday, and Thursday, 14:00–14:15
- Radio Vatican, Monday, Wednesday, and Saturday, 18:00–18:15
- Radio Rome, daily 20:00–20:15
- Radio Nacional de España, daily, 17:10–17:25.[99]

All of the programs were identified as the "Voice of the Supreme Committee for Liberation of Lithuania." One comment read:

In general the content of the radio programs is strongly anti–Communist. Their avowed purpose is to maintain the native traditions of the Lithuanian people in the face of enforced Sovietization. No attempt is made to accommodate the propaganda to operate within the framework of Communist indoctrination. The evidence available indicates that the Soviets have so far not made appreciable progress in eradicating Lithuanian traditions and the sense of Lithuanian nationality.

It must be recognized, however, that the VLIK is an organization of spontaneous origin and specific purposes, which may not always conform to the policy of the United States. Liberation of the Lithuanian SSR is and must remain the avowed policy of the group. Every effort is made to moderate, through case officer intercession, any excessively aggressive tendencies. So far, it has been possible to analyze in some detail only the scripts from Radio Rome. From the samples so far seen, their tone, from our point of view, is not offensive. In passing, it should be noted *in* this connection that the State Department still maintains diplomatic relations with the diplomatic representatives of the Baltic states, and has given no indication of readiness to great de jure recognition of the forced incorporation of the Baltic states by the USSR.[100]

The project renewal request and outline submitted by CIA's SR Division in May 1955, approved in August 1955 for FY 1956, contained very detailed information about Project AEPOLE, including CIA financial support:

The main task of this project is to subsidize VLIK efforts in the PP field by helping to develop and to maintain VLIK's psychological warfare section and broadcasts to the homeland. Other tasks to implement:

- Initiate preparatory work for black broadcast radio into the target area
- Keep alive Lithuanian cultural and political traditions by maintaining liaison with and supporting other Lithuanian émigré groups in addition to VLIK
- Rendering support and guidance for BLIK regular daily broadcasts to the homeland via Radio Rome, Radio Vatican and Radio Madrid.

## 6. Black Radio to the Baltic States

The candidate for chief editor of the VLIK Radio Section, while in training in Washington, will be given the cover of a research analyst. Upon his departure for German he is to assume his cover of a VLIK employee. The chief of the Madrid Radio Station is to be employed directly by VLIK and no cover arrangements for him are necessary.[101]

AEPOLE/14, the chief of the VLIK Radio Section in West Germany, and the chief of the Madrid Radio Station were witting of US Government interest only, i.e., not CIA support. The Chairman of VLIK, as well as the Chairman and key members of VLIK's Executive Committee were aware of CIA support. In the event that US interest in VLIK were discovered by the West German or Spanish Governments, this would have had no harmful effect on US foreign relations, since such interest had long been taken for granted by both countries.[102] CIA's association with and support of VLIK was viewed as a continuing activity and an integral part of its cold-war operations, so long as VLIK continued to be a viable instrument for the implementation of US Cold-War policy.[103]

The main support of VLIK was based on CIA "subsidization of their PP effort. In addition, CIA supported the VLIK effort by sending program guidance and material (in the original language or translated) for their broadcasts and other PP activities."[104]

CIA control of VLIK was through financial support with the possibility that it would be withdrawn if CIA determined that VLIK's productivity did not warrant further support. The head of Madrid Radio Station received an annual salary of $4,000 in FY 1956 and travel expenses of $1,200. CIA payments to VLIK from 1949 to the end of FY 1955 amounted to $112,294. For FY1955, VLIK received CIA financial support in the amount of $39,404. Subsidies paid to the radio stations Rome, Madrid, and Vatican amounted to $30,000 in FY1956.[105]

The request for Renewal Project AEPOLE for FY 1957 from the Chief, SR Division contained these achievements:

1. Provided propaganda material for radio broadcasts to Lithuania via, RIA, VOA, RFE (Polish Section), West German stations, Radio Rome, Radio Vatican and Radio Madrid.
2. Supported financially, via VLIK, the operation of 15.minute daily broadcasts in Lithuanian, beamed to Lithuania via Radio Rome, Radio Vatican and Radio Nacional (Madrid)
3. Supported financially, via VLIK, the operation in Germany of a daily service monitoring Lithuanian-language broadcasts emanating from Radios Vilnius.

Although these Lithuanian language radio language programs are still nominally supported by VLIK, they are in fact nearly completely dependent on CIA support.

To date it has been difficult to establish just what proportion of VLIK radio programs beamed to Lithuania via Radio Nacional, Radio Vatican, and Radio Rome eventually get through Soviet jamming and reaches the target audience. However, estimates indicate enough of the programs manage to bypass interference to contribute materially to the fulfillment of the objectives of the project.

The effectiveness of VLIK radio activities had been hampered to some effect be the fact that the VLIK administration in Germany lacked the talent to conduct these activities properly. VLIK has also been weakened in recent years be emigration of its personnel from Germany, inner strife, personnel jealousies, and some conflict with non-VLIK political factions among Lithuanian colonies in exile. It has there been decided by us that in order to revitalize VLIK and make it radio activities more effective, VLIK headquarters, including its radio section, should be moved to another location—preferably the U.S.—where the best talent among Lithuanian emigres is available.[106]

Changes in the administration of VLIK in West Germany were used by CIA to sever its covert relationship with the group but continue to directly subsidize the radio broadcasts. The effect of this was "salutary":

1. It forced VLIK out of its complacent lethargy,
2. It brought home to them the fact we are in business for results—not for charity.
3. It caused the new leaders of VLIK to seek and pay heed to our counsel.[107]

In addition, "an agreement has been extracted from the Chairman of VLIK to appoint with our consent five émigré leaders, irrespective of parties, to serve as a radio and propaganda policy guidance group. We expect at least three of these members to be out covert associates and all five would be subject to our influence."[108]

There continued to be a question about the effectiveness of the broadcasts, e.g., CIA's Chief of the Information Coordination Division wrote on March 27, 1957: "We have found that little evidence exists dated after 1954 to substantiate claims of either the program or technical effectiveness of Radio National."[109] The publication of VLIK's bulletin, and other PP activities, which were compatible with U.S. foreign policy objectives, included:

(a) To preserve the national identify of the Lithuanian people thereby helping them to resist assimilation into the Soviet society.
(b) To maintain among the Lithuanian people an attitude of irreconcilability toward International Communism and the Soviet regime dominating Lithuania today.
(c) To maintain and enhance the pro-Western and pro-American orientation of the Lithuanian people.
(d) To encourage revisionist tendencies among the Lithuanian Communists.
(e) To foster evolutionary changes by encouraging the Lithuania people to seek continuous concessions from the Soviet regime in Lithuania.
(f) To contribute by all possible means to the growth of intellectual ferment among the Lithuanian people.[110]

In the project renewal request for FY 1957, two objectives of AEPOLE were "to maintain the morale of the people of Lithuania, preserve and further stimulate their pro-Western attitudes and harass the Soviet regime in that country."[111] The "Operational mechanisms" of AEPOLE were: "Lithuanian section of Radio Madrid (Radio Nacional de España)" and "Supreme Committee for Lithuanian Liberation (a cover organization in New York), which sponsors the Lithuanian broadcasts from Radio Madrid."

By 1958, two half hour radio programs were prepared in Washington and Munich respectively. The Chief of CIA's Psychological and Paramilitary (PP) Staff wrote, "The present working arrangement should be improved in terms of cover, funding, and particularly guidance on policy and content of the broadcast." A new objective was included in the FY 1958 renewal request: "To seek out and encourage 'Titoist' tendencies in the Lithuanian Communist leadership." One of the accomplishments listed was

> direct CIA case officer contact was established with the Lithuanian program directors at Radio Nacional and Radio Rome, which were formerly supported by CIA indirectly through VLIK. They are now receiving from CIA modest monthly salaries and reimbursement for some operation expenses. In return for this assistance, they may be counted on to incorporate into their daily broadcast propaganda material that we provide of suggest. Although these Lithuanian language programs are still nominally supported by VLIK, they are in fact nearly completely dependent of direct CIA support.[112]

The FY1959 project action sheet for renewal of AEPOLE showed that CIA and VLIK had reached a rapprochement:

> Objectives: Facilitate evolutionary changes with the USSR by exploiting the major changes occurring in the Soviet hierarchy—to this end increase popular demands for greater freedom, aggravate frictions between Soviet and Satellite parties and governments, and induce popular doubts as to the validity of communism.
> 
> Disseminate facts and propaganda themes to the Soviet people inside the USSR through effective covert media, including radio; utilize selected émigré organizations for propaganda and political action.
> 
> The activities of AEPOLE were hampered by disunity within the Lithuanian emigration organization (VLIK), but this problem has now been satisfactorily resolved. SR Division is now working on improving the quality of the radio programs and also attempting to obtain a truer evaluation of the effectiveness of the radio program. The potential of this activity is greater than we have utilized and should be developed qualitatively.... AEPOLE should in no way be considered expendable but should receive concentrated attention both from headquarters and the field.[113]

The significant operation was that radio broadcasts from Radio Nacional de España continued daily with a 15-minute original broadcast and a 15-minute repeat program. It was planned to "improve the quality of Radio

Madrid's Lithuanian-language broadcasts in relation to US Government propaganda objectives ... with a greater degree of cooperation by Radio Madrid Lithuanian personnel with their Estonian and Latvian counterparts, and through a new series of specific propaganda directives."[114]

Project AEPOLE renewal request for FY 1960 included this "significant operational" events: "Radio broadcasts were continued from Radio Madrid with a 15-minute original broadcasts and a 15-minute repeat per day. Radio Rome broadcasts continued with a 20-minute program per day. An OSI report indicated that reception was technically on a par with VOA broadcasts. Last year a total of 95 reports on Radio Madrid and 80 reports on Radio Rome were obtained from the Balts and from Spanish repatriates who had listened to these broadcasts in the Soviet Union."[115]

The CIA decided to terminate AEPOLE in FY 1964 and broadcasts over Radio Nacional de España to Lithuania ceased on October 31, 1963. Radio liberty began broadcasting to Lithuania in 1975, before consolidation with Radio Free Europe as RFE/RL. Lithuanian broadcasts continued over RFE/RL in Prague, after the move from Munich in 1995, and over Voice of America until 2004.

# 7

# Black Broadcasts to Ukraine from Greece and RNE

## Radio Novaya Ukraina (New Ukraine), 1955–1959

On December 12, 1949, the Voice of America began broadcasting to Ukraine via shortwave radio; VOA was considered "White." On August 14, 1954, the Ukrainian Service of Radio Liberation (later Radio Liberty) began its first broadcast from Munich to Ukraine with these words: "Brothers and sisters! Ukrainians! We live abroad, but our hearts and minds are always with you. No iron curtain can separate us or stand in our way." Radio Liberty was considered "Gray." But these two radio stations were not the only ones the U.S. government used to broadcast to Ukraine as CIA's SR Division wanted clandestine radio broadcasts to Ukraine that were considered "Black."

In 1948, CIA's Office of Policy Coordination (OPC) selected the émigré organization Ukrainian Supreme Liberation Council (ZP/UHVR) as the "most reliable, best organized and operationally most experienced group for use in exploiting anti-Communist activity of the Ukrainian resistance group then active in the Ukraine."[1] For the next five years, CIA and ZP/UHVR conducted extensive joint foreign intelligence (FI) operations using the cryptonyms AEACRE and CARTEL and the political and psychological (PP) warfare operation AERODYNAMIC: propaganda leaflets and materials were smuggled into Ukraine or dropped by balloons. Agents were infiltrated into Ukraine, but most were killed or captured by the Soviet forces.

On June 17, 1950, ADPC Frank Wisner, approved OPC project PBCRUET: "The exploitation and expansion of the Ukrainian resistance movement.... To establish a 'black' radio transmitter outside (and possibly eventually inside) the USSR for broadcasts to the Ukraine."[2]

The immediate objective of PBCRUET was

to provide the ZPUHVR with sufficient funds, printing presses, and printing paper in order to assist this organization in carrying on psychological warfare activities directed against the Soviet regime and the Soviet forces of occupation. (Such operations, for instance, would include publication of a Ukrainian newspaper and leaflets, with overt distribution outside Ukraine and covert within.)[3]

The maximum objectives of PBCRUET included:

To assist the ZPUHVR and UHVR in developing the necessary channels for Escape and Evasion of U.S. fliers who may be forced down during possible future hostilities in Ukraine and other adjoining areas.[4]

In providing financial support for OPC activities envisaged in this project, and particularly for that portion subsidy of émigré personnel or organizations, the OSO and OPC field personnel will advise their Ukrainian émigré contacts that the funds are being supplied by various private sources in the United States who are interested in the Ukrainian national movement.

Communications—one-way coded messages via Voice of America, Radio Free Europe and other similar broadcasts.

Timetable 1950–1951

As soon as necessary approval can be obtained, a mobile shortwave broadcasting station will be established in Germany, Turkey, or some location.[5]

## The Setting up of Black Radio Broadcasting from Athens

CIA approval request, dated April 30, 1953, "Justification for SR (Soviet Russia) Division of Athens Radio Facilities for Clandestine Broadcasting to the USSR," listed the following as reasons for creating the new radio site:

There are no clandestine psychological warfare assets presently available through which we can reach the audience in these strategic areas. The people in these areas will be receptive targets for black broadcasts. In both areas anti–Soviet nationalism is a potent force and can be exploited. It was precisely in theme areas that anti–Soviet resistance forces arose during World War II, and the population has suffered since the end of the war from the MGB-MVD campaign to eradicate the remnants of these farces. Mass deportations have occurred in these areas since the war and have added to the hatred of the Soviet regime.

The same memorandum listed the aim of the "black" radio broadcasts:

[S]timulate and intensify discontent and disaffection to the Soviet regime and provide the target audiences with hope of ultimate liberation. This will be accomplished by means of broadcasts in the native language of the target audience, based on factual events and national and cultural history. These broadcasts will stimulate national consciousness among the minority groups addressed, and will urge them to maintain

## 7. Black Broadcasts to Ukraine from Greece and RNE

pride in the Individuality of their various national cultures. Concurrently the proposed broadcasts will encourage passive resistance, earning against premature uprisings but urging organized passive resistance, which can develop into something more active when conditions permit.[6]

The objectives of the clandestine radio project with the cryptonym RANTER were listed in a July 21, 1953, project outline:

> The objective of this project is to utilize broadcast time available on the KUBARK (CIA) radio installation PYREX at Athens, Greece, for the broadcast of a series of programs to be directed to:
> - Soviet officialdom,
> - Soviet military forces stationed in the Ukraine,
> - Indigenous civilian population of the Ukraine,
> - Underground movement,
> - Ukrainian Insurgent Army (UPA).

The tasks of the project were to:

> - Furnish evidence of outside sympathy and understanding for the Ukrainian peoples.
> - Intensify anti-regime disaffection by encouraging resentment, bitterness, and distrust of the Soviet regime and its personalities.
> - Maintain national consciousness among the Ukrainians and urge them to maintain pride in the individuality and heritage of their culture.
> - Create dissatisfaction among Ukrainian military personnel within the Soviet armed forces stationed in the Ukraine.
> - Create and intensify dissatisfaction among the Ukrainian civil authorities to the Soviet regime. The submitting division gave the following as why the black broadcasts were necessary: This project is based upon the need to make a more significant propaganda impact on this strategic target audience. At present the only PBPRIME (United States, i.e., Voice of America) and KUBARK (CIA) propaganda efforts directed to the target area consist of Voice of America broadcasts and the Radio Liberation effort to the Kiev area in the Russian language.
>
> The presentation of clandestine broadcasts, specifically tailored to the needs of the target audience delivered on a close and friendly basis, will augment the existing inadequate PBPRIME and KUBARK efforts.[7]

The July 1953 project outline amendment also listed the method of preparing the broadcasts. Scripts and tapes were to be prepared by a CIA covert operation in New York City: Prolog Research and Publishing Association, Inc. (CIA Cryptonyms QKTENURE and AETENURE):

It is proposed that the SR Division be authorized to plan a psychological warfare campaign to be implemented initially over the PYREX radio station located in Athens, Greece.

It is proposed that programs in the Ukrainian language be produced and recorded on magnetic tape in New York and flown to Athens for broadcast by personnel attached to PYREX. It is realized that programming from this distance is not as efficient and timely as it would be if located nearer the transmitter. However, this is the only means at present whereby immediate advantage can be taken of the PYREX facility. When future operation conditions permit the programming to be prepared closer to the transmitter site, this project's program activities will be transferred accordingly. At first three tapes a week for fifteen minutes each broadcast time will be prepared. With the increase in script output and availability of air time, the broadcasts can be expanded.[8]

During fiscal year 1954 the clandestine radio operation had been approved as a sup-project (AERANTER) of Project AERODYNAMIC and necessitated separate funding and CIA administration. It had the primary purpose of furthering "the PP efforts by inauguration of black radio transmissions directed at the Ukrainian SSR." It would "share transmitter time with similar type broadcasts presently made from the Athens base station." It was proposed that "programs in the Ukrainian language be produced and recorded on magnetic tape in New York and flown to Athens for broadcast by personnel attached to PYREX. It is realized that programming from this distance is not as efficient and timely as it would be if located nearer the transmitter. However, this is the only means at present whereby immediate advantage can be taken of the PYREX facility."[9]

Subproject RANTER had the following "advantages":

- It is possible to utilize the facilities of an established installation.
- It will provide a wedge which can be driven deeper between the Soviets and the Ukrainians and would exacerbate existing suspicions and antagonisms between the two ethnic factions.
- A psychological climate can be fostered which will be more favorable to the conduct of SR operations in the Soviet Ukraine. Soviet reaction to the broadcasts may indicate certain areas of vulnerability or sensitivity not heretofore recognized.[10]

RANTER had the following requirements:

- The establishment in New York City and/or other locations in the United States as may be necessary, of facilities for writing and producing a series of radio programs
- Procurement of equipment for recording these programs on magnetic tape. This tape will be pouched and flown to Athens for reproduction.
- The augmentation of a Ukrainian study group panel in New York.[11]

## 7. Black Broadcasts to Ukraine from Greece and RNE

The Study Group panel, which was supervised by one staff employee, who was experienced in psychological warfare activities, had the following duties:

- Write or assemble, record, and edit material which will be broadcast am/or held in reserve as a backlog for future broadcasts.
- Act as translators, researchers, writers, editors, and announcers.
- Collect and collate background and source materials in the form of overtly published books and periodicals and unclassified government information.
- Sterilize by rewriting and reattributing classified material for incorporation into the programs.[12]

Mykola Lebed, President of Prolog and CIA Principal Agent, (CIA cryptonym AECASSOWARY-2 and CASSAWARY-2) sent a "Ukrainian Broadcasting Policy Paper" in December 1954 that apparently for the first time mentioned the name "Nova Ukraina" (New Ukraine) for the proposed radio station. An officer of the SR PP Division commented on Lebed's paper on January 15, 1954, with these comments:

> [T]he program ... is Ukrainian, replete with national symbols and allusions. We especially like the idea of brief features dealing with the gnomic sayings of classical authors well-known in the Ukraine and assume that the writer intends to select phrases with political implications. Because of the fact of jamming, a scheme dividing the fifteen-minute program into brief and self-sufficient sections is sound. There would be no point in building the program around long involved themes the point of which would be obvious only at the end just as the jammer might be zeroing in. Brief and self-sufficient items would take advantage of gaps in the jamming and of fading of the jamming signals.
>
> The undersigned sees no reason why the name "New Ukraine" is not appropriate. It is submitted that we should take maximum advantage of the symbolic impact embodied in a voice which presumably speaks from the Ukraine and in the name and interest of the Ukrainian people themselves by identifying the station as frequently as possible, provided that it is consistent with jamming evasion techniques.[13]

One internal CIA document gave the background of Mykola Lebed: "The authorized Secretary of Foreign Affairs for the UHVR (Ukrainian Supreme Liberation Council), along with three other members of the UHVR, was sent to the West from the Soviet Ukrainian resistance movement in 1945 to make contact with Western intelligence representatives and to act in behalf of the homeland. The original group coopted a small number of other member when they arrived in the West to form the ZP/UHVR (the Foreign Representation of the UHVR), and established themselves in West Germany."[14]

On the question of music in the programs, CIA's Office of communications advised in January 1954 that the beam from Athens because of "side-band clipping" is designed to carry a male voice within a limited symphonic range and cannot carry all sounds equally well. This was done in order to maximize the power of the signal and the distance over which it would carry. Because of the "side-band clipping," the musical passage will sound fuzzy. It is felt, however, that a musical signature should be included in the program, ... provided that it can be transmitted in a low register around 500 cycles. A high-pitched musical signal carries a greater distance from the receiver than spoken words and could betray the listener.[15]

Going from the concept of a clandestine radio to the actual beginning of broadcasting to Ukraine was a relatively long and drawn out affair. CIA was frustrated for two years in reaching its goal of broadcasting clandestinely to Ukraine. One of the problems facing CIA in 1953 was that even though approval was received to begin clandestine radio broadcasting under the cryptonym AERODYNAMIC / RANTER, there was no professional staff of radio journalists, script writers, announcers, etc.

In February 1954, CIA falsely believed that the radio scripts and the first tapes for broadcasting would be ready within a month. On March 21, 1954, the SR division made a request to the Safehouse Procurement Office for a safehouse in New York City that would be: 6 rooms, detached, with a basement, in a middle-class neighborhood in Jackson Heights, Queens, Astoria, or Brooklyn.[16]

There was little progress in developing clandestine radio broadcasts until the end of 1954, so on January 27, 1955, there was meeting with CIA legendary officer Archibald Roosevelt, grandson of President Teddy Roosevelt, two other CIA officers, and Mykola Lebed. The meeting was summed up as

> they exchanged views of the AERODYNAMIC Project in general and, specifically, in order that Mr. Roosevelt might discuss with Lebed the Ukrainian Black Radio Broadcast—its present status and future possibilities. The meeting began with Mr. Roosevelt presenting his views or critique on the scripts. He pointed out: the scripts are too lengthy, feature wise. The male voice used in the broadcast tapes is not quite adequate. The contents of the scripts in my instances, does not seem quite timely, or effective enough to meet current developments in the Ukraine.
> 
> Lebed admitted that certain technical features of the scripts should be altered and improved. He said the Study Group was primarily composed of Eastern Ukrainians who had lived under the Soviet Regime their entire lives prior to coming to the West shortly after the end of World War II. He added, These people are well aware of Soviet reality and are competent in their respective fields and can produce the type of scripts.
> 
> He admitted, however, that while they may not have the latest word on many new changes in the Ukraine (although they do have access to material obtained from the Ukrainian Underground headquarters as late as 1953 and are provided with current Soviet publications), the basic criteria—the anti–Communist, anti–Bolshevik struggle and the quest for an independent Ukraine is really all that matters.
> 
> In concluding the discussion as to the future of the Black Radio broadcasts, Mr. Roosevelt made it clear that the decision to implement this phase of the Project has

## 7. Black Broadcasts to Ukraine from Greece and RNE 143

not yet been made and that the scripts, line to be followed, etc., is now under review and that a decision will be made in approximately two months, or possibly less. Mr. Roosevelt pointed out that he will pull no punches and that when a decision is reached—favorable or unfavorable—he will again meet with Lebed and make this decision known to him. In other words, there will not be a vague, general stall and a long period of indecision.

In the meantime, it was suggested that Lebed suspend making any further tapes and to divert the Study Group to other activities.[17]

On May 27–28, 1955, there was a CIA-Prolog meeting at the Raleigh Hotel in Washington, during which Lebed was advised to prepare at least three trial tapes prior to moving into full operation. Lebed expressed some reluctance due to the rejection of at least 30 tapes and scripts his group had prepared when originally granted the go-ahead. He stated that some of his key men were thinking of getting out of the Study Group because they saw no signs that their work was being put to good use. In any case, Lebed said he would make three tapes based on the restrictions presented to him several months ago by Mr. Roosevelt. CIA's liaison officer stressed the point that

> approval for the scripts and tapes in the black radio broadcasts have been in effect for over a year now and that money was being spent with no results. It was also pointed out that it was not up to him to push the Study Group and the ZP into doing something along this line when it is primarily for their advantage—they should have the initiative and the desire to see the thing through now that funds for this have been allocated. It was also pointed out that the project (they know there is such a thing) would be up for renewal at the end of the current fiscal year and that without some results there would be some difficulties in justifying the renewal at the same rate if at all.[18]

## Psychological Warfare Panel

In August 1955, at a meeting in the Statler Hotel in New York, Prolog president Lebed was told, "The study group is no longer in effect as it was not 'producing anything that is aiding in the immediate anti–Soviet struggle.' Those members who had comprised the defunct study group would now be shifted into a Psychological Warfare panel. Each individual would have his own responsibility; if he failed to satisfy the requirements he would be removed from the panel. The Psychological 'Warfare' Panel was to supply one fifteen-minute tape a week for broadcast from the PYREX facilities." August 22, 1955, was set as the deadline for receiving the first 14-minute broadcast tape.[19]

The first broadcast of radio Novaya Ukraina was made on September 25, 1955, with one 15-minute transmission daily. That was later increased to two scheduled broadcasts daily, which used two transmitter hours per day, or 60 hours per month.[20] CIA was unhappy with the first programs and in New York on October 5, 1955, there was a meeting with Lebed, the project Psychological Warfare Panel, and CIA to discuss the necessity of improving the contents of the radio scripts prepared by the group. According to CIA report:

> Getting down to the business of actual script writing, which would reflect the Ukrainian national interest without being the merchants of hate to everything Russian, we had considerable difficulty in reconciling the national Ukrainian interests of the group with the policy ... which precludes the extreme chauvinism. The produced scripts (five, six, and seven) were devoid of the former undertones of hatred against everything Russian and from this point of view they were deemed acceptable.
>
> The scripts produced were recorded at our suggestion in a fashion designed to enliven the presentation of material by be introduction of two additional voices, by cutting down the monologues, and by dramatization of the entire presentation. The previous tapes were recorded by a single voice end the resulting monotony in audio effect rendered the broadcasts dull and uninteresting. Because of the involved and detailed process of script editing, it has been decided that their final rendering will be accomplished with our immediate participation and that the croup will do the preparatory assembling of material.[21]

The project outline for AERODYNAMIC FY 1959 redocumentation and renewal request contained this comment:

> Operational Results During Calendar Year 1957.
> Radio Broadcast: two fifteen-minute programs daily, totaling over 1200 broadcasts beamed at the Soviet Ukraine from Radio PYREX in Athens. During 1957 the total number of transmittal hours was increased from 15 to 70 per month including repeat broadcast and random time. In addition, ZP/UHVR–controlled broadcasts over Radio Nacional, Madrid were beamed live fifteen minutes daily for a total of over 90 hours of broadcast time.[22]

## *Examples of Novaya Ukraina Programs*

Selected item from a Monthly Report of Project AERODYNAMIC March 1958:

> In addition to weekly summaries of world news and news of Ukrainian activities, the broadcasts included articles on the following themes:
> - Activities of Ukrainian emigration in the West disturb the Communist occupants of Ukraine.
> - Examples of Russian Imperialism in Ukraine.
> - Khrushchev in role of pacifist and humanist.
> - Russification of Ukraine on basis of new facts.[23]

Selected items from May 1958:

## 7. Black Broadcasts to Ukraine from Greece and RNE 145

Eight tapes were prepared by Prolog Associates during the Month of May and transmitted over Radio Pyrex for a total of 75 transmitter hours.

- Ten million Ukrainians in the RSFSR and Asia have no Ukrainian schools, newspapers or books, yet a new Ukrainian school has been built in New York at a cost of over 2 million dollars.
- Khrushchev states if is false to say Russia exploits other socialist nations.
- As a retort to Moscow's efforts to falsify Ukrainian history, Ukrainian émigrés in New York have to date published 10 volumes of M. Hrushevsky's History of Ukraine.
- The Ukrainian Shakespeare Society in Germany published in the Ukrainian language (unavailable in the USSR) a book of translations of all Shakespeare's sonnets, plus Romeo and Juliet.[24]

Some of the topics for the July 1958 broadcasts included:

- Hungarian school children are being arrested for participation in the 1956 revolution.
- Hungarian protests against the shooting of Imre Nagy continue.
- Khrushchev congratulates Arab nationalists but liquidates nationalists in Ukraine, Byelorussia, Lithuania and other nations
- World indignation is aroused by Russian attempts to capture Estonian, who succeeded in escaping from Soviet fishing vessel.[25]

Twelve tapes were transmitted in October 1958, including "special" tapes devoted to the commemoration of the 1956 Revolution in Hungary:

- The Hungarian Revolution. Comments on why and how?
- Excerpts from a letter written by a Hungarian author to artist Pablo Picasso. The Hungarian Revolution tore open the iron curtain and revealed to the free world the suffering of those living under Moscow rule.
- Ramifications and effects of the Hungarian Revolution on world opinion and emotions.
- Comments on how Moscow press falsified proceedings of Hungarian Revolution.[26]

Eight tapes were prepared in January 1959 at Prolog in New York, the following, in part, were included in the broadcasts:

- Commentary on the anti-religious campaign in the USSR.
- Moscow fears Communist revolution in Iraq in near future.
- Comments regarding the celebrations commemorating the forty-first anniversary of the free Ukrainian Republic.
- Soviets say Ukrainian students not compelled to study Russian language, but they permit no chance for advancement without it.[27]

According to the project Renewal Plan for FY 1959:

The radio broadcasts are attributed to a notional group of Ukrainian anti–Communists; There will be no connection, actual or implied, with any established Ukrainian group. Since the broadcast tapes are recorded in the United States and then flown to Athens and Greece, no physical security problems are envisaged in this operation.

> The existing headquarters of PROLOG ASSOCIATES in New York will serve as an office for preparation of the scripts.... Suitable backstopping is being set up to provide effective cover for all financial transactions between the Agency and PROLOG ASSOCIATES. Although AERODYNAMIC is sharing the facilities of PYREX, this Project will in no way conflict with other broadcasts from Athens over the same station.
>
> Existing facilities in Athens, Greece, and Madrid, Spain will be utilized for broadcasting. The Athens transmitters have a total power output of 2000 watts. The stations will have an audible radius of 1,300 miles under optimum conditions.[28]

The renewal for FY 1960, approved in March 1959, contained these comments about the clandestine broadcasts:

> Radio PYREX. Taped in New York by the AECASSOWARIES, under the title of NEW UKRAINE, an average of 80 broadcast hours per month have been sent over Radio PYREX carrying brief news items and commentary on political, religious, historical and cultural topics "which point up free Ukrainian political traditions and ethics to which the listening audience can subscribe." The themes are tailored toward the Soviet Ukrainian audience. Since Soviet Ukrainians in conversations "with Ukrainian emigres and with Western tourists have expressed disappointment in the excessive praise for the material wealth of Americans in VOA and Radio Liberation broadcasts, the content of NEW UKRAINE broadcasts is based on topic preferences expressed by the Soviet Ukrainians."[29]

In October 1959, although it was approved for renewal for FY 1960 that began in July 1959, CIA decided that clandestine radio broadcasting from Greece to Ukraine would be terminated. They had actually stopped during the two-day meeting at Camp David in September 1959 between U.S. President Eisenhower and Soviet Premier Khrushchev. Seventy-two hours monthly of Ukrainian-language programs had been prepared for broadcast over the Athens facilities prior to cessation of the broadcasts in October 1959.[30]

## Radio Nacional de España Ukrainian Broadcasts

The origins of CIA-RNE broadcasts to Ukraine can be traced to March 1956, when there were discussions between ZP/UHVR (Foreign Representation of the Ukrainian Supreme Liberation Council) and CIA regarding support of a political drive designed to organize a world-wide drive of raising nationalism as an ideology opposed to the Soviet brand of totalitarian Communism. Group members were to travel to Europe and the Middle East: Spain France, Belgium, Holland, England, Austria, Turkey, Greece, Syria, and Lebanon.

In Madrid, the ZP/UHVR was to contact the Ukrainian branch of Radio Nacional. The head of the branch was Dr. B. Tsimbalist, a personal

## 7. Black Broadcasts to Ukraine from Greece and RNE

friend of Dr. Vaysl Markus, a resident member of the Group in Paris. The Editor of *Suchasna Ukraine*, Dr. Stachiv, would be accompanied by Dr. Markus.

The editorial panel under Mykola Lebed in New York was in contact with Radio Madrid and received twelve radio scripts for comment. In March 1956, Lebed told his CIA contact at a meeting in New York:

> These broadcasts are following the general theme of Ukrainian national liberation, and they avoid chauvinistic attacks on the Russian nationals. However, their content is somewhat weak insofar as critical discussion of the defects of the Soviet system. The exposition of the problem of the Ukrainian population versus regime requires extensive study and continuous flow of information which at the present time is lacking in "Radio Nacional." The Ukrainian group of writers and editors in Madrid consists, for the most part, of the younger people who were educated by Jesuits in Madrid University.[31]

Lebed also said that the Ukrainian editors of the Radio Madrid broadcasts were anxious to establish contact with ZP/UHVR and wished to draw on its talent and resources in order improve their broadcasts.[32]

In August 1956, action was taken to have Prolog Associates gradually take over the Ukrainian broadcasts from Radio Nacional de España. The leader of the Ukrainian group producing the scripts for Radio Nacional, Tsymbalist, established liaison with Prolog Associates and offered to follow the leadership of Prolog Associates. Tsymbalist was expected to emigrate and settle in the United States. His position was be taken over by a representative of Prolog Associates Markus, who resided in Paris. The CIA clearance on Markus was implemented.[33] By the end of 1956, the Ukrainian desk at RNE was producing daily "live" broadcasts to Ukraine.

By 15 April 1957, CIA decided to reduce the support of ZP/UHVR in FY 1958, due to "the general reduction of the budget."[34] The reasoning was

> the Ukrainian Emigres who originally represented the underground resistance movement in USSR could no longer justify these claims. The current activities of Prolog Associates as a group fell into two categories; namely, Propaganda directed to the Ukrainian population in USSR and Political activities within the Ukrainian emigre circles in the free world. Within the first category could be included the following: Ideological guidance and technical support for Radio Madrid.[35]

In October 1957 the Prolog representative in Madrid brought a copy of the *Prolog Magazine* to the attention of a Radio Nacional executive, who was very interested in it and used its influence to have the article "Asian Renaissance" by Lev Shankowsky published in the *Radio Nacional Bulletin* in Spanish. This bulletin was distributed to Spanish ministers and members of the General Staff and others. At the same time the Arab Desk at Radio

Nacional translated the same article into Arabic and utilized it for their broadcasts to the Arab nations. The editor of the RNE Chinese Desk was also interested and had the article translated into Chinese. Both the Lebanese and Moroccan program directors also expressed interest in utilizing the article for their broadcasts.[36]

On October 14, 1957, in the Prolog offices in New York, Lebed informed his CIA case officer that he was in correspondence with one of the members of the ABN (Anti-Communist Bloc of Nations) mission on Formosa regarding broadcasts being beamed to the Soviet Union via the Nationalist Radio Network. The ABN representative asked for aid in obtaining suitable propaganda materials. Lebed obliged with a request that the group send copies of their radio scripts. He received a letter from ABN in which were enclosed the last two radio scripts in Ukrainian. He told his case officer that he would have the radio scripts translated and give them to him.[37]

Lebed met his CIA contact at the Prolog offices in New York in November 1957 and told him that he received information from Poland stating that the Ukrainian broadcasts from Radio Nacional were the best Ukrainian-language broadcasts from the West. The Ukrainian Section was headed by Dr. V. Tsymbalist, with occasional input from members of the small Ukrainian colony in Madrid. Another Ukrainian named Buchinsky (first name unknown), prepared two religious broadcasts in Ukrainian per week. Radio Nacional paid the Ukrainian Section approximately 1,000 pesos a month (approximately $25) but this was not sufficient for expenses. Prolog sent Tsymbalist at the rate of $50 per month and providing him with script material and records of Ukrainian music.[38]

In April 1958, Lebed told his CIA contact that Bogdan Tsymbalist, head of the Ukrainian section of Radio Nacional de España, had to immigrate to the United States in the near future, or he would lose his right to emigrate. A possible alternative was a trip to the United States for at least two weeks, which would allow him the possibility of returning to Spain and emigrating at a later date. Lebed planned to discuss this problem with him during the former's trip to Europe later this month.[39]

Mykola Lebed spent 6 days in Madrid in July 1958. Two days after his arrival, the Director of Radio Nacional was replaced by Gomez, considered to be pro–German and anti–American. Tsymbalist told Lebed that Gomez's advisor was a Yugoslav whose wife, a Russian and worked in the Madrid area. It was not known what changes would take place now that Gomez took over. Tsymbalist was hopeful that the Ukrainian broadcasts would be continued and told Lebed that would keep him informed of developments.[40]

In an internal CIA March 1959 report on the costs of the daily

## 7. Black Broadcasts to Ukraine from Greece and RNE 149

15-minute broadcasts over Radio Nacional, the total annual cost was $600 to "one individual located in Madrid, who directs the script writing and does the announcing. No salary paid."[41]

In November 1958, there was doubt about broadcasts over Radio Nacional to Ukraine:

> Regarding Radio Madrid, it is presently the intent of SR Division to send a case officer out to have local contact with any assets which we put on the ground in Madrid. The question raised was whether we know enough about individual we are subsidizing and particularly whether we have read the Radio Madrid scripts and would we come to any conclusion as to the quality of the propaganda output.[42]

The renewal of the AERODYNAMIC project for FY 1960, approved in March 1960, contained these comments about the clandestine broadcasts:

> Radio MADRID. Two 15-minute Ukrainian language programs have been broadcast daily over Radio Nacional de España in Madrid. Information received in correspondence and via tourists traveling to Poland indicates that the broadcasts are heard there and comments have been favorable. The content of these broadcasts is controlled via AECASSOWARY-2. Some radio script material is supplied by the ARCASSOWARY personnel in New York and by two of their contacts in Madrid, who do the actual broadcasts.
>
> The (redacted) requested for Radio MADRID will permit a, salary payment of (redacted) monthly for the full-time service of two AECASSOWARY representatives in Madrid. One has been in charge of the Ukrainian-language broadcasts over Radio Nacional de España. He helps in the mailing of the Ukrainian language INFORMATION BULLETIN from Spain to the USSR and is available for any operational opportunities, which may arise in or near Spain. He also "writes articles for the AECASSOWARY publications." An increase in the AECASSOWARY staff at Madrid becomes all the more important now that PYREX broadcasts will soon cease.[43]

Clandestine broadcasting to Ukraine from PYREX in Athens ended in October 1959.

The June 1985 report by the Comptroller General of the United States, "Nazi and Axis Collaborators were used to further U.S. Anti-Communist Objectives in Europe—Some Immigrated to the United States," listed Mykola Lebed as "Subject D" and gave a brief summary of the derogatory information against him:

> Subject D was used by U.S. intelligence in Europe after the war. Documentation reviewed shows that during the 1930s the subject, a member of an underground nationalist revolutionary organization, was convicted of complicity in planning the assassination of a high East European official (Polish Interior Minister Bronislaw Pieracki). Sentenced to death, he appealed his conviction. A higher court upheld the conviction but his sentence was subsequently commuted to life imprisonment. When the Nazis invaded this East European country (Poland), he was able to escape from

prison. During the war he was alleged to have cooperated with the Germans initially but later fought against them. He was also alleged to have committed terrorist acts and to have fought against the Communists.

The subject was considered extremely valuable by U.S. intelligence. Because of fear for his personal safety and his familiarity with U.S. intelligence operations, the CIA brought him to the United States under an assumed name.

In 1952, the Director of Central Intelligence, the Attorney General, and the Commissioner of INS agreed to admit the subject in the interest of national security without regard to his inadmissibility under any other laws.[44]

Because of this and other information, Lebed was the subject of numerous U.S. critical newspaper and magazine articles. Mykola Lebed died in Pittsburgh, Pennsylvania, on July 18, 1998.

# 8

# Focus on Russia
## Our Russia, Radio Free Russia and TsOPE

## Nasha Rossiya (Our Russia)

In the 1950s, CIAs Soviet Russia (SR) Division' project for clandestine radio broadcasting in Russian from Greece had CIA cryptonyms AECROAK and AEHANGOVER; the name of the radio station was Nasha Rossiya (Our Russia), which probably began shortwave broadcasting in 1954—the exact date is not known. The 1955 book *Broadcasting Stations of the World* listed Nasha Rossiya as a clandestine station using the Russian language; the 1953 edition did not list it.

The programs at first were tape recordings prepared by a CIA "panel" in the United States, air pouched to the CIA station in Athens, Greece, and then sent directly to the PYREX transmitting site for broadcasting. The procedure was then changed in 1957 with the tapes sent to a local contact, who processed the tapes and then sent them to PYREX for airing.

In September 1957, shortwave broadcasts from PYREX to the USSR aired from 07:00 to 07:30 a.m. and to Berlin from 9:30 to 10:00 p.m. The total number of broadcast hours for the month was 784 with a total number of tape runs 1,918.[1]

Soviet jamming of the Nasha Rossiya broadcasts that had begun in 1954 was so reduced, that in some cases, jamming began between five and 20 minutes after the broadcasts began or went off the air before the broadcasts ended. Many broadcasts were jammed by only one transmitter that meant the programs were audible in the target areas. The total of jamming free broadcast time was 57 hours, 34 minutes.[2]

On September 12, 1957, Nasha Rossiya began broadcasting "latest news and comments" programs that were locally prepared in Athens and the tapes were then sent to the CIA transmitting site for broadcasting

Monday through Thursday. Locally prepared tapes were then sent on Friday for weekend broadcasts, as there were no delivery of tapes on Saturdays and Sundays.³

In December 1957, the broadcasts times and lengths were changed from one 30-minute broadcast at 9:30 p.m. on one transmitter and one frequency, to one 15-minute broadcast on two transmitters and two frequencies at 9:45 p.m.⁴ The total number of tapes runs was 1,112 with the total number of broadcast hours at 761. News items prepared locally in Athens ran for 4 minutes. Some of the Nasha Rossiya programs included:

- Khrushchev's "refined" taste in clothing. (4½ minutes)
- Budapest, trial of General Maleter. (5½ minutes)
- Soviet distorted information and actual facts regarding the life of Negroes in the U.S. (6½ minutes)
- NATO Conference in Paris.
- Birth of Christ, and His influence on humanity in the course of nearly 2,000 years. (6 minutes)
- Highlights of anti–Communist struggle during 1957. (6½ minutes).⁵

Soviet jamming had been so reduced that 113 broadcast hours of Nasha Rossiya were broadcast free of jamming.⁶

No tapes were sent from Washington from December 10, 1957, to January 7, 1958, as they were held up by the local Army Post Office (APO) office. The AECROAK office in Athens had to use tapes from old broadcasts with additional news and comments.

According to the February 3, 1958, status report, "The fact that AECROAK has been given so much transmitter time (760 hours: average per/month) must be attributed to the effect of Headquarters post–Hungarian Revolution policy calling for greater emphasis on Russian language propaganda directed to Great-Russian elements in the USSR."⁷

In February 1958, a CIA staffer wrote to the Chief of the Soviet Russia Division bemoaning the lack of information about clandestine radio broadcasts as well as lack of enthusiasm at CIA headquarters for black radio operations:

> The weakest point of our radio activities has been almost complete lack of information regarding the degree of audibility and intelligibility of our broadcasts in the target areas. This uncertainty regarding the degree of penetration of Soviet jamming by our broadcasts has been responsible to a large degree for lack of enthusiasm toward our radio propaganda activities among Headquarters personnel. Consequently, radio propaganda has been demoted to the level of "marginal activities," with only a half-hearted effort being made to keep it going.
>
> This situation undoubtedly pleases the Soviets to no end, as the determination and the fury with which they have been jamming our broadcasts in order to prevent them from being heard by the Soviet people proves quite conclusively that they have great

## 8. Focus on Russia

fear for the effect these broadcasts may have on their people and their own fate if heard regularly.[8]

There was some concern in Athens that due to Greek government changes, "[I]t is anticipated that we will run into difficulty when trying to get the Russian language show on the air, as the Greeks feel that this may anger the local Soviet Ambassador." Moreover,

> at any rate, if the Russian language broadcasts are approved, they will have to be superficially of the most inoffensive nature—nothing openly anti–Soviet, mostly straight news. We are expected to furnish the programs. This will still allow us to give the Soviet listeners a considerable amount of information otherwise withheld from them making the effort worth our while. However broadcasts of this sort require careful study and selection of subject and skillful presentation.[9]

In February 1958, the broadcast scripts prepared in Athens included:

- U.S Sputnik "Alpha 58." (5½ minutes)
- Appeal to Soviet troops stationed in Romania in connection with peasants' uprisings. (4½ minutes)
- Opposition to Ulbricht in East Germany's Communist Party. (3½ minutes)
- Khrushchev's speech in Minsk. (10½ minutes)
- Khrushchev's grandiose plans covering the next 15 years. (3 minutes)
- Soviet Army Day. (8 minutes)
- Tenth Anniversary of Communist Regime in Czechoslovakia (4½ minutes)
- President Eisenhower's Reply to Bulganin Letter (11 minutes)[10]

According to a KGB May 1959 report, for April, "programs of the radio station 'Nasha Rossiya' (Our Russia) were listened to primarily at night time from 22:35–04:45 … in the suburbs of Kiev, Tbilisi and such cities as Kamensk-Uralsk, Serpukhov, Minsk, Borisov, Smolensk, Mozhaysk, Klin and others."[11]

Jamming continued to be a major issue for those in CIA involved in clandestine radio broadcasting, e.g., in July 1959:

> The big question has always been, however: are our broadcasts heard by a large enough number of people in the target areas to make the effort worthwhile? Or has the Soviet jamming system succeeded in preventing most of what we say in these broadcasts from reaching the ears of our potential listeners?
> This question for a long time has been burning the minds of those of us who have been directly connected with our black radio activities and who have always believed in radio propaganda as one of the most powerful weapons against communism, while others simply wanted to know, is the whole thing worth the money it costs? Yet, strangely enough no real effort has ever been made by KUBARK (CIA) to organize

monitoring of these broadcasts within the USSR despite the extensive travel in that country of a considerable number of people connected one way or another with KUBARK, and even some KUBARK personnel, not to mention the U.S. Government personnel stationed in Moscow.[12]

The details are not known but apparently when former Illinois Governor and presidential candidate Adlai Stevenson traveled to the USSR with this son in 1958, the son was asked to try and monitor Nasha Rossiya broadcasts to see if he could hear the call sign, even though he did not understand Russian.[13]

Nasha Rossiya programs were stopped for four weeks in October 1959 for analysis of its broadcasts. The transmitting site at Athens was described "as a base from which we can go on the air with unassigned frequencies, with propaganda broadcasts in various languages, without either prior or ex post facto censorship by local authorities."[14]

That month the responsible CIA unit for psychological operations proposed to phase out "black broadcasts to denied areas," including "regular news programs" to the USSR by October 31, 1959. Broadcasts of "fractional effort targeted at the USSR" were to continue, with "special broadcasts employing techniques, which only a clandestine station can use. For example, we would continue to into recordings of regular Soviet programs some subtle anti-Soviet propaganda We have found that this technique seems to avoid jammers and may produce a much more telling impact on the listener than a regular program."[15]

It is presumed that all broadcasts of Nasha Rossiya ceased in October 1959, or shortly thereafter, because *Broadcast Stations of the World* listed Nasha Rossiya as a clandestine station in Russian in the 1959 edition, but not in the 1960 edition.

## *Radio Free Russia*

### NTS

The initials NTS stand for "Narodno Trudovoi Soyuz—National Alliance of Russian Solidarists or National Labor Alliance" (in Russian: Национально Трудовой Союз, Народно-Трудовой Союз российских солидаристов—Narodno-Trudovoy Soyuz Rossiyskikh Solidaristov). The initials NTS were also used for two patriotic slogans "Nesem tiranam smert" (We are bringing death to tyrants) and "Nesem trudiashimsia svobodu" (We are bringing liberty to the workers).

CIA had a number of cryptonyms for NTS operations and projects, including: AEROSOL, AESAURUS / AENOBLE, AEGIDEON /

AENOBLE, QKDROOP, CARCASS, CABOCHE-1, PDGIDEON, and SHUBA-100.

NTS was founded in Belgrade, Kingdom of Yugoslavia, in 1928 (sometimes given at 1930) by a group of Russian exiles opposed to Soviet Communism. The ideology of NTS was strongly anti–Communist as expressed in its 1967 English language pamphlet:

> The NTS does not believe in opposing the Soviet regime by bomb throwing, sabotage and assassination. For although there is an inevitable conflict between the aspirations of the people for freedom and the firm intention of the Communist rulers to keep themselves in power, with time these aspirations will express themselves irresistibly on a mass scale. The philosophy of NTS is fundamentally Christian: Man should be his brother's keeper; one has an obligation to help people who are suffering oppression. The flexible and undogmatic "ideology" of NTS is called Solidarism.
>
> Unlike Communism, Solidarism provides a twentieth-century basis for dealing with present day issues. It rejects a purely materialistic approach to social, economic and political problems. It postulates that man, rather than matter, is the chief problem today. It rejects the concept of class warfare and hatred, and seeks to replace this dubious principle with the idea of co-operation (solidarity), brotherhood, Christian tolerance and charity. Solidarism believes in the innate dignity of the individual and seeks to safeguard as inalienable rights his freedom of speech, conscience and political organization. Solidarists in no way claim that their ideas represent the final answer to all problems, but they believe that man who is master of the atom bomb must also become master of himself and his destiny.[16]

The NTS ideology has been described as "anti–Western and anti-democratic." NTS has often been criticized for aligning itself with Nazi Germany in World War Two in the war against the USSR. After WWII, NTS set up its headquarters in Munich, Germany, and began publishing the newspaper "Possev" for its members.

Each member of NTS had to take an oath of allegiance, which was also heard in most of the NTS broadcasts:

> As a true and honest son of Russia, I give my word and swear to serve faithfully and devotedly, no matter what happens, the cause of Russia's freedom. I swear to be guided in everything I do by the honor and welfare of my Motherland and, at any cost, to carry out the instructions of the Revolutionary Staff of the NTS throughout the whole period of the revolutionary struggle.[17]

In August 1950, OPC's outline for the project proposed: "The OPC extend additional financial assistance, material support and operational guidance to NTS in order to facilitate expansion of its clandestine activities against the Soviet forces of occupation in Germany and Austria, and ultimately to facilitate penetration of the USSR"[18]: The immediate objectives of the project included:

a. To provide NTS with sufficient funds and policy guidance to enable it to increase its clandestine activities against the Soviet regime and, specifically, the Soviet occupation forces in Germany and Austria. The purpose of this campaign would be to undermine the morale and encourage defection, when we are prepared to handle it, of the Soviet occupation forces.

b. To provide NTS with sufficient funds and/or equipment to enable it to operate clandestine mobile short-wave stations along the border of the Soviet zones of Germany and Austria.[19]

Policy guidance and overall operational direction was provided by OPC headquarters, through the Chief Eastern European Division. $3,000 monthly was the expected financial support.[20]

The British Intelligence Service, SIS, began a cooperation with NTS in late 1950, and OPC had to coordinate its NTS operations with SIS until 1955. One of the British officers in Berlin at that time was George Blake, who would later defect to the USSR and be identified as a KGB officer. Thus the KGB was full informed about the NTS-CIA connection and NTS personnel in Berlin.[21]

According to one declassified CIA document: "Initial contact between this agency and NTS took place in May 1950 through support of NTS's anti-Soviet newspaper, *Possev*, which is published in Germany and distributed both overtly in Western Germany and covertly in Eastern Germany among Red Army personnel. NTS was not aware at the time that funds were supplied by a U.S. government source. Upon further appraisal of the NTS's operational potential and organization, this agency decided to contact NTS to discuss support of its overt and covert activities."[22]

## *Radio Free Russia*

In December 1950, NTS began broadcasting Radio Free Russia that was beamed at the Red Army in Eastern Germany from a station it owned and operated in the British Zone—the broadcast operation eventually moved into the U.S. Zone. The first transmitting station placed on a small truck was a small battery operated one of only 38 watts of power. There were no poles for the antennas, so trees were used instead.

The proposed OPC NTS Plan, April 9, 1951, read, in part:

Operation Radio

Problem: the preparation of opinion within Soviet territory facilitating the creation there of "molecules" of resistance, and direct contact with the revolutionary network net, both in the army of occupation and in the USSR proper.

1. Objectives. Regular daily broadcasts of propaganda material and of concrete instructions to existing "molecules" of resistance.

## 8. Focus on Russia

2. Implementation.
   (a) Procurement of two 1/2 kilowatt transmitters, one each for Berlin and Austria.
   (b) The development of radio-editorial work, which would include a station for monitoring of Soviet broadcasts, as well as a radio studio for the preparation of recordings for broadcasts.
   (c) Establishment, as a part of the staff, of a Propaganda Branch, which would control the material being broadcasts.
   (d) Study of the possibility of establishing a radio transmitter mounted on a sea-going vessel of small size.
   (e) Establishment of camouflage necessary for the security of the various stations.
   (f) Procurement of a 2 to 3 kilo-watt mobile station.[23]

One on CIA's earliest monitoring reports dated October 31, 1951, based on mid–July 1951 information listed the following
Subject: Clandestine Anti-Communist Radio Transmitter

- A radio broadcasting station which purports to represent "The Union of Nationalist Russians" and "Free Russia" has reportedly been transmitting programs in Russian and German languages for the past three months. The station is said to be located in Eastern Germany.
- The station devotes a large part of its broadcasting time to urging underground activities in the Soviet Army and sabotage in the Soviet industry.
- It comes on the air three times per day: at 10:30 a.m., 2 p.m., and 8 p.m. Beirut time, on either 45 or 47 meters. It sometimes shifts from one wavelength to the other during the same program. Its call sign is "N.T.S."[24]

The *Sydney Morning Herald* newspaper on Thursday, December 27, 1951, carried this article about NTS and Radio Free Russia by an unnamed Special Correspondent:

### Soviet Underground Grows in Europe

A strong "underground movement" led by Russian émigrés, is increasing the weight of Russian resistance to the Soviet police state. At the beginning of this year a new factor appeared in this struggle. N.T.S. established a mobile, unlicensed short-wave transmitter, "Free Russia." Each day it broadcasts anti–Communist propaganda in three languages: Russian, Ukrainian, and German. Being unrestrained by diplomatic relations with the Soviet Union, unlike "The Voice of America," NTS radio appeals to the Soviet Army and citizens to revolt. It sends out instructions on the organization of underground cells and their immediate tasks.

Soviet reaction was quick. The Soviet Ambassador in Vienna lodged a protest with the American authorities. The broadcasts of the radio station have ever since been jammed. To avoid this jamming, the station changes its wavelengths during the broadcasts, or transmits very close to those of the Soviet radio stations.

"Free Russia" also interferes in actual Soviet radio broadcasts. For example, a Soviet radio station, "Volga," the other day concluded its news commentary on life in Eastern Germany with the words, "The People's Democracy of Eastern Germany is strengthening daily. Under the vigilant eye of the M.V.D.," added the "voice" of "Free Russia."

The March 1952 NTS Operational Plan, "Petva-8," contained this passage:

> RADIO: This program called for the support of the present 1/2 kw station already in operation. In addition to this, support was asked for the construction of two other stations (1/2 kw) and one 2 kW station as well as mobile radio transmitters to be used along the border. We agreed that for all other operations, such as leaflet dissemination and clandestine radio activities, NTS would have responsibility for both effectiveness of operations and security; we would offer guidance and active assistance when we considered such to be necessary.[25]

In May 1952, there was a CIA evaluation of Radio Free Russia programs from February through December 1951. The analysis included this comment, "This, in general, seems to be very good propaganda."[26] The Progress Report for December 1952 included, "As soon as approval is granted for purchase of the necessary vehicles, Operation RADIO will be ready to get underway."[27]

CIA funding was given to NTS to enlarge the radio broadcast system. With the help of the CIA subsidized mobile transmitters, by May 1953 the original low NTS radio transmitting strength was increased by ten times and programs were broadcast simultaneously on three different shortwave wavelengths. One of the new pieces of equipment was a "control station" that allowed NTS technicians to monitor both Radio Free Russia and Soviet jamming simultaneously. The technicians would then change the Radio Free Russia slightly to avoid the jamming. NTS also had "listening posts" in Norway, Sweden, and Finland.

In May 1954, NTS head and co-founder of NTS Constantin Wasilevich Boldyreff (Konstantin Boldyrev—Константин Васильевич Болдырев) testified before the U.S. Senate Committee on the Judiciary and described Radio Free Russia. He said, in part:

> The underground has a clandestine model radio station, Free Russia. This is a black station and it has no inhibitions. It actually broadcasts on Soviet wavelengths whenever it can come, butting in, trying to use the pauses in the Soviet programs to throw in a slogan, and caustic remarks and a message, and so on.
>
> Then it also gives eight regular daily programs on its own wave-lengths, which are, of course, exposed to jamming, but it then moves to a neighboring wavelength, asking the listener to tune to it, and it takes some time for the Soviet jammers to tune their installations to a new wavelength. Thus, there is always a margin of a couple of minutes when the listener can get every word of the message and since the messages are always frequently repeated anyone who really has the persistence will get the entire message without fail.
>
> During maneuvers the tanks, for instance great facilities to listen to underground

## 8. Focus on Russia

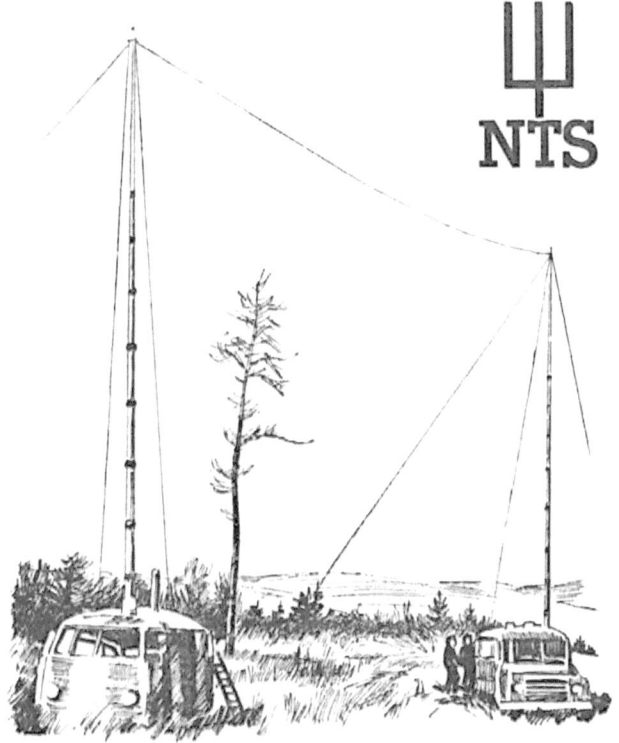

„Свободная Россия"
radio - station
„FREE RUSSIA"

**A Radio Free Russia QSL card for listeners to complete and forward to NTS.**

messages. This is what Radio Free Russia does. Of course, compared to the Voice of America, or BBC, it is a mosquito, but it has potential penetrative power incomparably greater than that of the Voice of America.[28]

By 1958, Radio Free Russia was on the air daily from 8:30 to 15:30, with one program in German to East Germany on Thursdays. The typical 20-minute program began with music from Tchaikovsky's Fifth Symphony and this announcement, which would slightly change over the years:

> NTS speaking. Attention. Attention!
> Within the USSR itself, radio still constitutes the only important means used currently to reach the Russian people. Jamming by the Russian radio of our broadcasts

continues to present a major problem. There was however, a perceptible increase in effectiveness of our radio resources in the last six months due to the inauguration of Radio Liberation and the stepped-up activity of Radio Free Russia. In addition to the radio, leaflet distribution was utilized to reach Soviet military forces stationed outside the USSR.

You are hearing the station Free Russia. Attention, Attention! Here is NTS speaking. Long live Freedom (Liberty).[29]

The programs consisted of brief news, comments on current affairs, ideological subjects, appeals and directions to revolutionary workers and NTS members in the USSR. Twice a week, Radio Free Russia broadcast a special program to Soviet soldiers stationed in East Germany.

In addition to instructions on how to organize revolutionary activities in the army, NTS broadcast lyrics to popular Soviet music, including: "Comrades on the Front: We have always played the game; Let your choice today be blunt—Russia's freedom is our aim."

Humor was included in programming, including, "Lenin was a Marxist—Stalin was a sadist—but Khrushchev is only a tourist."[30]

NTS attempted to place Radio Free Russia broadcasts on the wavelengths of Moscow radio stations. One reportedly successful attempt was when Radio Moscow was broadcasting an opera, with news of current events. The audience included officers of the Soviet army stationed in East Germany, who had gathered in the officer's mess. An NTS announcer cut into news announcements with sarcastic remarks and "Long live Freedom (Liberty)." As the program ended with "This is Radio Moscow. We have given you the latest news. Now you can hear the bells of the Kremlin tower." At this point, an announcer of NTS broke into the broadcast with, "You have also heard the underground radio station Radio Free Russia. Alliance of the Russian Solidarists speaking. Death to the tyrants! Freedom for the people."[31]

There was no way to measure the listening audience of NTS programs but hostile reactions of the Soviet government gave some indication of the effectiveness of the broadcasts. These reactions included kidnappings and attempted kidnapping of NTS member, murder attempts, and bombings of the NTS print shop and headquarters, as well the transmitting station in 1958, and antenna fields. One famous kidnapping of a NTS leader was that of Dr. Alexander Trushnovich on April 15, 1954, in West Berlin. He had been invited into an apartment of a man, who had assisted him for a few months. Trushnovich was never seen again. When police entered the apartment, they found it in disorder, with blood stains on the floor.[32]

Another kidnapping of the NTS leader was that of Valery Tremmel in Linz, Austria, in June 1954. He reportedly was drugged by two Soviet agents in his apartment and driven to the Soviet Sector of Vienna. An official Soviet statement said that he had been arrested while distributing pamphlets in Soviet Zone. He was sentenced to 20 years imprisonment and was never seen again.[33]

In addition to kidnapping and bombings, the Soviet KGB sent assassins to kill NTS leaders: "The KGB's 'Operation Rhein' gained world-wide notoriety in 1954, when the KGB Captain Nicolai Khokhlov was sent with two German agents to kill the NTS leader George Okolovich. Instead, Khokhlov went over to the NTS and disclosed the whole plot to Western Intelligence, handing over his famous cigarette-case pistol. In 1955 an East German called Wildprett was sent to kill the President of NTS, Dr. V.D. Poremsky, but he also gave himself up to the NTS."[34]

Gordon Young in his 1959 book, *The House of Secrets: Russian Resistance to the Soviet Union Today*, describes the broadcasting operation of Radio Free Russia in Germany:

> It was an idyllic scene that we encountered at last, in a peaceful apple orchard far out in the country. Under the shade of an apple tree a man in an open shirt was lying on an old mattress quietly smoking. (He was a relief technician waiting to go on duty.) Nearby was a plain fray-green fan from which came a series of noises, buzzes, and atmospheric walls. And standing by the wan gazing at the complicated radio dials and switches within was the inevitable small boy sucking a blade of grass. This was the control station, where the Free Russia emissions are received on two wavelengths simultaneously with the Soviet jamming. Inside the van sat a massive Russian technician, a former Soviet Navy sailor, watching the radio dials and speaking on a radio-telephone to the mobile transmitting van, sending continual instructions for slight adjustments to the wavelengths to dodge the Soviet interference. "It's not too bad this afternoon," he told me, "but the jamming gets really ferocious later in the evenings." Thanks to this van, the gift, I was told, of private American supporters of the NTS, the possibilities of efficient reception has been greatly increased. Some distance away from the van, under another apple tree, was the small electric generator providing the current for the van. No need any longer to rely on the primitive batteries with which the first transmitters were forced to operate and which always intended to expire at critical moments.
>
> The actual transmitting station we found about three miles away in the shadow of a farm—two large lorries incongruously surround by an assortment of chickens, dogs, cows, and ripening tomatoes.
>
> One set of programs of about 20 minutes is sent all day long, with intervals for about six hours a day, seven days a week.[35]

## Broadcasts to Cuba

After the Cuban missile crisis in October 1962, in November the U.S: based NTS operation began broadcasting Russian-language programs under the direction of Constantin Boldyreff from clandestine radio stations "Radio Libertad" and "Radio Caribe" to Soviet technicians and military stationed in Cuba. The broadcasts apparently originated out of the Dominican Republic and aired nightly at 22:45 simultaneously on three short-wave and five standard AM frequencies. Here is an excerpt from one of the broadcasts broadcast from Santo Domingo, Dominican Republic:

> Our Troops must be withdrawn from Cuba, where their presence provokes popular anger. Under no circumstances may our troops be used for the suppression of a popular revolt against Castro in Cuba. The oath of allegiance does not obligate our officers and men to submit to the orders to fire at the civilian population.[36]

Another program was addressed to the Soviet Commander in Chief in Cuba: "To shoot? Will you really order to shoot? To shoot ... and thereby to cover the name of our nation, you own name, with the disgraceful stain of murderer?"[37] Radio Free Russia always used "we" to signify that NTS and the Russian people were together.

The Soviet weekly newspaper *Golos Rodiny* (Voice of the Motherland) for Russians in East Germany wrote, "From the moment the Cuban conflict started, this 'Voice of a free Russia' has been croaking lies to disturb Soviet citizens in Cuba."[38]

## NTS on Taiwan

At a radio conference in Europe in 1953, representatives of Nationalist China and NTS met for the first time. Reportedly, the Chinese Nationalists were "favorably impressed with the work of NTS" and even supplied and planned to continue to supply NTS with materials for broadcasting and publications. Dr. Roman Redlich of NTS reportedly flew to Taiwan in late 1955 to establish his residence and work with the Chinese Nationalists in a "joint effort against Communism." In 1957, NTS received permission to broadcast out of Taiwan to the Eastern USSR via a powerful short-wave transmitter. Eventually, Radio Free Russia broadcast broadcast an average of ten hours daily.[39]

Redlich was succeeded by veteran NTS member Gleb Rahr, who arrived in 1957 or 1958 and remained there until 1960, when he moved to Japan to teach Russian at the University of Tokyo. In 1963, he returned to NTS in Germany, where he worked until 1974 (possibly the date that Radio Free Russia ceased broadcasting) before working for Radio Liberty in Munich. Rahr then wrote and recorded religious programs for Radio Liberty until it moved to Prague in 1995.

NTS also broadcast at one point over the Korean Broadcast System (KBS) in Seoul, Korea, twice daily 14:15–14:30 and 21:15–21:30.

In the mid–1960s, NTS in Germany also allowed "The Voice of Free Latvia" to broadcast one ten-minute program daily from 21:00 to 21:30 (original and repeat). This was done strictly on a financial basis, as there were ideological conflicts with the Latvian exile community and pro–Russia NTS. The Latvian émigré community did not financially support these broadcasts and they stopped in 1971 due to lack of funds.

### Effectiveness of NTS

It is difficult to estimate the effectiveness of NTS broadcasts due to paucity of audience research materials. That being said, the KGB took NTS seriously. The first example is a comment by the First Deputy of the KGB Chairman, S.K. Zvigun, during a meeting of KGB and Stasi (East German officers) in Moscow on November 13, 1969:

> Please allow me, Comrade Mielke, to express our thanks for your support so far in the fight against the anti–Soviet organization NTS [National Alliance of Russian Solidarists], various nationalist centers, and organizations in West Germany. We appreciate that you met with us in person and have placed such a strong emphasis on the fight against ideological subversion and are directing your personal attention to these issues…. [T]he enemy devotes major attention to anti–Soviet organizations and émigré associations. This concerns in particular the NTS. I again want to take the opportunity to thank you for your support in this regard.
> 
> Though various measures applied by the state security services, the NTS had already suffered heavy blows and was about to evaporate. Before Comrade Andropov took over the KGB leadership, we thought that the NTS was no longer active and operative attention was no longer required. However, later on we received new information about a re-activation of NTS activities. Several contact people have already been arrested in the Soviet Union. You certainly know about the trial. NTS activities remain a serious threat and operative work against them will have to resume.[40]

## Free Russia Fund

The 1967 NTS Information Pamphlet in English contained wording similar to the Free Europe Fund used in support of Radio Free Europe:

FREE RUSSIA FUND (Fund-raising for the NTS) NTS NEEDS YOUR HELP
  Russian Freedom Fighters—in the frontline of the battle against Communism—are protecting your freedom while fighting for theirs. They need your help! Trained, experienced, dedicated, they attack Communism where it is most vulnerable—inside the USSR and in Soviet outposts throughout the world. They use the weapons most dangerous to Communist—the truth … positive ideas of freedom … and practical means for achieving it in Russia and other captive countries.
  Donations should be sent to: NTS–FR Swiss Bank Association, Basel, Switzerland Conto No. XXX XXX or forwarded through any NTS members in your country.[41]

There is no available information on just when CIA decided to stop funding Radio Free Russia in Taiwan or in Germany. One unconfirmed report has it broadcasting in Germany until 1974.[42]

## TsOPE (ЦОПЭ)

CIA's created and controlled the Russian émigré organization "Central Association of Post-War Émigrés" (TsOPE—transliteration of ЦОПЭ-Центральное Объединение Послевоенных Эмигрантов) was founded in November 1952, most likely a result of CIA's frustration in the "labyrinthine maze" of uniting the alphabet soup of Russian émigré groups in Germany. CIA cryptonyms for TsOPE included:

- HBDUCKPIN,
- AEPAWN, and
- AEVIRGIL-1

According to one declassified CIA document, "TsOPE was created and is being supported and controlled by CIA in order to develop and utilize some of the human resources in the Russian anti–Soviet emigration in support of CIA's political and psychological objective of accelerating evolutionary changes in the character and policy of the Soviet regime."[43]

Through liaison with United States Escapee Program (USEP), Association of Friends of Russian Freedom (AFRF), Tolstoy Foundation, and other agencies, TsOPE assisted "the more unfortunate Russian emigrants, thereby helping to eliminate the deplorable conditions, which still represent a propaganda blot on the record of the West."

> Since CIA cannot finance welfare activity, TsOPE itself cannot grant direct welfare assistance. However, through overt contacts with the agencies mentioned above, TsOPE brings needy cases to the attention of appropriate officials, assists emigres to qualify for and obtain assistance—medical, vocational, food, etc.—and in general seeks to alleviate the situation of poverty and hopelessness attending the bulk of the post-war emigres. The organization thereby plays an important role in reducing one vulnerability in our psychological warfare effort, and in mobilizing emigre support of active anti–Soviet work.[44]

The name of the organization was changed in 1953 to Central Association of Political Émigrés from the USSR—Центральное объединение политических эмигрантов из СССР. The term "post war emigres" was eliminated basically because "there were not enough defectors to fill the ranks."[45]

TsOPE's headquarters was set up in Munich, Germany. According to one declassified CIA document, "From 11 to 14 November 1952, the Central Union of Post-War Émigrés held an organizational conference in Munich under covert CIA direction…. Western press recognized the potentialities of this organization as an anti-communist weapon. The fact that VOA, BBC, and Radio Liberation made an unprecedented number of excellent tape recordings for radio broadcasts beamed to the Soviet Union is an indication of the psychological warfare potential of TsOPE."[46]

## 8. Focus on Russia

CIA funding of TsOPE's activities were covered by double books are maintained; transmission of some funds is through banking channels, and the belief is fostered that support comes from anonymous donors; provision for membership dues also provides cover for some part of the finances. The possibility of initiating a large-scale drive for funds to provide at least a measure of overt and definite attributability to TsOPE's funds is currently being studied.

On some occasions, funds are also transferred through regular banking channels from Switzerland to TsOPE, solely as a cover device to add bona fide sources for income listed in TsOPE overt books. These books show only those expenditures, which can be easily traced.[47]

CIA full control of TsOPE was ensured since the organization was "entirely dependent of CIA financial support, and since the leaders of the organization have already learned to be depend heavily upon CIA guidance." In addition, "control of all aspects of the projects will be exercised by a KUBARK (CIA) senior case officer, who will deal directly with the president of the organization, with the editor of the publications, and if necessary with the president's Deputy for Welfare and Personnel."[48]

TsOPE's first "Chairman of the Presidium," i.e., president, was Grigory (Grigorii) Petrovich Klimov (CIA pseudonym: James N. Dussardie), a former Soviet army officer, who had defected to West Germany in 1947. In 1951 his book *Berliner Kreml* (The Kremlin of Berlin) was published in Germany and in 1953 the book was published in English as *The Terror Machine: The Inside Story of the Soviet Administration in Germany*. In 1955, Klimov resigned from TsOPE and emigrated to the United States.

At one point in the early Cold War, TsOPE members wrote and produced a weekly half-hour show over Voice of America studios in Munich titled "Life in the Free West through Our Eyes." TsOPE also was heavily involved in the printing and distribution of Boris Pasternak's novel *Dr. Zhivago* through mailings and personal contacts with Soviet visitors to the West.[49]

TsOPE also had chapters in Brussels, Paris, and Vienna. With the election in May 1958 of a new chairman and board of directors, CIA's SR Division turned its attention during FY 1959 toward tightening the organization through stronger internal executive control and supervision. The new chairman, Theodor Lebedev, "managed during the year to instill much-needed discipline within the organization, while broadening its appeal to anti–Soviet emigres in other areas. With the attraction of new members, the chairman has succeeded in his attempt to make the organization a dynamic and expanding group."[50]

TsOPE Chairman, Mikhail Dziuba, gave up his post in May 1958 because he was waiting only for the completion of the formalities that were delaying his emigration from Germany to the United States. After a few months, he expressed a desire that at the time of his emigration he was not to have anything further to do with the overt activity of TsOPE. After he arrived in the U.S. in September 1958, the TsOPE representative in the U.S. gave him advice and assistance in finding employment. He made no more demands from the CIA. His termination by mutual agreement was not expected to have an adverse effect on future project activity with TsOPE.[51]

The request for Project Renewal Fiscal Year 1958 contained these accomplishments:

- Produced and disseminated Russian language leaflets and a monthly magazine (Svoboda).
- Held propaganda meetings and press conferences.
- Engaged in psychological warfare against the Soviet target.
- Produced a weekly radio program over the Munich radio facilities of Voice of America. With its new resources TsOPE hopes to play a larger role in other areas of the world. Particular reference is made to the radio stations existing in such places as Madrid.[52]

In April 1959, through the TsOPE representative at Radio Nacional de España, the TsOPE brochure *The Soviet Naval Officer* was translated into Spanish with the approval of the Spanish Government, for distribution to various Spanish-speaking countries.

TsOPE was used by CIA not only for Foreign Intelligence (FI) operations, but also for Political and Psychological (PP) operations, including the launching of thousands of balloons and millions of propaganda leaflets from then West Berlin and Bavaria. During FY 1959 unknown circumstances forced CIA to move permanently a TsOPE leaflet balloon activity from Western Berlin to West Germany. The two TsOPE balloon teams continued their operations from West Germany, but both the number of East German visitors to the TsOPE Berlin office and the FI take declined sharply as a result of the discontinuation of ballooning from Berlin itself.

From July 1959 to March 1960, between twelve million and fifteen million leaflets a month were ballooned from West Germany to the Soviet Army concentration points in East Germany. Ballooning ceased in March 1960, before then TsOPE wrote, edited, and printed an average of six leaflets monthly.[53]

The Fiscal Year 1959 Project Renewal Request included these comments about radio broadcasting:

> During the past year TsOPE has been active participation in the Russian broadcast efforts of Radio Nacional de España, Radio Rome and Nationalist Radio on Formosa. Since initiation of these activities 62 15-minute TsOPE programs were broadcast from Formosa, 122 TsOPE scripts were broadcast over Radio Rome and 293 over Radio Nacional de España. In the latter case, a TsOPE radio propagandist has been accepted

## 8. Focus on Russia

as a regular employee of Radio Nacional and CIA is able to transmit guidance to the radio through this controlled asset. In addition to the scripts produced locally, TsOPE Munich transmits an average of 40 scripts a month to Madrid for broadcast over Radio Nacional.[54]

The Fiscal Year 1960 Project Renewal Request gave some details of TsOPE's radio broadcasting activities:

> The current objective of the project is to use this organization to sponsor the production and distribution of written propaganda and for the conduct of PP (political and psychological) operations against the USSR and its nationals at home and abroad. The organization produces books, magazines, brochures, articles, leaflets, radio scripts and broadcast tapes and directs them toward the Soviet target. TsOPE's contact in Radio Rome reported in the spring of 1959 that some 27 TsOPE radio scripts were then being used each month, in contrast to a much smaller number broadcast at the beginning of FY 1959, The TsOPE agent at RNE in Madrid got approximately 27 Russian scripts per month on the air, and he also supplied material for the Bulgarian, Estonian, and Latvian sections of RNE.
>
> The natural cover provided by TSOPE's status as a bona fide émigré organization, approved as a tax-free group by the West German Government, still applies.
>
> Radio scripts will continue to be sent to Madrid, Rome, and Formosa-and possibly to Turkey.[55]

The Chief, Munich Base sent a report to Chief, SR, dated June 29, 1960, that gave a precise summary of TsOPE's radio activities:

> The Radio Department AEVIRGIL provides radio scripts for three radio broadcasting stations; namely, the Rome Radio Station, Radio Madrid and the Chinese government station in Taiwan. The relationship with the Rome Radio Station is the best. The bulk of the Russian program of the Rome Station—outside of current news broadcasts—consist of AEVIRGIL scripts and of other material derived from AEVIRGIL periodicals and other publications. The chiefs of the Radio Station have expressed on a number of occasions their deep appreciation for AEVIRGIL cooperation. The heed of the Russian programs of the station stated that without AEVIRGIL impart she would net hem how she could accomplish her task become. the Italian government's financial support is so small that she seed net hove beam able to produce decent Russian language programs.
>
> The relationship with the management of Radio Madrid is not as satisfactory became of the attitude of the current chief of the station and of local conditions. Nevertheless, 20 to 25 Madrid scripts are being broadcast monthly by the Russian section of Radio Madrid, a somewhat larger number Is broadcast by the Bulgarian section and various members of scripts by the Estonian, Latvian and Polish sections. Besides, AEVIRGIL material is widely used for the daily bulletins distributed to the various sections of Radio Madrid. One monthly, completely AEVIRGIL program is also broadcast by the radio station.
>
> The Taiwan Radio Station obtains monthly four or more taped 15-minute AEVIRGIL programs.[56]

According to the FY 1961 Renewal Request: from July 1, 1959, through October 1960, the TsOPE radio team produced and forwarded 592 scripts to their Radio Rome contact and 649 scripts to their representative with Radio Nacional de España (an average of thirty-seven and forty scripts per month respectively). Seventy-two 15-minute radio programs were taped, sent to Taiwan, and transmitted over the Broadcast Corporation of China (BCC) facilities (approximately four a month). Of the scripts sent to Radio Rome, 297 were used, which, allowing for no reporting in two of the sixteen months involved, averages twenty-one per month.[57]

Of the material furnished to the TsOPE Madrid representative,

- 363 scripts were used by the Russian Section of RNE;
- 349 were translated and used by the Bulgarian Section;
- 96 by the Estonian Section;
- 7 by the Polish Section
- 7 by the Latvian Section
- Twelve scripts were used as background by Russian Section members other than the TsOPE representative;
- 70 items were used in special Radio España broadcasts;
- 214 items were translated into Spanish and printed in the RNE foreign section bulletin; and
- 15 special programs were broadcast in the name of TsOPE (one a month).
- The TsOPE representative himself also made one broadcast.[58]

TsOPE RNE broadcasts were "carefully conceived for the Soviet audience and directed toward specific objectives with definite principles; however, their effectiveness, the case officer adds, is limited by the inept content of most of the rest of the program. Both TSOPE representative and the Madrid Station are working toward a solution of this problem."[59]

From July 1, 1959, through October 1960, some TsOPE leaders received threatening or blackmail letters if they did not stop their activities. Attacks against the TsOPE office included stink bombs, landlord intimidations, leaflets, and telephone calls. The most serious cases of hostile actions were the December 1959 bombing of TsOPE headquarters in Munich and the attempted kidnapping of TsOPE member Kirstein in Berlin in July 1960.[60] However, in 1962, "through unexplained double-agent information, CIA aware of continuing Russian Intelligence Service interest in TsOPE; however, at the moment no serious or specific threat to the group's security is apparent."[61]

The TsOPE representative was not only involved with broadcasts over RNE but also in foreign intelligence activities:

> TsOPE representatives sent by the group's Munich Headquarters to other locales have been and can be used to even greater advantage by local CIA officers to support unilateral Agency operations. Instances of progress toward this objective were noted during the past year in Spain and Austria. In Spain the TsOPE representative, in addition

## 8. Focus on Russia

to his assigned work in the Russian Section of Radio Nacional España, introduced Madrid case officers to Spanish repatriates from the USSR, penetrated what the case officer calls "the key social organization to the future of Spain," the Sindicatos, and performed other informant functions possible because of his access to local targets.[62]

In Fiscal Year 1961, TsOPE Munich radio section produced approximately 1,000 scripts and 48 15-minute taped programs, which were broadcast by the BCC in Taiwan. while the former served as a basis for approximately 21 broadcasts a month over Radio Rome and 50 Russian-language broadcasts monthly over Radio Madrid. At Radio Madrid much of the TsOPE material was also translated and used for broadcasts to Satellite countries.[63]

TsOPE's contribution to Radio Rome and the BCC site Taiwan remained at the same level during FY 1961 as during FY 1960; however, there was an increase in the amount of TsOPE material used at RNE. The TsOPE Madrid Representative's gradually increasing influence on the program content can be seen by the following figures on RNE's use of TsOPE material:

|  | FY1960 | FY1961 |
|---|---|---|
| No. of scripts sent from Munich to Madrid | 489 | 607 |
| Russian Section Broadcasts | 277 | 417 |
| Bulgarian Section | 249 | 550 |
| Estonian Section | 61 | 57 |
| Polish Section | 6 | 6 |
| Latvian Section | 5 | 2 |
| TsOPE Broadcasts | 12 | 12 |
| Items in RFE's foreign section bulletin | 148 | 292[64] |

According to a 1962 project review, there were 305 TsOPE international members, with the majority in Germany (132), Belgium (97), USA (24), and Israel (19). There was an "affiliate" group in Sweden with 17 persons, who conducted anti–Soviet activities in Sweden. The objective of TsOPE's radio section was, "To collect and prepare anti–Soviet propaganda for broadcast to the Soviet Union, China and other countries in the Soviet orbit." Seventy to 75 scripts per month were accepted by TsOPE "from a variety of authors all over the world." These scripts were edited, translated when necessary, and sent to Madrid, Rome, and Taiwan for broadcasting.[65]

## Termination of the CIA-TsOPE Broadcasts

In 1961 and 1962, there was debate at CIA concerning the future of TsOPE. The future plans of TsOPE were described as

While we recognize that there are severe inherent limitations on the long-range viability of TsOPE as a political organization, dependent as it is on the organizational and propaganda-writing abilities of a very few people who cannot be replaced should they die or become sick, the propaganda assets of the organization are the only ones of their kind over which we exert full control and which can be used any way we desire in pursuit of CIA aims. To terminate the project now would deprive us of this asset before we ever tried to get the most out of realistically and in the face of a foreseeable need for as many assets as possible to reach the people in the Soviet Union.[66]

The argument did not prevail and Project AEVIRGIL and TsOPE operations were terminated in the summer 1963 for the following reasons:

- TsOPE's usefulness has been superseded by events and because the CIA personnel and resources allotted to its support could now be used more effectively in other forms of CA (Covert Action) activity.
- In the past decade TsOPE's leadership has grown old.
- As their years in the West increased, their understanding of and appeal to the Soviet man has inevitably decreased.
- Internal dissension has arisen within the group;
- Strategic members have resigned either under pressure or voluntarily; and there are no new, fresh members of the emigration who can be readily found to replace the old.
- Many of the group's activities have been curtailed by lack of personnel, budget reductions during recent years, or simply, external circumstances.
- Radio Rome ceased broadcasting in Russian.

A review of AEVIRGIL production as reflected in renewals of past years indicates that the project did justify its existence and did serve for almost a decade as a mainstay in the total SR/CA (Soviet Russia/Covert Action) effort.[67]

The final figures of radio broadcasts for fiscal year 1962 were:

- 240 broadcasts over Radio Rome (prior to the time Russian-language broadcasting was discontinued);
- 1613 broadcasts over Radio Madrid (in Russian, Bulgarian, Estonian and Polish)[68]

## *Kidnapping of Gottfried Burghardt*

Project CARRERA originated as a subproject of CIA's East European (EE) Division's Project REDCAP on October 3, 1953, under control of the Berlin Operations Base (BOB).[69] Its purpose was "to further the REDCAP program by means of exploiting the REDCAP leads resulting from the distribution of AEPAWN propaganda." REDCAP was "the planned collection of information on Soviet personnel stationed abroad for the purpose of personal exploitation, including defection inducement." The background was listed as "it is believed that an AEPAWN office in Berlin provides the best and most logical channel for following up REDCAP leads derived from the TsOPE propaganda distribution, by enabling recipients of this propaganda to contact an overt office on safe ground."⁷⁰

The objective of Project CARRERA was "to set up a Berlin office using the name of AEPAWN for cover and to install a REDCAP agent in the office for the purpose outlined above." There were two tasks listed in the project outline:

1. To receive, debrief, and obtain an initial impression of the motives willingness, etc., of visitors who, having received AEPAWN propaganda, come to the office on their own initiative to supply intonation or REDCAP leads or to aid the anti–Communist cause
2. To arrange for contact between leads so developed and REDCAP operational personnel of Berlin Operations Base.⁷¹

Personnel in the CARRERA office included:

1. The case officer was a Russian-born contract agent employed by CIA since 1951 under the cover of a "Department of Army civilian employee," and
2. Gottlieb Burghardt, Primary Agent (PA), a 54-year-old Russian-born German citizen residing in Berlin as a political refugee since 1951; bilingual in Russian and German; no previous intelligence training; cautious, security conscious, excellent listener. He had been security cleared on August 12, 1953.⁷²

Gottlieb Burghardt was born on April 22, 1899. One CIA cryptonym for Gottlieb Burghardt was AECADILT-1. Burghardt's wife, Ilse, also worked in the TsOPE office with cryptonym AECADILT-2.

The coordination of CARRERA activity was between the TsOPE case officer in Munich and the Chief of REDCAP in Berlin. The SR Division was the coordinating element at CIA headquarters.

In May 1954, the Berlin Operations Base requested 300 DM to purchase and maintain for four months a "police dog" for Burghardt's protection as it was believed "the Soviets may contemplate abducting Burghardt. His apartment had been broken into and ransacked."⁷³ In October 1954, BOB decided to move the Burghardt and his wife into a new apartment. The request for additional money included this statement, "Burghardt has been the subject of previous RIS (Russian Intelligence Service) attempts in the past."⁷⁴

In November 1954, the Frankfurt Chief of Mission presented a request to Headquarters for the renewal of Project CARRERA, including a request for a second Principal Agent:

> The project has demonstrated in the past its value as a tool of REDCAP activities. The experience of the first year, and particularly of the last months, shows a constantly rising number of contacts and leads attracted by the CARRERA office. Regardless of his energy and dedication, Burghardt, who is assisted only in the German-language clerical work by Ilse Burghardt, is not able any longer to cope efficiently with the increased work load. In several instances favorable opportunities for both the gathering of intelligence data and defection inducement have been explored less thoroughly than such leads would warrant. It appears imperative to assign an additional principal agent to this project, who could take over a part of the operational load.[75]

Burghardt's main function was to "manage the office, debrief, screen, and select the most promising leads." The second Principal Agent would "explore and develop these leads, especially those which, for security and operational reasons, could be best handled outside the office." The CARRERA project developed into "a highly workable tool for the implementation of REDCAP objectives, strengthening also the political prestige of AEVIRGIL as an active fighting group of anti–Communist Soviet refuges." The project's listed objectives were:

- Gathering of military and political intelligence data on SOPG troops and personnel;
- Gathering of data concerning the morale and attitudes of SOPG and Soviet civilian personnel;
- Gathering of data on Soviet installations in the Soviet zone of occupation.
- Inducement of defection (both physical and in place) among SOPG personnel.
- Promotion of general anti–Communist ideas among Soviet personnel in Germany and support of defection inducement by distribution of AEVIRGIL propaganda.[76]

Burghardt's background was listed as

> Russo-German emigre. Perfect command of both languages. In World War II fought on the German side in a Cossack unit and had experience of low-level tactical military intelligence. After World War II employed in an East-German trade organization which supplied Soviet military units. At that time had connections with BIS (British Intelligence Service), which he severed when he refugeed to West Berlin.
> Character-wise stable, Sober, extremely diligent and dedicated to anti–Communist political work among Russians. Slow but methodical debriefer, sober and factual reporter. Inspires confidence to low and medium-level contacts
> Was selected for the job in 1953 simply because he was cleared and available but developed to be the most suitable agent to fill the job and contributed essentially to the methodic conduct of the project in 1953–1954.[77]

It was noted that Burghardt, "Has no cover since he is openly employed with the TsOPE office. In social contacts he poses as a translator in subordinate position." And, "the principal agent has a strong ideological motivation. The material factor is very secondary though the fact that his present activities provide him with a steady job and salary after a protracted period of unemployment is an additional motivational factor."[78]

Burghardt's contacts with his Soviet zone based collaborators took place by pre-arranged meetings in West Berlin, mostly in TsOPE's office, sometimes outside in public places.

The justification for the security expenses of $250.00 were given as:

> In view of the increased risk and hazards involved in (Burghardt's) work, the following amount must be provided to cover security expenses (moves from one abode to another), acquisition of protective means, etc.
>
> No special commitments have been made to either (Burghardt) or (his wife) but it is felt at this Base that Burghardt's reliable and courageous performance on two occasions and the almost constant danger of abduction involved in his daily work require that some commitments be made at this time.
>
> It is recommended to provide in case of any violence committed by the opposition against Burghardt (serious physical injuries, death or abduction and resulting in a protracted lack of earnings) for a compensation in the amount of $1,250.00 to be payable to his wife in a lump sum in in such amounts which will be agreed upon this organization and his wife.[79]

The January 1955 project extension also request included this comment:

> The field office Outline, containing the request for renewal, incorporates numerous changes, including requests for additional funds and personnel. However, in view of the increasing and continuing attempts by the RIS to penetrate the CARRERA office in Berlin, EE feels that additional provisions should be made to protect the Principal Agent and the provisions mew proposed in the renewal are inadequate. We are querying the Field on proposals for increased protection. Meanwhile, the Field has requested and EE agrees that the Principal Agent deserves an increase in salary of $25.00 per month.[80]

The April 1955 project renewal request for the period 1 April 1955 through 31 March 1956, included the statement that in November 1954, the TsOPE office was burglarized and some case files stolen. Because Burghardt later was threatened by an anonymous phone call and letter, physical security measures to him and his wife were undertaken. These included the purchase of a vehicle, which was justified as

> the need for this vehicle arises out of operational requirements, security considerations, and from considerations for the welfare of a principal agent, whose welfare is believed to be in jeopardy. The use of this vehicle ... is intended to allow the principal agent a means of transportation necessary to accomplish the large number of meetings which arise outside of the project office. The principal agent is exposed because of his overt association with the project office. To date he has been entirely

dependent on public transportation, which are considered inadequate because he is exposed to physical danger and possible abduction. It should be pointed out that the principal agent has already received an anonymous threat against his life. The principal agent has no direct contact with the Berlin Operations Base; and because of his overt connections with the project office, he would immediately blow any station quasi-personal vehicle he might use.[81]

The July 1955 Amendment to Project CARRERA had this comment:

> The workload of the AECARRERA office has been progressively increasing and Burghardt has been handling this increased workload without complaint and at the expense of his physical well-being. In order to meet this heavy contact schedule, he has been on duty evenings and weekends. The field feels that even with the addition of an assistant, Burghardt will continue to carry a heavy work schedule since he will spend more time with individual contacts and follow leads with greater persistence.[82]

## Kidnapping

On December 15, 1956, at 7 p.m., Gottlieb Burghardt went to keep an operational contact meeting with DDR contact Waltraud RICHTER. The next day Ilse Burghardt reported that her husband was missing. CIA could not understand Burghardt's failure to take the necessary precautions in going to a night meeting alone with a suspect contact.[83]

A short second page article in the East Berlin newspaper *Berliner Zeitung* on December 18, 1956, mentioned that Burghardt was reportedly seized on an East Berlin street by pedestrians when he was molesting them. He also was alleged to be drunk and carrying a pistol. The story was viewed by CIA as an East Germany MFS or Soviet KGB effort to cover the kidnapping in event that Burghardt was to be used publicly later in which case his presence in East Berlin would have to be explained.[84]

Ilse Burghardt wrote a letter to Attorney Wolfgang Vogel on January 2, 1957, asking him for his help in the case. He agreed and they met for the first time on January 30, 1957. Subsequently, Wolfgang Vogel reportedly stated he had learned from DDR authorities that Burghardt was kidnapped and he was to be tried under Article 6 of the DDR Constitution which includes espionage activities.[85]

The West Berlin police took an active part in the investigation and put four people in custody, who allegedly formed an MFS kidnap team that was originally given the assignment by the MFS to kidnap Burghardt. Another team was organized and given the assignment according to the testimony of one of the people in custody.

The Berlin Operations Base tried to do all it could to aid Burghardt, e.g., "No psychological / propaganda activity was undertaken pending determination of the best tactics to be utilized in the case: a. a statement

## 8. Focus on Russia 175

that Burghardt kidnapped made at time of incident and we in fact have nothing more to say now, and b. on balance we feel strong play this stage would force DDR court to throw book at Burghardt in self-justification.... [W]e are attempting via police keep lid on previous kidnap plot. Plan use this as counter blast ... this might catch them off balance and upset prearranged plans thus benefit."[86]

All key personalities in the DDR with whom Burghardt and TsOPE had contact, were notified of Burghardt's kidnapping and each contact individually decided what action would be in their best personal interests. TsOPE offered limited aid toward political recognition if they decide to seek refuges status in the West. Burghardt's kidnapping culminated a three-year history of RIS interest and action against him.

The trial of Gottlieb Burghardt began at the end of June 1957. He was charged with working for the American intelligence service from 1951 to 1953 and then for TsOPE against the DDR. The trial lasted three days and was not open to the public. He was sentenced to 14 years imprisonment. Burghardt reportedly admitted that he had at least 35 active agents in the DDR. Vogel's pro-forma appeals of the sentence were for naught. After the trial, Vogel again met with Ilse Burghardt. An unidentified TsOPE member was also there and asked Vogel if he could arrange for a prisoner exchange. Vogel did bring up the possibility with the DDR but in April 1958, this was declined.[87]

He was finally released from prison in August 1964, when he was among the first 70 prisoners released by the DDR in exchange for money from West Germany. Vogel personally drove Burghardt to West Berlin; the other ex-prisoners were taken in three buses to West Germany.[88] Burghardt's fate afterwards is not known.

# 9

# Clandestine Radio to Byelorussia and to Slovakia

## Byelorussia

In the early Cold War, short-wave broadcasts to the Byelorussian Soviet Socialist Republic (BSSR) via Radio Nacional de España in Madrid, Spain, not only were unsupported by CIA but also many requests for Agency financial support were consistently rejected—although CIA supported the exile group in other activities

The post–World War II Byelorussian emigration in Western Europe was split into two organizations:

- BZR/BCR (Beloruska Zentralna Rada or Byelorussian Central Council) (CIA cryptonym AETOMAC-1)
- BNR (Beloruska Nationalna Rada, Byelorussian National Council or Council of the Byelorussian Peoples Republic) based in Paris, France.

The BZR/BCR, which was created during the World War II German occupation of Byelorussia and supported by the Germans, was headed by Radislaw (Radoslav) Ostrowsky (AETOMAC-2).[1]

The head of the BNR was Mykola Abramtchik,[2] who was also the head of the Paris-based Byelorussian Liberation Union. One CIA officer made this comment about BNR:

> As best as could be determined, BNR is not an official organization but a rather vague and loose association of individuals with nationalistic aspirations to a common homeland, who recognize Abramtchik as president of their government in exile. Abramtchik is President also of the Paris Bloc (a political center for non–Russian ethnic groups).... Many members of this group, unpaid as they are for their BNR activities, are regular employees of such organizations as Radio Liberty.[3]

## 9. Clandestine Radio to Byelorussia and to Slovakia

From 1951 to 1962, CIA financially supported and used the BNR émigré/exile group in the United States and Europe. CIA Cryptonyms used for various projects were: AEACRE, AEDEPOT, AEPRIMER, AEQUOR, AEREADY, AECAMBISTA, CHAURUS, CAMBISTA, CAMPOSANTO. The number 1 after the cryptonym referred to the BNR itself, e.g., AECAMBISTA-1.

CIA operations against the BSSR began in the summer 1951, when CIA initiated a joint Office of Special Operations (OSO)-Office of Policy Coordination (OPC) Foreign Intelligence (FI) project (cryptonym AEQUOR). The project included agent infiltration operations in BSSR to establish contact with partisan groups and set up support bases for future operations (cryptonym CAMPOSANTO). CIA's Munich Combined Soviet Operations Base (CSOB) was the responsible field unit. OSO and OPC shared equally in all expenses related to the recruitment, training, compensation, equipment and dispatch and exfiltration of agents into and out of Byelorussia.[4]

Another OPC project was subsidy for a weekly newspaper *The Fatherland (Batskaushchina)* published in c. 3,000 copies in Munich, a number of which were sent into Poland and the BSSR. The newspaper first appeared in 1946 but lack of continual funds forced it to appear irregularly. OPC began subsidizing it in 1951.[5] There were three themes OPC wanted covered in the newspaper:

- Anti-Bolshevism first and foremost
- Pro-Americanism in the sense that American action in defense of the free world would be explained to the readers as an antidote to Soviet propaganda,
- Belorussian nationalism, which while not inciting against the Great Russians or objecting to federation with them, would demand that Belorussia be given local autonomy wherein they would be ruled by their own people, freely elected.[6]

The OPC subsidy totaled DM 2,300 for every two issues published.[7]

## BNR and Voice of America

In November 1951 Mikola Abramtchik told his CIA-BNR case officer:

> Abramtchik commented that with Alexander Barmine, a died-in-the-wool Great Russian, as the head of the Slavic language section, the Byelorussian VOA programs would be un–Byelorussian in content and that therefore so long as Barmine retains his position it would probably be wiser to have no Byelorussian broadcasts at all rather than thinly-disguised Great Russian propaganda in Byelorussia.[8]

On February 25, 1952, CIA Deputy Chief, SR and one other officer met with Abramtchik, who claimed that he was told that in the event of a change in the direction of the Voice of America, CIA would arrange an interview for Abramtchik with whomever might become responsible for the broadcasts. Abramtchik said that a change in direction had now taken place, and he "would like to have a crack at talking the program director into introducing programs in Byelorussian."[9]

Abramtchik added that had been previously told by the "notoriously Russophile program directors" that no broadcasts in Byelorussian were contemplated because all Byelorussia could understand either Russian or Polish. Abramtchik said that this was not the case, and at any rate, a statement of this sort was an affront to Byelorussian national pride. By extension, this policy implied that the Byelorussians, as a cultural and political group, were not worth bothering with.[10] Abramtchik added:

> The VOA policy of precluding Byelorussian broadcasts is laid to the influence of Russian chauvinists who are well entrenched in the VOA set-up. Official U.S. policy, as it manifests itself through the State Department, is censured for showing preference for Russians over other Eastern Slavs, for naively trusting the fairmindedness of Russians in positions of authority and for the failure on the part of Native Americans to understand the problems of Eastern Europe.[11]

The Voice of America only broadcast to Byelorussia for approximately one-year, in 1956–1957.

## BNR and Radio Liberation

On March 3, 1953, CIA sponsored Radio Liberation from Bolshevism began broadcasting in Russian to the USSR. Implementation of Project AEQUOR required close coordination with AmComLib (Radio Liberty) to avoid any adverse effects on either project. The Coordination Committee of Non-Russian Organizations (Ukrainians, Georgians, Azerbaijani, North Caucasians, Armenians, and Byelorussians) met in Paris in April and delegated Abramtchik the authority to conduct further discussions with AMCOMLIB in New York.[12] In October 1953, BNR leader Mykola Abramtchik told AMCOMLIB:

> The opposition to him is centered in a group of emigres, which takes strong issue with him on the matter of collaboration with the American Committee. This group is angered by what it terms "capitulation" to the American Committee in connection with the plans for the formation of a Byelorussian Section of Radio Liberation. The group looks upon this as a renunciation of the 30-odd years of struggle of the Byelorussia for the reconstruction of the Byelorussian State, and particularly considers it to be due to the pressure of those who do not believe that the Byelorussians have any right to an independent state.[13]

## 9. Clandestine Radio to Byelorussia and to Slovakia 179

Abramtchik also said, "About one-fourth of the members of the Byelorussian Rada will desert with its followers. About three-fourths will remain with him and will be prepared to collaborate on Radio Liberation."[14]

In November 1953, CIA Case Officer met Abramtchik in Munich and reported that the American Committee had granted BNR an opportunity to utilize the facilities of Radio Liberation for broadcasts in the Byelorussian language. Initially the Byelorussian section of RL, consisting of five persons, would make only one 15-minute broadcast daily: the material transmitted will be anti–Bolshevik struggle and would fall within the political purview established by AMCOMLIB. There would be one announcer, one secretary, and/or translator and three researchers, all of whom would be paid a full salary by Radio Liberation.[15]

At the February 9, 1954, meeting with the case officer, Abramtchik was critical of AMCOMLIB in general and with Admiral Stevens in particular. He said that Admiral Stevens had only been in Moscow and was prone to accept the Russian point of view and was being badly advised by "Russophiles."[16] Radio Liberation began transmitting programs to Byelorussia on May 24, 1954.

Project AEQUOR PP activity then focused on subsidizing the Byelorussian language newspapers internationally.

Abramtchik wanted also to use Radio Nacional de España (RNE) in Madrid to broadcast in the Byelorussian language and for years lobbied CIA to financially those broadcasts at a cost of $4,000 annually. The responses were always negative. He tried again in August 1957, when he requested $500.00 per month for a 15-minute broadcast.[17]

Abramtchik was told in November 1957 of CIA headquarters decision not to financially support RNE Byelorussian language broadcasts. He made another plea asking that CIA not reject underwriting the salary costs for the Byelorussian employees, which in itself would permit them to make the broadcasts. Abramtchik asked that CIA agree to subsidize two scriptwriters and accordingly reduced his budget request from $4,000 to $2,400 (representing salaries for two writers at $100 each per month). According to Abramtchik, Byelorussians in Poland and the BSSR had written to RNE stating that the radio's Polish broadcasts were heard clearly in their areas.[18]

In September 1958, CIA did not approve BNR's broadcasting in RNE because

> at the present for the reason that that facility has undergone a personal change, which is inimical to our interests. The situation is a serious one and it is felt that we should not attempt to enlarge the number of participants in that undertaking less such expansion prove to be acutely detrimental to the Radio Madrid undertaking. Should the situation at Radio Madrid ameliorate, or should BNR developments warrant, the subject

of BNR participation in Radio Madrid will be discussed anew and if approved, will be encompassed with AEQUOR via project amendment.[19]

BNR Byelorussian language broadcasts over Radio Nacional de España began on January 1, 1959, under the BNR's own expense: funds for the two broadcasters were raised from "taxes" collected from BNR members in Munich and in the United States.[20]

On May 30, 1959, CIA-BNR case officer told Abramtchik, who was visiting Munich, that CIA headquarters' decision was not to support the BNR participation in the RNE broadcasts. The case officer reported that Abramtchik accepted this news with great regret and again asked that this decision be reconsidered. He added, in Abramtchik's opinion, "the BNR portion of the Radio Madrid broadcasts are even more effective CIA P&P material than the Radio Liberation broadcasts, particularly since the former are tailored to appeal to the nationalistic aspirations of the Byelorussian minority nationality group, whereas the latter are closely controlled and must adhere to policies, which are not popular with the minority nationalities, e.g. evasion self-determination issue, a line adopted to avoid offending the Great Russians, et cetera."[21]

The renewal request of AEQUOR Project dated July 16, 1959, included the following:

> Byelorussian language broadcasts over Radio Madrid are directed to the BSSR and to the Byelorussian colonies in Poland. Technical reception of these broadcasts in Poland is known to be good. Various letters have been received from Poland proving that these Byelorussian broadcasts are listened to assiduously.
>
> The BNR has been able to continue these broadcasts to the present day only by levying a tax on each gainfully employed member of the BER in Europe with the hope that CIA would see fit to continue this going and effective PP effort. CIA funds requested by the BNR for this effort have been in the modest sum of $4000 per year in order to pay the salaries of two BNR employees who devote their full time on these broadcasts and to cover all other costs of broadcasting.
>
> It should be noted that there are no other Byelorussian nationalist broadcasts in the Byelorussian language in existence. (NOTE: The Byelorussian broadcasts over Radio Liberation are not nationalist in content and are strictly controlled to accord with a non-offensive policy toward the nationality issue.) The Spanish government is not currently censoring these broadcasts over Radio Madrid.
>
> It should also be reiterated that our BNR contacts, quite unlike most other emigre contacts engaged in PP activities, have repeatedly offered to publish and broadcast anything and everything CIA wants. We have made little or no use of this offer.[22]

In the request for the Project AEQUOR renewal for FY 1960, the "analysis of effectiveness" of these early broadcasts read:

> Fifteen-minute programs are transmitted twice daily. Two BNR adherents prepare the programs under extremely primitive conditions, but reports from legal travelers indicate that the programs are received at least as far as the Byelorussian colonies

## 9. Clandestine Radio to Byelorussia and to Slovakia 181

in eastern Poland. It is likely that they are also heard in Byelorussia. Soviet jamming is said to be erratic and only moderately effective. The cost of the broadcasts is borne entirely by BNR, although CIA support has been requested.... Many members of the group, unpaid as they are for their AECAMBISTA activities, are regular employees of such organizations as Radio Liberty.[23]

Abramtchik traveled to Washington in June 1960 and met with the CIA case officer. He again was told his request was under consideration. A survey was then made of the effectiveness of the programs. The Chief of the SR Division sent a message to the Chief of Station in Germany that gave a summary of the Abramtchik request.

> He stated that unless outside financial help is forthcoming, this activity has to be dropped. He asked for a yearly subsidy of $4000.00 for the program (two daily 15-minute broadcasts). This figure he broke down into monthly remuneration of $170.00 each for the two BNR staffers and their wives, who also help to produce the programs. Abramtchik said that two families are currently receiving 100 pesetas (about $25.00) a month from the Spanish Government and that the remainder of their support has been collected from members and supports of BNR in Europe and North America, including $850.00 out of his own pocket last year. Abramtchik stated that this support could not continue much longer. The request for financial aid was linked to by Abramtchik with the assertion that Radio Madrid is an effective CIA instrument. He submitted several letters, which indicated that Radio Madrid is definitely heard in Eastern Poland. These letters also purported to show that the program is well received by Byelorussians in Poland. We are currently checking into other sources of information on the effectiveness of Radio Nacional and will give serious consideration to Abramtchik's request shortly.[24]

The Chief of Station for Germany sent a report to CIA headquarters dated June 2, 1960, that the "radio segment of AEQUOR" was the least deserving of CIA support, since

> a. It stands to be less effective that reading matter or personal contact.
> b. It is actually at the mercy of the Spanish authorities and could be shut off at a moment's notice.
> c. It is in the midst of re-organizing, and we do not yet know if it will be redirected along lines that we would wish to support.
> d. It has been run so far without CIA support.
> e. It represents a type of activity, which (as you know) tends to be regarded by the CIA Staff as an uneconomic expenditure of assets in all but the most demonstrably effective cases. This being the situation, too much emphasis on the radio angle could understandable prejudice acceptance of the whole thing.
>
> We are accordingly in approximate agreement with the distribution of funds suggested by Headquarters that nothing be allotted for radio broadcasts.[25]

The FY 1961 project renewal request from SR/3 contained this comment:

> Abramtchik has made repeated impassioned pleas for support of BNR now self-supported broadcasts over Radio Madrid to the extent of $4,000 per annum. It is

felt that the AEQUOR program is not comprehensive enough to justify such a subsidy; nor is the quality of overall Radio Madrid programming sufficiently high to recommend such an undertaking.[26]

On July 8, 1960, Cord Meyer, CIA's Chief of International Organizations Division sent a memorandum to the DCI in which he detailed a meeting between Abramtchik and a member of the Contacts Division on June 30, 1960: "Mr. Abramtchik solicited Agency financial support for 'émigré activities' to be conducted by the Paris Bloc ... he stated that NTS and TsOPE receive appropriate financial support from CIA and he implied that the American Committee for Liberation is supported by the same source."[27]

Abramtchik visited Munich in August 1960 and repeated his request for CIA financial support for BNR radio broadcasts over Radio Madrid. The Chief of Base, Munich sent a message to Chief, SR on October 6, 1960, with this comment, "Since the past year has produced no new indications of the effectiveness of the broadcasts behind the Iron Curtain, we, unfortunately are in no better position to judge on the merits of this proposal than a year ago."[28]

The project renewal request for FY 1961 contained this comment: "As best could be determined BNR is not an official organization but a rather vague and loose association of individuals with nationalistic aspirations for a common homeland who recognize Abramtchik as president of their organization in exile.... It should be recognized, however, that Abramtchik is not the sole pretender to leadership of the Belorussian emigration, and even in that segment of the emigration which recognizes him as president, his influence if not unchallenged."[29]

On February 12, 1961, the Chief, Munich Operations Group (MOG), sent a message to Chief, SR, that included this scathing comment: "We recommend that the project be terminated or transferred to BGACTRESS. It is demoralizing to the officers concerned to handle a project as amorphous, unproductive, implausible, and uncooperative as this. Furthermore, it does our local reputation no good to be considered so gullible."[30]

CIA never did financially support the Madrid broadcasts to Byelorussia and decided in August 1961, to terminate project AEQUOR effective December 30, 1961, for the following reason: "The project is being terminated for lack of evidence that it is contributing significantly to the fulfillment of Agency objectives. The Field concurs in this judgment. That the project has had some effect in the Cold War is true, but it is not believed that its effectiveness merits continued investment of Agency funds."[31]

On October 27, 1961, CIA told BNR in Munich that its monthly subsidy would be terminated. Abramtchik visited Munich on November

6, 1961, and BNR informed him of the decision.³² After the meeting, the Chief SR wrote, Abramtchik "probably lacks the personality, the perseverance, and the imagination to organize any significant program by his group of contact operations. However, it is probably better to direct his efforts toward such activity than to discourage him completely, or on the other hand to encourage his rather pitiful wanderings from one conference to another, in search of an evanescent union of anti-communist forces, to which his group in its present state, could probably contribute very little in any case."³³

Abramtchik traveled to the United States in January 1962, and wanted to personally meet with CIA Director John McCone and, and tell him that his subordinates "stabbed his organization in the back" and "terminated" the Belorussian project out of ignorance.³⁴ The meeting did not take place and Abramtchik returned to Europe, effectively cutting off all known remaining connections to CIA.

Mikola Abramtchik remained as President of the Rada of the Belorussian Democratic Republic in Exile until he died on May 25, 1970; he is buried in Paris, France.

## White Legion Radio to Slovakia

In 1945, the US Army set up the 430 CIC Detachment in Vienna, Salzburg, and Linz, Austria, with the primary function of "denazification" and searching to arrest "Nazi war criminals" and put them on trial. Austria after the World War II was crowded with "displaced persons" (DPs) who had been liberated from concentration camps or were former forced laborers in German factories. CIC was then tasked with screening these displaced persons, with the goal of returning them to their respective homelands or after 1948 to the USA. With the completion of the Iron Curtain, CIC Austrian operations evolved into intelligence gathering in Czechoslovakia and Hungary through the use of couriers to infiltrate into and exfiltrate from both.

## White Legion Movement

One CIC intelligence gathering operation reportedly was Project WACO, which involved CIC using anti–Communist agents in Czechoslovakia 1948–1949 to gather intelligence and recruit new agents behind the Iron Curtain. CIC recruited Jozef (Josef) Vicen and Jozef Mikula to be leading members of the agents used 1948–1949 in Slovakia. Vicen was born in Slovakia on December 14, 1921, in Homa Streda, a town bordering Hungary and spoke fluent Slovak as well as Hungarian.[35]

## White Legion Radio

Josef Vicen escaped to Austria from Czechoslovakia in May 1946. The radio station known as the "White Legion Radio" went into operation in April 1950 in cooperation with the suport of the CIC. The programs were broadcast live from a studio in the "Villa Mayer" in Ried /Innkreis in the American Zone in Upper Austria. The CIC staff also lived in the villa. The range of the low-powered transmitter on shortwave was estimated to be about 300 kilometers so that it was able to reach a large part of Slovakia and Moravia.[36]

In March 1951, White Legion Radio was reported on the air on the short-wave 46-meter band on Saturdays at 17:00 and Sundays at 08:30 and 13:00. The site had to be relocated at least 3 times for "security reasons starting in May 1951 and went off the air as it moved to Griedkirchen in 1951, to Wissenback am Attersee in 1952, and to Bad Mitterndorf in 1953."[37]

CIA did not finance the White Legion radio station, but OPC in Karlsruhe sent a message on January 7, 1952, to Chief Foreign Division, OPC Headquarters in Washington on the subject of "developments re Bela Legia Radio Station":

> This operation was given three months probationary period to prove itself, and having apparently succeeded in doing so with the allowed time, we are continuing our support, at least until such time as other instructions are received.
> Coincidently with the end of the trial period we were notified by (redacted) that he had received approval from OPC to undertake support of the radio and broadcast personnel for the purpose of filling the propaganda vacuum in Slovakia.
> 
> a. OPC will initially undertake support of the Bela Legia radio in the form of a subsidy for a period of two months, during which time they will observe the modus-operandi of the Bela Legia group and attempt to assay the value of the broadcasts. Continuance of the subsidy will be dependent on results of these studies.
> b OPC does not wish to be involved with any direction of operations of the group nor with logistical support other than financial. Secure housing of the radio proper will be provided through an OPC representative in Austria, or, if this proves impossible, rent will be paid for a house to be located by the Bela Legia.
> c. OPC desires only very general control of the broadcasts, which will take the form only of setting general tone. To accomplish this, OPC will monitor the broadcasts, and receive broadcast transcripts.
> d. Target date for resumption of Bela Legia broadcasts is to be 15 January, dependent of results of meeting to be held between OPC, Bela Legia representatives of 7 January.[38]

## Arrest and Trial of White Legion Members

In 1951, the new manager of the White Legion radio station, Catholic Priest Kamil Sumichrast in the Benedictine Monastery in Salzburg, sent Ernest Strečanský, Alexander Tihlárik, and Jozef Krutý to Slovakia with the aim of creating a reporting group of the White Legion.[39]

In July 1952, a Slovak Catholic priest visited a displaced persons camp in Wels, Austria and told a refugee about the arrest of five men, who reportedly had attempted to cross from Austria into Czechoslovakia. The refugee then told a CIC agent based in Salzburg, who in turn wrote a report on July 30, 1952, which read, in part:

> During the period of late June and early July 1952, the following named Czechoslovak refugees who had previously fled the CSR to the comparative safety of the US Zone of Austria were apprehended and arrested by the StB ... as they attempted to return to the CSR for unknown reasons:

- Ernest Strečanský,
- Peter Pavlovič,
- Anton Časta,
- Alexander Tihlárik and
- Jozef Krutý[40]

The names were checked against CIC files in Austria and a summary report was written by CIC Special Agent (S/A) Clyde E. Taylor on July 30, 1952. One CIC agent report received was dated November 6, 1951, and read, in part: "Strechansky, Ernest, Possible Czech Intelligence Personality, ... as an employee of Radio Free Europe in Salzburg was asking suspicious questions of CSR refugees concerning their anti–Communist acquaintances. He was known to have exhibited considerable interest in the 'White Legion,' an anti–Communist organization comprised of Czechoslovak refugees, and the KOVANDA Group, which allegedly gathers intelligence information for a US agency in Germany."[41]

Another CIC report, "Radio Free Europe—Theft of Documents," dated December 10, 1951, mentioned "Strechansky, who had been employed at RFE as a secretary allegedly confiscated some confidential documents from the RFE office in Salzburg." The CIC report dated April 4, 1952, read, in part, "Slovaks Allegedly Operating on behalf of the RIS in Austria, Oliver Stankovsky is allegedly in the employ of one Ernest Strechansky and is paid 2,000 Schillings as well as room and board."

CIC special agent Taylor, concluded his report with: "The above, information is submitted because the undersigned believes that if the five named refugees have actually been intercepted by Czech authorities they will, after debriefing, attempt to trade them their freedom in exchange for their acceptance to work as Czech intelligence operatives in the US Zone of Austria. In the event that any of the above-mentioned personalities appear in Salzburg they will be subjected to a detailed interrogation in an effort to prove or disprove whether they are actually operating for the CIS."[42]

The five White Legion men were put on trial June 23-24,1953, pled guilty, and were sentenced to long prison terms:

- Strečanský 16 years
- Casta 16 years
- Tihlarik 15 years
- Kruty 15 years
- Pavlovič 25 years[43]

## The White Legion 8

The case of "The White Legion 8" appeared in a CIA intelligence report in October 1952:

> Members of Slovak "White Legion" tried for espionage and terrorism. The Slovak radio reported Wednesday that eight members of the anti-State organization "White Legion" were being tried in Kosice on charges of organized terrorism and espionage "in the service of the American warmongers" in various districts of Eastern Slovakia. One of the accused stated that he acted on the incitement of foreign broadcasts carried on the "White Legion" radio.
> Comment: The "White Legion" is a strongly anti-Communist Slovak resistance movement whose main activity to date appears to consist of a twice-a-week Slovak language broadcast beamed into Czechoslovakia from Austria. These broadcasts resumed last April after a lapse of about 18 months, and monitored broadcasts have been heard to urge the Slovaks to "do everything possible to hinder police investigations" and to avoid certain named Communist agents.[44]

Prague Radio reported on the trial and an Associated Press report on the trial was carried by newspapers in the United States and gave more details:

> Four Get Death Sentence As American Spies VIENNA, Austria—(AP)
> A Communist court in Kosice, Czechoslovakia, has convicted four persons of being members of an underground partisan ring and American spies, and sentenced them to death, Radio Prague announced today. The court sentenced a fifth man to life Imprisonment and three others to prison terms from 15 to 25 years. The Prague broadcast said the eight-man group was accused of terrorism, murder and with having "followed the orders of the White Legion radio station, with the aim of reinstating a Nazi-type Slovak state." ... "White Legion 8" (after the White Legion led by Jozef Vicen) and the sentence was declared at the beginning of October 1952 (death sentences for Michal Mihók, Ján Rešetko, Bohumil Grúber, and František Bodnár). 4 Other people were sentenced to life prison, 25, 18 and 15 years.[45]

The Supreme Court in Prague confirmed the sentence on December 10, 1952, and the death sentences were carried out on April 21, 1953, in Prague.

A CIA Information Report on Czechoslovakia dated April 16, 1953, included this information on the "White Legion station, which was said to broadcast in Slovakia":

> This was a program of what for lack of any exact data.... The White Legion broadcast on short waves. Because of the danger of detection, it must be assumed that the transmitter was installed on a truck or other moveable object and changed its position between broadcasts. Probably for fear of detection, broadcasts were infrequent and highly irregular in terms of time and duration, but limited to evening hours. The signal was probably not very strong.[46]

A CIA Information Report dated June 17, 1953, included this information:

> The most popular foreign broadcast in Slovakia is that of the "White Legion," the clandestine radio station in Austria., followed closely by the Slovak station in Rome. These two stations transmit in the Slovak language and for the Slovak people.[47]

Lubomir Gleiman described in his memoirs, *From the Maelstrom: The White Legion Radio*:

> The Radio of the White Legion gave the impression of operating in the mountains of Central Slovakia. The programs were in no-way anti–Czech, but concentrated on the anticommunist offensive. The items were remarkably fresh and actual, often quite detailed. One point proved of crucial importance. The activity of the White Legion was completely autonomous; any individual or group could act in the name of the Legion, as long as it was of anticommunist persuasion and refrained from individual or group violence. The purpose of the whole activity was not only intelligence gathering, but also corrosive, ridiculing the nature of the whole system. It was to expose hypocrisy, double-think and corruption, especially of those most vocal and publicly exposed power brokers of the over-stretched imperial hubris of Moscow.[48]

Gleiman also described one ingenious way Radio Free Europe received information Slovakia:

> In the village of Stara Lubonva, in the Tatra region, there was a telephone booth with such and such number. The point was that if one placed a call from within Czechoslovakia to the number of the telephone booth and dial an additional number, he or she would then get a number in Munich and pay the local charges in Stara Lubonva. It so happened that when the Father Anton Hlinka, succeed the distinguished Rev. Dr. Jozef Rudinsky, as Catholic Chaplin in Radio Free Europe, the connection became operational, directly to his home phone number in Munich. Thus, Radio Free Europe was receiving important news within a matter of a few minutes.[49]

According to the October 20, 1953, CIA report entitled Resistance Potential of Czechoslovakia, "The White Legion (Biela Legie) operated in Slovakia as late as the fall of 1952. This group delivered its anti-communist messages via radio within Czechoslovakia only. It was made up of well-organized personnel from all walks of life and that it moved all over Slovakia in spreading its message ... it was liquidated in fall of 1952."[50]

Imrich Kružliak, Josef Sramek, Viktor Magdolen. Beluska were part of The White Legion radio station and after its closure, they joined Radio Free Europe in Munich. On July 23, 1954, Kružliak wrote a letter to Vicen telling him to apply for a position of announcer with RFE in Munich. Vicen was to write his application in English, send it to NCFE in New York, include the fact that he had worked for Americans, include names of those with whom he worked and add that he had worked for White Legion Radio. The reply dated August 17, 1954, was that there was an open position in the evaluation section and he was to apply for that, which he did the next day. At the end of September he received the answer: "There was no vacancy to suit his qualifications." However, he did work occasionally for the Free Europe Press as a translator/writer on the leaflet-balloon program "Operation Veto" to Czechoslovakia, but he was not given a permanent position as Dr. Zdenek Suda, who then directed the program, thought he was "too separatist."[51]

## Kidnapping of Josef Vicen

Reportedly, there was an attempt by the Soviet and Czechoslovak Intelligence Services to kidnap Vicen from Austria in 1949. Despite the shutdown of the "White Legion" radio, its most prominent exponent, Jozef Vicen, remained a top priority target for the Czechoslovakian State Security Service.[52]

As early as 1955, the Czechoslovak State Security (StB) and the Hungarian Secret Service (AVH) forged the plan of kidnapping Jozef Vicen (Code Name Eva). Action plans were discussed and agreed upon. Agents who had a friendly contact with Vicen were to play an important role: while the StB relied on Hubert S. alias, "Arno," the Hungarian AVH initially wanted to use its agent "Budavari." After the negotiations between the two secret services, the StB agreed with the Hungarian plan.

Vicen was lured into the restaurant Gasthaus zur Wegscheide in Floridsdorf, in the Soviet Zone of Austria, to meet "Arno." They had at least three glasses of Cognac and decided to leave the restaurant. Vicen paid the bill and he and Arno left the restaurant together. Hardly on the street, Vicen lost consciousness and woke up in a car. But by then he had already crossed the border into Czechoslovakia in in the back seat of the car, where he was injected with a drug. He was driven to the Prague prison Ruzyně.

In custody and after countless interrogations Vicen decided to cooperate with the StB. Trading with the Czech prosecutors was simple: information or his life. At least 180 people reportedly were arrested because of his statements, which reportedly totaled almost 1,000 pages. In the subsequent staged trial, Jozef Vicen was sentenced to 25 years in prison. Austria protested the action and there was newspaper coverage in Austria of the trial. He was released in 1968 and worked in manual labor jobs until he retired. He also published his autobiography, *Vo víroch rokov, 1938–1988,* and was active in Slovakia as a former political prisoner until he died in 2008.

## Ferdinand Ďurčanský, Radio Barcelona, "The Voice of Free Slovakia"

Ferdinand Ďurčanský was born in 1906 near Zilina, Slovakia, then a part of the Austro-Hungarian Empire. He graduated from the Law School of Komenskeho University in Bratislava. He also studied law in Paris and returned to Bratislava to conclude his studies for a Doctorate of Laws degree and practiced law in Bratislava. In 1936 he founded the magazine *Nastup (The Attack),* which has been described as fascist, anti–Semitic. In February 1938, he participated in the agreement between Slovakia, Hungary, and Sudeten-Germans on a joint action plan against the Czech government in Prague. Czechoslovakia was divided as federal state with autonomous regional governments in Slovakia and Ruthenia. On March 12, 1939, Ďurčanský and Monsignor Josef Tiso traveled to Berlin to meet with Hitler 2 days later, German troops invaded Bohemia and Slovakia was declared an independent nation.

Ďurčanský became Minister of Foreign Affairs. He concluded an agreement in August 1939 with Germany that established a military zone in Slovakia, which helped the German invasion of Poland on September 1, 1939. Ďurčanský also signed an agreement with Germany to send forced labor to Germany and permitted the German army to occupy important Slovak factories.

Ďurčanský lost his cabinet posts in July 1940 for not fully explained reasons. For the next four years he practiced law in Bratislava and managed a chemical factory. In April 1945 as the Soviet army moved in Slovakia, he and others escaped to Austria. Reportedly, he escaped with 150 kilograms of morphine.

In 1945, Ferdinand Ďurčanský escaped from Austria to Rome, with his wife and two children. When Karel Sidor of the Slovak League of America (SLA) declined to share with him funds that were collected from Slovak nationals abroad, Ďurčanský organized the Slovak Action Committee

(Slovenský Akćny Vybor—SAV) on January 15, 1946, to work for an independent Slovakia. Ďurčanský also lived in a Jesuit monastery in Frascati near Rome, then in Grottaferrata in the College of Oriental Priests and in the Vatican.

In 1946, the United Nations War Crimes Commission listed Ďurčanský as a war criminal, but extradition requests by the Czechoslovak government under President Benes was refused by Italy on the grounds that the Treaty of 1921 between the two countries did not apply to political criminals. In December 1946, a trial against Ďurčanský was opened in Prague, and on April 15, 1947, he was sentenced to death in absentia as a war criminal. There was apparently a failed attempt to kidnap him in Rome in August and bring him back to Czechoslovakia for trial.

In November 1946, Ďurčanský began his attempts to enter the USA when he registered him-self and his family with the American Consulate in Naples, Italy on the Czech quota waiting list. He applied for a visa in January 1947 but it was declined.

He sailed from Naples, Italy to Buenos Aires, Argentina, under the pseudonym Nandor Vilcek.[53] Ďurčanský moved to Argentina, supposedly as the invitation of Evita Peron. and in 1948 Argentina refused his extradition to Czechoslovakia.

Slovak refugees Dezider Murgaš and Eduard Moščovič, reportedly on the initiative of Ferdinand Ďurčanský, assembled a radio from parts purchased on the black market from the US Army's stock at the end of winter 1946. Another Slovak refugee R. Dilong went to Salizano, Italy about 100 km from Rome to worship in a Franciscan Monastery. A local priest and convinced anti-Communist placed the radio in the parish house; the church tower acted as an antenna. Radio Barcelona was the call sign and it only had power of 1Kw. Since the station was illegal in Italy, authorities began looking for it.[54]

Radio Barcelona broadcast daily from 22:00 to 22:30 in Slovak on the 44.5-meter band and from 23:00 to 23:30 in English on the 16 and 19-meter bands to the United States. Czechoslovak authorities monitored and recorded the broadcast on March 20, 1947; the last known broadcast was on April 19, 1947.[55] The Czechoslovak Ministry of National Defense report in May 1947, concluded that the radio station was operating from a "British military base near Udine, a city in north-eastern Italy."[56]

The "Voice of the Slovak Republic" radio station, first heard on April 16, 1947, spoke on behalf of the Slovak Action Committee. The broadcast of May 18, 1947, included: "Calling all Slovaks to remain faithful to the ideals of national independence ... those who remain faithful to these ideals will reap the fruit of liberation; those who betray them must be Spanish Radio Nacional." It spoke in behalf of Slovak separatism and

## 9. Clandestine Radio to Byelorussia and to Slovakia 191

used the slogan, "This year over to the attack! Every trace of the Second Czechoslovak Republic will be erased." Listeners were encouraged to write "SAV" (Slovenský Akćny Vybor—Slovak Action Committee) in all public places in Slovakia. The broadcast of May 20, 1947, included, "Preparations for a revolt are already underway ... a rising is in preparation against the Communist government.... Insurgent troops are already being organized."[57]

The radio station "For Free Slovakia" began on November 27, 1948, from Braunau, Austria, operated by Jozef Čačko. It broadcast for two hours on Saturday and Sunday. The U.S. Army's CIC reportedly confiscated the radio and "For Free Slovakia" ended.[58]

On March 12, 1949, Ďurčanský created the Slovak Liberation Committee (Slovensky oslobodzovaci vybor—SOV) to replace the Slovak Action Committee.

Ďurčanský arranged for renewal of the radio station in Austria on December 5, 1950, that broadcast on Tuesdays and Fridays on 12:45 a.m. on the short-wave band of 40 meters. The program began and ended with the playing of the Slovak Republic's national anthem in World War II and included the statement: "By fighting Communism we are fighting for the restoration of the Slovak Republic." The first program was not jammed.

Reportedly, the Austrian Transmitter Group West in the French zone broadcast in short-wave from Innsbruck to Slovaks in the displaced persons camps. Similar broadcasts were made in Czech, German, Hungarian, Romanian, and Serb/Croat.[59]

Ďurčanský returned to Europe on or about May 20, 1952, from Argentina and proceed to Innsbruck, Austria. He requested a visa for Germany, but it was refused by the Combined Travel Board (German and American intelligence services). He then proceeded to Paris, where he received a 3-month French visa, before returning to Germany.

A Free Europe Committee memorandum in May 1952 gave some details about Ďurčanský:

> Our continuing study of the various attacks on PEROUTKA (head of the Czechoslovak Desk of RFE) indicates that they are inspired by agents of two political adventurers and agitators, namely General PRCHALA and Dr. Ferdinand DURCANSKY ... DURCANSKY'S fulminations and vilifications of many prominent Czechs regularly appear in obscure newspapers published in the Czech or Slovak language in various centers of Czech emigration.[60]

In the Slovak émigré newspaper in the United States in 1952, *Slovåk v Amerike*, there was a notice announcing the broadcasting of a short-wave radio transmitter on 45 meters daily at 1900 hours, Central European Time. The notice named John Kutasovic as trustee and urged readers to contribute funds for the radio station. The alleged new transmitter called itself the

"Voice of the Slovak Republic," and proclaimed to be the sole defender of Slovak rights. A CIA memorandum dated June 14, 1952, concluded:

> We strongly believe that direct or indirect American help for Ďurčanský is not only unsound politically and morally, but also will greatly complicate our problems here.... [A]nd, in the case of DYCLEAN (CIA)—are in strong opposition to Ďurčanský and will wish to divert their strength to sabotaging and penetrating him, if permitted to do. Psychological warfare operations will be rendered almost useless, as too much conflicting material will be poured into a small target.
>
> We respectfully submit ... that it will serve no substantial interest of DYCLAIM (OSO) to support Ďurčanský through indirect subsidizations paid to ZIPPER (Gehlen Organization-ORG) for the purpose.
>
> With respect to the solicitation of funds in SLOVAK V AMERIKE, if in fact the alleged radio is a hoax, solicitors might be urged to sue the paper for fraud. Hrobek might write an article demanding proof, or some other less indirect but equally effective method used to kill the fund-raising.[61]

In 1953, Ďurčanský was living in Munich, Germany, and tried and failed to set up another radio station in Augsburg, Germany, with the assistance of the German Intelligence organization (Gehlen organization—ORG). Ďurčanský sent a letter dated February 18, 1953, to William (Bill) Griffith, Political Advisor of RFE in Munich, in which he wrote in part:

> Because it is generally in the interest of every follower of the principles of Freedom and Democracy that resistance against Communism and Moscow's imperialism be strengthened, and because the realization of these principles behind the Iron Curtain is a pre-condition for peace may I be allowed to remind you that a successful achievement of these aims requires to organize a special Slovak section-desk-in the radio station of the National Committee for a Free Europe in Munich, which would in no way be dependent on the Czechs but would have the same working capacity as the Czech desk.
>
> The Slovak Liberation Committee would gladly cooperate with the National Committee for a Free Europe if we would be given the democratic opportunity of broadcasting those ideals of which the Independence of the United States was born and which alone can form the basis of progress, happiness and peace in the World.[62]

A copy of his letter was sent to the United States High Commissioner in Bonn, James B. Conan.

From 1952 to 1958 Ďurčanský's acted in an advisory capacity to the German Gehlen Organization (ORG), supplying them with information on Czechoslovakia. In March 1953, ORG told CIA that the illegal radio broadcasts would not be made but they would continue working with Ďurčanský—he had the code name "Professor" with ORG. The Gehlen Organization explained to CIA field office that "Other than a basic discussion with members of the Sudeten German group (Landsmanshaft) three months ago about a joint anti–Communist transmission to Czechoslovakia, there has been no preparation in this direction. The discussion has to be recognized as having failed. This involved private negotiations of the PROFESSOR without any direct or indirect involvement of the ORG."[63]

In 1958, Ďurčanský was listed as the President of the Presidium of the People's Council of the Anti-Bolshevik Bloc of Nations (ABN) based in Munich. On February 10, 1959, Ďurčanský arrived in New York. He told an Associated Press reporter that he was visiting New York to promote a plan for "The disintegration of the Soviet empire." He said that he was a spokesman for ABN and intended to go the United Nations and then Washington, D.C., for promotion of his plan.[64] He traveled to Cleveland, Ohio, and gave an interview to the *Cleveland Plain Dealer* newspaper that was published on Sunday, February 15, 1959. The headline read, "Red Defeat Seen through Aid to Rebels."

After returning to Munich, Ďurčanský continued to be active politically but on lower and quieter scale by writing articles for Germany newspapers and magazines.

Dr. Ferdinand Ďurčanský died in Munich on March 21, 1974, and was buried there. In 2011, a bust was erected in his hometown of Rajec, Slovakia. This led to protests by various groups and was condemned by the Slovak government but was not removed.

## Killing of Matúš Černák

One of Ďurčanský's listed associates was Matúš Černák—former Slovak Minister to Berlin in World War II, Slovak National Council Abroad (SNCA) representative in Germany and a listed CIA informant.[65] Ďurčanský and Černák, were joint authors of a statement criticizing Radio Free Europe for "suppressing the majority (i.e., Slovaks). recruiting personnel among communists, betraying routes of escape from Czechoslovakia, and demoralizing their listeners with American jazz."[66]

Matúš Černák was killed by a package bomb that exploded in a Munich post office on July 5, 1955. There was widespread media coverage of his death, e.g., in Germany, United States, and Australia. He was buried in Munich, in a ceremony attended by German Chancellor Konrad Adenauer. In 1991, his remains were sent to Prague.

On April 13, 1959, in Vienna, Austria, there was a four-hour meeting between an unidentified Czechoslovak intelligence officer and a CIA officer. That was followed up by a message to CIA headquarters about the meeting, part of which included:

> Czech IS did blow up Matus Cernak. Op conceived and run by IS man RUDOLF BALOUN, who was under CTK cover. Bomb made in Prague, delivered to unknown agent, probably a German, by BALOUN in meadow near Hallein, Austria. (Redacted)

drove the car and third man, probably Lubomir KUBICEK, who then of TDY from Prague, went along. Agent did not know package contained bomb. Mailed it as instructed. When newspapers headlined Cernak death, agent got jitters, came Vienna, went to Legation and was packed off to CSSR. (Redacted) says purpose bombing was to create dissension between Slovak separatists and Czech nationalists in Munich immigration. Adds bombing not now totally taboo, such proposals no longer approved.[67]

The Bavarian State Criminal Office promised 5,000, and later 10,000 DM for providing any information that would lead to arrest and prosecution. The police investigation revealed that the explosive package had been filed at the post office at Frankfurt's Main Station. It was reportedly sent by a man between the ages of 40–45, 1.65–1.70 cm tall, slim figure, dark hair, with a dark beard, and reportedly spoken in broken German with a Slavic accent.

Circumstantial evidence points to the agent, who allegedly mailed the package to Černák, as Kurt Baumgartner, code name "Berthelot." Reportedly, when Baumgartner read the news in the newspapers about the circumstances of the bombing, he panicked and immediately went to Austria to the Czechoslovak Embassy and was transported to Czechoslovakia. He lived quietly in Prague in an apartment provided by StB, received monthly payments, provided translations and gave German lessons, until his death in 1987.

His StB case officer, Ladislav Kubiček ("Kautský") reportedly was awarded 2,000 Czech Crowns for "successful implementation of operative actions abroad."[68]

# Conclusion

This book has detailed the use of clandestine radio broadcasts as an integral part of the psychological and political (PP) warfare operations of CIA in the "battle for men's minds" of those who found themselves behind the Iron Curtain in the post–World War II years. In some cases, foreign intelligence operations (FI), i.e., penetration of agents into the target countries, were used to gather information about the audibility of these clandestine radio broadcasts. There was no way of polling the audience in the respective countries, so in some cases, foreign intelligence, including interviews of those persons in the West, who had listened to the broadcasts gave CIA information to decide if the radio broadcasts were cost effective. In other cases, penetration of agents for intelligence purposes into the target countries ceased early in the Cold War in favor of psychological and political warfare via radio, and printed matter, that continued until the collapse of Communism.

Did the clandestine, surrogate radio broadcasts have the intended effect on the listeners? Did they make a difference? The questions remain unanswered as they go beyond the scope of this book. The answers lie in further research on the indigenous listeners, who remained behind the Iron Curtain, especially Communist Party apparatchiks. Readers of this book can use it as a steppingstone for further research and analysis in media studies and Cold War historiography. This is not the final book on the subject of radio broadcasts, black, gray, and white, as some government and personal archives continue to be opened to researchers. For example, CIA has released millions of classified documents, but millions remain classified and closed. In many cases in Eastern Europe, inculpatory files were destroyed completely, or in the case of the former East German Stasi files, it will be years before the shredded documents are readable.

The Cold War Iron Curtain dividing East from West Europe is long gone, but in the world today there are still countries closed to active political opposition. Studies of the Cold War remain relevant and provide lessons learned to those willing to oppose repressive governments. The objectives of CIA's political and political warfare were finally achieved in 1989 in Eastern Europe and in the Soviet Union in 1991. Unfortunately, since the euphoric times, some countries are slipping back into undemocratic governments.

To repeat the Marshall Mcluhan quote from the Preface: "Radio affects most people intimately, person-to-person, offering a world of unspoken communication between writer-speaker, and the listener. That is the immediate aspect of radio. A private experience." Internet is a wonderful development in the exchange of ideas in the "global village," but not everyone has access to it, and the various social media outlets are basically impersonal with shorthand sentences and "selfie" photographs that do not attempt to provoke the reader to action or contemplation.

In 2009, I began my internet blog Cold War Radio Vignettes (https://coldwarradios.blogspot.com), and by December 2020 the number of pageviews exceeded 400,000, including 25,000 from Russia, 9,000 from Ukraine, and 5,000 from China. That shows to me, that there is considerable interest in the use of radio broadcasts in the Cold War. The reader is encouraged to look at the posts and leave comments or questions, which I do my best to answer.

# Appendix A
## Selected CIA Cryptonyms

AEBALCONY—(1960–62) was designed to use U.S. citizens with Baltic language fluency in "mounted" and "piggy-back" legal traveler operations into Soviet-occupied Estonia, Latvia, and Lithuania.

AEBASIN/AEROOT (1953–60) supported Estonian émigrés and émigré activities against the Estonian SSR.

AECAMBISTA-1—Byelorussian National Council (BNR).

AECASSOWARY-1—ZP/UHVR, Foreign Representation of the Ukrainian Liberation Council.

AECAVATINA-1—Stefan Bandera (also CAVETINA-1).

AECOB—AECOB, approved in 1950, was a vehicle for foreign intelligence (FI) operations into and within Soviet Latvia and involved infiltration and exfiltration of black agents and the recruitment of legally resident agents in the USSR, especially Latvia. ZRLYNCH was approved in 1950 for use of the Latvian Resistance Movement, which had been formed in 1944, as a vehicle for clandestine activities within the USSR. ZRLYNCH was renewed in 1952 as a part of AECOB, which then provided both FI and political and psychological (PP) activities. AECOB / ZRLYNCH PP project was terminated in 1955. AECOB FI project was terminated in 1959.

AEFLAG (1955–62) was aimed at people of the Latvian SSR.

AEFREEMAN—(1953–64), which included AEBASIN/AEROOT (1953–60), AEFLAG (1955–62), and AEPOLE (formerly AECHAMP [1949–59]), was designed to strengthen resistance to communism and harass the Soviet regime in the Baltic countries. These projects provided intelligence and operational data from Baltic countries through radio broadcasts, mailing operations, liaison with émigré organizations, political and psychological (PP) briefings for legal travelers and exploitation of other media such as demonstrations.

## Appendix A

AEGEAN—AEGEAN (formerly CAPSTAN) provided FI (foreign intelligence) from the Baltic States and USSR using support bases developed in the Lithuanian SSR as transit points. AEGEAN/CAPSTAN work continued under Project AECHAMP

AEGIDEON—AESAURUS / AENOBLE (initially AEROSOL, renamed AEGIDEON / AENOBLE in 1958) operation (1950–61) maintained communications with agents of the National Alliance of Russian Solidarists (Narodno Trudovoi Soyuz or NTS [CABOCHE-1, PDGIDEON, SHUBA-100]). Operation RADIO was a mobile covert radio operated by NTS for propaganda into East Zone.

AEMARSH—(1953–59) involved collecting foreign intelligence on the Soviet regime in Latvia through sources residing in the Latvian SSR, legal travelers, and all possible legal means. The Institute for Latvian Culture (AEMINX) was established as a cover facility engaged in the preservation and development of Latvian national culture and collection of information on Latvian national life.

AEPOLE (formerly AECHAMP [formerly BGLAPIN]) (1949–59) targeted the Lithuanian SSR.

AERODYNAMIC—(formerly CARTEL, ANDROGEN, AECARTHAGE) (1949–70) refers to CIA support for ZP/UHVR (Ukrainian Supreme Liberation Council), which began in 1949.

AESAURUS—AESAURUS / AENOBLE (initially AEROSOL, renamed AEGIDEON / AENOBLE in 1958) operation (1950–61) maintained communications with agents of the National Alliance of Russian Solidarists (Narodno Trudovoi Soyuz or NTS [CABOCHE-1, PDGIDEON, SHUBA-100]). NTS was founded in 1930s by Russian émigrés with extreme rightest and anti–Semitic views and collaborated closely with the Nazis in Russia, providing local administrators, propagandists, and informants. NTS rebuilt itself in 1945 as an anti–Soviet émigré organization inside the USSR and with its own newspaper "Possev." This project sought the development and exploitation of NTS agents as long-term hot war assets and as sources of operational positive and psychological intelligence. The Project included Operation CARCASS, training/dispatch into USSR of agents to organize resistance groups and collect FI; Operation SPAIN to establish NTS groups in US zone/Germany and Austria against Soviet occupation forces through propaganda, defection, resistance, and collecting FI; Operation RADIO to establish a mobile covert radio operated by NTS for propaganda into East Zone. See also QKDROOP.

AETENURE—Prolog Research Corporation, the New York publishing arm of Project QRPLUMB.

AETERRACE—Ukrainian Society for Foreign Studies, which was the Munich office of QRPLUMB and published the monthly journal *Suchasnist*.

AEVIRGIL—(1953–63) provided a controlled, anti-communist émigré organization for political and psychological activities against the Soviet target. The particular émigré organization, which was called the Central Association of Post-War Émigrés (TsOPE) and located in Munich, produced and disseminated Russian language leaflets and a monthly magazine (Svoboda), held propaganda meetings and press conferences, and was engaged in psychological warfare against the Soviet target.

AMCOMLIB—American Committee for the Liberation of the Peoples of Russia (AMCOMLIB) was a part of Project QKACTIVE. PBAFFIRM (cryptonym). PBCHORD (cryptonym for Munich Office of AMCOMLIB).

ANDROGEN—CIA support for ZP/HUVR (Ukrainian Supreme Liberation Council).

AQUATIC—CIA Technical Services Division (TSD)

BGACTRESS—CIA International Organizations Division (IOD)

BGCANE—Office of Policy Coordination (OPC)

BGCONVOY—(Formerly QKSTAIR) (1950–55) was the basic political and psychological (PP) and paramilitary (PM) program against Bulgaria with the objective of conducting psychological warfare (PW) operations against the Bulgarian regime and establishing in the country resistance organizations capable of PM activity of various types. BGCONVOY also provided for the development and exploitation of the Principal Agent, Ivan Docheff, who was leader of the Bulgarian National Front, and the newspaper published by the group.

BGFIEND—a country project for the purpose of selecting, training, and infiltrating indigenous agents into Albania to effect and support resistance activities for the purpose of overthrowing the Communist controlled government in Tirana. This project also included the support of the National Committee for a Free Albania, which consisted of a group of Albanians in exile who represented various political factions, but who were all dedicated to the liberation of their country from Communist control. In this connection the project included the support of propaganda activities, i.e., leaflets, publication of an Albanian newspaper (Shqiperia) and support of Voice of Free Albania. Cryptonym changed to OBOPUS in 1953.

BGRHYTHM—CIA Office of Policy Coordination (OPC). Other cryptonyms for OPC included: BGCANE, DYCLAVIER, DYCLIP, DYCLUCK, FJCAPE, KNOBBY, VLKIVA, ZACACTUS.

BGSPEED (sub project of BGFIEND)–Purchase of vessel for purpose of offshore transmission of propaganda into Albania.

CABOCHE-1—National Alliance of Russian Solidarists (Narodno Trudovoi Soyuz [NTS]), which reportedly was founded in the 1930s by Russian émigrés with extreme rightest and anti-Semitic views and collaborated closely with the Nazis in Russia, providing local administrators, propagandists, and informants. The NTS rebuilt itself on purely anti-Communist grounds in 1945. After the war, the NTS has its own newspaper "Possev." See also AESAURUS, QKDROOP

CAMBISTA-1—Byelorussian National Council (BNR)

CARCASS—Operation CARCASS, training/dispatch into USSR of agents to organize resistance groups and collect FI; Operation SPAIN to establish NTS groups in US zone/Germany and Austria against Soviet occupation forces through propaganda, defection, resistance, and collecting FI;

CASSOWARY-1—Ukrainian émigré organization, ZP/UHVR, Foreign Representation of the Ukrainian Supreme Liberation Council.

CHARITY—OBDURATE (formerly OBSTACLE, Plan CHARITY) (1954-56), incorporated into OBLONG in 1956, exploited the intelligence potential of a significant Albanian émigré group in Rome (Balli Kombetar).

CHAURUS—Byelorussian Liberation Union in Paris that was headed by Mikola Abramtchik

DTORIC—National Committee for Free Europe (NCFE), Free Europe Committee

DYCLEAN—CIA Office of Special Operations (OSO)

DYCLEMATIC—CIA Office of Special Operations (OSO)

EDUCATOR—(1949-50) was a psychological warfare project and provided the production and dissemination of covert propaganda against the Soviet Union and its satellites using radio broadcasts and printed material.

FJHAKI—Estonia.

FJMACHINE—Free Europe Exile Relations (FEER), a Division of the Free Europe Committee, Inc. James McCargar was European Director of FEER (1955-58).

FJSTEAL—Union of Soviet Socialist Republics.

HARVARD—(1951-65) was designed initially to provide safehouse and operational aid facilities for CIA activities in Germany. In 1952, the

## Selected CIA Cryptonyms

HARVARD mission was expanded to include the rehabilitation and resettlement of defectors, agents, and agent-trainees.

HBCHEST—Sweden.

HBCLOUD—Latvia.

HTNEIGH—HTNEIGH provided support to National Committee for Free Albania (NCFA) as CIA's overt vehicle for political, psychological, paramilitary activities against Albania.

JAGUAR—British Intelligence Service.

JBCLOUD—Latvia.

JBCREOLE—Voice of America (VOA).

JKLANCE—Central Intelligence Agency.

LCFLUTTER—Polygraph test.

LCHOMELY—Operations from Germany into Estonia.

LCIMPROVE—Information concerning Soviet Intelligence Services worldwide.

OBHUNT and OBSIDIOUS (sub-project of OBOPUS/BGFIEND)— Infiltration of agent teams into Albania via air drops or overland to organize underground resistance, establish safe houses, collect operational intelligence, and to spread propaganda.

OBOPUS—National Committee for Free Albania. OBOPUS (formerly BGFIEND) (1949-58) was initially a joint US-British covert action program designed to overthrow the Soviet dominated regime of Enver Hoxha in Albania and evolved into establishing and exploiting National Committee for Free Albania (NCFA), propaganda media, infiltration agents, and economic warfare.

OBSIDIOUS—Infiltration missions into Albania via airdrops or overland to organize underground resistance, establish safe houses, collect operational intelligence, and to spread propaganda. These missions were associated with Project BGFIEND.

OBTEST (sub project of OBOPUS/BGFIEND)—Clandestine radio broadcasts into Albania.

OBTUSE (sub-project of OBOPUS/BGFIEND)—PP activity against Albania. Distribution of leaflets, printed matter & small quantity of selected consumer goods via overflights and limited mail campaign.

ODOPOL—U.S. Army Counterintelligence Corps (US Army CIC or CIC).

OGIVE—CIA Office of Special Operations.

PBAFFIRM—American Committee for the Liberation of the Peoples of Russia (AMCOMLIB), which is a part of Project QKACTIVE.

# Appendix A

PBCHORD—Munich Office of the American Committee for the Liberation of Peoples of Russia (AMCOMLIB).

PBCHUTE—Lithuania.

PBGIDEON—National Alliance of Russian Solidarists (Narodno Trudovoi Soyuz [NTS]).

QKACTIVE—(1951-71), operating through a proprietary cover organization (American Committee for the Liberation of the People of the USSR [AMCOMLIB] [PBAFFIRM]), sought to conduct overt anti-Soviet activities to weaken the Soviet regime and thereby reduce its threat to world security through radio broadcasts (Radio Liberty).

QKBROIL—(1951-54), which was superseded by Project SHELLFIRE in 1954, was a program to encourage the Rumanian people to resist communism; to establish a clandestine underground in Rumania to hamper Soviet/satellite military operations and to serve as a nucleus for wartime resistance; to undermine the political, economic, and military structure of communist Rumania; to develop a National Committee for a Free Europe (NCFE) Political Center (Rumanian National Refugee Organization) as cover for overt activities and a covert operational support arm for OPC operations.

QKCOAST—Baltic States.

QKDEMON (formerly UMPIRE, EDUCATOR) (1949-50) was a psychological warfare project and provided the production and dissemination of covert propaganda against the Soviet Union and its satellites using radio broadcasts and printed material.

QKDROOP—(1950-52) provided funds, material support, and operational guidance to the National Alliance of Solidarists (NTS or Natsionalny Trudovoi Soyuz).

QKIVORY—TPTONIC (formerly QKIVORY) refers to National Committee for a Free Europe (NCFE) and its subcommittees (NCFE was changed to Free Europe Committee—FEC) in1954.

QKSTAIR—BGCONVOY (formerly QKSTAIR) (1950-55) was the basic political and psychological and political (PP) and paramilitary (PM) program against Bulgaria with the objective of conducting psychological warfare (PW) operations against the Bulgarian regime and establishing in the country resistance organizations capable of PM activity of various types.

QRDYAMIC—QRDYNAMIC/QRPLUMB (formerly AEBEEHIVE) (1970-91) superseded Project AERODYNAMIC and supported the Ukrainian émigré organization ZP / UHVR (Ukrainian Supreme Liberation Council) with a New York publishing arm called Prolog Research Corporation (QRTENURE, AETENURE) and a Munich Office, Ukrainian Society for Foreign Studies (QRTERRACE, AETERRACE), publisher of the monthly journal Suchasnist. CIA terminated QRPLUMB after the fall of the Berlin Wall in 1991 and provided funds to enable Prolog to transition to a privately funded company.

REDBIRD—Operations involving the illegal return of defectors and émigrés to USSR as agents.

REDBLOCK—CIA Soviet Division. Other cryptonyms included REDCOAT, REDLEG and REDTOP.

REDCAP—(1951-65) was the planned collection of information on Soviet personnel stationed abroad for the purpose of operational exploitation, including defector inducement.

SGPSALM—Latvian Resistance Movement.

SGSWIRL—Polygraph Test.

SHELLFIRE—(1951-54), which was superseded by Project SHELLFIRE in 1954, was a program to encourage the Rumanian people to resist communism; to establish a clandestine underground in Rumania to hamper Soviet/satellite military operations and to serve as a nucleus for wartime resistance; to undermine the political, economic, and military structure of communist Rumania.

SHUBA-100—National Alliance of Russian Solidarists (Narodno Trudovoi Soyuz [NTS]).

TPFEELING—Radio Free Europe.

TPLINGO—Radio Liberation / Liberty.

TPTONIC—(Formerly QKIVORY) refers to National Committee for a Free Europe (Free Europe Committee in 1954) and its subcommittees.

UMPIRE—QKDEMON (Formerly UMPIRE, EDUCATOR) (1949-50) was a psychological warfare project and provided the production and dissemination of covert propaganda against the Soviet Union and its satellites using radio broadcasts and printed material.

VALUABLE—British operations in Albania.

VLKIVA—Office of Policy Coordination.

ZACABIN—CIA Office of Special Operations.

ZRLYNCH—AECOB, approved in 1950, was a vehicle for foreign intelligence (FI) operations into and within Soviet Latvia and involved infiltration and exfiltration of black agents and the recruitment of legally resident agents in the USSR, especially Latvia. ZRLYNCH was approved in 1950 for use of the Latvian Resistance Movement, which had been formed in 1944, as a vehicle for clandestine activities within the USSR. ZRLYNCH was renewed in 1952 as a part of AECOB, which then provided both FI and political and psychological (PP) activities. AECOB / ZRLYNCH PP project was terminated in 1955. AECOB FI project was terminated in 1959.

ZYCACTUS—Office of Policy Coordination.

*Source: Second-release-lexicon, Research Aid: Cryptonyms and Terms in Declassified CIA Files, https://www.archives.gov/files/iwg/declassified-records/rg-263-cia-records/second-release-lexicon.pdf [last viewed December 2020].*

# Appendix B
## *National Security Council Directive 5412/2*

NSC 5412/2 Washington Undated
COVERT OPERATIONS

1. The National Security Council, taking cognizance of the vicious covert activities of the USSR and Communist China and the governments, parties and groups dominated by them, (hereinafter collectively referred to as "International Communism") to discredit and defeat the aims and activities of the United States and other powers of the free world, determined, as set forth in NSC directives 10/2[2] and 10/5[3], that, in the interests of world peace and U.S. national security, the overt foreign [Page 747] activities of the U.S. Government should be supplemented by covert operations.

2. The Central Intelligence Agency had already been charged by the National Security Council with conducting espionage and counterespionage operations abroad. It therefore seemed desirable, for operational reasons, not to create a new agency for covert operations, but, subject to directives from the NSC, to place the responsibility for them on the Central Intelligence Agency and correlate them with espionage and counter-espionage operations under the over-all control of the Director of Central Intelligence.

3. The NSC has determined that such covert operations shall to the greatest extent practicable, in the light of U.S. and Soviet capabilities and taking into account the risk of war, be designed to:
    (a) Create and exploit troublesome problems for International Communism, impair relations between the USSR and Communist China and between them and their satellites, complicate control within the USSR, Communist China and

their satellites, and retard the growth of the military and economic potential of the Soviet bloc.

(b) Discredit the prestige and ideology of International Communism, and reduce the strength of its parties and other elements.

(c) Counter any threat of a party or individuals directly or indirectly responsive to Communist control to achieve dominant power in a free world country.

(d) Reduce International Communist control over any areas of the world.

(e) Strengthen the orientation toward the United States of the peoples and nations of the free world, accentuate, wherever possible, the identity of interest between such peoples and nations and the United States as well as favoring, where appropriate, those groups genuinely advocating or believing in the advancement of such mutual interests, and increase the capacity and will of such peoples and nations to resist International Communism.

(f) In accordance with established policies and to the extent practicable in areas dominated or threatened by International Communism, develop underground resistance and facilitate covert and guerrilla operations and ensure availability of those forces in the event of war, including wherever practicable provision of a base upon which the military may expand these forces in time of war within active theaters of operations as well as provision for stay-behind assets and escape and evasion facilities.

4. Under the authority of Section 102(d)(5) of the National Security Act of 1947, the National Security Council hereby directs that the Director of Central Intelligence shall be responsible for:

(a) Ensuring, through designated representatives of the Secretary of State and of the Secretary of Defense, that covert operations are planned and conducted in a manner consistent with United States foreign and military policies and with overt activities, and consulting with and obtaining advice from the Operations Coordinating Board and other departments or agencies as appropriate.

(b) Informing, through appropriate channels and on a need-to-know basis, agencies of the U.S. Government, both at home and abroad (including diplomatic and military representatives), of such operations as will affect them.

5. In addition to the provisions of paragraph 4, the following provisions shall apply to wartime covert operations:

## National Security Council Directive 5412/2

(a) Plans for covert operations to be conducted in active theaters of war and any other areas in which U.S. forces are engaged in combat operations will be drawn up with the assistance of the Department of Defense and will be in consonance with and complementary to approved war plans of the Joint Chiefs of Staff.

(b) Covert operations in active theaters of war and any other areas in which U.S. forces are engaged in combat operations will be conducted under such command and control relationships as have been or may in the future be approved by the Department of Defense.

6. As used in this directive, "covert operations" shall be understood to be all activities conducted pursuant to this directive which are so planned and executed that any U.S. Government responsibility for them is not evident to unauthorized persons and that if uncovered the U.S. Government can plausibly disclaim any responsibility for them. Specifically, such operations shall include any covert activities related to: propaganda; political action; economic warfare; preventive direct action, including sabotage, anti-sabotage, demolition; escape and evasion and evacuation measures; subversion against hostile states or groups including assistance to underground resistance movements, guerrillas and refugee liberation groups; support of indigenous and anti-communist elements in threatened countries of the free world; deception plans and operations; and all activities compatible with this directive necessary to accomplish the foregoing. Such operations shall not include: armed conflict by recognized military forces, espionage and counterespionage, nor cover and deception for military operations.

7. Except as the President otherwise directs, designated representatives of the Secretary of State and of the Secretary of Defense of the rank of Assistant Secretary or above, and a representative of the President designated for this purpose, shall hereafter be advised in advance of major covert programs initiated by CIA under this policy or as otherwise directed, and shall be the normal channel for giving policy approval for such programs as well as for securing coordination of support therefor among the Departments of State and Defense and the CIA.

8. This directive supersedes and rescinds NSC 10/2, NSC 10/5, NSC 5412, NSC 5412/1, and subparagraphs "a" and "b" under the heading "Additional Functions [Page 749] of the Operations Coordinating Board" on page 1 of the President's memorandum for the Executive

Appendix B

Secretary, National Security Council, supplementing Executive Order 10483.

*Source: Eisenhower Library, Special Assistant to President for National Security Affairs Records, President's Papers. Top Secret. This directive was transmitted to the NSC under cover of a December 28 note from NSC Executive Secretary Lay. Lay stated that the President had approved the directive on the same date. Foreign Relations of the United States, 1950–1955. The Intelligence Community, 1950–1955, Document 250, https://history.state.gov/historicaldocuments/frus1950-55Intel/d250 [accessed December 2020].*

# Appendix C
*Radio Nacional Propaganda Broadcasts*

~~SECRET~~

OFFICIAL DISPATCH  DISPATCH No.: MGW-A-172
Date: 30 May 1949
To: (*redacted*)
From: (*redacted*)
Subject: Radio Nacional Propaganda Broadcasts
REF:FF-CWUHG and MGW-A-136

1. Reference is made to the two above dispatches concerning the possibility of EDUCATOR supplying our Madrid office with background material for broadcasts to the Soviet Union and satellite areas over Radio Nacional.
2. Since receiving your dispatch, we have studied the matter not only in regard to the immediate problem of applying background material but also relative to the larger, long range possibility of utilizing Radio Nacional as a channel for operational broadcasts, to which EDUCATOR creative personnel in Germany might contribute both program material as well as programs themselves, including possibly special recordings.
3. Information here indicates that Madrid is heard reasonably well in satellite areas, although I would like to have the benefit of any monitoring reports which you may have obtained on the subject. If the station does in fact reach satellite areas with reasonable satisfactory audibility and if the Spanish Government, through proper covert arrangements, is willing to place the facilities and broadcast time of the station at the disposal of *(redacted)* this would clearly open up the possibility of using Madrid as an operational

outlet for broadcasts, either sponsored by or accordingly produced by the U.S. Government.

4. In regard to (cover), through negotiations with the proper Spanish Government levels, I should think a suitable operational cover could be arranged—as, for example, the Spanish Government, in its desire to oppose religious persecutions in satellite countries, has accorded broadcasting time to refugee Catholic groups in Spain in order to permit them to talk to their fellow countrymen.

5. In regard to (policy control), periodic policy guidance from the home office, together with close monitoring watch over the broadcasts, should provide adequate policy control, especially if the cover and security of the operation are well maintained and the U.S. Government is not linked in any way to the broadcasts.

# Appendix D
## Frank Wisner Memorandum, November 22, 1950

~~SECRET~~

22 November 1950

MEMORANDUM FOR: DEPUTY DIRECTOR
OF CENTRAL INTELLIGENCE

SUBJECT: Radio Free Europe

1. At the meeting of the directors of the National Committee for a Free Europe in New York on Thursday evening, November 2nd, attended by the Deputy Director of Central Intelligence and the Assistant Director for Policy Coordination, the Committee was asked to reexamine its radio activities and prepare a statement of the aims and objectives of Radio Free Europe for study by the Deputy Director of Central Intelligence. Two comprehensive memoranda and other materials have been received in response to this request.
2. The following is a summary of these reports, together with our own additional views and refinements.
    a. Essentially an instrument of psychological warfare, Radio Free Europe's purpose is to prevent, or at least to hinder, the cultural, political and economic integration of the satellite states with the Soviet Union.
    b. Sponsored by a group of citizens, Radio Free Europe provides a channel over which individuals, both foreigners in exile and American citizens, can speak to the people behind the Iron Curtain. Unhampered by official status, Radio Free Europe supplements but takes care not to compete with or duplicate the Voice of America. Programs are sent out in intimate colloquial languages on a far wider selection of subjects that the Voice of

America as an agency of the government is in a position to use, and Radio Free Europe can move into the area of gray or even black propaganda should the situation warrant it.
c. To accomplish its purpose in bringing hope to our friends and confusion to our enemies, Radio Free Europe has been developing programs aimed at:
   (1) Keeping alive the hope of liberation in the satellite states and telling the various peoples that they are not forgotten by the free world;
   (2) Stimulating and increasing the difficulties of the satellite regimes in their efforts to achieve full control of production and economic integration with the USSR;
   (3) Creating doubts and fears among the quislings of the satellites by character assassination and talk of ultimate retribution, and at the same time drawing a distinction between Communist puppets and those who follow the party line in order to survive, thereby encouraging high level defections among the latter;
   (4) Developing an atmosphere favorable to the grown of resistance movements, for ultimate exploitation in war, or, at a propitious moment, in peacetime.
d. Programs totaling 7½ hours per day are currently going out in five languages to Bulgaria, Czechoslovakia, Hungary, Poland and Rumania. These programs are devoted approximately one-third to news and two-thirds to so-called features, ranging from political satires to controlled speeches by exiles. As a result of five months' experiences, emphasis has shifted from the use of distinguished political and intellectual exiles, whose personal prejudices and protracted absence from their native lands render them of questionable current value, to timely news items and commentary slanted to accomplish Radio Free Europe's purposes.
e. The production of five different language programs per day is the task of the New York office. Whenever possible scripts are written by exiles and edited by the American staff. By this means, the programs are kept local in character and more in keeping with the taste of their audiences. Of primary concern is the development and maintenance of an adequate flow of information from behind the Iron With Curtain, since local news in the satellites is as interesting as world news. Because of the dangers of being caught listening, all programs must have special appeal if they are to hold their audience.

f. With only one low powered transmitter for use in less than five months, it is too early to judge the effectiveness of the effort. There are about 69,000,000 people living in the target area, and the best information available indicates that they have about 3,100,000 receiving sets equipped to receive short and/or medium wave transmission. This ratio of approximately 33 people per set varies widely between countries, there being five people per set in Czechoslovakia, compared with over seventy people per set in Bulgaria and Romania. However, in all these countries a grape vine process plays an important role in the dissemination of information, particularly information of a startling nature, and although relatively few persons may actually hear a broadcast, the contents appear to spread with great rapidity. This seems to be a consequence of the almost total obstruction of the normal flow of news from abroad. About the only measure of the results of Radio Free Europe's broadcasts to date is the relatively frequent public denunciation of them in the satellite areas. The state radio stations in both Hungary and Rumania have imitated certain of our programs in an effort to reply to the information carried. Also, we understand that Radio Leipzig has announced that any West German who works for Radio Free Europe will be hanged after the "liberation" of Germany.
g. Present plans call for an extension of facilities to permit broadcasting six hours per day per country and the necessary expansion of research and writing personnel to produce the programs needed for this schedule. In addition, the present delay of about 30 hours between the receipt of a news item and the broadcasting thereof, will be materially reduced by the establishment of a programs office in Germany where much of the work now don in New York can be carried on.
h. Supplementing the 7½ short wave transmitter now operating in Frankfurt, a 135 kw medium wave transmitter located near Munich will be completed next year. Two GE 100kw short wave and four RCA 50 kw short wave transmitters are on order for delivery in the first half of 1951. Two of the 50 kws will be placed near the Frankfurt area, thereby giving complete coverage of the target area from Germany. The final location of the remaining units depends on various technical and political considerations, but the general plan is to set up a second line facility in North Africa, Portugal, or the Azores to provide both better coverage and also a reserve to fall back on in case for any reason we are forced out of the German locations.

## Appendix D

i. The original budget of Radio Free Europe for the fiscal year 1850/51 has been tentatively amended under date of 24 August 1950 as follows: (redacted) Final approval of this amended budget is sought at this time in order that the program of expansion may be carried through. Of the (redacted) requested for Capital Expenditures, (redacted) has already been transferred, leave (redacted) still to be remitted.

j. The annual operating cost indicated above at (redacted) will not, of course, apply to the current fiscal year, as this sum is for a full year's operation of all the proposed new facilities, which even if approved immediately, will not be in operation in their entirety until late spring. At the present time, operating expenses are running at (redacted) per month, or an annual rate of (redacted) per year, some employees have already been added in anticipation of the enlarged operation.

k. The equipment to be installed under this plan has been specified by the Committee's advisor, Mr. Peter S.G. Mero, an independent radio consultant, with the concurrence of A.D. Ring and Company, who are likewise consultants in this field. This has been supervised by Mr. Robert Lang, Director of Radio Free Europe. To verify their conclusions, our special radio consultant, Commander Graveson spent some time in New York last week reviewing these plans and specifications, and his report is expected daily.

l. The present regulations of the National Production Authority requiring manufactures to give precedence to Defense Orders may seriously interfere with the acquisition of the new equipment and steps are being taken to expedite this procurement.

Frank G. Wisner<br>
Assistant Director for Policy Coordination

Source: "Wisner Update on Radio Free Europe," November 22, 1950, History and Public Policy Program Digital Archive, Obtained and contributed to CWIHP by A. Ross Johnson. Cited in Ch. 1, n. 39, of his book Radio Free Europe and Radio Liberty, CIA mandatory declassification review document number MORI 1137561. https://digitalarchive.wilsoncenter.org/document/114350 [last viewed December 2020].

# Appendix E
### Extracts from 1953 Jackson Report on Radio Free Europe— National Committee for Free Europe

~~TOP SECRET~~

Report to the President by the President's Committee on International Information Activities

[WASHINGTON,] June 30, 1953. [Here follow a table of contents and a list of appendices, of which all but Appendix II are printed.] [...] National Committee for a Free Europe

The National Committee for a Free Europe (NCFE) was created by CIA in 1949 with the following purposes:

1. to create an institution in which the émigrés from the satellite nations could find employment which would utilize their skills and, at the same time, document for the world at large the actions of the satellite governments and Soviet Russia;
2. to utilize the political figures of such emigrations as rallying points and as symbols of unified opposition to communism in this country and abroad;
3. to relieve the Department of State of the need to deal with émigré political leaders whom they could not endorse as "Governments in Exile" at a time when the United States officially recognized the satellite governments; and
4. generally to "aid the non-fascist, non-communist leaders in their peaceful efforts to prepare the way toward the restoration in Eastern Europe of the social, political, and religious liberties, in which they and we believe."

The activities of NCFE fall into six categories: the organization and support of refugee political groups; Radio Free Europe (RFE), which broadcasts from Munich and Portugal to the eastern European satellites; projects on eastern Europe; the Free University in Exile located at Strasbourg; the compilation of an information digest of current developments behind the Iron Curtain; and assistance to refugees from the satellites now residing in western Europe.

In the fiscal year 1953 $\_\_\_\_$ was allotted for the support of these activities. Most of this support was furnished by CIA. Of this amount $\_\_\_\_$ was allocated to RFE, $\_\_\_\_$ to the Free University in Exile, and $\_\_\_\_$ to the support of the other activities conducted by NCFE. The following personnel are engaged in these operations: RFE: 252 Americans and 1,526 aliens; Free University in Exile: 8 Americans and 45 aliens; other activities: 183 Americans and 345 aliens.

The bulk of available evidence indicates that RFE is widely heard, particularly in its three primary target areas, Czechoslovakia, Hungary and Poland, and that its programs are well received by its audience. There is less agreement on the effectiveness of other NCFE activities. Efforts to form national councils composed of political leaders from the various emigrations have largely been frustrated by the bickering and jealousies common to émigré politicians. The Free University in Exile, which was established to train refugee students for future leadership in their own countries after liberation, has found it difficult to provide proper motivation and the whole project is currently under reexamination. The research and news-gathering activities provide material for broadcasting operations and are also a source of information regarding developments behind the Iron Curtain. Aid to satellite refugees in western Europe, which is designed to supplement the activities of regular relief agencies by assisting refugees to adapt to their new environment while preserving their national consciousness and national culture, is a program now in its initial phases.

In the original plan the various national councils were to be responsible for broadcasts over RFE facilities to their respective countries. Since the complexities and rivalries of émigré politics made the organization of national councils difficult, it was decided to set up RFE on a non-political basis. Émigré staffs were hired for competence rather than political affiliation and programs to various countries are now identified as the Voice of Free Czechoslovakia, Poland, and so on. Although this reason for the national councils no longer exists, they do have potential value in exile relations. If the émigré leaders are prepared to create national councils of their own volition, NCFE should assist them to engage in such propaganda activities as they may be qualified to conduct. Primary attention, however, should be given to the broadcasting phase of NCFE activities. The

Committee recommends that the rest of these activities be reviewed by CIA to determine whether they should be continued or modified.

As in the case of the Russian emigration, support operations which enable refugees from the satellites to live decently either in the United States or in western Europe have a certain long-term value even though their short-range advantages are not apparent. These individuals might constitute a useful cadre in the event of hostilities in eastern Europe and the research work they do may prove of value, both now and in the future, if suitable arrangements can be made for better distribution of the results to appropriate agencies.

Certain specific problems arise in connection with NCFE activities, particularly RFE. There is first the question of cover. It has been suggested that, because the present cover has worn thin, RFE's official connections be freely admitted. Such a course, however, would vitiate the principal reason for the existence of RFE as a separate organization. So long as its government connections are not officially admitted it can broadcast programs and take positions for which the United States would not desire to accept responsibility. The Committee believes that the present cover is adequate for this purpose.

A second problem is the question of relations with the West German Government. RFE's European headquarters and several of its transmitting facilities are located in West Germany. By the very nature of its activities it is inevitable that there should be conflict between the interests of RFE and those of the large number of ethnic Germans who have been displaced from their homes in eastern Europe. These German refugees are critical of some of the eastern Europeans employed on RFE and frequently disagree with the political solutions which are advocated or implied with respect to the future organization of this area. They constitute a compact political pressure group in western Germany and are in a position to influence the attitude of the Bonn Government. This will be a continuing problem and may be expected to become more acute as Germany moves toward full sovereignty. It is therefore imperative that every effort be made by RFE to work out and maintain the best possible relations with the Bonn Government.

The Report of the President's Committee on International Information Activities, June 30, 1953.

Source: *Eisenhower Library, White House Office records, "Project 'Clean Up.'"*

# Appendix F
Extracts from 1953 Jackson Report on Radio Liberty

## The American Committee for Liberation from Bolshevism, Inc.

The Committee was founded in 1951 for the purpose of attempting to utilize the forces of the Soviet emigration against the Soviet regime. The Committee is under CIA sponsorship and guidance, and has not attempted to raise funds publicly, which would assist in providing plausible cover for its activities. Policy has been determined in close coordination with the Department of State.

The American Committee has assumed that the most effective propaganda against the Soviet regime can be conducted by former Soviet nationals speaking in the name of a united emigration. Proceeding on this assumption, a great deal of time and effort has been expended in attempting to bring together in one political center the diverse political groups existing in the emigration, which themselves have no leader of recognized stature.

The difficulties in the way of accomplishing this aim are twofold: first, the extreme hostility existing between Great Russian groups and those composed of the various non-Russian peoples of the Soviet Union; and second, basic political differences between Marxist and non-Marxist elements in the emigration, regardless of nationality. After long and arduous negotiations, agreement was finally reached in October 1952 for the formation of a coordinating center composed of four Great Russian and five nationality groups. The entire right wing of the Great Russian emigration and such important minority groups as the Ukrainians and Byelorussians have thus far held aloof.

## Extracts from 1953 Jackson Report on Radio Liberty

It is the declared purpose of the American Committee to proceed with propaganda activities utilizing the present coordinating center, and to attempt gradually to broaden the base of the center by the inclusion of additional groups as circumstances permit. Activities of the center include Radio Liberation, a Russian-language station which went on the air from Munich on March 1, 1953, broadcasting initially to Soviet occupation forces in Germany and Austria, and a Russian Institute intended to utilize the knowledge and skills present in the emigration for research on the Soviet Union. A newspaper, addressed primarily to the Soviet emigration and published in the name of the coordinating center, is planned.

In the fiscal year 1953 $_____ was allotted for support of this project. Of this figure $_____ was for Radio Liberation and $_____ for the conduct of the other activities of the Committee. Ninety-six Americans and 218 aliens were employed.

The results to date have not been noteworthy. Undoubtedly more rapid progress could have been made if the idea of a political center had been abandoned and activities on the RFE pattern begun without regard to political considerations. From the outset there have been many advocates of such a course who argued that the whole history of the Russian emigration since 1917 has demonstrated the futility of attempting to persuade its diffuse elements to coalesce in a common undertaking. The prevailing view, however, has been that the psychological impact of a united voice of the Soviet emigration would so much outweigh that of a station under transparent foreign control that the time and effort expended on the formation of a coordinating center were justified.

In a situation short of war the project can probably make its greatest contribution by de-emphasizing its political activities and devoting its major effort to the improvement of broadcasts from Radio Liberation. This station should use Soviet émigrés in an effort to weaken the Soviet regime and should concentrate on the Soviet military, government officials, and other groups in the population which harbor major grievances against the regime. Present plans call for the provision of new transmitting facilities in Spain. It is important that these or other facilities be developed in order to enable Radio Liberation to reach a wide audience within the Soviet Union.

Pending a final determination of its effectiveness, we believe that the activities of the American Committee should be continued. Because results can be expected in the immediate future only from broadcasting, however, it is recommended that major attention should be concentrated on Radio Liberation. Expenditures on the coordinating center can be reduced but should be maintained at a level adequate to keep the organization in being, without active efforts to broaden the base of the center. If through the efforts of the present membership of the center additional émigré groups can be persuaded to participate, such moves should receive the encouragement and support of the Committee.

The Report of the President's Committee on International Information Activities, June 30, 1953.

*Source: Eisenhower Library, White House Office records, "Project 'Clean Up.'"*

# Appendix G
## Termination of Voice of Free Albania Broadcasts— Termination of HTGRUBBY Broadcasts

~~SECRET KAPOK~~

Dispatch No. SGAA-31592
Date: 7 March 1958

TO: Chief, SE
FROM: Chief of [redacted]
References; [redacted] 17771, 9 December 1957
[redacted] 17984, 6 January 1950
SUBJECT: General—Plans / OBTEST
Specific—Considerations on the Termination of HTGRUBBY

Synopsis: Since the Branch does not have a qualified PSXCH Case Officer and Headquarters cannot provide one, we have reluctantly agreed to suspend HTGRUBBY

1. The two cited references imply, by their suggested employment of the various assets available to the Branch, that continuation of the NATCOM program has assumed a position of priority over other activities in which we might be gainfully employed. These references have been discussed with [redacted]who concur with the Branch view that acceptance of Headquarters' recommendations would not only disrupt any attempt at a balanced Fl/PSYCH program against Albania but would in fact virtually eliminate Fl and HTGRUBBY coverage of Albania.
2. The operation and management of a single PP radio program is a difficult task, even when there is a qualified PSYCH officer available

with an indigenous staff to assist him. Headquarters has expressed precisely this opinion in both DIR 06881 and DIR 10899. It is obvious that the NATCOM program cannot be run properly for any long period of time unless the proper guidance, direction, and support is given to ATPLEBE. To be effective, the program must be timely in its presentation; it must offer concrete and realistic proposals which can be acted upon by the listening audience thereby bringing about desired changes. The program must always be within the limits imposed upon KUBARK by existing PBPRIME policy. Only a Staff Officer can have access to all of the material available at the [redacted] which covers his area of activity—and can therefore properly carry out his responsibility. Furthermore, a full time Staff Officer is necessary in order to inject new life and ideas into the programs so that they avoid becoming stereotyped, meaningless and so deteriorated in quality that they reflect adversely on this Station and on KUBARK. Therefore, essentially, the problem is to find a Staff Case Officer if we are to maintain NATCOM.

3. ...
4. We believe nevertheless that a good PSYCH program is probably the only means at our disposal—short of paramilitary or open conflict—of exerting external influences to attempt to bring about any desired changes in Albania. There is no question in our minds that a properly oriented program will also assist in the conduct of FI activities. In a country like Albania, where we have no other means of getting the message across, we have to rely on the radio—also an essential channel in a possible eventual "hot" situation. Because of our strong beliefs here, we, have, at the expense of other Branch activities, maintained for approximately eight months, both the NATCOM and HTGRUBBY programs without a PSYCH officer. In [redacted] 9801, we advised you that, with the existing personnel assigned to the Branch, we found it impossible to maintain two radio programs. We stated that we would begin to phase out HTGRUBBY and that we would put NATCOM on an irregular basis. We sincerely hoped that we could continue a curtailed PSYCH program over an extended period thus affording Headquarters additional time to obtain a qualified PSYCH officer. Our belief that a PSYCH officer would be made available was based on the grounds that Headquarters was also of the opinion that a PSYCH effort should be maintained. [redacted] 117771, 9 December 1957, has made it clear from an administrative point of view that a PSYCH officer is not available. Necessarily then, much of our case officer time will be used up on PSYCH activities and only the barest minimum time can be devoted to Albanian

Fl operations. In view of the above, we must therefore presume that in terms of KUBARK policy, continuation of NATCOM takes precedence over Fl coverage of Albania and that for all practical purposes, our Fl responsibility will require only a token effort.

5. Per DIR 06740, 6 February 199, we are therefore suspending HTGRUBBY effective 28 February 1958. AIBERM, AIPOET, and RNADUANA are being returned to the United States.
6. NATCOM, under the supervision of [redacted] will be continued on as regular a basis as possible with existing means. It is understood, however, that we are not in a position to guarantee the highest quality programs at all times. Furthermore, since AlPLEBE has mentioned to on two different occasions that he is experiencing increasing difficulty in keeping the National Socialist attitude, it appears that we must inevitably expect that the tone of the programs will slowly approach a certain neutral position between National Socialism and outright anti–Communism. Since there is no doubt in the Field concerning AIPLEBE's knowledge of the Albanian scene and his extremely facile mind, we plan to capitalize on this transition. Our expectations and our future planning are based on the gradual change-over of NATCOM to a sophisticated and possibly cynical criticism of the regime which is founded on everyday facts rather than on Leninist dogma.

# Appendix H
## *Personal History of Ferdinand Durčansky*

Name: Durcansky, Ferdinand
Summary of Available Personality Information     2 November 1954
Personal History Excerpts

    Free Europe Committee Relationship: Subject as a leading Slovak separatist, has frequently criticized the programs and personnel of RFE and the Council of Free Czechoslovakia (CFC) (see Allegations)

    In the Spring of 1945, Subject escaped to Rome. When Karel SIDOR and the Slovak League of America (SLA) declined to share with him funds collected from Slovak nationals abroad, Subject organized the Slovak Action Committee (SAC) to work for an independent Slovakia (RI/201 21 Mar 51; State/BID, Sep 54). Between 1945 and 1947 he was reported broadcasting to Slovakia from radio "Barcelona," located at various times in Austria, in Udina, Italy, and on a ship in the Bay of Naples (RI/201 20 Nov 51; I&R [redacted] files, SO/SSD, 28 Oct 54).

    In June 1947 Subject was reported broadcasting to Slovakia from either Austria or Italy, although a Prague newspaper stated on June 18, 1947, that his station had recently gone off the air. In September he was reported broadcasting again, this time from either Austria or Bavaria (State/NW, Sep 54). Early in 1953 he was said to be on the point of installing a transmitter near Augsburg for broadcasting to Slovakia; he is presently living in Munich, according to the latest report (IO, FEC list of émigré organizations, mid–1954).

...

    Allegations against Radio Free Europe and Council of Free Czechoslovakia (CFC)

    1. Subject wrote a letter in 1948 to General Lucius Clay denouncing Mikulas FERJENCIK and others members of the CFC...

## Personal History of Ferdinand Durčansky

2. Documents published by Subject's Slovak Liberation Committee in Munich and London accuse the NCFE of pointing its radio programs toward subjugating the interests of the Slovak people, and of employing Czechs who formerly collaborated with the Communists (RI/201, 20 Mar 52).
3. A State Department dispatch reported that the stimulus behind criticism of the personnel and programs of the Czech Desk of RFE seemed to be coming from the SLC (RI/201, 1 Apr 52).
4. An Free Europe Committee memorandum stated:

   Our continuing study of the various attacks on PEROUTKA (head of the Czech Desk of RFE) indicates that they are inspired by the agents of two political adventurers and agitators namely General PRCHALA and Dr. Ferdinand DURCANSKY.... His (subject's) fulminations and vilifications of many prominent Czech's regularly appear in obscure newspapers published in the Czech or Slovak language in various centers of Czech emigration... (RI/201, 15 May 52)....

5. Subject is alleged to have accused the Council of Free Czechoslovakia (CFC) of acting in secret understanding with the Prague government (i.e., with the present Communist government of Czechoslovakia) (State/BID, Sep 54).
6. Subject and Matus CERNAK, the SNCA representative in Germany, were joint authors of a statement criticizing RFE/Munich for suppressing the majority (i.e. Slovaks), recruiting personnel among communists, betraying routes of escape from Czechoslovakia, demoralizing their listeners with American jazz, and so on (IO undated)
7. In a letter to Mr. GRIFFITH (probably William Griffith, Policy Advisor, RFE/Munich) subject stated that the broadcasts of RFE "propagate ... the Czechoslovak conception which is being regarded by the Slovak people as one of the causes of its present plight and which, according to absolutely reliable information from Slovakia, conflicts with the will of the Slovak people" (IO file #345, 18 Feb 52).

...

In March 1953 ZIPPER (Gehlen Organization) denied that Subject was operating a black radio in Augsburg under German sponsorship, but in June 1953 they reiterated the fact that they would continue to work with him.

# Chapter Notes

## Chapter 1

1. "The Report of The President's Committee (Jackson Committee) on International Information Activities," June 30, 1953, /special Collection/helms/pdf/jacksn_report.pdf, https://www.cia.gov/library/readingroom/document/5076de59993247d4d82b59ab [last viewed December 2020].
2. Jean Edward Smith, *Lucius D. Clay: An American Life* (New York: Henry Holt, 1990), p. 285.
3. CIA Historical Staff Chronology 1946–65, Volume 1 1946–1955, p. 21, https://www.cia.gov/library/readingroom/document/cia-rdp85b00803r000200050002-6 [last viewed December 2020].
4. A photocopy of this directive can be found in Michael Warner, ed., *CIA Cold War Records: The CIA under Harry Truman*, "Psychological Operations, NSC 4-A," (Washington, DC: CIA, 1994), pp. 175–177. See also, National Security Council (NS) Truman Administration (1947–53). https://fas.org/irp/offdocs/nsc-hst/nsc-4.htm [last viewed December 2020].
5. Ibid.
6. Foreign Relations of the United States, 1945–1959, "Emergence of the Intelligence Establishment," *Emergence of the Intelligence Establishment*, Document 269, https://history.state.gov/historicaldocuments/frus1945-50Intel/d269 [last viewed December 2020].
7. Ibid.
8. Ibid.
9. Ibid.
10. "George F. Kennan and the Office of Policy Coordination at the CIA, 1948–50" by Douglas Selvage, Yale University. A paper presented at the Annual Conference of the Society for Historians of American Foreign Relations at National Archives II, College Park, Maryland, on June 18, 1998, p. 4.
11. "Memorandum from the Chief of the Special Procedures Group (Cassady) to the Deputy Chief of the Special Procedures Group (Dulin)," 11 March 1948, *Emergence of the Intelligence Establishment*, op. cit., Document 261.
12. Selvage, op. cit.
13. Ibid.
14. OPC began with its establishment on September 1, 1948, and ended on August 1, 1952, when it was merged with the Office of Special Operations (OSO) into a combined directorate, which became known as the Clandestine Services of Central Intelligence Agency.
15. The full text of NSC 10/2 is reproduced as Document 292, *Foreign Relations of the United States, 1945–1950, Emergence of the Intelligence Establishment*, https://history.state.gov/historicaldocuments/frus1945-50Intel/d292 [last viewed December 2020].
16. See full details of Wisner's experiences in Romania in Evan Thomas, *The Very Best Men: Four Who Dared: The Early Years of the CIA* (New York: Simon & Schuster, 1995).
17. Memorandum from the director of the Policy Planning Staff, Department of State (Kennan) to the assistant director for Policy Coordination, Central Intelligence Agency (Wisner), Washington, 6 January 1949, *Emergence of the Intelligence Establishment*, op. cit., Document 308.
18. Ibid., 215–6.
19. "U.S. Government Officials Discuss

Émigré Broadcasts to Eastern Europe," August 26, 1948, History and Public Policy Program Digital Archive, obtained and contributed to CWIHP by A. Ross Johnson. Cited in his book *Radio Free Europe and Radio Liberty*, Ch. 1 p. 13, CIA mandatory declassification review document number C05458947. http://digitalarchive.wilsoncenter.org/document/114321.

20. Memorandum to ADPC, Subject; Umpire Project. QKDEMON PROJECT OUTLINE VOL. 1_0001, https://www.cia.gov/library/readingroom/document/5197c261993294098d50d899 [last viewed December 2020].

21. Source: Document 306, Office of the Historian, FRUS, 1945–1050, Emergence of the Intelligence Establishment, https://history.state.gov/historicaldocuments/frus1945-50Intel/d306 [last viewed December 2020].

22. https://www.cia.gov/library/readingroom/document/519a2b76993294098d50f599 [last viewed December 2020].

23. *Ibid.*
24. *Ibid.*
25. *Ibid.*

26. Gerald Miller, "Office of Policy Coordination 1948–1952," pp. 10–11 (Undated) https://www.cia.gov/library/readingroom/document/0000104823 [last viewed December 2020]. The report was reproduced and edited in CIA's *Studies in Intelligence*, Vol. 17, No. 2-S, Summer 1973.

27. Minutes of Princeton meeting 5/10–5/11/52. White House, 10 May 1952. U.S. Declassified Documents Online, http://tinyurl-1galegroup-1com-1p8zkmg0s0a51.zugang.nationallizenzen.de/tinyurl/BUYwD8 [last opened July 2020]. The Psychological Strategy Board issues a restrained revision of the Princeton Statement adopted at a May 1952 meeting at Princeton on psychological operations [copy available in the Hoover Archives]. "Revised Princeton Statement [on American Foreign Policy]," July 16, 1952, History and Public Policy Program Digital Archive, obtained and contributed to CWIHP by A. Ross Johnson. Cited in Ch. 2, n. 25 in his book *Radio Free Europe and Radio Liberty*, CIA mandatory declassification review document number C01441015. http://digitalarchive.wilsoncenter.org/document/114470 [last viewed December 2020].

28. *Ibid.* Lewis Galantiere was NCFE counselor, William E. Griffith was policy adviser to RFE's European director.

29. *Ibid.*
30. *Ibid.*
31. *Ibid.*

32. "The Report of The President's Committee (Jackson Committee) on International Information Activities," op. cit.

33. *Ibid.*
34. *Ibid.*

35. Official Dispatch OPC Headquarters, QKDEMON VOL. 4_0168, https://www.cia.gov/library/readingroom/document/5197c261993294098d50d869 [last viewed December 2020]. Extracts in Appendix C.

36. *Ibid.*

37. "Monitoring of AEHANGOVER and AERODYNAMIC Broadcasts," July 9, 1959, AERODYNAMIC VOL.17 (Operations)_0040, https://www.cia.gov/library/readingroom/document/519a2b76993294098d50f4c2 [last viewed December 2020].

38. *Ibid.* See Appendix IV, Recommendations, p. 119

39. Foreign Relations of the United States, 1958–1960, Eastern Europe; Finland; Greece; Turkey, Volume X, Part 2 Document 18 [last viewed December 2020].

40. *Ibid.*
41. *Ibid.*

42. "Stasi Note on Meeting with KGB Officials, 13 November 1969," November 13, 1969, History and Public Policy Program Digital Archive, Office of the Federal Commissioner for the Stasi Records (BStU), MfS, MfS, SdM 577, p. 88–110. Translated from German for CWIHP by Bernd Schaefer. http://digitalarchive.wilsoncenter.org/document/115714 [last viewed December 2020]. For more information about "Radio Baikal"and "Radio Caucasas," see Chapter 1.

43. . "Free Russia" is examined in Chapter 8, and "Free Ukraine" is covered in Chapter 7.

44. Second Release Lexicon, p. 49. AEHUNTER was probably the cryptonym for the Georgian National Democrats.

45. "Progress Report for period 11–30 Sept. 1957," October 29, 1957, AERODYNAMIC VOL. 15 (Operations)_0043, https://www.cia.gov/library/readingroom/document/519a2b7d993294098d5105c8 [last viewed December 2020].

46. "Progress Report for period 1–31 December 1957," AERODYNAMIC VOL.

15 (Operations)_0045, https://www.cia.gov/library/readingroom/document/519a2b7d993294098d5105ee [last viewed December 2020].

47. "Progress Report for period 1–28 February 1958," March 20, 1958, AERODYNAMIC VOL. 15 (Operations)_0066, https://www.cia.gov/library/readingroom/document/519a2b7d993294098d5105e0 [last viewed December 2020].

48. KGB Report, op. cit.

## Chapter 2

1. The phrase was developed by the Advertising Council for the Radio Free Europe Fund annual solicitation drives in the early 1960s: "Give Now To ... Radio Free Europe, The American People's Counter-Voice to Communism."

2. William E. Griffith, Radio Free Europe Policy Director, 1952–1958, "RFE—Four Essential Ingredients of Its Success," February 15, 1952, File RFE-Policy Matters General 1950–1956, Box 286, RFE/RL Corporate Records, Hoover Institution Archives (hereinafter HIA).

3. Headquarters OPC Message 170-CWUEG, to OPC Heidelberg, Germany, May 20, 1949, QKDEMON VOL.4_0140, https://www.cia.gov/library/readingroom/document/5197c261993294098d50d7f8 [last viewed December 2020].

4. Memorandum from Karlsruhe to Policy Coordination, November 5, 1948, QKDEMON VOL. 2_0009, https://www.cia.gov/library/readingroom/document/5197c261993294098d50d97e [last viewed December 2020].

5. Message from Chief of Station Karlsruhe to Chief, SPG, November 16, 1948, "Work Accomplished and Present Status of Umpire of Germany," https://www.cia.gov/library/readingroom/document/5197c261993294098d50d933 [last viewed December 2020].

6. Ibid.

7. Message from Policy Coordination to OPC Karlsruhe, December 7, 1948, QKDEMON VOL. 2_0019,https://www.cia.gov/library/readingroom/document/5197c261993294098d50d8d8 [last viewed December 2020].

8. Message from OPC Karlsruhe to Policy Coordination, December 28, 1948, QKDEMON VOL. 2_0031, https://www.cia.gov/library/readingroom/document/5197c261993294098d50d8e9 [last viewed December 2020].

9. Message from Karlsruhe to Policy Coordination, February 23, 1949, QKDEMON VOL. 2_0150, https://www.cia.gov/library/readingroom/document/5197c261993294098d50d916 [last viewed December 2020].

10. Message Policy Coordination to OPC Karlsruhe, March 14, 1949, QKDEMON VOL. 2_0194, https://www.cia.gov/library/readingroom/document/5197c261993294098d50d8b9 [last viewed December 2020].

11. Message OPC Karlsruhe to Policy Coordination, March 17, 1949, QKDEMON VOL: 3_0008, https://www.cia.gov/library/readingroom/document/5197c260993294098d50d778 [last viewed December 2020].

12. Message OPC Karlsruhe to Policy Coordination, March 31, 1949, QKDEMON VOL. 3_0064, https://www.cia.gov/library/readingroom/document/5197c260993294098d50d778 [last viewed December 2020].

13. Memorandum to Mr. Wisner, February 6, 1949, QKDEMON VOL. 2_0106, https://ia801300.us.archive.org/15/items/QKDEMONVOL2-0106/QKDEMON%20%20%20VOL.%202_0106.pdf [last viewed December 2020].

14. Message from Policy Coordination to OPC Heidelberg, June 9, 1949, QKDEMON VOL. 4_0190, https://ia801306.us.archive.org/11/items/QKDEMONVOL4-0190/QKDEMON%20%20%20VOL.%204_0190.pdf [last viewed December 2020].

15. Memorandum for: COP, December 29, 1949, QKDEMON VOL. 4_0220, https://ia800204.us.archive.org/5/items/QKDEMON/QKDEMON%20%20%20VOL.%204_0220.pdf [last viewed December 2020].

16. Dwight D. Eisenhower, "Crusade for Freedom," Denver, Colorado, 4 September 1950, Dwight D. Eisenhower Presidential Library, Museum and Boyhood Home, Abilene, Kansas, https://www.eisenhowerlibrary.gov/sites/default/files/file/pre_presidential_speeches.pdf [last viewed December 2020].

17. Dewitt C. Poole to Allen Dulles, September 28, 1950, https://www.cia.gov/library/readingroom/docs/

DOC_0000480977.pdf [last viewed December 2020].

18. *Ibid.*

19. "Letter from DeWitt C. Poole to William H. Jackson," 25 October 1950, National Committee for a Free Europe, Inc., 1949–1950, Allen W. Dulles Papers; Policy Papers, Department of Rare Books and Special Collections, Princeton University Library, https//findingaids.edu/collections/MC019/c00736 [last viewed December 2020].

20. https://www.cia.gov/library/readingroom/document/0001137561 [last viewed December 2020].

21. Secret Report Attachment to Memorandum by the Undersecretary of State for Public Affairs (Edward W. Barrett) to Deputy Secretary of State (Mathews, January 24, 1951, FRUS 1951, Vol. IV, Part 2, pp. 1206–1208, http://images.library.wisc.edu/FRUS/EFacs2/1951v04p2/reference/frus.frus1951v04p2.i0010.pdf [last viewed December 2020].

22. *Ibid.*, Document No. 611, pp. 1217–1218.

23. *Chronicle-Express*, Pann Van, New York, May 17, 1951, p. Six-A.

24. RFE/RL Collection, HIA.

25. Memorandum to the Executive Secretary of the National Security Council (Lay), Subject: Third Progress Report on NSC 59/1, "The Foreign Information Program and Psychological Warfare Planning, Foreign Relations, 1950.1955, Document 57, https://history.state.gov/historicaldocuments/frus1950-55Intel/d57#fn:1.5.4.2.10.164.14.32.2 [last viewed December 2020].

26. Origins v3—MIT, web.mit.edu/CIS/pdf/Panel ORIGINS.

27. Memorandum from Robert J. Hooker of the Policy Planning Staff to the Director of the Policy Planning Staff (Nitze) Washington, March 26, 1951, *Foreign Relations, 1950–1955*, Document 59, https://history.state.gov/historicaldocuments/frus1950-55Intel/d59 [last viewed December 2020].

28. *Ibid.*

29. For a detailed look in English: Dr. Igor Lukes, "KAMEN: A Cold War Dangle Operation with an American Dimension, 1948–52," *Studies in Intelligence*, Vol. 55, No. 1 (Extracts, March 2011), https://www.cia.gov/library/center-for-the-study-of-intelligence/csi-publications/csi-studies/vol.-55-no.-1/kamen-a-cold-war-dangle-operation-with-an-american-dimension-1948-1952.html, [last viewed December 2020]. In the Czech language, military historian Dr. Prokop Tomek wrote a detailed article about KAMEN and the major player Amon Tomasoff, "Adventurer in the Service of Communists" (Amon Tomašoff—dobrodruh ve službách komunistů) in SECURITAS IMPERII 12, Sborník k problematice 50. Let," pp. 5 -28. The most detailed study of the subject can be found in two books in Czech by Václava Jandečková: *Kámen: Svědectví hlavního aktéra akce "Falešné hranice" u Všerub na Domažlicku*, Nakladatelství Českého lesa (2014) and Falešné hranice: *Akce "Kámen": Oběti a strůjci nejutajovanějších zločinů StB 1948–1951* (2018). In addition, she wrote a detailed article in English: "OPERATION "Kámen"—VŠERUBY 1948: New Revelations in the Case of the Fake Czech Border to Germany," *Journal for Intelligence, Propaganda and Security Studies* (JIPPS) Vol. 7, No. 1 (2013), 49–68.

30. Lukes, op. cit., p. 9.

31. "Operation Kámen," op. cit., p.64. She obtained from Liška's family in Canada a copy of his report on the operation that he gave to the CIC before leaving Germany.

32. Lukes, op. cit. Karel Koecher, a native of CSSR and a naturalized U.S. citizen, was arrested in New York in November 1984 on charges of spying for the Czechoslovak Intelligence Service (CIS). He was alleged to have been sent to the West on a mission of infiltrating the CIA and providing classified information to the CIS. There was mention in the press that Koecher was once a consultant to RFE and that he said that he sent material to RFE while he was still in CSSR. He pled guilty and was sentenced to life imprisonment, but the sentence was commuted if he left the USA and never returned. His wife was arrested for refusing to cooperate with the federal investigation. Both were "swapped"" in Berlin in February 1986 for the former Soviet dissident Scharansky and other dissidents jailed behind the Iron Curtain. There was a lot of publicity about their arrest and trial and subsequent return to Czechoslovakia. Amon Tomašoff died of brain cancer in 1953.

33. Document 658, FRUS 1951, Vol. IV, Part 2, p. 1316.

34. Memorandum of Conversation,

Washington, January 17, 1952, Foreign Relations, 1950–1955, Document 100. Washburn had been head of the public relations department for General Mills, Inc., in Minneapolis before joining the Crusade for Freedom. He went on to become deputy director of the U.S. Information Agency from 1953 to 1961 and later served on the Federal Communications Commission from 1974 to 1982.

35. Memorandum to the Executive Secretary of the National Security Council (Lay) Washington, undated. Third Progress Report on NSC 59/1, "The Foreign Information Program and Psychological Warfare Planning Document. Foreign Relations, 1950–1955, Document No. 57.

36. William E. Griffith, op. cit.

37. Quoted in A. Ross Johnson, *Radio Free Europe and Radio Liberty: The CIA Years and Beyond*, p. 42.

38. Griffith, op. cit.

39. Alan A. Michie, *Voices Through the Iron Curtain: The Radio Free Europe Story* (New York: Dodd, Meade, 1963), p. 30.

40. David L. Hollyer, "The Saga of the Cold War's MB50," *Radio World*, January 15, 2003. Hollyer was an engineer for Radio Free Europe.

41. Stanley Leinwoll, "Freedom's Radio," *Electronics Now*, September 1997, pp. 46–53.

42. Radio Romania in December 2020 was still using the 855 kHz frequency with a 250 kW transmitter located at Țâncăbești, Romania.

43. RFE/RL Collection, HIA.

44. Arch Puddington, *Broadcasting Freedom: The Cold War Triumph of Radio Free Europe and Radio Liberty* (Lexington: University Press of Kentucky, 2000), pp. 48–49. The quote also appeared in *The American Spectator*, p. 75, Joseph Shattan, "Saturday Evening Club," 2000. Also, Nancy DeWolf Smith, "Radio Days Revisited," *Wall Street Journal*, May 19, 2000, and *Wall Street Journal*, "Beaming Some Light into the Darkness," June 5, 2000.

45. "Personalities at Kender-Lenszovogyar, Ujszeged," 24 October 1951, HU OSA 300-1-2-9627; Records of Radio Free Europe/Radio Liberty Research Institute: General Records: Information Items; Open Society Archives at Central European University, Budapest, http://hdl.handle.net/10891/osa:c850e1f7-feff-4b97-a4b7-053065f13d64 [last viewed December

2020]. Translation provided by Janos Kund, former staffer of RFE/RL.

46. RFE/RL Collection, HIA.

47. RFE/RL Corporate Records, Washington, D.C

48. Dispatch from Chief of Base, Munich, to Chief, EE, January 24, 1956, https://www.cia.gov/library/readingroom/docs/LISZKA%2C%20BELA_0014.pdf [last viewed December 2020].

49. From 1948 to 1956, the Hungarian secret police was known as the State Protection Authority (Államvédelmi Hatóság, ÁVH).

50. Cable Muni 2608, Munich to Director, December 9, 1955, https://www.cia.gov/library/readingroom/docs/LISZKA%2C%20BELA_0006.pdf [last viewed December 2020].

51. Ibid.

52. Chief of Base, Pullach, to Chief of Base, Munich, February 20, 1956, https://www.cia.gov/library/readingroom/document/519697ec993294098d50cc48 [last viewed December 2020].

53. English translation, Attachment D to EGMA-20450, https://www.cia.gov/library/readingroom/document/519697ec993294098d50cc4c [last viewed December 2020].

54. English translation of Letter from "Erzei," March 5, 1956, LISKA, BELA_0020, https://www.cia.gov/library/readingroom/document/519697ec993294098d50cc46 [last viewed December 2020].

55. LISZKA, Bela_0022.

56. LISZKA, Bela_0023.

57. LISZKA, Bela_0030.

58. LISKA, Bela_0020, op. cit.

59. Chief of Base, Munich, to Chief, EE Status Report, August 6, 1956, https://www.cia.gov/library/readingroom/document/519697ec993294098d50cc43 [last viewed December 2020].

60. Ibid., Case Officer Comment No. 4.

61. TPTONIC was the CIA project cryptonym for the National Committee for Free Europe (NCFE), a project administered by the Directorate of Plans International Organization Division (IOD). NCFE was the parent organization of RFE, which had the cryptonym TPFEELING.

62. Memorandum from Deputy Director of Security (Investigations and Support) to Chief, CI /OA, https://www.cia.gov/library/readingroom/docs/LISZKA%2C%20BELA_0039.pdf [last viewed December 2020].

63. Results of Local Processing, Received April 10, 1957, LISKA, BELA_0042, https://www.cia.gov/library/readingroom/document/519697ec993294098d50cc4e [last viewed December 2020].

64. RFE Internal Memorandum from William Griffith to Richard Condon, dated December 5, 1956, "Policy Review of Voice for Free Hungary Programming, October 23 November 1956." It surfaced in 1996 and was reprinted (without supporting appendices) in Csaba Bekes, Malcolm Byrne, and Janos M. Rainer, *The 1956 Hungarian Revolution: A History in Documents* (Budapest: CEU Press, 2002). What were not published, however, are three appendices to this report. Appendix I contains the summary evaluation of each individual program, Appendix II evaluates the performance of the individual Hungarian Service broadcasters and Appendix III contains excerpts of the written RFE policy guidance for the period. The review covered 308 programs or 70 percent of all non-news broadcast coverage during the period. A copy of the memorandum with all three appendices can be found in the RFE/RL Collection, HIA. Copies of the authentic "logging" tapes (the programs recorded as broadcast over the RFE transmitters at Biblis ,Germany, with German post office date/time signals) of RFE Hungarian (and the other RFE languages) for the period October 19-November 13, 1956, are available at the Hoover Institution, the Szechenyi National Library in Budapest, and the Federal German Archives in Koblenz on 367 CDs in MP3 format.

65. *Ibid.*

66. Quoted in Michael Nelson, *War of the Black Heavens: The Battles of Western Broadcasting in the Cold War*, p. 73.

67. "The Revolt In Hungary A Documentary Chronology of Events Based Exclusively on Internal Broadcasts By Central And Provincial Radios," https://www.cia.gov/library/readingroom/document/cia-rdp80b01676r001000010035-4 [last viewed December 2020].

68. Letter to honorable Herbert Hoover, Jr., Acting Secretary of State, from DCI Allen W. Dulles, November 26, 1956, with Press Release of Joseph C. Grew, https://www.cia.gov/library/readingroom/document/cia-rdp80b01676r002600100037-5 [last viewed December 2020].

69. *New York Times*, January 26, 1957.

70. *U. N. Review,* United Nations, *Report of the Special Committee on the Problem of Hungary,* June 20, 1957.

71. Cord Meyer, *Facing Reality: From World Federalism to the CIA* (New York: Harper and Row, 1980), p. 127.

72. George Urban, *Radio Free Europe and the Pursuit of Democracy: My War within the Cold War* (New Haven: Yale University Press, 1997), Chapter 16, p. 219.

73. "MUN-22 September Crypto Message," 5 September 1968, HU OSA 298–1-2-50–1166; Records of Free Europe Committee: President's Office: Encrypted Telex Communication between FEC New York and RFE Munich; Open Society Archives at Central European University, Budapest, permanent url: http://hdl.handle.net/10891/osa:5efe8614-0f88-486c-a159-157fec78b4b3 [last viewed December 2020].

74. "MUN-51 August Crypto Message," 21 August 1968, HU OSA 298–1-2-50–1005; Records of Free Europe Committee: President's Office: Encrypted Telex Communication between FEC New York and RFE Munich; Open Society Archives at Central European University, Budapest, permanent url: http://hdl.handle.net/10891/osa:edae4bb4-8083-4464-9bba-21472856c06b [last viewed December 2020].

75. "MUN-57 August Crypto Message," 21 August 1968, HU OSA 298–1-2-50–0999; Records of Free Europe Committee: President's Office: Encrypted Telex Communication between FEC New York and RFE Munich; Open Society Archives at Central European University, Budapest, permanent url: http://hdl.handle.net/10891/osa:73326cc3-9b77-4336-9364-105661d2b8ea [last viewed December 2020].

76. "MUN-83 August Crypto Message," 23 August 1968, HU OSA 298–1-2-50–0969, Records of Free Europe Committee: President's Office: Encrypted Telex Communication between FEC New York and RFE Munich; Open Society Archives at Central European University, Budapest, permanent url: http://hdl.handle.net/10891/osa:e575ff57-809c-43a4-8105-ddfbce66e206 [last viewed December 2020].

77. "MUN-90 August Crypto Message," 24 August 1968, HU OSA 298–1-2-50–0962;

Records of Free Europe Committee: President's Office: Encrypted Telex Communication between FEC New York and RFE Munich; Open Society Archives at Central European University, Budapest, permanent url: http://hdl.handle.net/10891/osa:29797b5a-e562-453b-99daea191160f253 [last viewed December 2020].

## Chapter 3

1. "Office of Policy Coordination History of American Committee for Liberation," August 21, 1951, History and Public Policy Program Digital Archive, Obtained and contributed to CWIHP by A. Ross Johnson. Cited in Ch. 1, n. 60, in his book *Radio Free Europe and Radio Liberty*, CIA mandatory declassification review document number C01441005, http://digitalarchive.wilsoncenter.org/document/114354 [last viewed December 2020].

2. The Report of The President's Committee (Jackson Committee) on International Information Activities, June 30,1953: Project "Clean Up," *Foreign Relations, 1952–54*, Vol. 2, International Information Activities (Washington, D.C.: U.S. Department of State).

3. "Radio Liberty Editorial Policies Defined," January 22, 1953, History and Public Policy Program Digital Archive, obtained and contributed to CWIHP by A. Ross Johnson. Cited in his book *Radio Free Europe and Radio Liberty*. CIA mandatory declassification review document number C01434009. A nearly identical unredacted RL policy document, dated February 11, 1953, is available in the Hoover Archives and is cited in Ch. 1, n. 85, http://digitalarchive.wilsoncenter.org/document/114471 [last viewed December 2020].

4. For more details in Russian about Vinogradov and the first Radio Liberation personalities and broadcasts, "History of the First Broadcast" by Ivan Tolstoi, https://www.svoboda.org/a/24918117.html [last viewed December 2020].

5. James Critchlow, *Radio Hole in the Head: Radio Liberty: An Insider's Story of Cold War Broadcasting* (Washington, D.C.: American University Press, 1995), p. 59.

6. "CIA Criticizes American Committee for Liberation Policies," May 18, 1953, History and Public Policy Program Digital Archive, Obtained and contributed to CWIHP by A. Ross Johnson. Reference in Ch. 1, p. 32, in his book *Radio Free Europe and Radio Liberty*, CIA mandatory declassification review document number C05459035, http://digitalarchive.wilsoncenter.org/document/114473 [last viewed December 2020].

7. The Report of The President's Committee (Jackson Committee) on International Information Activities, June 30,1953, op. cit.

8. William Henry Chamberlin, "Émigré Anti-Soviet Enterprises and Splits," *Russian Review*, Vol. 13, No. 2, April 1954, p. 92.

9. *Ibid*.

10. See the author's book *Cold War Radio: The Dangerous History of American Broadcasting in Europe, 1950–1989* (Jefferson, NC: McFarland, 2009), Chapter 2, for more details.

11. CIA Information Report, https://www.cia.gov/library/readingroom/docs/CIA-RDP78-04864A000100100063-0.pdf [last viewed December 2020].

12. "KGB Report: On the State of Jamming Anti-Soviet Radio Programs of Foreign Radio Stations," May 19, 1959, History and Public Policy Program Digital Archive, Archives of the Central Committee of the Communist Party of the Soviet Union. Obtained by Michael Nelson, translated by Volodymyr Valkov, http://digitalarchive.wilsoncenter.org/document/121546 [last viewed December 2020].

13. *Radio Liberty Annual Report, July 1, 1973—June 30, 1974*. RFE/RL Collection HIA.

14. Radio Liberty Press Release, January 10, 1964, RFE/RL Collection, HIA.

15. Shortwave broadcasting from this site would continue until May 25, 2001. Exactly 27 years after the first broadcast, on March 23, 2006, the huge transmitter towers, some of which reached a height of over 500 feet, were demolished in a live Spanish television broadcast.

16. Isaac Patch, *Closing the Circle: A Buckalino Journey Around Our Time* (Wellesley, MA: Wellesley College Printing Services, 1966), p. 256.

17. *Ibid*.

18. Patch, op. cit., p. 257.

19. Patch, p. 261.

20. Patch, p. 262.

21. National Security Council Intelligence Directive No. 13, January 19, 1950. *Foreign Relations of the United States, 1950–1955*, Document 252, https://history.state.gov/historicaldocuments/frus1950-55Intel/d252 [last viewed December 2020].
22. *Ibid.*
23. *Ibid.*
24. Project Outline—HARVARD, Attachment to Memorandum from John A. Bross, Chief, Eastern Europe Division, to Chief, Foreign Intelligence, January 1956, https://www.cia.gov/library/readingroom/document/5197c265993294098d50e2c4 [last viewed December 2020].
25. Eric Thomas Chester, *Covert Network: Progressives, the International Rescue Committee and the CIA* (New York: M.E. Sharpe, 1995, and Routledge, 2018), p. 78.
26. *The New York Times*, Special Report, February 19, 1951, p. 24.
27. *Montana Standard*, Butte, Montana, Monday February 19, 1951, p. 2.
28. Joseph E. Persico, *Casey: The Lives and Secrets of William J. Casey: From the OSS to the CIA* (New York: Viking, 1990), p. 128.
29. Frank R. Barnett, "America's Strategic Weakness—Redefection," *The Russian Review* 15, No. 1 (1956), 29–36.
30. McKinney Russell, The Association for Diplomatic Studies and Training, *Foreign Affairs Oral History Project*, May 1, 1997, https://www.adst.org/OH%20TOCs/Russell,%20McKinney.toc.pdf. This interview was updated but not edited in 2009: https://adst.org/wp-content/uploads/2013/12/Russell-McKinney-H.-Sr.-2009.pdf [last viewed December 2020].
31. Appendix I, Stricter Enforcement of Refugees' Transportation Loan Repayments Needed, General Accounting Office, GAO/NSIAD-85–86, March 8, 1986.
32. M. Packman, Reds and Redefection. *Editorial research reports 1956* (Vol. II). Washington, DC: CQ Press. Retrieved from http://library.cqpress.com/cqresearcher/cqresrre1956110700 [last viewed December 2020].
33. "Psychological Operations Plan for Soviet Orbit Escapees, Phase A (Code Name ENGROSS)," Psychological Strategy Board, Washington, D.C. December 20, 1951, p. 5. https://www.archives.gov/files/declassification/iscap/pdf/2012-089-doc1.pdf [last viewed December 2020].

34. "Assignment America," Inez Robb, *Crescent News*, Defiance, Ohio, March 24, 1953.
35. *Ibid.*
36. *Ibid.*
37. Normal Lindhurst Hostel Popular With Red Deserters, *The Portsmouth Times*, Portsmouth, Ohio, January 10, 1955, p. 6.
38. *Ibid.*
39. Memorandum dated February 24, 1955, from Acting Chief, International Organization Division, to Deputy Director Plans. , groom/document/5197c263993294098d50dd76 [last viewed December 2020].
40. Inez Robb, "Assignment America," *The Daily Courier*, Connellsville, Pennsylvania, Wednesday, March 18, 1953, p. 8.
41. *Ibid.*
42. Report from Chief of Base, Munich, September 11, 1957, https://www.cia.gov/library/readingroom/document/5197c262993294098d50dc2a [Last viewed June 2018].
43. *Ibid.*
44. Memorandum from Chief, SR/3 to IO/C/Plans, Subject: Proposed Termination of USEP Contracts with Small Voluntary Agencies. September 7, 1960, https://www.cia.gov/library/readingroom/document/5197c265993294098d50e2ae [last viewed December 2020].
45. *Ibid.*
46. *Ibid.*
47. *Ibid.*
48. *Billboard*, "2 Red Jazzmen Are U.S.'-Sit-Ins,'" November 7, 1964.
49. John S. Wilson, "2 Russian Jazzmen Make Club Debut," *The New York Times*, November 3, 1964.
50. Boris Midney, Discography at Discogs, https://www.discogs.com/artist/142519-Boris-Midney [last viewed December 2020].
51. Message from Chief, EE, to Chief of Station, Germany, March 6, 1964, https://www.cia.gov/library/readingroom/document/5197c265993294098d50e2c0 [last viewed December 2020].
52. Memorandum for Assistant Deputy Director (Plans) from Chief Foreign Intelligence, Subject Project HARVARD Renewal, https://www.cia.gov/library/readingroom/document/5197c265993294098d50e2c0 [last viewed December 2020].
53. HARVARD Project Renewal, July 11, 1963, https://www.cia.gov/library/

readingroom/document/5197c265993294 098d50e2c7 [last viewed December 2020].

54. Message from Chief, EE to Chief, CSB, Frankfurt, July 29, 1964https://www.cia.gov/library/readingroom/document/5197c265993294098d50e2b4 [last viewed December 2020].

55. "Memorandum for the 303 Committee, Washington, January 27, 1969," *Foreign Relations, 1969–1976*, Vol. 29, Document 28, 93.

56. "Nixon Approves Continuation of Radio Liberty," December 29, 1969, History and Public Policy Program Digital Archive, obtained and contributed to CWIHP by A. Ross Johnson. Cited in Ch. 8, n. 25, in his book *Radio Free Europe and Radio Liberty*, CIA mandatory declassification review document number C01441044. Published as document 23, FRUS, 1969–76, XXIX, http://digitalarchive.wilsoncenter.org/document/115128 [last viewed December 2020].

57. "Memorandum for the Record," *Foreign Relations, 1969–1976*, Document 147, 457.

58. "Memorandum from the President's Assistant for National Security Affairs (Kissinger) to President Nixon," *Foreign Relations, 1969–1976*, Document 149. Tab A is a copy of the CIA report. https://history.state.gov/historicaldocuments/frus1969-76v12/d149 [last viewed December 2020].

59. *The Right to Know: Report of the Presidential Study Commission on International Radio Broadcasting* (Washington, D.C.: U.S. Government Printing Office, February 5, 1973), https://ia802609.us.archive.org/29/items/TheRightToKnow/TheRightToKnow.pdf [last viewed December 2020].

60. *Ibid.*
61. *Ibid.*
62. *Ibid.*

## Chapter 4

1. Outline Plan for Project Code Name QKSTAIR, OPC Form No. 1103, https://www.cia.gov/library/readingroom/docs/BGCONVOY_0001.pdf [last viewed December 2020].

2. *Ibid.*
3. *Ibid.*
4. Memorandum July 9, 1950, Subject: Information regarding existing mobile propaganda equipment, https://www.cia.gov/library/readingroom/docs/BGCONVOY_0002.pdf [last viewed December 2020].

5. Project Financial Data, QKSTAIR, Fiscal Period July 1, 1951, through June 30, 1952, https://www.cia.gov/library/readingroom/docs/BGCONVOY_0005.pdf [last viewed December 2020].

6. Memorandum, July 17, 1950, Subject: Cover Problems Pertaining to QKSTAIR, https://www.cia.gov/library/readingroom/docs/BGCONVOY_0003.pdf [last viewed December 2020].

7. Медийната война срещу комунизма в България: Радио "Горянин" [The Media War against Communism in Bulgaria: Radio "Goryanin"], Extree Centre Point, Tuesday, April 19, 2011, http://www.extremecentrepoint.com/archives/8008 [last viewed December 2020]. Translated by Bulgarian historian Vanya Petkova.

8. Monthly Project Status Report, SC/PC/2, Bulgaria, BGCONVOY_0006, https://www.cia.gov/library/readingroom/document/5197c269993294098d50eda1 [last viewed December 2020].

9. EE-1, Report of Operations for the Quarter Ended June 30, 1951, OBOPUS BGFIEND VOL_17 (BGFIEND OPERATIONS) 0047, https://www.cia.gov/library/readingroom/document/519a2b7a993294098d50fe5e [last viewed December 2020].

10. Monthly Project Status Report, BGCONVOY, July 1951, BGCONVOY_0007, https://www.cia.gov/library/readingroom/document/5197c269993294098d50eda0 [last viewed December 2020].

11. Monthly Project Status Report for Month of August 1951, QKSTAIR, Bulgaria, BGCONVOY_0008, https://www.cia.gov/readingroom/document/5197c269993294098d50eda7 [last viewed December 2020].

12. Monthly Project Status Report for Month of September 1951, QKSTAIR, Bulgaria, BGCONVOY_0009, https://www.cia.gov/readingroom/document/5197c269993294098d50ed9e [last viewed December 2020].

13. *Ibid.*

14. Radio Free Europe Information Item 12114, "Rumors of Resistance Rife in Bulgaria" November 30, 1951, http://hdl.handle.net/10891/osa:2e22d061-c02a-4b35-

99ee-5343a2cb0d2f [last viewed December 2020].

15. Monthly Project QKSTAIR Status Report for Month of October 1951, BGCONVOY_0010, https://www.cia.gov/library/readingroom/document/5197c269 993294098d50edaf [last viewed December 2020].

16. Monthly Project BGCONVOY Status Report for Month of November 1951, BGCONVOY_0011, https://www.cia.gov/library/readingroom/document/5197c269 993294098d50edb5 [last viewed December 2020].

17. Война срещу комунизма в България: Радио "Горянин" [The Media War against Communism in Bulgaria: Radio "Goryanin"], op. cit.

18. Monthly Project BGCONVOY Status Report for Month of January 1952, BGCONVOY_0013, https://www.cia.gov/library/readingroom/document/5197c269 993294098d50edb0 [last viewed December 2020].

19. Monthly Project BGCONVOY Report for Month of February 1952, BGCONVOY_0014, https://www.cia.gov/library/readingroom/document/5197c269 993294098d50edc3 [last viewed December 2020].

20. Monthly Project BGCONVOY Status Report for Month of April 1952, BGCONVOY_0015, https://www.cia.gov/library/readingroom/document/5197c269 993294098d50edc9 [last viewed December 2020].

21. Monthly Project BGCONVOY Status Report for Month of September 1952, BGCONVOY_0019, https://www.cia.gov/library/readingroom/document/5197c269 993294098d50eda3 [last viewed December 2020].

22. *Ibid.*

23. Monthly Project BGCONVOY Status Report for Month of October 1952, BGCONVOY_0020, https://www.cia.gov/library/readingroom/document/5197c269 993294098d50eda2 [last viewed December 2020].

24. Project BGCONVOY Status Report December 1952, BGCONVOY_0022, https://www.cia.gov/library/readingroom/document/5197c269993294098d50edb7 [last viewed December 2020].

25. Project BGCONVOY Status Report April 1953, BGCONVOY_0026, https://www.cia.gov/library/readingroom/docu ment/5197c269993294098d50edc6 [last viewed December 2020].

26. Project Status Report, May 1953, BGCONVOY_0027, https://www.cia.gov/library/readingroom/document/5197c269 993294098d50edc5 [last viewed December 2020].

27. BGVONGOY Monthly Status Report, January 1953, BGCONVOY_0023, https://www.cia.gov/library/readingroom/document/5197c269993294098d50edbb [last viewed December 2020].

28. Project BGCONVOY Status Report, February 1953, BGCONVOY_0024, https://www.cia.gov/library/readingroom/document/5197c269993294098d50edb1 [last viewed December 2020].

29. Project BGCONVOY Status Report, March 1953, BGCONVOY_0025, https://www.cia.gov/library/readingroom/docu ment/5197c269993294098d50edaa [last viewed December 2020].

30. BGCONVOY_0026, op. cit.

31. BGCONVOY_0027, op. cit.

32. Project BGCONVOY Status Report, June 1953, BGCONVOY_0028, https://www.cia.gov/library/readingroom/docu ment/5197c269993294098d50edab [last viewed December 2020].

33. *Ibid.*

34. BGCONVOY Project Status Report, July 1953, BGCONVOY_0029, https://www.cia.gov/library/readingroom/docu ment/5197c269993294098d50edba [last viewed December 2020].

35. *Ibid.*

36. Project BGCONVOY Progress Report, September 1953, BGCONVOY_0031, https://www.cia.gov/library/readingroom/document/5197c269993294 098d50edb3 [last viewed December 2020].

37. Project BGCONVOY Progress Report, October 1953, BGCONVOY_0032, https://www.cia.gov/library/readingroom/document/5197c269993294098d50edad [last viewed December 2020].

38. Project BGCONVOY Progress Report, November 1953, BGCONVOY_0033, https://www.cia.gov/library/readingroom/document/5197c269993294 098d50edc0 [last viewed December 2020].

39. Project BGCONVOY Progress Report, December 1953, BGCONVOY_0034, https://www.cia.gov/library/readingroom/document/5197c269993294 098d50edc7 [last viewed December 2020].

40. Project BGCONVOY Progress

Report, January 1954, BGCONVOY_0035, https://www.cia.gov/library/readingroom/document/5197c269993294098d50edac [last viewed December 2020].
41. Project BGCONVOY Progress Report, November 1954, BGCONVOY_0045, https://www.cia.gov/library/readingroom/document/5197c269993294098d50edbf [last viewed December 2020].
42. Project BGCONVOY Status Report, February 1954, BGCONVOY_0036, https://www.cia.gov/library/readingroom/document/5197c269993294098d50eda6 [last viewed December 2020].
43. Project BGCONVOY Outline, June 28, 1954, BGCONVOY_0037, https://www.cia.gov/library/readingroom/document/5197c269993294098d50eda5 [last viewed December 2020].
44. Ibid.
45. Ibid.
46. Dispatch from Chief (redacted) to Chief, EE, Chief, SR, October 2, OBOPUS BGFIEND VOL.10_0031, 1959, https://www.cia.gov/library/readingroom/document/519a2b7a993294098d50fcf7 [last viewed December 2020]. And, Message from Chief, EE, Phasing Out of Black Broadcasts to Denied Areas, OBOPUS BGFIEND VOL.10_0032, 1959, https://www.cia.gov/readingroom/document/519a2b79993294098d50fcec [last viewed December 2020].
47. *State Security and the Hostile Radio Stations*, The Committee for Disclosing the Documents and Announcing Affiliation of Bulgarian Citizens to the State Security and the Intelligence Services of the Bulgarian National Armed Forces (CDDAABCSSIB-NAF), Sofia, 2014, pp. 236–341, https://comdos.bg/media/DVD14.pdf [last viewed December 2020]. Selected documents translated from Bulgarian by historian Vanya Petkova.
48. Ibid.
49. Ibid.
50. Ibid.
51. RFE Information Report, Item No. 7212, September 17, 1951, Clandestine Radio Transmitters, http://hdl.handle.net/10891/osa:0c498509-a1a2-4fda-aa4e-3709d7abf72c [last viewed December 2020].
52. Ibid.
53. RFE Information Report, Item No. 5990/52, May 9, 1952, Resistance, Underground, Clandestine Radio Transmitter, http://hdl.handle.net/10891/osa:e99c2ba0-340a-49a7-85a6-53bc0f7a9fe2 [last viewed December 2020].
54. Ibid.
55. Undated and unsigned proposal to institute covert operations within Communist-held Romania, QKBROIL_0005, https://www.cia.gov/library/readingroom/document/5197c261993294098d50d9a0 [last viewed December 2020].
56. Undated Project Outline QKBROIL, QKBROIL_0009, https://www.cia.gov/library/readingroom/document/5197c261993294098d50d99f [last viewed December 2020].
57. Project QKBROIL Outline approved by ADPC, August 28, QKBROIL_0012, 1951, https://www.cia.gov/library/readingroom/document/5197c261993294098d50d988 [last viewed December 2020].
58. Undated Brief Historical Resume, QKBROIL_0002, https://www.cia.gov/library/readingroom/document/5197c261993294098d50d9a1 [last viewed December 2020].
59. Ibid.
60. Ibid.
61. Project QKBROIL Analysis, June 22, 1951, QKBROIL_0008, https://www.cia.gov/library/readingroom/document/5197c261993294098d50d999 [last viewed December 2020].
62. Project QKBROIL Outline approved by ADPC, QKBROIL_0012, op. cit.
63. https://www.cia.gov/library/readingroom/docs/QKBROIL_0007.pdf [last viewed December 2020].
64. Report of Operations for the Quarter Ended June 30, 1951, OBOPUS BGFIEND Vol. 17_0047, https://www.cia.gov/library/readingroom/document/519a2b7a993294098d50fe5e [last viewed December 2020].
65. Briefing for Chief, SE, Subject QKBROIL Project, January 1952, https://www.cia.gov/library/readingroom/docs/QKBROIL_0023.pdf [last viewed December 2020].
66. QKBROIL_0012, op. cit.
67. QKBROIL_0023, op. cit.
68. Memorandum for Chief, QKBROIL, September 28, 1951, Subject: Phasing of Implementation of Project, QKBROIL_0015, https://www.cia.gov/library/readingroom/document/5197c26

1993294098d50d997 [last viewed December 2020].

69. 85 manuscript boxes of Brutus Coste's papers, 1940–1985, are located at the Hoover Institution Archives, Stanford University, California. The papers include "Correspondence, dispatches, memoranda, reports, press releases, speeches and writings, conference proceedings, financial records, and printed matter, relating to Romanian diplomacy during World War II; discussion of Romania at the Paris Peace Conference of 1946; Romanian and other Eastern European émigré affairs; postwar anti-communist movements, especially the Assembly of Captive European Nations and the Truth about Romania Committee; and the status of human rights in Romania and elsewhere in Eastern Europe."

70. Aims of QKBROIL Operations—1952, January 9, 1952, QKBROIL_0022, https://www.cia.gov/library/readingroom/document/5197c261993294098d50d98f [last viewed December 2020].

71. Ibid.

72. QKBROIL_0002, op. cit.

73. Ibid.

74. Undated project QKBROIL Outline, QKBROIL_0029, https://www.cia.gov/library/readingroom/document/5197c261993294098d50d9a7 [last viewed December 2020].

75. Request for Radio Policy Guidance, November 8, 1954, OBOPUS BGFIEND VOL.10_0003, https://www.cia.gov/readingroom/document/519a2b7a993294098d50fd03 [last viewed December 2020].

76. Undated Project QKBROIL (probably July 1954), outline copy in poor quality, QKBROIL_0001, https://www.cia.gov/library/readingroom/document/5197c261993294098d50d99e [last viewed December 2020].

77. Radio Romania, 23/10/2015, http://www.rador.ro/2015/10/23/aici-radio-paris/ [last viewed December 2020].

78. Radio Romania International, 2010-11-01, "Exil și anticomunism prin radio," October 25, 2010, http://old.rri.ro/arh-art.shtml?lang=2&sec=40&art=68012 [last viewed December 2020].

79. Ibid.

80. Ibid.

81. Ibid. Translations provided by Liviu Tofan, former news chief and assistant director of the Romanian Broadcast Department of Radio Free Europe.

82. Memorandum to Chief SR, Subject: Specific Information Requested by Headquarters, February 18, 1958, AERODYNAMIC VOL. 15 0054, https://www.cia.gov/library/readingroom/document/519a2b7d993294098d5105e6 [last viewed December 2020].

83. Ibid.

84. Dispatch to Chief EE, Chief SR, Phasing Out of Black Broadcasts to Denied Areas, October 2, OBOPUS BGFIEND VOL.10_0031, 1959, https://www.cia.gov/library/readingroom/document/519a2b7a993294098d50fcf7 [last viewed December 2020].

*Chapter 5*

1. Project BGFIEND Report, November 1951, OBOPUS BGFIEND VOL.2_0035, https://www.cia.gov/library/readingroom/document/519a2b76993294098d50f3f4 [last viewed December 2020].

2. Memorandum for ADPC, Subject: Revaluation of the Project BGFIEND, November 29, 1949, OBOPUS BGFIEND VOL.2_0015, https://www.cia.gov/library/readingroom/document/519a2b76993294098d50f3d1 [last viewed December 2020].

3. Project BGFIEND Report, November 1951, OBOPUS BGFIEND VOL.2_0035, https://www.cia.gov/library/readingroom/document/519a2b76993294098d50f3f4 [last viewed December 2020].

4. Ibid.

5. Project Outline, Project BGSPEED, OBOPUS BGFIEND VOL.12_0014, https://www.cia.gov/library/readingroom/document/519a2b79993294098d50fc70 [last viewed December 2020].

6. OBOPUS BGFIEND VOL. 2_0015, op. cit.

7. Review of BGFIEND, February 8, 1950, OBOPUS BGFIEND VOL.2_0018, https://www.cia.gov/library/readingroom/document/519a2b76993294098d50f3ec [last viewed December 2020].

8. Memorandum for the File, Subject: The Present and Future Potential of the Propaganda Broadcasting Vessel OBOPUS BGFIEND VOL.12_0009, https://www.cia.gov/library/readingroom/document/519a2b79993294098d50fc67 [last viewed December 2020].

9. OBOPUS BGFIEND VOL.12_0014, op. cit.

10. Memorandum for the Executive, December 22, 1949, OBOPOUS BGFIEND VOL. 12_0008, https://www.cia.gov/library/readingroom/document/519a2b799932940 98d50fc7d [last viewed December 2020].
11. OBOPUS BGFIEND, VOL12_0009, op. cit.
12. Report of Operations for the Quarter Ended 30 June 1951, OBOPUS BGFIEND, VOL.17_0047, https://www.cia.gov/library/readingroom/document/519a2 b7a993294098d50fe5e [last viewed December 2020].
13. Memorandum For: NSO, Subject: BGFIEND—Acquisition of Propaganda Broadcasting Vessel, April 21, 1950, OBOPUS BGFIEND VOL.12_0011, https://www.cia.gov/library/readingroom/document/519a2b79993294098d50fc7b [last viewed December 2020].
14. Ibid.
15. Ibid.
16. Memorandum for FB-1, Subject: BGFIEND Propaganda Vessel, May 4, 1950. OBOPUS BGFIEND VOL.12_0012, https://www.cia.gov/library/readingroom/document/519a2b79993294098d50fc71 [last viewed December 2020].
17. Ibid.
18. Ibid.
19. Cover Sheet of Outline Plan for Project EE-10.1, Code Name BGSPEED, OBOPUS BGFIEND VOL.12_0014, https://www.cia.gov/library/readingroom/document/519a2b79993294098d50fc70 [last viewed December 2020].
20. Memorandum for: The Executive Committee, September 28, 1951, OBOPUS BGFIEND VOL.12_0030, https://www.cia.gov/library/readingroom/document/519a2 b79993294098d50fc73 [last viewed December 2020].
21. Ibid.
22. Ibid.
23. Memorandum for: ADPC, Subject: BGSPEED, June 12, 1950, OBOPUS BGFIEND VOL.12_0014, https://www.cia.gov/library/readingroom/document/519a2 b79993294098d50fc70 [last viewed December 2020].
24. Memorandum to ADPC from Chief, Communications Division, Subject: Technical Fitness of BGFIEND Installation, June 7, 1951, OPOPUS BGFIEND VOL.12_0020, https://www.cia.gov/library/readingroom/document/519a2b79993294 098d50fc5b [last viewed December 2020].

25. Memorandum for Read Admiral Leslie C. Stevens, Chief JSPD, JCS, Subject: Security Considerations in Preparation of Covert Vessel *Irmay*, January 24, 1951, OBOPUS BGFIEND VOL.12_0018, https://www.cia.gov/library/readingroom/document/519a2b7a993294098d50fd08 [last viewed December 2020].
26. Ibid.
27. "Considerations on the Termination of HTGRUBBY," SGAA-31592, March 7, 1958, OB VOL. 10_0023, https://www.cia.gov/library/readingroom/document/519a2b7a993294098d50fd08 [last viewed December 2020].
28. Memorandum for the Record, Subject: Final Report on the JUANITA's Mission, OBOPUS BGFIEND VOL.12_0031, https://www.cia.gov/library/readingroom/document/519a2b79993294098d50fc5d [last viewed December 2020].
29. Ibid.
30. Ibid.
31. Ibid.
32. Message to: ZACACTUS (OPC), August 23, 1951, Subject; KMHYMNAL, OBOPUS BGFIEND VOL.12_0024, https://www.cia.gov/library/readingroom/document/519a2b79993294098d50fc60 [last viewed December 2020].
33. Memorandum for Assistant Director, Office of Communications, Subject: Report on Project BGFIEND (SS JUANITA), March 4, 1952. The Memorandum included an attachment: "Report on BGSPEED—Summary of Principal Failures and Reasons for Them."OBOPUS BGFIEND VOL.12_0034, https://www.cia.gov/library/readingroom/document/519a2 b79993294098d50fc76 [last viewed December 2020].
34. Memorandum for: The BGSPEED File, Subject: Disposal of Yacht "Juanita," February 28, 1955, OBOPUS BGFINED VOL. 12_0041, https://www.cia.gov/library/readingroom/document/519a2b79 993294098d50fc80 [last viewed December 2020].
35. Project Approval Sheet, Cryptonym OBTEST, Approved July 16, 1954,OBOPUS BGFIEND VOL.10_0001, https://www.cia.gov/library/readingroom/document/519a2 b7a993294098d50fcfb [last viewed December 2020].
36. CIA Information Report, Albanian Clandestine Radio Station, Distributed November 30, 1951, https://www.cia.

gov/library/readingroom/document/cia-rdp82-00457r009200380004-9 [last viewed December 2020].

37. CIA Information Report, Clandestine Station Radio Free Albania, distributed December 3, 1951, [last viewed December 2019]. https://www.cia.gov/library/readingroom/document/cia-rdp80-00809a000500730246-5. [last viewed December 2020].

38. Summary of BGFIEND 1952 Operations, February 5, 1953, OBOPUS BGFIEND VOL.24_0023, https://www.cia.gov/library/readingroom/document/519a2b7c993294098d51029d [last viewed December 2020].

39. Ibid.

40. Memorandum to DYCLUCK (OPC), July 7, 1952, OBOPUS BGFIEND VOL.22_0042, https://www.cia.gov/library/readingroom/document/519a2b7c993294098d510225 [last viewed December 2020].

41. Report on Albania, September 1953, OBOPUS BGFIEND VOL.26_0030, https://www.cia.gov/library/readingroom/document/519a2b78993294098d50f99e [last viewed December 2020].

42. Facsimile and translated text of the leaflet defection message, OBOPUS BGFIEND VOL.8_0038, https://www.cia.gov/library/readingroom/document/519a2b79993294098d50fcad [last viewed December 2020].

43. OBOPUS BGFIEND VOL.26_0030, op. cit.

44. Monthly Activity Report, June 15, 1954 to July 13, 1954, OBOPUS BGFIEND VOL.28_0009, https://www.cia.gov/library/readingroom/document/519a2b78993294098d50f946 [last viewed December 2020].

45. Ibid.

46. Review of Albanian CIA Activities During 1955 and General Plans for 1956, April 19, 1956, OBOPUS BGFIEND VOL.10_0006, https://www.cia.gov/library/readingroom/document/519a2b799932940 98d50fcf1 [last viewed December 2020].

47. Ibid.

48. Ibid.

49. Project Status Report, Project OBLIVIOUS, 1–31 January 1956, OBOPUS BGFIEND VOL.30_0001, https://www.cia.gov/library/readingroom/document/519a2b7e993294098d5107d5 [last viewed December 2020].

50. Radio Announcement Leaflet, OBOPUS BGFIEND, VOL.8_0021, https://www.cia.gov/library/readingroom/document/519a2b79993294098d50fc8d [last viewed December 2020].

51. OBOPUS BGFIEND VOL.30_0016 [last viewed December 2020].

52. Summary Request for Renewal, FY July 1, 1957 thru June 30, 1958, SE Division, Yugoslav / Albania Branch Project Cryptonym OBTEST, OBOPUS BGFIEND VOL.10_0016, https://www.cia.gov/library/readingroom/document/519a2b7a993294098d50fd01 [last viewed December 2020].

53. Ibid.

54. 1957 Year-end Progress Report, Subject: Psych/Albania, 12 February 1958, to Chief SE OBOPUS BGFIEND VOL.30_0064, https://www.cia.gov/library/readingroom/document/519a2b7e993294098d5107e0 [last viewed December 2020].

55. Ibid..

56. Ibid.

57. Memorandum March 4, 1958, Considerations on the Termination of HTGRUBBY (VOFA), OBOPUS BGFIEND VOL.10_0022, https://www.cia.gov/library/readingroom/document/519a2b7a993294098d50fd00 [last viewed December 2020].

58. Memorandum for Chief SE Division from Chief, International Organizations Division, Undated, OBOPUS BGFIEND VOL. 10_0019, https://www.cia.gov/library/readingroom/document/519a2b79993294098d50fcf5 [last viewed December 2020].

59. Plans/OBTEST, June 5, 1958, OBOPUS BGFIEND VOL.10_0025, https://www.cia.gov/library/readingroom/document/519a2b7a993294098d50fd07 [last viewed December 2020].

60. Notification of Project Approval, FY 1959, October 7, 1958, OBOPUS BGFIEND VOL.10_0026, https://www.cia.gov/library/readingroom/document/519a2b79993294098d50fcf2 [last viewed December 2020].

61. Review of OBTEST/1 Operations, , April 9, 1959, OBOPUS BGFIEND VOL.10_0028, https://www.cia.gov/library/readingroom/document/519a2b7a9932940 98d50fcfa [last viewed December 2020].

62. Phasing out of Black Broadcasts to Denied Areas, October 2, 1959, https://www.cia.gov/library/readingroom/document/519a2b7a993294098d50fcf7,OBOPUS VOL.10_0031 [last viewed December 2020].

## Chapter 6

1. SR Project Outline, AEBASIN PP, for FY 1955, SR Division. AEFREEMAN_0008, https://www.cia.gov/library/readingroom/document/5197c264993294098d50e168 [last viewed December 2020].
2. Meeting at Mr. Barrett's House on Tuesday Evening November 23, 1951, to discuss USIE-OPC Relationships, Washington. Foreign Relations of the United States, the Intelligence Community 1950–1955, Document 94, https://history.state.gov/historicaldocuments/frus1950-55Intel/d94 [last viewed December 2020].
3. Quoted in Jonathan H. L'Hommedieu, "Baltic Language Broadcasting: Émigré Politics and American Cold War Radios," *Baltic Language Broadcasting*, p. 97, "Comparison of costs incurred operating RFE to Czechoslovakia and the Baltic countries per radio set," Internal RFE memorandum, August 12, 1953, RFE/RL corporate records collection, Hoover Institution Archives, Box 152, Folder 11.
4. Project LCHOMELY, Attachment A, Project Outline, AEROOT AEBASIN_0005, AEFREEMAN_0005, https://www.cia.gov/library/readingroom/document/5197c269993294098d50ed97 [last viewed December 2020].
5. Undated OPC Message, REDTOP QRBASIC, Kalins, Bruno Vol.2_0069, https://www.cia.gov/library/readingroom/document/51966ec9993294098d50a79e [last viewed December 2020].
6. AEFREEMAN_0008, op. cit.
7. Project Outline AEBASIN, October 16, 1952. AEROOT AEBASIN_0007, https://www.cia.gov/library/readingroom/document/5197c269993294098d50ed5a [last viewed December 2020].
8. *Ibid.*
9. AEFREEMAN_0008, op. cit.
10. Memorandum for Chief, IO Division from Chief IO/1, Project Proposal—AEBASIN, September 30, 1954, AEFREEMAN_0010, https://www.cia.gov/library/readingroom/document/5197c264993294098d50e157 [last viewed December 2020].
11. Evaluation of AEBASIN Broadcasts, January 23, 1956, AEFREEMAN_0019, https://www.cia.gov/library/readingroom/document/5197c264993294098d50e15a [last viewed December 2020].
12. Request for Renewal FY 1957, June 1956, AEFREEMAN_0022, https://www.cia.gov/library/readingroom/document/5197c264993294098d50e16b [last viewed December 2020].
13. Description, Project AEBASIN, Renewal 1957, AEFREEMAN_0026, https://www.cia.gov/library/readingroom/document/5197c264993294098d50e149 [last viewed December 2020].
14. Request for PP Project Renewal, FY 1959, AEFREEMAN_0036, https://www.cia.gov/library/readingroom/document/5197c264993294098d50e159 [last viewed December 2020].
15. *Ibid.*
16. *Ibid.*
17. *Ibid.*
18. Project AEBASIN (consolidated into unified Project AEFREEMAN), Project Action Sheet, November 18, 1958, AEFREEMAN_0035, https://www.cia.gov/library/readingroom/document/5197c264993294098d50e162 [last viewed December 2020].
19. Request for Project AEBASIN Renewal, FY 1960, AEFREEMAN_0042, https://www.cia.gov/library/readingroom/document/5197c264993294098d50e171 [last viewed December 2020].
20. *Ibid.*
21. *Ibid.*
22. *Ibid.*
23. Request for Project AEBASIN Renewal FY 1961, AEFREEMAN_0044, https://www.cia.gov/library/readingroom/document/5197c264993294098d50e17b [last viewed December 2020].
24. ODYOKE was CIA cryptonym for U.S. government. Request for Project AEBASIN FY 1962, AEFREEMAN_0047, https://www.cia.gov/library/readingroom/document/5197c264993294098d50e175 [last viewed December 2020].
25. Request for Renewal of Project AEFREEMAN, FY 1963, AEFREEMAN_0052, https://www.cia.gov/library/readingroom/document/5197c264993294098d50e146 [last viewed December 2020].
26. Project Renewal 1964, Termination of Project AEFREEMAN June 30, 194, AEFREEMAN_0055. https://www.cia.gov/library/readingroom/document/5197c264993294098d50e172 [last viewed December 2020].
27. AEFREEMAN_0052, op. cit.
28. *Ibid.*
29. AEFREEMAN_0055, op. cit.
30. *Ibid.*

31. For a concise history of Estonian language broadcasts over VOA, visit http://www.vabaeestisona.com/index.php/news-in-english/1070-the-voice-of-america-and-its-estonian-service-a-concise-history-1951-2004--sp-3631.html [last viewed December 2020].
32. Project Outline AEFLAG, Request for Funds January 1, 1957, through June 30, 1957, AEFLAG_0009, https://www.cia.gov/library/readingroom/document/5197c263993294098d50df1a [last viewed December 2020].
33. Memorandum to Deputy Director (Plans), Subject: Administrative Plan for SR Division Proprietary Project AEMARSH, AEMARSH DEVELOPEMENT AND PLANS_0003, https://www.cia.gov/library/readingroom/document/5197c269993294098d50ee45 [last viewed December 2020].
34. *Ibid.*
35. Operational Plan for Latvian Language Program on Radio Madrid, July 18, 1955, AEFLAG_0004, https://www.cia.gov/library/readingroom/document/5197c263993294098d50df16 [last viewed December 2020].
36. *Ibid.*
37. *Ibid.*
38. *Ibid.*
39. *Ibid.*
40. *Ibid.*
41. *Ibid.*
42. *Ibid.*
43. *Ibid.*
44. *Ibid.*
45. AEFLAG_0009, op. cit.
46. Memorandum for: PP/C/OPS from Chief Information Coordination Division, March 27, 1957, AEFREEMAN_0030, https://www.cia.gov/library/readingroom/document/5197c264993294098d50e155 [last viewed December 2020].
47. Addendum to Project AEFLAG Revision of Renewal Level for FY 1958, AEFLAG_0011, https://www.cia.gov/library/readingroom/document/5197c264993294098d50e156 [last viewed December 2020].
48. Project Outline AEFLAG, January 1957, AEFREEMAN_0031, https://www.cia.gov/library/readingroom/document/5197c264993294098d50e161 [last viewed December 2020].
49. *Ibid.*
50. Project Action Sheet, AEFLAG, Renewal for FY 1958, November 27, 1957, AEFREEMAN_0034 [last viewed December 2020].
51. AEFLAG_0011, op. cit.
52. *Ibid.*
53. Project Renewal AEFLAG for FY 1960, AEFREEMAN_0043 [last viewed December 2020].
54. AEFREEMAN_0045, op. cit.
55. Termination of Project AEFREEMAN in FY 1964, AEFREEMAN_0055, https://www.cia.gov/library/readingroom/document/5197c264993294098d50e172 [last viewed December 2020].
56. *Ibid.*
57. Even though the CIA pseudonym Cleveland O. Hahn is used, Launags' full biography can be read at LAUNAGS, FREDs VOL.1_0015, https://www.cia.gov/library/readingroom/document/519697ec993294098d50cbb8 [last viewed December 2020].
58. Memorandum for Assistant Deputy Director for Plans, January 19, 1965, LAUNAGS, FREDS VOL. 4_0023, https://www.cia.gov/library/readingroom/document/519697ef993294098d50d28e [last viewed December 2020].
59. Memorandum October 1, 1959, Subject: CHURGIN, Raymond S., LAUNAGS, FREDS VOL. 3_0055, https://www.cia.gov/library/readingroom/document/519697ef993294098d50d2ba [last viewed December 2020].
60. Memorandum from SR / COP / PP to Chief , FI/ Plans, Subject; Temporary Assignment of Louis G. GOLTEDGE to PP Activity, November 8, 1955, LAUNAGS, FREDS VOL.2_0092, https://www.cia.gov/library/readingroom/document/519697eb993294098d50cb3d [last viewed December 2020].
61. *Ibid.*
62. Memorandum, September 9, 1955, Subject; CHURGIN, Raymond S., LAUNAGS, FREDS VOL.3_0050, https://www.cia.gov/library/readingroom/document/519697ef993294098d50d2aa [last viewed December 2020].
63. SINGER was the pseudonym of the treasurer of LCI. "Review of my activities in 1956 /57" LAUNAGS, FREDS Vol.1_0026, https://www.cia.gov/library/readingroom/document/519697ec993294098d50cbb6 [last viewed December 2020].
64. Memorandum January 18, 1965, Subject: Freds. Z. Launags Possible Repatriation to Latvia, LAUNAGS, FREDS

## Notes—Chapter 6 243

VOL.4_0022, https://www.cia.gov/library/readingroom/document/519697ee993294098d50d236 [last viewed December 2020].
65. Memorandum for: Security Support Division, Subject: Amendment to Security Clearance for Raymond S. CHURGIN, LAUNAGS, FREDS VOL.2_0126, https://www.cia.gov/library/readingroom/document/519697ec993294098d50cb8f [last viewed December 2020].
66. LAUNAGS, FREDS VOL.3_0055, op. cit.
67. Ibid.
68. Ibid.
69. Ibid.
70. Memorandum for: The Record, November 31, 1959, Meeting with Raymond S.C. on Sunday, November 15, 1959, LAUNAGS, FREDS VOL.3_0059, https://www.cia.gov/library/readingroom/document/519697ef993294098d50d2e0, [last viewed October 1959].
71. LAUNAGS, FREDS VOL.4_0022, op. cit.
72. Ibid.
73. Memorandum for General Counsel from David E. Murphy, Chief, SR Division, August 17, 1967, LAUNAGS, FREDS VOL.4_0097, https://www.cia.gov/library/readingroom/document/519697ef993294098d50d27a [last viewed December 2020].
74. Ibid.
75. Ibid.
76. Ibid.
77. Memorandum for Director, DCS, Subject Case 32254—Fred Z. Launags, December 24, 1968, LAUNAGS, FREDS VOL 4_120, https://www.cia.gov/library/readingroom/document/519697ef993294098d50d24a [last viewed December 2020].
78. Copies of the weekly newspaper *Brīvā Latvija* are available on microfilm at the Library of Congress, Washington, D.C. LCCN permalink https://lccn.loc.gov/sn92068342 [last viewed December 2020].
79. Extension of Project AECHAMP (PP portion), February 19, 1954, AEFREEMAN_0005, https://www.cia.gov/library/readingroom/document/5197c264993294098d50e16c [last viewed December 2020].
80. Use of Lithuanian Resistance Group (Outline proposal for discussion with OPC representatives), June 8, 1949, AECHAMP VOL.1_0002, https://www.cia.gov/library/readingroom/document/5197c263993294098d50df15 [last viewed December 2020].

81. Basic Plan, Cryptonym AEGEAN, October 1950, AECHAMP VOL.1_0008, https://www.cia.gov/library/readingroom/document/5197c263993294098d50df0f [last viewed December 2020].
82. Ibid.
83. Ibid.
84. Field Project Outline Plan, Project AEGEAN, AECHAMP VOL.1_003, https://www.cia.gov/library/readingroom/document/5197c263993294098d50df05 [last viewed December 2020].
85. STUDY, REVIEW, ANALYSIS of all CAPSTAN AGENTS' PERSONAL HISTORIES, CONTACTS and ASSOCIATIONS, March 23, 1953, AECHAMP VOL. 1_0022, https://www.cia.gov/library/readingroom/document/5197c263993294098d50df07 [last viewed December 2020].
86. Ibid.
87. Ibid.
88. Memorandum, Subject: Information on Survival of REDSOX agent, May 14, 1956, AECHAMP VOL 2_0050, https://www.cia.gov/library/readingroom/document/5197c264993294098d50dfca [last viewed December 2020].
89. Memorandum for Chief, FI: AMENDMENT to AECHAMP (FI) Project, September 15, 1953, AECHAMP VOL. 2_0020, https://www.cia.gov/library/readingroom/document/5197c264993294098d50dfbc [last viewed December 2020].
90. Allotment of Funds to CAPSTAN-FI and Basic Plan, July 24, 1952, VOL.1_0016, https://www.cia.gov/library/readingroom/document/5197c263993294098d50df03 [last viewed December 2020].
91. Memorandum May 14,1953, Subject, Cryptonym Change for Project CAPSTAN, AECHAMP VOL.1_0023, https://www.cia.gov/library/readingroom/document/5197c263993294098d50df0a [last viewed December 2020].
92. Memorandum September 9, 1953, Subject: Summary Report as of 1 July 1953—AECHAMP PP Activities, AECHAMP VOL.2_0019]. https://www.cia.gov/library/readingroom/document/5197c264993294098d50dfd8 [last viewed December 2020].
93. Ibid.
94. Ibid.
95. AEFREEMAN_0005, op. cit.
96. Ibid.
97. Ibid.
98. Memorandum February 14, 1955,

Subject: Project AECHAMP/PP—Amendment No. 1, AEFREEMAN_0013, https://www.cia.gov/library/readingroom/document/5197c264993294098d50e169 [last viewed December 2020].
99. Memorandum August 4, 1955, Subject: AEPOLE Project, AEFREEMAN_0015, https://www.cia.gov/library/readingroom/document/5197c264993294098d50e163 [last viewed December 2020].
100. Ibid.
101. Project Outline, Project AEPOLE, May 12, 1955. Approval August 19, 1955, AEFREEMAN_0016, https://www.cia.gov/library/readingroom/document/5197c264993294098d50e177 [last viewed December 2020].
102. Ibid.
103. Ibid.
104. Ibid.
105. Ibid.
106. Request for Renewal August 21, 1956, Project AEPOLE, FY 1957, AEFREEMAN_0025, https://www.cia.gov/library/readingroom/document/5197c264993294098d50e14c [last viewed December 2020].
107. Ibid.
108. Ibid.
109. Memorandum for: PP/C/OPS from Chief Information Coordination Division, March 27, 1957, Project AEFLAG, AEFREEMAN_0030, https://www.cia.gov/library/readingroom/document/5197c264993294098d50e155 [last viewed December 2020].
110. Request for PP Project Renewal, FY 1959, AEPOLE, AEFREEMAN_0038, https://www.cia.gov/library/readingroom/document/5197c264993294098d50e177 [last viewed December 2020].
111. Description, Project AEPOLE, FY 1957 Renewal, SR-2/Lithuania, AEFREEMAN_0028, https://www.cia.gov/library/readingroom/document/5197c264993294098d50e15f [last viewed December 2020].
112. Request for Renewal for FY 1958, October 21, 1957, AEFREEMAN_0033, https://www.cia.gov/library/readingroom/document/5197c264993294098d50e148 [last viewed December 2020].
113. Project AEPOLE (Consolidated into Project AEFREEMAN), Project Action Sheet, November 24, 1958, Renewal for FY 59, AEFREEMAN_0037, https://www.cia.gov/library/readingroom/document/5197c264993294098d50e14e [last viewed December 2020].
114. Renewal of Projects AEPOLE, AEFLAG, and AEBASIN, September 21, 1961, AEFREEMAN_0047, https://www.cia.gov/library/readingroom/document/5197c264993294098d50e175 [last viewed December 2020].
115. Request for Project Renewal, For FY 1960, Approval March 7, 1960, AEPOLE, AEFREEMAN_0041, https://www.cia.gov/library/readingroom/document/5197c264993294098d50e15e [last viewed December 2020].

## Chapter 7

1. CIA Cryptonyms for supporting ZP/UHVR included: AERODYNAMIC, CARTEL, CASSOWARY-1, ANDROGEN, AECARTHAGE, QRPLUMB. CIA released 1,338 files related to AERODYNAMIC operations.
2. Joint OSO/OPC AERODYNAMIC and PBCRUET Project Outline, FY 1951 (July 1, 1959 through June 30, 1950), https://www.cia.gov/library/readingroom/document/519a2b75993294098d50f142 [last viewed December 2020].
3. Project Outline, March 27, 1950, AERODYNAMIC VOL 1_0004, https://www.cia.gov/library/readingroom/document/519a2b77993294098d50f7a0 [last viewed December 2020].
4. Ibid.
5. Ibid.
6. Ibid.
7. Project Outline Clearance Sheet, Project Cryptonym AERODYNAMIC / RANTER, July 21, 1953, AERODYNAMIC VOL.1_0130, https://www.cia.gov/library/readingroom/document/519a2b77993294098d50f7ba [last viewed December 2020].
8. Ibid.
9. Amendment to Project AERODYNAMIC, July 21, 1953, https://www.cia.gov/library/readingroom/document/519a2b77993294098d50f7ba [last viewed December 2020].
10. Ibid.
11. Ibid.
12. Ibid.
13. Memorandum to SR/CPP, "Comments on Ukrainian Policy Paper by CASSOWARY 2," January 15, 1954, AERODYNAMIC VOL. 11 (Operations)_0038, https://www.cia.gov/library/readingroom/document/519a2b74993294098d50f08c [last viewed December 2020].

14. David E. Murphy, Chief, Soviet Bloc Division, Memorandum to John Warner, Legislative Counsel, April 11, 1967, AERODYNAMIC VOL. 36 (OPERATIONS)_0036.pdf, https://www.cia.gov/library/readingroom/document/519a2b74993294098d50ef7f [last viewed December 2020].

15. Message from Chief of Base, Munich, to Chief, EE. January 12, 1954, Subject; AECASSOWARY 1 Newspaper, AERODYNAMIC VOL: 11 (OPERATIONS)_0037, https://www.cia.gov/library/readingroom/document/519a2b74993294098d50f0a5 [last viewed December 2020].

16. Request for procurement of safehouse for AERODYNAMIC Project, AERODYNAMIC VOL. 2_0002, https://www.cia.gov/library/readingroom/document/519a2b78993294098d50f888 [last viewed December 2020].

17. Memorandum for the Record, Subject: Meeting with AECASSOWARY 2 and AECASSOWARY 15, AERODYNAMIC Vol. 43, Contact Reports_0063, https://www.cia.gov/library/readingroom/document/519a2b79993294098d50fc01 [last viewed December 2020].

18. Memorandum for the Record, Subject: Contact Report—Meeting with AECASSOWARY 2, 4, and 15, AERODYNAMIC VOL. 43 CONTACT REPORTS_0067, https://www.cia.gov/library/readingroom/document/519a2b79993294098d50fc13 [last viewed December 2020].

19. Contact Report, "Meeting with AECASSOWARY 2 on 11 August 1955," AERODYNAMIC VOL:43 Contact Reports_0070, https://www.cia.gov/library/readingroom/document/519a2b79993294098d50fc46 [last viewed December 2020].

20. Communications Annex Renewal, August 4, 1958, AERODYNAMIC VOL. 3_0016, https://www.cia.gov/library/readingroom/document/519a2b78993294098d50f909 [last viewed December 2020].

21. Contact Report, October 5, 1955, AERODYNAMIC VOL. 43 CONTACT REPORTS_0071, https://www.cia.gov/library/readingroom/document/519a2b79993294098d50fc14 [last viewed December 2020].

22. FY 1959 Renewal and Redocumentation, AERODYNAMIC VOL.3_0022, https://www.cia.gov/library/readingroom/document/519a2b78993294098d50f8a8 [last viewed June 2009].

23. Monthly Report, March 1, 1958, to March 31, 1958, AERODYNAMIC VOL.15_0070, https://www.cia.gov/library/readingroom/document/519a2b7d993294098d5105af [last viewed December 2020].

24. Monthly Report, May 1, 1958, to May 31, 1958, AERODYNAMIC VOL.16_0003, https://www.cia.gov/library/readingroom/document/519a2b7d993294098d51059a [last viewed December 2020].

25. Monthly Report July 1, 1958, to July 31, 1958, AERODYNAMIC VOL.16_0019, https://www.cia.gov/library/readingroom/document/519a2b7d993294098d51056a [last viewed December 2020].

26. Monthly Status Report, October 1, 1958, to October 31, 1958, AERODYNMAIC VOL.16_0048, https://www.cia.gov/library/readingroom/document/519a2b7d993294098d510593 [last viewed December 2020].

27. Monthly Status Report, January 1, 1959, to January 30, 1959, AERODYNAMIC VOL.16_0063, https://www.cia.gov/library/readingroom/document/519a2b7d993294098d510592 [last viewed December 2020].

28. Renewal FY 1959 & Redocumentation, AERODYNAMIC VOL. 3_0021, https://www.cia.gov/library/readingroom/document/519a2b78993294098d50f8aa [last viewed December 2020].

29. Request for Project Renewal for FY 1960, AERODYNAMIC VOL. 3_0053, https://www.cia.gov/library/readingroom/document/519a2b78993294098d50f8f4 [last viewed December 2020].

30. Project Renewal for FY 1961, AERODYNAMIC Vol. 3_0078, https://www.cia.gov/library/readingroom/document/519a2b78993294098d50f912 [last viewed December 2020].

31. Proposed Political Action memorandum, March 13, 1956, AERODYNAMIC VOL: 2_0052 https://www.cia.gov/library/readingroom/document/519a2b78993294098d50f83b [last viewed December 2020].

32. *Ibid.*

33. Project Status Report, 15 August–15 September 1956, AERODYNAMIC VOL.2_0069, https://www.cia.gov/library/readingroom/document/519a2b78993294098d50f883 [last viewed December 2020].

34. Memorandum April 29, 1957 to SR/COP/PP, AERODYNAMIC VOL.

2_0093, https://www.cia.gov/library/readingroom/document/519a2b78993294098d50f85f [last viewed December 2020].
35. Ibid.
36. Memorandum for the Record, Contact with AECASSOWARY-2, October 16, 1957, AERODYNAMIC VOL.43 CONTACT REPORTS_0119, https://www.cia.gov/library/readingroom/document/519a2b79993294098d50fc3f [last viewed December 2020].
37. Ibid.
38. AERODYNAMIC Vol. 44 CONTACT REPORTS_0004, https://www.cia.gov/library/readingroom/document/519a2b79993294098d50fb82 [last viewed December 2020].
39. Memorandum, Contact with AECASSOWAR-2 at Prolog Office, March 24-26, 1958, AERODYNAMIC VOL.44 CONTACT REPORTS_0013, https://www.cia.gov/library/readingroom/document/519a2b79993294098d50fb8b [last viewed December 2020].
40. Memorandum for the Record, Contact with AECASSOWARY-2 and 27, July 16-17, 1958, AERODYNAMIC Vol. 44 CONTACT REPORTS_0020, https://www.cia.gov/library/readingroom/document/519a2b79993294098d50fb97 [last viewed December 2020].
41. AERODYNAMIC VOL.3_0038 [last viewed December 2020].
42. Memorandum for the Record, November 29, 1958, AERODYAMIC VOL. 3_0028, https://www.cia.gov/library/readingroom/document/519a2b78993294098d50f90b [last viewed December 2020].
43. Request for Project Approval FY 1960, February 9, 1960, AERODYNAMIC Vol. 3_ 0053, https://www.cia.gov/library/readingroom/document/519a2b78993294098d50f8f4 [last viewed December 2020].
44. Nazi and Axis Collaborators were used to Further U.S. Anti-Communist Objectives in Europe—Some Immigrated to the United States, https://www.gao.gov/assets/150/142984.pdf [last viewed December 2020].

## Chapter 8

1. Progress Report for period 11-30 September 1957, AERODYNAMIC VOL. 15 (Operations)_0043, https://www.cia.gov/library/readingroom/document/519a2b7993294098d5105c8 [last viewed December 2020].
2. Ibid.
3. Ibid.
4. Ibid.
5. Progress Report for period 1-31 December 1957, AERODYNAMIC VOL. 15 (Operations)_0045, https://www.cia.gov/library/readingroom/document/519a2b7d993294098d5105ee [last viewed December 2020].
6. Ibid.
7. Ibid.
8. Dispatch SGAA 74-126-40, February 19, 1958, AERODYNAMIC VOL. 15 (Operations)_0054, https://www.cia.gov/library/readingroom/document/519a2b7d993294098d5105e6 [last viewed December 2020].
9. Ibid.
10. Progress Report for Period 1-28 February 1958, AERODYNAMIC VOL. 15 (Operations)_0066, https://www.cia.gov/library/readingroom/document/519a2b7d993294098d5105e0 [last viewed December 2020].
11. For more details of the May 1959 KGB report on Jamming: Public Policy Program Digital Archive, Archives of the Central Committee of the Communist "KGB Report, 'On the State of Jamming anti-Soviet Radio Programs of Foreign Radio Stations,'" May 19, 1959, History and Party of the Soviet Union. Obtained by Michael Nelson, translated by Volodymyr Valkov. http://digitalarchive.wilsoncenter.org/document/121546 [last viewed December 2020].
12. Message from Director, October 14, 1958, AERODYNAMIC VOL. 17 (Operations)_0040, https://www.cia.gov/library/readingroom/document/519a2b76993294098d50f4c2 [last viewed December 2020].
13. Ibid.
14. Dispatch EKAA-1389 to Chief, EE, and Chief, SR, Approval Request, "Phasing Out of Black Broadcasts to Denied Areas," October 2, 1959, OBOPUS BGFIEND Vol. 10_0031, https://www.cia.gov/library/readingroom/document/519a2b7a9932940 98d50fcf7 [last viewed December 2020].
15. Ibid.
16. NTS 1967 English language Information Pamphlet, p. 15, https://en.wikisource.org/wiki/National_Alliance_of_Russian_Solidarists_(1967) [last viewed December 2020].

17. Gordon Young, *The House of Secrets: Russian Resistance in the Soviet Regime Today* (New York: Duell, Sloan, and Pierce, 1959), p. 38.
18. Project Outline, August 28 1950, QKDROOP_0001, https://www.cia.gov/library/readingroom/document/5197c261993294098d50da02 [last viewed December 2020].
19. *Ibid.*
20. *Ibid.*
21. *Battle Ground Berlin*, p. 110.
22. Memorandum January 7, 1952, to Chief, SR Division, AESAURUS AENOBLE VOL. 1_0014, https://www.cia.gov/library/readingroom/document/5197c269993294098d50eed7 [last viewed December 2020].
23. "Proposed Plan Submitted by AEROSOL (1)," AESAURUS AENOBLE VOL. 1_0004, https://www.cia.gov/library/readingroom/document/5197c26a993294098d50eee0 [last viewed December 2020].
24. CIA Information Report, October 31, 1951, "Clandestine Anti-Communist Radio Transmitter," pdf, https://www.cia.gov/library/readingroom/document/cia-rdp82-00457r009100420008-1 [last viewed December 2020].
25. AESAURUS AENOBLE VOL. 1_0027, https://www.cia.gov/library/readingroom/document/5197c26a9932940 98d50eeef [last viewed December 2020].
26. Evaluation of Radio Free Russia, May 8, 1952, https://www.cia.gov/library/readingroom/document/cia-rdp80-01065a000600020091-0 [last viewed December 2020].
27. Progress Report for December 1953, Great Russian Section, AESAURUS AENOBLE VOL. 2_0003, https://www.cia.gov/library/readingroom/document/5197c269993294098d50eeba [last viewed December 2020].
28. Constantin W. Boldyreff was born August 8, 1909, in Gatchina, Russia, and died in Valley Cottage, New York on July 14, 1995. He was buried in the Novo-Diveevo Russian Orthodox Cemetery, Nanuet, New York. His testimony is taken from *Hearings on "Strategy and Tactics of World Communism,* May 18 and 27, 1954, Part 1 (Washington, D.C.: U.S. Government Printing Office, 1954), p. 19.
29. Young, op. cit., p. 2.
30. Young, p. 73.
31. Young, p. 76.
32. Young, pp. 20–22.
33. Young, p. 23.
34. NTS 1967 English language Information Pamphlet., op. cit.
35. Young, pp. 69–70.
36. "To Ivan in Cuba: Now Hear This!" *Life*, April 12, 1963.
37. *Ibid.*
38. *American Legion Magazine*, April 1966, Vol. 80, p. 40. The article was written by Eugen Lyons, the first president of the Radio Liberation Committee (AmComLib).
39. *Proceedings of the Tenth Conference, Taipei, Taiwan, Republic of China, November 23–27, 1964.* Asian Peoples' Anti-Communist League, 1965.
40. "Stasi Note on Meeting with KGB Officials, 13 November 1969," History and Public Policy Program Digital Archive, Office of the Federal Commissioner for the Stasi Records (BStU), MfS, MfS, SdM 577, p. 88–110. Translated from German for Cold War International History Project by Bernd Schaefer. http://digitalarchive.wilsoncenter.org/document/115714 [last viewed December 2020].
41. NTS Information Pamphlet, p. 18.
42. For more information about NTS, see Benjamin Tromly, "The Making of a Myth: The National Labor Alliance, Russian Émigrés, and Cold War Intelligence Activities," *Journal of Cold War Studies*, Winter 2016, Vol. 18, No. 1, Pages 80–111.
43. Request for PP Project Renewal, FY 1959, Division Project Clearance Sheet, April 20, 1960. AEVIRGIL VOL.3_0032, https://www.cia.gov/library/readingroom/document/5197c268993294098d50eb87 [last viewed December 2020].
44. Project AEVIRGIL Outline September 29, 1954, AEVIRGIL VOL. 3_0008, https://www.cia.gov/library/readingroom/document/5197c268993294098d50eb7b [last viewed December 2020].
45. Message from Chief of Base, Frankfurt, to Chief SR, June 26, 1962. AEVIRGIL VOL. 2_0042. https://www.cia.gov/library/readingroom/document/5197c268993294098d50eb76 [last viewed December 2020].
46. DD/P Project Outline Clearance Sheet, HBDUCKPIN, AEVIRGIL VOL. 3_0006, https://www.cia.gov/library/readingroom/docs/AEVIRGIL%20VOL.%203_0006.pdf [last viewed December 2020].
47. AEVIRGIL VOL. 3_0008, op. cit.
48. Project Outline HBDUCKPIN, February 18, 1953. From Chief of Base, Munich, to Chief, EE, AEVIRGIL VOL.

3_0005, https://www.cia.gov/library/readingroom/docs/AEVIRGIL%20VOL.%203_0005.pdf [last viewed December 2020].

49. TsOPE distributed *Dr. Zhivago* copies at the 1958 World's Fair in Brussels. For example, at the 1958 Brussels World Fair 365 copies were distributed, https://www.cia.gov/library/readingroom/document/0005795687. The CIA released 99 documents describing its role in the publishing and distribution of the novel: https://www.cia.gov/library/readingroom/collection/doctor-zhivago.

50. Renewal of Project AEVIRGIL, FY 1960, February 29, 1960, AEVIRGIL VOL. 3_0032. https://www.cia.gov/library/readingroom/document/5197c268993294098d50eb87 [last viewed December 2020].

51. *Ibid.*
52. *Ibid.*
53. Project Outline, September 29, 1954, AEVIRGIL VOL. 3_0008, https://www.cia.gov/library/readingroom/docs/AEVIRGIL%20VOL.%203_0008.pdf [last viewed December 2020].
54. Summary Request for Renewal Fiscal Year 1959, AEVIRGIL VOL. 3_0031. https://www.cia.gov/library/readingroom/document/5197c268993294098d50eb80 [last viewed December 2020].
55. AEVIRGIL VOL. 3_0032, op. cit.
56. Report from Chief, Munich Base, to Chief, SR, June 29, 1960. AEVIRGIL VOL. 2_0012, https://www.cia.gov/library/readingroom/document/5197c268993294098d50eb5b [last viewed December 2020].
57. Renewal of Project AEVIRGIL FY 1961, AEVIRGIL VOL. 3_0033, https://www.cia.gov/library/readingroom/document/5197c268993294098d50eb78 [last viewed December 2020].
58. *Ibid.*
59. *Ibid.*
60. *Ibid.*
61. Report: Soviet Activities Against the Emigration, January 4, 1962, AEVIRGIL VOL. 1_0045, https://www.cia.gov/library/readingroom/document/5197c268993294098d50ebb1 [last viewed December 2020].
62. AEVIRGIL VOL.3_0033, op cit.
63. Message from Director to Munich, Frankfurt, Berlin, AEVIRGIL VOL. 3_0034, https://www.cia.gov/library/readingroom/document/5197c268993294098d50ebc2 [last viewed December 2020].
64. *Ibid.*
65. AEVIRGIL VOL. 2_0042, op. cit.
66. AEVIRGIL VOL. 1_0045. op. cit.
67. Request for Amendment and Termination of Project AEVIRGIL,AEVIRGIL VOL. 3_0035, https://www.cia.gov/library/readingroom/document/5197c268993294098d50eb7c [last viewed December 2020].
68. *Ibid.*
69. Project Outline, Berlin Operations Base, October 3, 1953, AECARRERA_0002, https://www.cia.gov/library/readingroom/document/5197c263993294098d50def5 [last viewed December 2020].
70. *Ibid.*
71. AECARRERA_0002, op. cit.
72. *Ibid.*
73. Message from Berlin Operations Base (BOB) to EE, March 17, 1954, AECARRERA_0004, https://www.cia.gov/library/readingroom/document/5197c263993294098d50dec2 [last viewed December 2020].
74. *Ibid.*
75. *Ibid.*
76. *Ibid.*
77. *Ibid.*
78. *Ibid.*
79. *Ibid.*
80. Memorandum from EE/FI/C to Chief, Foreign Intelligence (FI) Plans, January 15, 1955, AECARRERA_0006, https://www.cia.gov/library/readingroom/document/5197c263993294098d50dee0 [last viewed December 2020].
81. Memorandum for the Record, Justification for Vehicle, Project AECARRERA, April 20, 1955, AECARRERA_0009, https://www.cia.gov/library/readingroom/document/5197c263993294098d50ded1 [last viewed December 2020].
82. Memorandum to Chief FI, Plans, Amendment to AECARRERA Project, July 13, 1955, AECARRERA_0014, https://www.cia.gov/library/readingroom/document/5197c263993294098d50dee6 [last viewed December 2020].
83. Progress Report, January 1–31, 1957, AEVIRGIL VOL.1_0010, https://www.cia.gov/library/readingroom/document/5197c268993294098d50eba6 [last viewed December 2020].
84. *Ibid.*
85. Norbert F. Pötzl, *Basar der Spione: Die geheimen Missionen des DDR-Untenhandlers Wolfgang Vogel* (Hamburg: Spiegel Buchverlag, 1997), p. 54.

86. AEVIRGIL VOL..1_0010, op. cit.
87. Pötzl, op. cit., p. 60.
88. Pötzl, op. cit., p. 61.

## Chapter 9

1. Radoslaw Ostrowsky is also transliterated as Radaslau Astrouski or Radoslow Ostrowski.
2. CIA cryptonyms CAMBISTA 4 and AECAMBISTA 4. The name is also spelled as Mikola Abramchik.
3. Request for PP Project Renewal 1960, AEQUOR VOL. 3_0062, https://www.cia.gov/library/readingroom/document/5197c269993294098d50ed30 [last viewed December 2020].
4. Memorandum for the ADPC, Subject: Project AEQUOR, August 30, 1951, AEQUOR VOL. 1_0007, https://www.cia.gov/library/readingroom/document/5197c269993294098d50ec9c [last viewed December 2020].
5. Memorandum for Chief, SR, Subject: A Review of the Byelorussian National Council /BNR), March 17, 1958 AEQUOR VOL. 3_0022, https://www.cia.gov/library/readingroom/document/5197c269993294098d50ed44 [last viewed December 2020].
6. Extract from message 221, CMGWU, Subject; CSOB/Bi-weekly Report #1, July 9, 1951, AEQUOR VOL. 1_0004, https://www.cia.gov/library/readingroom/document/5197c269993294098d50ecb8 [last viewed December 2020].
7. Monthly Progress Report, June 1-30, 1952, July 2, 1952, AEQUOR VOL. 1_0024, https://www.cia.gov/library/readingroom/document/5197c269993294098d50ecab [last viewed December 2020].
8. Contact with Mikola ABRAMTCHIK, November 7, 1951, ABRAMTCHIK, Mikola_0028, https://www.cia.gov/library/readingroom/document/519a2b7b993294098d510094 [last viewed December 2020].
9. Contact Report, April 1, 1952, ABRAMTCHIK, MIKOLA_0040, https://www.cia.gov/library/readingroom/document/519a2b7b993294098d51003f [last viewed December 2020]. BGACTRESS was CIA's International Organizations Division (IOD), which oversaw both Radio Free Europe and Radio Liberty, for example.
10. Ibid.
11. Ibid.
12. "Conference with Mikola ABRAMTCHIK," November 7, 1951, ABRAMTCHIK, MIKOLA_0069, https://www.cia.gov/library/readingroom/document/519a2b7b993294098d51003f [last viewed December 2020].
13. Dispatch from Chief, SR to Chief, Munich Operations Group, Subject: Current Status of Project AEQUOR, June 2, 1961, AEQUOR VOL. 3_0075, https://www.cia.gov/library/readingroom/document/5197c269993294098d50ed31 [last viewed December 2020].
14. Ibid.
15. Memorandum for Chief, SR Division, Subject: Termination of Project AEQUOR, August 29, 1961, AEQUOR VOL. 3_0076, https://www.cia.gov/library/readingroom/document/5197c269993294098d50ed34 [last viewed December 2020].
16. Dispatch to Chief, WE, Subject: Meeting with AECAMBISTA/4, December 4, 1971,AEQUOR VOL. 3_0078, https://www.cia.gov/library/readingroom/document/5197c269993294098d50ed1e [last viewed December 2020].
17. Message from Frankfurt to Director, September 3, 1957, AEQUOR VOL. 3_0009, https://www.cia.gov/library/readingroom/document/5197c269993294098d50ed46 [last viewed December 2020].
18. Memorandum from Chief of Base, Frankfurt, to Chief, SR, Contact Report, November 21, 1957, AEQUOR VOL. 3_0013, https://www.cia.gov/library/readingroom/document/5197c269993294098d50ed2e [last viewed December 2020].
19. Message from Chief, SR, to Chief of Base, Frankfurt, Subject; AEQUOR Finances FY 1959, September 3, 1959, AEQUOR VOL. 3_0036, https://www.cia.gov/library/readingroom/document/5197c269993294098d50ed0a [last viewed December 2020].
20. Dispatch from Chief of Base, Frankfurt, to Chief, SR, Subject: AEQUOR Progress Report, April 1, 1959, AEQUOR VOL. 3_0049, https://www.cia.gov/library/readingroom/document/5197c269993294098d50ed20 [last viewed December 2020].
21. Message from Chief of Base, Frankfurt, to Chief, SR, June 18, 1959, AEQUOR VOL. 3_0055.
22. AEQUOR VOL. 3_0056, https://www.cia.gov/library/readingroom/document/5197c269993294098d50ed0d [last viewed December 2020].
23. AEQUOR VOL. 3_0062, op. cit.

24. Dispatch from Chief, SR, to Chief of Base, Munich, Chief of Station, Germany, June 8, 1960, AEQUOR VOL. 3_0064, https://www.cia.gov/library/readingroom/document/5197c269993294098d50ed15 [last viewed December 2020].

25. Dispatch from Chief of Station, Germany, to Chief, SR, Comments on Renewal of AEQUOR, June 2, 1960, AEQUOR VOL. 3_0065, https://www.cia.gov/library/readingroom/document/5197c269993294098d50ed2b [last viewed December 2020].

26. Renewal of Project AEQUOR, June 1,1960, to June 30, 1961, AEQUOR VOL. 3_0071, https://www.cia.gov/library/readingroom/document/5197c269993294098d50ed40 [last viewed December 2020].

27. Memorandum for Director of Central Intelligence, Subject: Request for Financial Support by Belorussian Émigré Leader, July 8, 1969, AEQUOR VOL. 3_0066, https://www.cia.gov/library/readingroom/document/5197c269993294098d50ed12 [last viewed December 2020].

28. Dispatch from Chief, Munich Base, to Chief, SR, Review of Project AEQUOR, October 6, 1950, AEQUOR VOL. 3_0068, https://www.cia.gov/library/readingroom/document/5197c269993294098d50ed27 [last viewed December 2020].

29. AEQUOR VOL. 3_0071, op. cit.

30. Dispatch from Chief, Munch Operations Group, to Chief, SR, February 12, 1961, AEQUOR VOL. 3_0069, https://www.cia.gov/library/readingroom/document/5197c269993294098d50ed08 [last viewed December 2020].

31. AEQUOR VOL. 3_0076, op. cit.

32. Dispatch from Chief, SR, to Chief, Munich Operations Group, Subject: Current Status of Project AEQUOR, AEQUOR VOL. 3_0075, https://www.cia.gov/library/readingroom/document/5197c269993294098d50ed31 [last viewed December 2020].

33. Dispatch to Chief, WE, Subject: Meeting with AECAMBISTA/4, December 4, 1961, AEQUOR VOL. 3_0078, https://www.cia.gov/library/readingroom/document/5197c269993294098d50ed1e [last viewed December 2020].

34. Memorandum for the Record, January 18, 1962, AEQUOR VOL. 3_0081, https://www.cia.gov/library/readingroom/document/5197c269993294098d50ed26 [last viewed December 2020].

35. There is little available in English about the White Legion. That being said, there are some details, for example, in Vladimír Varinský, "Anti-Communist Activities of the Exile White Legion and its Operation by the State Security in Slovakia," *European Researcher*, No. 1 (16), 2012, http://www.erjournal.ru/journals_n/1327215695.pdf [last viewed December 2020].

36. Beata Katrebova Blehova: "An beiden Ufern der March. Der antikommunistische Widerstand der Weissen Legion." In: Stefan Karner and Michal Stehlík (eds.), *Österreich. Tschechien. Geteilt—getrennt—vereint. Beitragsband und Katalog der Niederösterreichischen Landesausstellung* (Schallaburg, 2009), pp. 252–255.

37. Radio Free Europe Field Report, Salzburg/Wels/Klagenfurt area field office, 15 September 1951, HU OSA 200–1-2–6888, [Electronic Record] http://hdl.handle.net/10891/osa:bb44f8db-7327-4151-9482-33a835942a16 [last viewed December 2020].

38. Bolschwing, VOL. 2_0002 [last viewed December 2020].

39. Varinský, op. cit.

40. Agent Report, 30 July 30, 1952, by Clyde E. Taylor, S|A, 430th CIC Sub-Det "A" Salzburg, Subject: Arrest of Czech Refugees by StB in the CSR, BOLSCHWING, OTTO (VON) VOL. 2_0031.pdf, https://www.cia.gov/library/readingroom/document/519a6b25993294098d510dc7 [last viewed December 2020].

41. Ibid.

42. Ibid.

43. Ibid.

44. Current Intelligence Digest, 3 October 1952, CIA Office of Current Intelligence. https://www.cia.gov/library/readingroom/document/cia-rdp79t01146a001300090001-9 [last viewed December 2020].

45. *Tucson Daily Citizen*, Tucson, Arizona, October 6, 1952, p. 4; *The Courier-Journal*, Louisville, Kentucky, October 4, 1952, p. 5.

46. CIA Information Report, Reception of Western Broadcasts; Underground Radio, April 18, 1953, https://www.cia.gov/library/readingroom/document/cia-rdp80-00809a000500010228-5 [last viewed December 2020].

47. CIA Information Report: Slovak Reaction to VOA Broadcasts, June 17, 1953, CIA-https://www.cia.gov/library/readingroom/document/cia-rdp80-

00810a001400310007-5 [last viewed December 2020].

48. Lubomir Gleiman, *From the Maelstrom: A Pilgrim's Story of Dissent and Survival in the Twentieth Century,* Chapter 18, "From Nationalism to Anti-Imperialism. Vicen and Biela Legia (The White Legion), " Author House Publishing, 2011.

49. *Ibid.*

50. CIA Information Report, Czechoslovakia, Popular Moral and Resistance to the Communist Regime, October 20, 1953, https://www.cia.gov/library/readingroom/document/cia-rdp82-00046r000200280005-4 [last viewed December 2020].

51. Beata Katrebova Blehova, Rádio Slobodná Európa a Svetový kongres Slovákov, in Peter Jašek, (ed.), *Svetový kongres Slovákov v zápase proti komunistickému režimu* (Bratislava: Ústav Pamäti Národa, 2018), pp. 184–207. This is a book compilation of the presentations at a conference in Bratislava, June 17, 2015. Dr. Zdenek Suda worked for RFE in Munich 1954–1968. Dr. Imrich Kruzliak worked for the Radio Free Europe in Munich from 1951 to his retirement in 1980.

52. Varinsky, op. cit., p. 51.

53. Summary of available Personality Information, November 2, 1954, DURCANSKY, FERDINAND VOL. 2_0028, https://www.cia.gov/library/readingroom/document/519a6b26993294098d5110ae [last viewed December 2020].

54. Petr Kubik, "Slovenský exil v Itálii 1945–49," *Securitas imperii Studie,* No.21 (02/2012) p. 40 (In Czech), https://www.ustrcr.cz/data/pdf/publikace/securitas-imperii/no21/026-047.pdf [last viewed December 2020].

55. *Ibid.*

56. *Ibid.*

57. Central Intelligence Group, Intelligence Report, "Voice of the Slovak Republic," CIA-RDP78-04864A000100020012–5.

58. Peter Kubik, op. cit.

59. Information from Foreign Documents or Radio Broadcasts, December 5, 1950, Slovak Clandestine Station, https://www.cia.gov/library/readingroom/document/cia-rdp78-04864a000200010002-6 [last viewed December 2020].

60. DURCANSKY, FERDINAND VOL. 2_0028, op. cit.

61. Report on the Slovak Committee for Liberation and the Slovakian National Council, June 2, 1951, DURCANSKY, FERDINAND VOL.1_0058, https://www.cia.gov/library/readingroom/document/519a6b27993294098d5110ef [last viewed December 2020].

62. Foreign Service Dispatch, From Hight Commissioner, Germany to Department of State, Washington, March 10, 1953, DURCANSKY, Ferdinand VOL.2_0017, https://www.cia.gov/library/readingroom/document/519a6b26993294098d511088 [last viewed December 2020].

63. March 30, 1953, Report of Gehlen Organization, DURCANSKY, FERDINAND VOL.2_0020, https://www.cia.gov/library/readingroom/document/519a6b26993294098d5110a2 [last viewed December 2020].

64. Memorandum for the Chief, International Organizations Division, February 12, 1959, DURCANSKY VOL.2_0041, https://www.cia.gov/library/readingroom/document/519a6b26993294098d511098 [last viewed December 2020].

65. DURCANSKY, FERDINAND VOL. 2_0028, op. cit.

66. *Ibid.*

67. Message from CIA Vienna to Washington April 15, 1959, PEKELSKY, VLADIMIR VOL.2_0028, https://www.cia.gov/library/readingroom/document/519bdeda993294098d5157fa [last viewed December 2020].

68. Radek Schovánek, Když vraždí estébáci, Center for Documentation of Totalitarian Regimes, https://www.minulost.cz/cs/kdyz-vrazdi-estebaci [last viewed December 2020]. The most detailed article about the murder of Cernak is in Czech: Prokop Tomek, "Kdo zabil Matúše Černáka?" [Who Killed Matúše Černáka], *Pamat Naroda,* 01–2009, https://www.upn.gov.sk/sk/pamat-naroda-012009/ [last viewed December 2020].

# Bibliography

Alexeyeva, Ludmilla. *U.S. Broadcasting to the Soviet Union*. New York: Helsinki Watch Committee, 1986.
Bethell, Nicholas. *The Great Betrayal: The Untold Story of Kim Philby's Greatest Coup*. London: Hodder and Stoughton, 1984.
Bischoff, Anna, and Zusanna Jürgens, ed. *Voice of Freedom—Western Interference? 60 Years of Radio Free Europe*. Güttingen: Vendenhoeck & Ruprecht, 2015.
Board for International Broadcasting. *Annual Reports*. Washington, D.C.
Bower, Tom. *The Red Web: MI6 and the KGB Master Coup*. London: Aurum, 1989.
Browne, Donald R. *International Radio Broadcasting: The Limits of the Limitless Medium*. New York: Praeger, 1982.
Carruthers, Susan L. *Cold War Captives: Imprisonment, Escape, and Brainwashing*. Berkeley: University of California Press, 2009.
Critchlow, James. *Radio Hole-in-the-Head/Radio Liberty: An Insider's Story of Cold War Broadcasting*. Washington, D.C.: American University Press, 1995.
Dulles, Alan. *The Craft of Intelligence*. Westport, CT: Greenwood, 1963.
Felix, Christoper [pseudonym for James McCargar]. London: Madison, 1963.
Fischer, George, ed. *Russian Émigré Politics*. New York: Free Russian Fund, 1951.
*Foreign Relations of the United States, 1945–1959: Emergence of the Intelligence Establishment*. Washington, D.C.: Government Printing Office, 1996.
Frolik, Josef. *The Frolik Defection: The Memoirs of an Intelligence Agent*. London: Lee Cooper, 1975.
Gati, Charles. *Failed Illusions: Moscow, Washington, Budapest and the 1956 Hungarian Revolt*. Stanford, CA: Stanford University Press, 2006.
Grose, Peter. *Operation Rollback: America's Secret War Behind the Iron Curtain*. Boston: Houghton Mifflin, 2000.
Hersh, Burton. *The Old Boys: The American Elite and the Origins of the CIA*. St. Petersburg, FL: Tree Farm, 2002.
Holt, Robert T. *Radio Free Europe*. Minneapolis: University of Minnesota Press, 1958.
Jackson, Wayne G. *Allen Welsh Dulles as Director of Central Intelligence, February 26, 1953–November 29, 1961*. CIA Historical Study, 1973.
Jandečková, Václava. *Kámen: Svědectví hlavního aktéra akce „Falešné hranice" u Všerub na Domažlicku*. Nakladatelství Českého lesa, 2014.
Johnson, A. Ross. *Radio Free Europe and Radio Liberty: The CIA Years and Beyond*. Stanford: Stanford University Press, 2010.
Kadar Lynn, Katalin. *The Inauguration of Organized Political Warfare: Cold War Organizations Sponsored by the National Committee for Free Europe / Free Europe Committee*. Saint Helena, CA: Helena History, 2013.
Kovrig, Bennet. *Of Walls and Bridges: The United States and Eastern Europe*. New York: New York University Press, 1991.
Lendvai, Paul. *The Bureaucracy of Truth: How Communist Governments Manage the News*. London: Burnett, 1981.

Lucas, Scott. *Freedom's War: The American Crusade against the Soviet Union.* New York: New York University Press, 1999.
Lurie, Mark. *Galantiere: The Lost Generation's Forgotten Man.* West Palm Beach, FL: Overlook, 2017.
Meyer, Cord. *Facing Reality: From World Federalism to the CIA.* New York: Harper and Row, 1980.
Michener, James A. *The Bridge at Andau.* New York: Random House, 1957.
Michie, Allan. *Voices Through the Iron Curtain: The Radio Free Europe Story.* New York: Dodd, Mead, 1963.
Mickelson, Sig. *America's Other Voice: The Story of Radio Free Europe and Radio Liberty.* New York: Praeger, 1983.
Mosley, Leonard. *Dulles: A Biography of Eleanor, Allen, and John Foster Dulles and Their Family Network.* New York: Dial, 1978.
Muravchik, Joshua. *Exporting Democracy: Fulfilling America's Destiny.* Washington, D.C.: American Enterprise Institute, 1991.
Nelson, Michael. *War of the Black Heavens: The Battles of Western Broadcasting in the Cold War.* Syracuse, NY: Syracuse University Press, 1997.
Parta, R. Eugene. *Discovering the Hidden Listener: An Assessment of Radio Liberty and Western Broadcasting to the USSR During the Cold War.* Stanford: Hoover Institution, 2007.
Powers, Thomas. *The Man Who Kept the Secrets: Richard Helms and the CIA.* New York: Pocket, 1991.
Prados, John. *Safe for Democracy: The Secret Wars of the CIA.* Chicago: Ivan R. Dee, 2006.
Price, James R. *Radio Free Europe: A Survey and Analysis.* Washington, D.C.: Congressional Research Service, Library of Congress, 1972.
Puddington, Arch. *Broadcasting Freedom: The Cold War Triumph of Radio Free Europe and Radio Liberty.* Lexington: University of Kentucky Press, 2000.
*Report of the Presidential Study Commission on International Radio Broadcasting: The Right to Know.* Washington, D.C.: Government Printing Office, 1973.
Saunders, Frances Stonor. *The Cultural Cold War: The CIA and the World of Arts and Letters.* New York: New, 1999.
Seagrave, Sterling. *Yellow Rain: A Journey Through the Terror of Chemical Warfare.* London: Abacus, 1982.
Short, K.R.M., ed. *Western Broadcasting Over the Iron Curtain.* London: Croom Helm, 1986.
Sosin, Gene. *Sparks of Liberty: An Insider's Memoir of Radio Liberty.* University Park: Pennsylvania State University Press, 1999.
Starr, Richard F., ed. *Public Diplomacy: USA versus USSR.* Stanford, CA: Hoover Institution, 1986.
Steven, Stewart. *Operation Splinter Factor.* Philadelphia: J.B. Lippincott, 1974.
Szabo, Miklos, *Professional Emigres,* Budapest: Pannonia, 1959.
Thomas, Evan. *The Very Best Men: Four Who Dared: The Early Years of the CIA.* New York: Simon & Schuster, 1995.
Tyson, James L. *U.S. International Broadcasting and National Security.* New York: Ramapo, 1983.
Urban, George. *The Nineteen Days: A Broadcaster's Account of the Hungarian Revolution.* London: Heinemann, 1957.
———. *Radio Free Europe and the Pursuit of Democracy: My War within the Cold War.* New Haven, CT: Yale University Press, 1997.
Warner, Michael, ed. *CIA Cold War Records: The CIA Under Harry Truman.* Washington, D.C.: CIA, 1994.
Washburn, Philo C. *Broadcasting Propaganda: International Radio Broadcasting and the Construction of Political Reality.* Westport, CT: Praeger, 1992.
Wettig, Gerhard. *Broadcasting and Detente: Eastern Policies and Their Implications for East-West Relations.* London: C. Hurst, 1977.
Wheland, Joseph G. *Radio Liberty: A Study of Its Origins, Structure, Policy, Programming and Effectiveness.* Washington, D.C.: Congressional Research Service, Library of Congress, 1972.

Wiener, Tim. *Legacy of Ashes: The History of the CIA*. New York: Doubleday, 2007.
Wilford, Hugh. *The Mighty Wurlitzer: How the CIA Played America*. Cambridge, MA: Harvard University Press, 2008.
Young, Gordon. *The House of Secrets: Russian Resistance to the Soviet Regime, Today*. New York: Duell, Sloan, and Pearce, 1959.

# Index

Abrahamovič, Evzen 33
Abramtchik, Mikola 176–183, 200
AEACRE 137, 177
AEBALCONY 197
AEBASIN 110–114, 197
AEBEEHIVE 202
AECADILT-1 171
AECADILT-2 171
AECAMBISTA 177, 181, 196
AECAMBISTA-1 197
AECARTHAGE 198
AECASSOWARY 147–149, 197
AECAVATINA 197
AECHAMP 129, 130, 197
AECOB 197, 203–204
AEDEPOT 177
AEFLAG 117, 120–121, 197
AEFREEMAN 113, 115–116, 197
AEGEAN 127–128, 198
AEGIDEON 155, 198
AEHANGOVER 161
AEHAWKEYE-1 122
AEMANTILLA 61
AEMARSH (Latvia) 117–121, 198
AEMINX (ILC) 117, 198
AENOBLE 155, 198
AEPAWN 164, 179–171
AEPOLE 130–133, 135–136, 197
AEQUOR 177–182
AERANTER 140
AEREADY 177
AERODYNAMIC 140
AEROSOL 155, 198
AESAURUS 155, 198
AETENURE 139, 198
AETERRACE 199
AETOMAC 176
AEVIRGIL 174, 167, 170, 172, 199
AEZERO/1 120
AIPLEBE 105

Albania 3, 12, 18, 67, 76–77, 79, 84, 89–107, 198
Allen, George 18–19
Altschul, Frank 26–27
AMCOMLIB 4, 52, 54, 178–179, 199, 201
American Friends of Russian Freedom (AFRF) 56–63, 164
ANDROGEN 198–199
AQUATIC 198
Army Security Agency (ASA) 21–23
Austria 7, 13, 37–38, 45–46, 51, 59, 147, 155–157, 160, 168, 183–189, 191, 193, 198–200
AVH—Allam Vedelmi Hatosag 4, 37–41, 188
AVO—Allam Vedelmi Osztal 4

Baltics 108, 121, 127
"Barbara" 25, 68, 79
Barrett, Edward 28
Baumgartner, Kurt ("Berthelot") 164
Belgium 147, 169
Beloruska Nationalna Rada (BNR) 176, 177–183, 197, 200
Beloruska Zentralna Rada (BZR) 176
Berle, Adolphe 15
Berlin 1, 7–8, 13, 40, 46, 52, 58, 74, 101 130, 151, 156–157, 160, 165, 168, 170–174, 189, 193, 203
Berukshtis, Igor 62
BGACTRESS 192, 199
BGCANE (OPC) 199
Board of the Democratic Resistance Movement 127
BGCONVOY 69, 71, 87, 199, 202
BGFIEND 84, 89, 90, 92, 94, 199–200, 201
BGLAPIN 128
BGRYTHYM 199
BGSPEED 92, 94, 97–99, 200
"Black Radio" 2, 18–19, 24, 35, 67, 79, 81,

# 258 Index

83, 84, 106–109, 111, 124, 129, 138, 140, 142, 152–154, 225
Boldyreff, Constantin (Boldyrev Konstantin) 158
British Intelligence Service (SIS) 90–91, 94, 95, 156, 172, 201, 203
Bulgaria 2, 4, 13, 17–18, 25, 45, 61, 65, 67–79, 81, 83–84, 87, 93, 100, 167–170, 199, 202, 212, 213
Bulgarian National Committee 68
Burghardt, Gottfried 170–175
Butenas, Julijonas 128–129
Byelorussian Central Council (BCR) 176

CABEZONE 63
CABOCHE-1 (NTS) 155, 198, 200
CAMANTILLA 63
CAMBISTA-1 177, 181, 197, 200
CAMPOSANTO 177
CAPSTAN 129
CARCASS 155, 198, 200
"Carola" 29
CARRERA (AECARRERA) 171–172
Casey, William (Bill) 57–58
Cassady, Thomas C. 8–10
CASSOWARY-1 141, 149, 200
Časta, Anton 185–186
Central Association of Post-War Émigrés (TsOPE) 53, 100, 151, 164–171, 173, 195, 192, 199
Černák, Matúš 193–194
Chamberlin, William Henry 52
CHARITY 200
CHAURUS 177, 200
Churgin Raymond S. 123–124
Clay, Lucius D. 7–8, 11, 224
Counterintelligence Corp (CIC) 4, 32, 183–186, 191, 201
Cuba 35, 161–162
Czechoslovakia 13–14, 15, 17, 21, 25, 29, 31–33, 44–45, 54, 64,-65, 74, 108, 183–190, 192–194

Davies, John Paton 9–10
Defector Reception Center (DFC) 57, 61–63
DIE—Directia de Informatii Externe (Romania) 4
Directorate of State Security (Bulgaria— DS) 69, 71, 77
Dr. Zhivago 165
DS—Drazven Sigurnost (Bulgaria) 4, 69, 71, 77
DTORIC (NCFE) 200
Dubrovsky, Sergey 50–51
Dulles, Allen 11, 15, 27, 47, 60
Durand, Dana 51

Ďurčanský, Ferdinand 189–193, 224–225
DYCLAVIER 199
DYCLEAN 192, 199, 299
DYCLEMATIC 200
DYCLIP (OPC) 199
DYCLUCK (OPC) 199
Dziuba, Mikhail 165

"Eagle" 35
EDICT 22
EDUCATOR 16–17, 21–22, 24, 200, 202–203, 209
Eisenhower, Pres. Dwight David 26–27
Eisenhower, Milton 65
Estonia 2, 108–116, 122, 136, 145, 167–170, 197, 200–201

Farago, Ladislas 36–37
Fatalibey, Abo 52
Finland 13, 129, 158
FJHAKI (Estonia) 200
FJSTEAL (USSR) 200
Free Europe Committee (FEC) 4, 25, 27, 42–44, 47, 74, 81–84, 100, 103–104, 191–192, 200, 202–203
Free Russia Fund 163
Furtseva, Yekaterina 18

Gleiman, Lubomir 187
Goodman, Sheba 58
Greenwood Project 21–22, 24
Griffith, William (Bill) 14, 34

HARVARD 30, 57, 63, 200–201
HBCHEST (Sweden) 201
HBCLOUD (Latvia) 201
HBDUCKPIN 164
Helms, Richard (CIA) 64, 130
Hillenkoetter, Roscoe 8, 12
Holmes, Leslie 92, 94
Hristo Botev 75–79
HTGRUBBY 102, 221–223
HTNEIGH 201
Hulick, Charles C. 13
Hungary 2, 13, 17, 25, 31, 35–43, 45, 79, 145, 183

Institute for Latvian Culture (ILC) 117, 120

Jackson, C.D. 14–15, 24
Jackson, William Harding 15, 27–28
JAGUAR 201
JBCLOUD (Latvia) 201
Juanita 94–98

Kampus, Roberts 118–119
Karas, Alex 52

# Index

Kennan, George 8–11, 47
KGB (Kommitet Gosudarstvenoi Bezopastnosti) 19–20, 45, 53, 60, 153, 156, 161, 163, 174
Khokhlov, Nicolai 161
Kissinger, Henry 62
KLIMOV, Grigory (Grigorii) 165
KMHYMNAL 94
KNOBBY (OPC) 199
Krutý, Josef 185
KUBARK (CIA) 105, 139, 153–154, 165
Kubiček, Ladislav ("Kautsky") 194
Kukauskas-Lukis, Jonas 128

Lampertheim 22–23, 50, 68, 79
Latvia 2, 107, 115–126, 136, 182, 167–169, 197–198, 201, 203–204
Launags, Freds Ziedonids 121–126
LCFLUTTER 201
LCHOMELY 109–110, 201
LCIMPROVE 201
Lebed, Mykola 141–144, 148–150
Lebedev, Theodor 165
Lindhurst, Norman 59–50
Liška, Stanislav 32
Liszka, Bela von 37–41
Lithuania 2, 61, 108, 115–116, 121, 126–136, 145, 197–198, 202
Luksa, Juozas Albinas 128
Lyons, Eugene 47, 57

Marine Biological Research Institute (MBRI) 93
Marshall, George C. 10–11, 13
Meyer, Cord 43, 105, 111, 182
Midney, Boris 62
Mikula, Jozef 183
Munich 15, 25–26, 29, 34–35, 37–38, 40–41, 44, 46, 51–55, 58, 60, 66, 111, 116, 121, 127–128, 130, 135–137, 155, 162, 164–169, 171, 177, 179–180, 182–183, 187–188, 192–194, 199, 202, 203
Munich Operational Base (MOB) 38, 127, 177
Murphy, David E. 124

Nasha Rossiya (Our Russia) 18, 151–154
National Alliance of Russian Solidarists (NTS) 50, 53, 154–163, 182, 198, 200
National Committee for Free Europe (NCFE) 14, 15–16, 27–28, 31, 34, 38, 72, 82–86, 102, 104–105, 109–110, 188, 200
National Security Council 5, 8, 10, 56, 72, 74, 202, 205–208
Nationalist Socialist Radio (NATCOM) 104–106
Nixon, Pres. Richard M. 64–65

Novaya Ukraina 143, 144
NTS 50, 53, 154–163, 182, 198, 200

OBHUNT (Albania) 201
OBOPUS (Albania) 199, 201
OBSIDIOUS (Alblania) 201
OBTEST (Albania) 102, 106–107, 201
OBTUSE (Albania) 201
ODOPOL (CIC) 201
ODYOKE 115
Office of Policy Coordination (OPC) 4–5, 10–13, 16–17, 21–24, 47, 67–68, 70–71, 81, 84, 86, 88, 90–94, 97–98, 100, 110, 122, 127–129, 137–138, 156, 177, 185, 199, 202
Offie, Carmel 11, 13
OGIVE (OSO) 201
Operation Focus 38
Operation Radio (NTS) 158
Operation Stone (Akce Kámen) 31–32
Ostrowsky, Radislaw (Radoslav) 176

Pasternak, Boris 165
Patch, Isaac 54–56
Pavlovič, Peter 185–186
PBAFFIRM 199, 201
PBCHORD 199, 202
PBCHUTE (Lithuania) 202
PBCRUET 137–138
PBGIDEON (NTS) 202
PBPRIME 139
Peroutka, Ferdinand 29, 191
Petva-8 158
Plechavicius, Paulius 128
Poole, Dewitt 27–28
Poremsky, V.D. 161
Possev 155–156
Project Menthol 75
Project Metaphor 75–77
Project Troy 30–31
Prolog Associates 139, 141, 143, 145–148, 198, 203
Psychological Strategy Board (PSB) 59
Psychological Warfare Panel 143
Purre, Helene 109
PYREX 145, 151

QKACTIVE 19, 201, 202
QKBROIL (Romania) 82–85, 202
QKCOAST (Baltic States) 110, 202
QKDEMON 21, 202–203
QKDROOP (NTS) 155, 198, 200, 202
QKIVORY 192, 292
QKSTAIR 68
QRDYNAMIC 202
QRPLUMB 198–199, 202–203
QRTENURE 139, 198, 203
QRTERRACE 198, 202

Radio Barcelona 189
Radio Free Europe 1–2, 5, 7–8, 11, 14–16, 18, 21, 23, 25–29, 31, 33–45, 47, 51, 57–59, 63–65, 68–70, 74, 79–84, 86, 100, 103–106, 108–109, 111, 116, 121, 136, 138, 147, 163, 185, 187, 193, 200, 202–203, 211–216, 224
Radio Free Russia 18–19, 156–163
Radio Goryanin 67–79
Radio in the American Sector (RIAS) 7–8, 130
Radio Kavkaz (Caucasus) 18–19
Radio Liberation 50–51, 54, 58
Radio Liberty 2, 5, 8, 16, 18, 23, 28, 39, 47–49, 51, 53–55, 57, 59, 61–66, 94, 115–116, 121, 136–137, 154, 160, 162, 176, 181, 202–203
Radio Madrid 114, 147
Radio Nacional de España 16–17, 108, 112–114, 117, 119–121, 131–136, 144, 146–149, 166–169, 176, 179–181, 190, 209
Radio Nova Ukraina (New Ukraine) 18, 137, 141, 143–144
Radio Osvobodoshdenie (Liberation) 18
Radio Pyrex 145–146
Radio Rome 115, 121, 130, 132–136, 166–170
Radio Vatican 114, 130–134
Rahr, Gleb 162
Ramparts 64
RANTER 139–140, 142
REDBIRD 203
REDBLOCK (CIA) 203
REDCAP 170–172, 203
REDCOAT 203
REDLEG 203
Redlich, Roman 162
REDSOX 19, 122, 126
REDTOP 203
REI, August 109–110
Robb, Inez 60
Roosevelt, Archibald 142–143
Rose, Karoly 37–41
Ruddock, Merret 13
Russell, McKinney 58

Sargeant, Howland 55
SGPSALM 203
SGSWIRL 203
SHELLAC 85
SHELLFIRE 86, 202–203
SHUBA-100 155, 198, 293
Sigurimi 103
Sirvys, Albinas 128
Slovakia 3, 183–193
Special Procedures Branch (CIA) 8
Special Procedures Group (CIA) 8, 21

StB—Statni Bezpecnost 6, 32–33, 185, 188–189, 194
Stevens, Leslie C. 94
Strečanský, Ernest 185
Sumichrast, Kamil 185
Sweden 119, 122, 127–128, 158, 169, 201

Taiwan (Formosa) 53
Tigrid, Pavel 29
Tihlárik, Alexander 185
Tolstoy, Mrs. Ivan 57
Tolstoy Foundation 57
TPFEELING 203
TPLINGO 202
TPTONIC 41, 202–203
Trumpis, Benediktas 128
TsOPE 164–170

UHVR 141
UJDROLLERY 38
Ukraine 2–3, 18–19, 137–149, 196
UMPIRE 9, 11–12, 21–22, 24–25, 202–203
Union of Soviet Socialist Republics (USSR) 2, 3, 5, 8, 11, 13–14, 16, 18–19, 44, 47–51, 55–56, 60, 62, 64, 57, 78, 80, 88, 90, 105, 110, 126–127, 131–132, 135, 137–138, 145–147, 151–156, 160, 162–164, 167, 169, 178, 198–199, 200, 203–205, 212
United States Escapee Program (USEP) 59
Urban, George 44

Valahu, Mugur 86–88
VALUABLE 91, 96, 150, 203
Varga, Bela 36
Vicen, Josef 183–184, 188–189
Vinogradov, Boris 50–51
VLIK (Vyriausiasis Lietuvos išlaisvinimo komitetas) 127–129, 131–134
VLKIVA (OPC) 203
Voice of America (VOA) 1, 7–8, 11, 18–19, 21, 25–26, 30, 34–35, 53, 72, 81, 86–87, 91, 108–109, 116, 129, 136–139, 157, 159, 165–166, 176–178, 201
Voice of Bulgarian Resistance 67
Voice of Estonian Freedom 113–114
Voice of Free Albania (VOFA) 91, 98–101, 103–105, 199
Voice of Free Hungary 35
Voice of Free Latvians 118
Voice of Free Slovakia 189, 191
Voice of National Resistance (Romania) 80
Voice of the Forest (Vocea Padurii) 79

Walker, Colonel 23
Walsch, Gen. Robert LeGrow 24

## Index

WEMCA 18
White Legion 183–188
"Winds of Freedom" 31
Wisner, Frank 10–13, 24, 27–28, 47, 51, 67, 81, 90–91, 93–94, 128, 130, 137, 211, 213–214, 227

ZACABIN (OSO) 203
Zhukov, Yuri 18–19
ZIPPER 192, 224
ZP/UHVR 137
ZRLYNCH 197, 203–204
Zvigun, S.K. (KGB) 19
ZYCACTUS (OPC) 204

www.ingramcontent.com/pod-product-compliance
Lightning Source LLC
Chambersburg PA
CBHW021350300426
44114CB00012B/1166